Pro Cryptography and Cryptanalysis

Creating Advanced Algorithms with C# and .NET

Marius Iulian Mihailescu
Stefania Loredana Nita

Apress®

Pro Cryptography and Cryptanalysis: Creating Advanced Algorithms with C# and .NET

Marius Iulian Mihailescu
Bucharest, Romania

Stefania Loredana Nita
Bucharest, Romania

ISBN-13 (pbk): 978-1-4842-6366-2
https://doi.org/10.1007/978-1-4842-6367-9

ISBN-13 (electronic): 978-1-4842-6367-9

Managing Director, Apress Media LLC: Welmoed Spahr
Acquisitions Editor: Joan Murray
Development Editor: Laura Berendson
Coordinating Editor: Jill Balzano

Cover image designed by Freepik (www.freepik.com)

Distributed to the book trade worldwide by Springer Science+Business Media LLC, 1 New York Plaza, Suite 4600, New York, NY 10004. Phone 1-800-SPRINGER, fax (201) 348-4505, e-mail orders-ny@springer-sbm.com, or visit www.springeronline.com. Apress Media, LLC is a California LLC and the sole member (owner) is Springer Science + Business Media Finance Inc (SSBM Finance Inc). SSBM Finance Inc is a **Delaware** corporation.

For information on translations, please e-mail booktranslations@springernature.com; for reprint, paperback, or audio rights, please e-mail bookpermissions@springernature.com.

Apress titles may be purchased in bulk for academic, corporate, or promotional use. eBook versions and licenses are also available for most titles. For more information, reference our Print and eBook Bulk Sales web page at www.apress.com/bulk-sales.

Any source code or other supplementary material referenced by the author in this book is available to readers on GitHub via the book's product page, located at www.apress.com/9781484263662. For more detailed information, please visit www.apress.com/source-code.

Printed on acid-free paper

To our families

Table of Contents

About the Authors

Marius Iulian Mihailescu, PhD is the CEO of Dapyx Solution Ltd., a company focused on security- and cryptography-related research. He has authored and co-authored more than 50 articles, journal contributions, and conference proceedings, and three books related to security and cryptography. He lectures at well-known national and international universities, teaching courses on programming, cryptography, information security, and other technical topics. He holds a PhD (thesis on applied cryptography over biometrics data), an MSc in information security, and and an MSc in software engineering.

Stefania Loredana Nita, PhD is a software developer and researcher at the Institute for Computers. Prior to that she was an assistant lecturer at the University of Bucharest, where she taught courses on advanced programming techniques, simulation methods, and operating systems. She has authored and co-authored more than 15 papers and journals, most recently *Advanced Cryptography and Its Future: Searchable and Homomorphic Encryption,* as well as two books. She holds a PhD (thesis on advanced cryptographic schemes using searchable encryption and homomorphic encryption), an MSc in software engineering, a BSc in computer science, and a BSc in mathematics.

About the Technical Reviewer

Doug Holland is a software engineer and architect at Microsoft Corporation and holds a Masters degree in software engineering from the University of Oxford. Before joining Microsoft, he was awarded the Microsoft MVP and Intel Black Belt Developer awards.

Introduction

Information represents one of the most important aspects that need to be taken into consideration when complex systems are designed and implemented, such as business, organizations, and military operations. Information that falls into the wrong hands can be a disaster and can lead to a huge loss of business or catastrophic results. In order to secure communication, cryptology (cryptography and cryptanalysis) can be used to cipher information.

Due to the rapid growth of electronic communication, the issues in information security are increasing every day. Messages that are exchanged over worldwide, publicly accessible computer networks must be protected and retained and must also have protection mechanisms against manipulation. Electronic business requirements consist of having digital signatures that are recognized by the law. With the help of modern cryptography, we have solutions to all of these problems.

This book was borne from cryptography courses (theoretical and applied cryptography) given to students (graduate and undergraduate levels) in computer science at the University of Bucharest and Titu Maiorescu University; business experience at national and international companies; ethical hacking best practices; and security audits. The book it is intended to cover the most advanced cryptography and cryptanalysis techniques together with their implementations using C# and the .NET Framework, giving a practical perspective, helping readers to think of cryptography and cryptanalysis techniques in terms of practice. Some of the implementations in C# will be given using the new features of C# 8.0 (see Chapter 6). As an advanced and exhaustive book, serving as a comprehensive guide to the most important topics in security information, cryptography, and cryptanalysis, the book can be used for a wide range of purposes and areas by multiple professionals, such as security experts with their audits, military experts and personnel, ethical hackers, teachers in academia, researchers, software developers, and software engineers when security and cryptographic solutions need to be implemented in a real business software environment; student courses (undergraduate and graduate levels, master degree, professional and academic doctoral degree); business analysts, and many more.

Cryptography and Cryptanalysis

We consider it useful to define some of the main notions we will work with throughout the book.

CRYPTOGRAPHY represents the defensive side of cryptology. Its main objective is to create and design the cryptographic systems and their rules. Cryptography can be seen as the art of protecting the information by transforming it into an unreadable format called cipher text.

CRYPTANALYSIS represents the offensive side of cryptology. Its main objective is to study the cryptographic systems with the goal of providing necessary characteristics in such a way as to fulfill the function for which they have been designed. Cryptanalysis has the possibility to analyze the cryptographic systems of third parties through the cryptograms realized with them, in such way that breaking them obtains useful information for their business purposes. The people who are dealing with this field are known as cryptanalysts, code breakers, or ethical hackers.

CRYPTOLOGY represents the science or art of secret writings. Its main objective is to protect and defend the secrets of the data and the confidentiality of the information with the help of cryptographic algorithms.

The book examines all three sides from a practical side with references to the theoretical background by illustrating how a theoretical algorithm should be exploited and spread in order to be implemented.

Book Structure

The book has 24 chapters divided within three parts (see Table 1): Part I – Foundational Topics (Chapters 1-9), Part II – Cryptography (Chapters 10-17), and Part III – Cryptanalysis (18-24). Figure 1 shows how to read the book and what chapters depend on each other.

In *Part I - Foundations (Chapters 1-9)*, the book covers a beginner-to-advanced level, from theoretical to practical: the fundamental concepts of cryptography (*Chapter 1*). In *Chapter 2,* we cover a collection of basic key elements on complexity theory, probability theory, information theory, number theory, abstract algebra, and finite fields.

Chapters 3 and *Chapter 4* deal with integer arithmetic and floating-point arithmetic processing and algorithms. The importance of these chapters is quite vital, and other chapters and algorithm implementations are dependent on the content of these chapters.

In *Chapter 5,* we discuss the newest features and enhancements of C# 8.0. We present how the features and enhancements play an important role in developing cryptography and cryptanalysis algorithms and methods. We cover readonly members, default interface methods, pattern matching enhancements, how to use the new type of declarations, static local functions, disposable ref types, nullable reference types, asynchronous streams, indices and ranges, null-coalescing assignments, unmanaged constructed types, stackalloc in nested expressions, and enhancement of interpolated verbatim strings.

Chapter 6 covers the most important guidelines for secure coding, focusing on the balance between security and usability in most expected scenarios by using trusted code. We also cover sensitive topics such as securing state data, security and user input, security-neutral code, and library codes that expose the protected resources.

Chapter 7 covers the cryptography model and cryptographic services for .NET. Vital topics include .NET Framework basic implementations, object inheritance, how cryptography algorithms are implemented, stream design (the`CryptoStream` class), configuring cryptography classes, how to choose cryptography algorithms, generating the keys for encryption and decryption, storing asymmetric keys in a key container, cryptographic signatures, ensuring data integrity using hash codes and functions, creating and designing cryptographic schemes, encryption of XML elements with symmetric keys, assuring and guaranteeing interoperability of the applications between different platforms, such as Windows to Linux and vice-versa, and many other important related topics.

Chapter 8 covers the architecture of the `System.Security.Cryptography` namespace and how it can be used during coding. The chapter discusses cryptographic services, secure encoding and decoding of data, and operations (hashing, random number generation, message authentication, etc.).

Chapter 9 discusses in detail several cryptographic libraries (e.g. NSec, Bouncy Castle, Inferno, and SecureBlackbox) which are open source and have a higher level of trustiness. They can be used during the development process or as an example and source of inspiration for implementing your own algorithms.

In ***Part II – Pro Cryptography (Chapters 10-17)***, the book covers the most important frameworks that are developed in C# and .NET, such as elliptic-curve cryptography (*Chapter 9*). The discussion is conducted further with advanced cryptography topics (*Chapters 11-17*) by presenting practical implementations and showing how to treat such advanced topics from a theoretical mathematical background to a real-life environment.

Chapter 10 discusses Cryptography Next Generation (CNG), which helps us to implement the Elliptic Curve Diffie-Hellman (ECDH) algorithm and perform the necessary cryptographic operations.

Chapter 11 uses the Lattice Cryptography Library for implementation, pointing out the importance for post-quantum cryptography. Implementations of key exchange protocols proposed by Alkim, Ducas, Poppelmann, and Schwabe [1] will be discussed. Also, an instantiation of the Chris Peikert key exchange protocol [2] will be discussed. We reiterate that the implementation is based on a novel technique for computing, known as the Number Theoretic Transform, in order to apply errorless, fast convolution functions over successions of integer numbers.

Chapter 12 and *Chapter 13* discuss two advanced cryptography topics, homomorphic and searchable encryption. For searchable encryption (SE), in *Chapter 12*, we give a brief implementation and solution in C# for SE by pointing out the advantages and disadvantages and by eradicating the most common patterns from encrypted data. In *Chapter 13*, for homomorphic encryption (HE), we examine the implementation of HElib (Homomorphic Encryption Library) by using the design and implementation proposed in 2013 by Shai Halevi and Victor Shoup in [3].

Chapter 14 introduces the issues raised during the implementation of (ring) learning with errors cryptography mechanisms. We give a lattice-based key exchange protocol implementation— a library that is used for experimentation purposes.

Chapter 15 introduces new concepts behind the transposition of the theory of chaos-based cryptography into practice. The results and outputs of the chapter represent an important advance of cryptography as it is a new topic which hasn't received proper attention until now.

Chapter 16 presents solutions for implementing securing methods for big data analytics, access control methods (key management for access control), attributed-based access control, secure search, secure data processing, functional encryption, and multi-party computation.

Chapter 17 discusses the security issues raised about applications that are running in a cloud environment and how they can be resolved during the designing and implementation phase.

In *Part III – Pro Cryptanalysis (Chapters 18-24)*, we deal with advanced cryptanalysis topics and we show how to pass the barrier between theory and practice, and how to think of cryptanalysis in terms of practice by eliminating the most vulnerable and critical points of a system or software application in a network or distributed environment.

Starting with *Chapter 18* we provide an introduction to cryptanalysis by presenting the most important characteristics of cryptanalysis.

Chapter 19 starts by showing the important criteria and standards used in cryptanalysis, how the tests of cryptographic systems are made, the process of selecting the cryptographic modules, the cryptanalysis operations, and classifications of cryptanalysis attacks.

In *Chapter 20* and *Chapter 21*, we show how to implement and design linear, differential, and integral cryptanalysis. We focus on techniques and strategies whose primary role is to show how to implement scripts for attacking linear and differential attacks.

Chapter 22 presents the most important attacks and how they can be designed and implemented using C# and .NET. We examine the behavior of the software applications when they are exposed to different attacks and we exploit the source code. We discuss software obfuscation and we show why this is a critical aspect that needs to be taken into consideration by the personnel involved in implementing process of the software. Also, we show how this analysis can lead to machine learning and artificial intelligence algorithms that can be used to predict future attacks over the software applications that are running in a distributed or cloud environment.

In *Chapter 23*, we go through text characterization methods and their implementation. We discuss chi-squared statistic; identifying unknown ciphers; index of coincidence; monogram, bigram, and trigram frequency counts; quadgram statistics as a fitness measure; unicity distance; and word statistics as a fitness measure.

Chapter 24 presents the advantages and disadvantages of implementing the cryptanalysis methods, why they should have a special place when applications are developed in distributed environments, and how the data should be protected against such cryptanalysis methods.

Table 1. *Book Structure*

Part	Chapter Number	Chapter Title
Part I **Foundations** **(Foundational Topics)**	1	Cryptography Fundamentals
	2	Mathematical Background and Its Applicability in Cryptography
	3	Large Integer Arithmetic
	4	Floating-Point Arithmetic
	5	What's new in C# 8.0
	6	Secure Coding Guidelines
	7	Cryptographic Services in .NET
	8	Overview of the *System.Security.Cryptography* Namespace
	9	Cryptography Libraries in C# and .NET
Part II **Pro Cryptography**	10	Elliptic-Curve Cryptography
	11	Lattice-Based Cryptography
	12	Searchable Encryption
	13	Homomorphic Encryption
	14	(Ring) Learning with Errors Cryptography
	15	Chaos-Based Cryptography
	16	Big Data Cryptography
	17	Cloud Computing Cryptography
Part III **Pro Cryptanalysis**	18	Getting Started with Cryptanalysis
	19	Cryptanalysis Attacks and Techniques
	20	Linear and Differential Cryptanalysis
	21	Integral Cryptanalysis
	22	Attacks
	23	Text Characterization
	24	Implementations of Cryptanalysis Methods

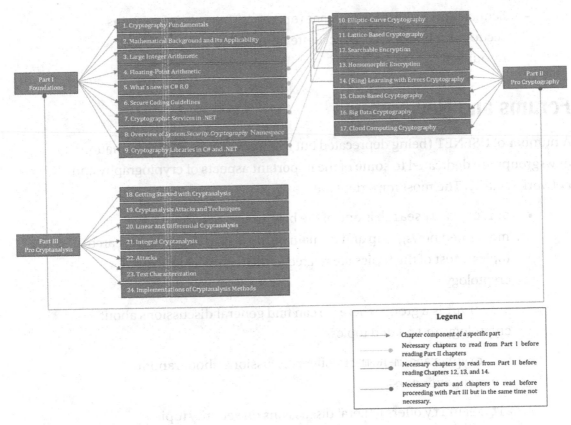

Figure 1. *A roadmap for readers and professionals*

Internet Resources

There are a number of very important resources available on the Web that can be useful for this book and help the readers keep up with the advancements and progress in the field.

- Bill's Security Site, `https://asecuritysite.com/`, contains multiple implementations of cryptographic algorithms. The website is maintained by Bill Buchanan, Professor at the School of Computing at Edinburgh Napier University.

- Books by William Stallings [4] including *Cryptography and Network Security*, `http://williamstallings.com/Cryptography/`. The site includes various important sets of tools and resources that the author updates frequently, keeping in step with the most important advances in the field of cryptography.

- Schneier on Security, `www.schneier.com/`. The website contains sections on books, essays, accurate news, talks, and academic resources.

Forums and Newsgroups

A number of USENET (being deprecated but it still contains useful information) newsgroups are dedicated to some of the important aspects of cryptography and network security. The most important are

- `sci.crypt.research` is one of the best groups to follow. It is a moderated newsgroup and its main purpose is to deal with research topics. Most of the topics are related to the technical aspects of cryptology.

- `sci.crypt` is a group where we can find general discussions about cryptology and related topics.

- `sci.crypt.random-numbers` offers discussions about random number generators.

- `alt.security` offers general discussions on security topics.

- `comp.security.misc` has general discussions on computer security topics.

- `comp.security.firewalls` has discussions about firewalls and other related products.

- `comp.security.announce` is a source for CERT news and announcements.

- `comp.risks` holds discussions about the public risks from computers and users.

- `comp.virus` offers moderated discussions about computer viruses.

Also, there are a number of forums that deal with cryptography topics and news that are available on the Internet. The most important are

- Reddit – Cryptography News and Discussions [5]: This forum group contains general information and news about different topics related to cryptography and information security.

- Security forums [6] cover a vast amount of topics and discussions about computer security and cryptography.

- TechnGenix – Security [7]: One of the most updated forums with news related to cryptography and information security. The group is maintained by leading security professionals in the field.

- Wilders Security Forum [8]: The forum contains discussions and news about the vulnerabilities of software applications due to bad implementations of cryptographic solutions.

- Security Focus [9]: The forum contains a series of discussions about the vulnerabilities raised by implementations of cryptographic algorithms.

- Security InfoWatch [10]: The discussions are related to data and information loss.

- TechRepublic – Security [11]: The forum contains discussions about practical aspects and methodologies that can be used when software applications are designed and implemented.

- Information Security Forum [12]: A world-leading forum in the fields of information security and cryptography. The forum contains conferences, hands-on and practical tutorials, solving solutions to security and cryptographic issues.

Standards

Many of the cryptographic techniques and implementations described in this book are in accordance with the following standards. These standards have been developed and designed to cover management practices and the entire architecture of security mechanisms, strategies, and services.

The most important standards covered by the current book are

- **National Institute of Standards and Technology (NIST)**: NIST represents the U.S. federal agency that deals with standards, science, and technologies that are related to the U.S. government. Excepting the national goal, the NIST Federal Information Processing Standards (FIPS) and the Special Publications (SP) have a very important worldwide impact.

- **Internet Society**: ISOC represents one of the most important professional membership societies with organizational and individual membership worldwide. The society provides leadership on issues relating to the future perspective of the Internet and applications that are developed using security and cryptographic mechanisms, with respect for the groups that are responsible, such as the Internet Engineering Task Force (IETF) and the Internet Architecture Board (IAB). The mentioned organizations develop Internet standards, known and published as RFCs (Requests for Comments).

- **ITU-T**: The International Telecommunication Union (ITU) represents one of the most powerful organizations within the United Nations System. Together with governments and the private sector, it coordinates and administrates the global telecom networks and services. ITU-T represents one of the three sectors of ITU. The mission of ITU-T consists of the production of the standards that cover all the fields of telecommunications. The standards proposed by ITU-T are known as Recommendations.

- **ISO:** The International Organizations for Standardization (ISO) represents a world-wide federation that contains national standards bodies from over 140 countries. ISO is a nongovernmental organization with the goal of promoting the development of standardization and activities that are related with a view to facilitate the international exchange of services to develop cooperation with intellectual, scientific, and technological activities. The results of the ISO are as international agreements published as International Standards.

Conclusions

We are living in the era of unimaginable evolution and incredible technologies that enable the instant flow of information at any time and to any place. The secret lies in the convergence process of the computer with the networks—a very important key force in the evolution and development of these incredible technologies.

In this introduction, we outlined the objectives of the book and their benefits. We successfully showed the mission of the book, addressing the practical aspects of cryptography and information security and its main intention of using the current work. The process of using systems that build advanced information technologies has been shown to have a deep impact on our lives every day. All the technologies prove to be pervasive and ubiquitous.

The book represents the first practical step of translating the most important theoretical cryptography algorithms and mechanisms into practice through one of the most powerful programming languages, C#).

In this introduction, you learned the following:

- The difference between cryptography, cryptanalysis, and cryptology was explained in order to eliminate confusion.

- The book structure was discussed in order to help the reader to easily follow the content. Also, a roadmap was presented to the reader with the goal of showing the dependencies of each chapter and what is necessary for each chapter to be followed. Each chapter was presented in detail, presenting its main objective.

- This chapter included a list of newsgroups, websites, and USENETs, resources where the readers can keep themselves updated with the latest news in fields of cryptography and information security.

- This chapter listed the most important standards used in the fields of cryptography and information security. The reader is now familiar with the process and how each standard works.

Bibliography

[1] Alkim, E., Ducas, L., Pöppelmann, T., & Schwabe, P. (2016). Post-quantum key exchange—a new hope. In 25th {USENIX} Security Symposium ({USENIX} Security 16) (pp. 327-343).

[2] Peikert, C. (2014, October). Lattice cryptography for the internet. In international workshop on post-quantum cryptography (pp. 197-219). Springer, Cham.

[3] Halevi, S., & Shoup, V. (2013). Design and implementation of a homomorphic-encryption library. IBM Research (Manuscript), 6, 12-15.

[4] Stallings, W., Cryptography and Network Security - Principles and Practice. 5 ed. 2010: Pearson. 744.

[5] Reddit. Cryptography News and Discussions. Available from: www.reddit.com/r/crypto/.

[6] Forums, Security. Available from: www.security-forums.com/index.php?sid=acc302c71bb3ea3a7d631a357223e261.

[7] TechGenix, Security. Available from: http://techgenix.com/security/.

[8] Wilders Security Forums. Available from: www.wilderssecurity.com/.

[9] Security Focus. Available from: www.securityfocus.com/.

[10] Security InfoWatch. Available from: https://forums.securityinfowatch.com/.

[11] TechRepublic – Security. Available from: www.techrepublic.com/forums/security/.

[12] Information Security Forum. Available from: www.securityforum.org/.

PART I

Foundational Topics

CHAPTER 1

Cryptography Fundamentals

Introduction

The history of cryptography is very long and interesting. For a complete non-technical reference of cryptography, we recommend *The Codebreakers* [1]. The book presents cryptography from its initial use by the Egyptians around 4,000 years ago to recent history when it played a vital role in the outcome of both world wars. The book was written in **1963** and covers aspects of history that were significant in terms of the development of cryptography. Cryptography is seen as an art and it is associated with diplomatic services, military personnel, and governments. Cryptography has been used as a tool for protecting strategies and different secrets related to national security.

The most important development in the history of cryptography was in **1976** when Diffie and Hellman [2] published the work paper entitled "New Directions in Cryptography." The paper introduced the concept that revolutionized how cryptography was seen: public-key cryptography. The authors also introduced a new and ingenious method for key exchange. The security of the method is based on the intractability of the discrete logarithm problem. At that time, the authors didn't have a practical implementation of the public-key encryption scheme, an idea that was very clear and started to generate significant interest in the cryptographic community. Starting in **1978**, the first implementation of a public-key encryption and signature scheme was proposed by Rivest, Shamir, and Adleman (nowadays known as RSA [3]). The RSA scheme is based on the intractability of factoring large integers. If we are doing a parallel between integer factorization from RSA and Shor's Algorithm, we will observe that the last algorithm will run in polynomial time for quantum computers and it will represent an important challenge to any cryptography approach that is based on the hardness assumption of

© Marius Iulian Mihailescu and Stefania Loredana Nita 2021
M. I. Mihailescu and S. L. Nita, *Pro Cryptography and Cryptanalysis*,
https://doi.org/10.1007/978-1-4842-6367-9_1

factoring large integers [62]. The application of factoring large integers and its purpose has increased the number of the methods for factoring. In **1980,** there were important advancements in this area but none of them showed any improvements for the security of RSA. A very important class of practical public-key schemes was found and proposed in **1985** by ElGamal [4]. His schemes are also based on the problem of the discrete logarithm.

The most important and significant contribution provided by public-key cryptography is represented by the digital signature. In **1991,** the ISO/IEC 9796 international standard for digital signatures was adopted [5]. The standard is based on the RSA public-key scheme. In **1994,** the United States government adopted the Digital Signature Standard, a powerful scheme based on the problem of the discrete logarithm.

Nowadays, searching for new public-key scheme, improvements on the current cryptographic mechanisms, and designing new proofs for security are still happening and continue to bring significant improvements.

The goal and purpose of this book is to explain the latest updates of the principles, techniques, algorithms, and implementations of the most important aspects of cryptography in practice. The focus is on the aspects that are most practical and applied. You will learn about the aspects that represent issues and we will point to references in literature and best practices that provide solutions. Due to the large volume of material covered, most of the results will be accompanied by implementations. This also serves to not obscure the real nature of cryptography. The book offers strong material for both implementers and researchers. The book describes algorithms and software systems with their interactions.

Information Security and Cryptography

In this book, the term and concept of *information* can be understood as *quantity.* In order to make an introduction to cryptography and its applications through algorithms and implementation technologies (such as C#), you need to understand the issues that are related to information security. All parties who participate in a certain transaction must have the confidence that specific objectives that are associated with the information security have been followed. The objectives are listed in Table 1-1.

A set of protocols and mechanisms has been created in order to deal with the issues raised by information security when the information is send by physical documents. The objectives of the information security can be achieved as well through mathematical algorithms and protocols, requiring at the same time procedural techniques and following the laws by achieving the result that is desired. As an example, let's consider the privacy of letters, which is provided by sealed envelopes that are delivered by a legitimate mail service. The physical security of the envelope has its own limitations and laws are established in such way that if mail is open by someone who is not authorized to do so, they can be charged with a criminal offense. There are cases when that security is achieved not only through the information itself but also through the paper document that records the originality of the information. As an example, consider paper currency, which requires special ink and material in order to avoid and prevent the forgery of it.

Table 1-1. *Security Objectives*

Security Objective	Description
Privacy/confidentiality	Keeping the secrecy of the information from those who are not authorized to see it
Signature	A way to bind the signature to an entity (e.g. document)
Authorization	Sending from one entity to another, representing an official authorization to do or be something
Message authentication	Known as the authentication origin of data; some texts use as a definition the corroboration of the information source
Data integrity	The process of making sure that the information has not been altered by an unauthorized person or through other unknown means
Entity authentication/ identification	Comparing the identity of an entity (e.g. computer, person, credit card, etc.).
Validation	A way of providing timeliness for authorization in order to use or manipulate the information or resources
Certification	Represents the acknowledgement of information by a trusted entity
Access control	The process of restricting resources to privileged entities
Certification	Acknowledgement of information by a trusted certification

(continued)

5

Table 1-1. (*continued*)

Security Objective	Description
Timestamping	A record that represents the time of creation or the existence of information
Witnessing	A way of verifying the creation of existence of information represented by an entity who is different from the creator
Receipt	Represents an acknowledgment that the information has been received
Ownership	A way to provide an entity with the legal right to use or transfer a specific resource to other entity
Confirmation	Represents the acknowledgement that services have been provided with success or not
Revocation	The process of retraction of a certification or authorization
Non-repudiation	The process of preventing the denial of other previous commitments or actions
Anonymity	The stashing process of the identity of an entity involved in a specific process

Conceptually speaking, the way information is stored, registered, interpreted, and recorded hasn't changed too much. The ability to copy and modify information represents one of the most important characteristics of manipulating information that has been changed significantly.

One of the most important tools used in information security is represented by the *signature.* It represents a building block for multiple services such as non-repudiation, data origin authentication, identification, and witnessing.

In a society based on electronic communication, achieving information security implies fulfilling requirements based on legal and technical skills. At the same time, there is no guarantee that the objectives of information security can be met accordingly. The technical part of information security is assured by *cryptography.*

Cryptography represents the discipline that studies mathematical techniques that are related to information security such as confidentiality, integrity (data), authentication (entity), and the origin of the authentication. Cryptography doesn't consist only of providing information security, but also in a specific set of techniques.

Cryptography Goals

From the list of objectives related to information security listed in Table 1-1, the next four represent the basis of a framework that will help others to be derived:

- Privacy/confidentiality (Definition 1.5 and 1.8)

- Data integrity (Definition 1.9)

- Authentication (Definition 1.7)

- Non-repudiation (Definition 1.6)

Let's consider each of the objectives separately and see their own goal and purpose:

- *Confidentiality* represents a service that is used to protect the content of information from those who are not authorized to see it. There are different approaches to providing confidentiality, from mathematical algorithms to physical protection that will scramble the data in an incomprehensible mode.

- *Data integrity* represents a service that deals with the unauthorized alteration of data. In order to assure the integrity of the data, one needs to have the ability to detect data manipulation by parties that are unauthorized.

- *Authentication* represents a service that occupies an important role in the authentication of the data or application and that deals with *identification*. The function is applied on both sides of the entity that deals with the information. It is necessary that both parties that are participating in the communication present their identity to each other (the parties involved could be a person or a system). The information that is delivered and transferred over a communication channel should be certified as to origin, data content, time sent, etc. Based on these reasons, this aspect of cryptography is divided in two major subfields: *authentication of the entity* and *data origin authentication*. The *data origin authentication* offers data integrity.

- *Non-repudiation* is represented by a service that helps prevent an entity from denying previous actions.

  When a conflict exists because an entity denies certain actions were taken, there is a sinew that can resolve the situation that is necessary.

One of the fundamental goals of cryptography is to make sure that the four areas listed above are addressed properly on both sides, theory and practice.

The book will describe a number of fundamental *cryptographic tools*, also known as *primitives*, which are used in providing information security. Examples of primitives are described as encryption schemes (Definition 1.5 and 1.8), hash functions (Definition 1.9), and schemes for digital signatures (Definition 1.6). In Figure 1-1, we have provided a schematic depiction of the cryptographic primitives and how they intersect and relate. Many of the cryptographic primitives depicted in Figure 1-1 are covered in this book, followed by practical implementations. The primitives should pass through an evaluation process with respect for the following criteria:

- *Level of security.* The level of security is quite difficult when we have to quantify it. It can be seen as the number of operations necessary to defeat the proposed objective. Usually the level of security is defined based on the volume of work that is necessary to defeat the objective.

- *Functionality.* In order to meet different information security objectives, the primitives need to be combined.

- *Operation methods.* The primitives, when they are applied in different ways and with different inputs, usually develop different characteristics. One primitive is capable of providing very different functionality that depends on the mode of operation.

- *Performance.* The concept of performance refers to the efficiency that a primitive can offer in a specific and particular mode of operation.

- *Ease of implementation.* This concept represents a process more than a criterion of achieving the primitive in practical usage.

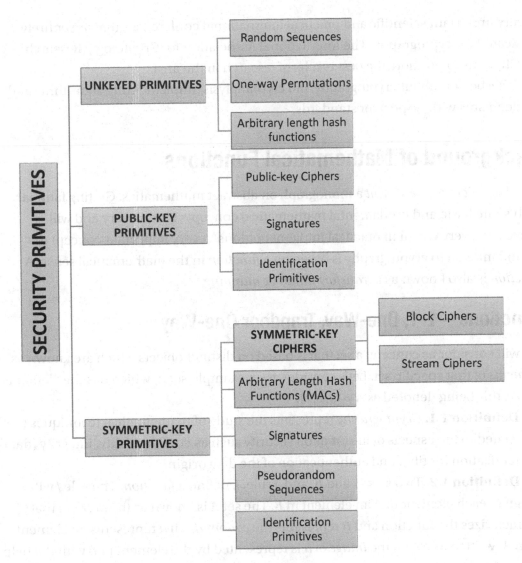

Figure 1-1. *Cryptographic primitives taxonomy*

The importance of various criterions depends very much on the application and resources that are available.

Cryptography has been seen as an art practiced by many practitioners and professionals who have conceive different ad-hoc techniques with the goal of meeting important information security requirements. In the last twenty years, we have seen a period of transition of the discipline from art to science. Currently, there are a couple of very important scientific and practical international conferences that are entirely dedicated to cryptography. The International Association for Cryptologic Research (IACR) aims to promote the best results of research in the area.

This book is about cryptography and cryptanalysis, implementing algorithms and mechanisms with respect for standards.

Background of Mathematical Functions

This *book does not represent* a monograph on abstract mathematics. Getting familiar with some basic and fundamental mathematical concepts is necessary and will prove to be very useful in practical implementations. A very important concept that is fundamental to cryptography is based on a *function* in the mathematical sense. A *function* is also known as a *transformation* or *mapping*.

Functions – 1-1, One-Way, Trapdoor One-Way

We will consider as concept, a *set* that is based on distinct objects which are known as *elements* of that specific set. Let's consider as an example set A, which has the elements a, b, c, this being denoted as $A = \{a, b, c\}$.

Definition 1.1. *Cryptography* represents the study of mathematical techniques that are related to the aspects of information security such as confidentiality, integrity (data), authentication (entity), and authentication of the data origin.

Definition 1.2. Two sets, A and B, and a rule, f, define a *function*. The rule f will assign to each element in A an element in B. The set A is known as the *domain* that characterizes the function and B represents the *codomain*. If a represents an element from A, written as $a \in A$, the *image* of a is represented by the element in B with the help of rule f; the image b of a is noted by $b = f(a)$. The standard notation for function f from set A to set B is represented as $f: A \rightarrow B$. If $b \in B$, and then we have a preimage of b, which is an element $a \in A$ for which $f(a) = b$. The entire set of elements in B, which has at least one preimage, is known as the *image* of f, noted as $Im(f)$.

Example 1.3. *(function)* Consider the sets $A = \{a, b, c\}$ and $B = \{1, 2, 3, 4\}$, and the rule f from A to B as being defined as $f(a) = 2, f(b) = 4, f(c) = 1$. Figure 1-2 shows a depiction of the sets A, B and the function f. The preimage of the element 2 is a. The image of f is $\{1, 2, 4\}$.

Example 1.4. *(function)* Let's consider the following set of $A = \{1, 2, 3, \ldots\ldots, 10\}$ and consider f to be the rule that for each $a \in A$, $f(a) = r_a$, where r_a represents the remainder when a^2 is being divided by 11.

$$f(1) = 1 \qquad f(6) = 3$$

$$f(2) = 3 \qquad f(7) = 5$$

$$f(3) = 9 \qquad f(8) = 9$$

$$f(4) = 5 \qquad f(9) = 4$$

$$f(5) = 3 \qquad f(10) = 1$$

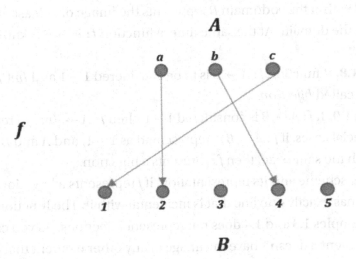

Figure 1-2. *Function f from a set A formed from three elements to a set B formed from five elements*

The image of f is represented by the set $Y = \{1, 3, 4, 5, 9\}$.

Think of the function in terms of the scheme (in the literature, it's known as the *functional diagram*) as depicted in Figure 1-2, where each element from domain A has precisely one arrow originating from it. For each element from codomain B we can have any number of arrows as being incidental to it (including also zero lines).

Example 1.5. *(function)* Let's consider the following set defined as $A = \{1, 2, 3, ..., 10^{50}\}$ and consider f to be the rule $f(a) = r_a$, where r_a represents the remainder in the case when a^2 is divided by $10^{50} + 1$ for all $a \in A$. In this situation, it is not feasible to write down f explicitly as we did in Example 1.4. This being said, the function is completely defined by the domain and the mathematical description that characterize the rule f.

1-1 (One-to-One) Functions

Definition 1.6. We can say that a function or transformation is $1 - 1$ (one-to-one) if each of the elements found within the codomain B are represented as the image of at most one element in the domain A.

Definition 1.7. We can say that a function or transformation is *onto* if each of the elements found within the codomain B represents the image of at least one element that can be found in the domain. At the same time, a function $f : A \to B$ is known as being onto if $Im(f) = B$.

Definition 1.8. If function $f : A \to B$ is to be considered $1 - 1$ and $Im(f) = B$, and then the function f is called *bijection*.

Conclusion 1.9. If $f : A \to B$ is considered $1 - 1$, then $f : A \to Im(f)$ represents the bijection. In special cases, if $f : A \to B$ is represented as $1 - 1$, and A and B are represented as finite sets with the same size, then f represents a bijection.

Based on the scheme and its representation, if f represents a bijection, then each element from B has exactly one line that is incidental with it. The function shown and described in Examples 1.3 and 1.4 does not represent bijections. As you can see in Example 1.3, element 3 doesn't have the image of any other element that can be found within the domain. In Example 1.4, each element from the codomain is identified with two preimages.

Definition 1.10. If f is a bijection from A to B, then it is a quite simple matter to define a bijection g from B to A as follows: for each $b \in B$ we will define $g(b) = a$ where $a \in A$ and $f(a) = b$. The function g is obtained from f and it is called an *inverse function* of f and is denoted as $g = f^{-1}$.

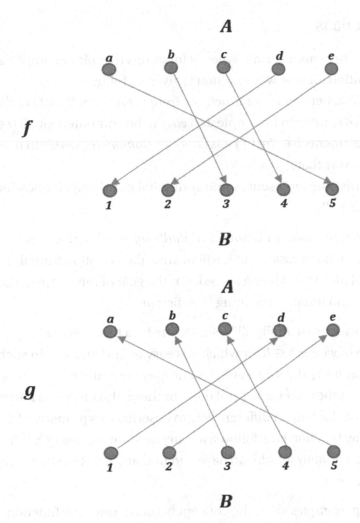

Figure 1-3. *Representation of bijection f and its inverse, g = f⁻¹*

Example 1.11. *(inverse function)* Let's consider the following sets of $A = \{a, b, c, d, e\}$ and $Y = \{1, 2, 3, 4, 5\}$, and consider the rule f which is given and represented by the lines in Figure 1-3. f represents a bijection and its inverse, g, is formed by reversing the sense of the arrows. The domain of g is represented by B and the codomain is A.

Keep in mind that if f represents a bijection, f^{-1} is also a bijection. The bijections in cryptography are used as tools for message encryption and inverse transformations are used for decryption. The fundamental condition for decryption is for transformation to be bijections.

One-Way Functions

In cryptography, there are a certain types of functions that play an important role. Due to the rigor, a definition for one-way function is given as follows.

Definition 1.12. Let's consider function f from set A to set B that is called a *one-way* function if $f(a)$ proves to be simple and *easy* to be computed for all $a \in A$ but for "essentially all" elements $b \in Im(f)$ it is *computationally infeasible* to manage to find any $a \in A$ in such way that $f(a) = b$.

Note 1.13. This note represents some additional notes and clarifications of the terms used in Definition 1.12.

1. For the terms *easy* and *computationally infeasible* a rigorous definition is necessary but it will distract the attention from the general idea that is being agreed. For the goal of this chapter, the simple and intuitive meaning is sufficient.

2. The phrase "essentially all" refers to the idea that there are a couple of values $b \in B$ for which it is easy to find an $a \in A$ in such way that $b = f(a)$. As an example, one may compute $b = f(a)$ for a small number of a values and then for these, the inverse is known by a table look-up. A different way to describe this property of a one-way function is as follows: for any random $b \in Im(f)$, it is computationally feasible to have and find any $a \in A$ in such way that $f(a) = b$.

The following examples show the concept behind a one-way function.

Example 1.14. *(one-way function)* Consider $A = \{1, 2, 3, ..., 16\}$ and let's define $f(a) = r_a$ for all the elements $a \in A$ where r_a represents the remainder when 3^x will be divided with 17.

a	1	2	3	4	5	6	7	8	9	10	11	12	13	14	15	16
$f(a)$	3	9	10	13	5	15	11	16	14	8	7	4	12	2	6	1

Having a number between 1 and 16, it is quite easy to look and find the image of it under f. Without having the table in front of you, for example, for 7 it is hard to find a given that $f(a) = 7$. If the number that you are given is 3, then is quite easy to see that $a = 1$ is what you actually need.

Keep in mind that this represents an example that is based on very small numbers. The important aspect here is that there is a difference in the volume of work to compute $f(a)$ and the amount of work to find a given $f(a)$. Also, for large numbers, $f(a)$ can be efficiently computed using the square-and-multiply algorithm [20], where the process of finding a from $f(a)$ is harder to find.

Example 1.15. *(one-way function)* A *prime number* represents a positive integer bigger than 1 whose positive integer divisors are 1 and itself. Choose the following primes of p = 50633, q = 58411, compute $n = pq = 50633 \cdot 58411 = 2957524163$, and let's consider $A = \{1, 2, 3, ..., n - 1\}$. We define a function f on A by $f(a) = r_a$ for each $a \in A$, where r_a represents the remainder when x^3 is divided by n. For example, let's consider $f(2489991 = 1981394214$ since $2489991^3 = 5881949859 \cdot n + 1981394214$. Computing $f(a)$ represents a simple thing to be done, but reversing the procedure is quite difficult.

Trapdoor One-Way Functions

Definition 1.16. A *trapdoor one-way function* is defined as a one-way function $f: A \rightarrow B$ with the additional property that by having extra information (known as *trapdoor information*) it will become feasible to find and identify any given $b \in Im(f)$, with an $a \in A$ in such way that $f(a) = b$.

In Example 1.15, we show the concept of a trapdoor one-way function. With extra information about the factors of $n = 2957524163$ it will become much easier to invert the function. The factors of 2957524163 are large enough that finding them by hand computation would be difficult. With the help of any computer software we can find the factors quite quickly. If, for example, we have very large distinct prime numbers (each number having around 200 decimal digits), p and q, with today's technologies, it's quite difficult even with the most powerful computers to find p and q from n. This is the well-known problem entitled as *integer factorization problem, which for quantum computers will not represent an issue.*

One-way and trapdoor one-way functions represent the basic foundation for public-key cryptography. These concepts are very important and they will become much clearer later when their application to cryptographic techniques are implemented and discussed. It is quite important to keep these abstract concepts from this section in mind as the concrete methods and the main foundation for the cryptography algorithms that will be implemented later within this book.

Permutations

Permutations represent functions that are in cryptographic constructs.

Definition 1.17. Consider S to be a finite set formed of elements. A *permutation p* on S represents a bijection as defined in Definition 1.8. The bijection is represented from S to itself as $p: S \rightarrow S$.

Example 1.18. This example represents a permutation example. Let's consider the following permutation: $S = \{1, 2, 3, 4, 5\}$. The permutation $p: S \rightarrow S$ is defined as follows:

$$p(1) = 2, \; p(2) = 5, \; p(3) = 4, \; p(4) = 2, \; p(5) = 1$$

A permutation can be described in different ways. It can be written as above or as an array as

$$p = \begin{pmatrix} 1 & 2 & 3 & 4 & 5 \\ 3 & 5 & 4 & 2 & 1 \end{pmatrix},$$

in which the top row of the array is represented by the domain and the bottom row is represented by the image under p as mapping.

As the permutations are bijections, they have inverses. If the permutation is written as an away (second form), its inverse will be very easily to find by interchanging the rows in the array and reordering the elements from the new top row and the bottom row. In this case, the inverse of p is defined as follows:

$$p^{-1} = \begin{pmatrix} 1 & 2 & 3 & 4 & 5 \\ 5 & 4 & 1 & 3 & 2 \end{pmatrix}$$

Example 1.19. This example represents a permutation example. Let's consider A to be the set of integers $\{0, 1, 2, ..., p \cdot q - 1\}$ where p and q represent two distinct large primes. We need to suppose also that neither $p - 1$ nor $q - 1$ can be divisible by 3. The function $p(a) = r_a$, in which r_a represents the remainder when a^3 is divided by pq can be demonstrated and shown as being the inverse perumutation. The inverse permutation is computationally infeasible by computers nowadays, unless p and q are known.

Involutions

Involutions are known as functions having their own inverses.

Definition 1.20. Let's consider a finite set of S and f defined as a bijection S to S, noted as $f: S \rightarrow S$. In this case, function f will be noted as the *involution* if $f = f^{-1}$. Another way of defining this is $f(f(a)) = a$ for any $a \in S$.

Example 1.21. This example represents an involution case. In Figure 1-4, we depict an example of involution. In Figure 1-4, note that if j represents the image of i, then i represents the image of j.

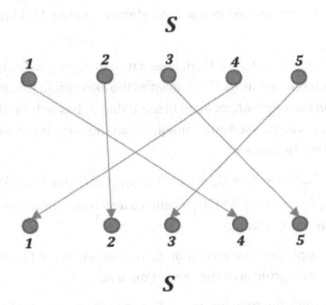

Figure 1-4. *Representation of an involution with a set of S with five elements*

Concepts and Basic Terminology

When we deal with the scientific study of the cryptography discipline, we see that it was built on hard and abstract definitions born from fundamental concepts. In this section, we will list the most important terms and key concepts that are used in this book.

Domains and Codomains Used for Encryption

- $\mathcal{A}$ is represented as a finite set known as the *alphabet of definition*. Let's consider as an example, $\mathcal{A} = \{0,1\}$, which is the binary alphabet, which is a frequently used as a definition.

- $\mathcal{M}$ represents a set known as the *message space*. The message space contains the strings of symbols from an alphabet, $\mathcal{A}$. As an example, $\mathcal{M}$ may contain binary strings, English text, French text, etc.

- $\mathcal{C}$ represents the set known as the *ciphertext space*. $\mathcal{C}$ contains strings of symbols from an alphabet, $\mathcal{A}$, which is different from the alphabet defined for $\mathcal{M}$. An element from $\mathcal{C}$ is called *ciphertext*.

Encryption and Decryption Transformations

- $\mathcal{K}$ is a set known as the *key space*. An element within $\mathcal{K}$ is known as a *key*.

- Each element from $\mathcal{K}$, $e \in \mathcal{K}$, defines a unique bijection from $\mathcal{M}$ to $\mathcal{C}$ which is noted as E_e. E_e is known as the *encryption function* or *encryption transformation*. Keep in mind that E_e has to be a bijection if the process is reversed and a unique clear message is recovered for each distinct ciphertext.

- For each $d \in \mathcal{K}$, we have D_d, which is a bijection from $\mathcal{C}$ to $\mathcal{M}$ (for example, $D_d : \mathcal{C} \to \mathcal{M}$). D_d is called a *decryption function* or *decryption transformation*.

- When we apply the transformation E_e to message $m \in \mathcal{M}$, it is usually known as *encrypting m* or the *encryption of m*.

- When we apply the transformation D_d to a ciphertext c, it is known as *decrypting c* or the *decryption of c*.

- The *encryption scheme* is based on a set, $\{E_e : e \in \mathcal{K}\}$, that represents the encryption transformations and a corresponding set, $\{D_d : d \in \mathcal{K}\}$, which are the decryption transformations that have the property that for each $e \in \mathcal{K}$ there is a unique key $d \in \mathcal{K}$ in such that $D_d = E_e^{-1}$; so $D_d(E_e(m)) = m$ for all $m \in \mathcal{M}$. The encryption scheme is also referred to as a *cipher*.

- The keys represented by e and d are in the above definitions known as a *key pair* and in some documentation are noted as (e, d). In some cases, e and d could be the same.

- In order to *construct* an encryption scheme, we must select a message space $\mathcal{M}$, a ciphertext $\mathcal{C}$, a key space $\mathcal{K}$, a set of encryption transformations $\{E_e : e \in \mathcal{K}\}$, and a corresponding set of decryption transformations $\{D_d : d \in \mathcal{K}\}$.

The Participants in the Communication Process

Starting with Figure 1-5 the following terminology is defined:

- An *entity* or *party* represents someone or something who sends, receives, or manipulates the information. In Figure 1-5, *Alice* and *Bob* are represented as entities or parties, as computers, etc.

- A *sender* represents an entity in a two-party communication. It represents the rightful transmitter of the information. In Figure 1-5, the *sender* is represented by *Alice*.

- A *receiver* represents an entity in a two-party communication. It represents the intended recipient of information. In Figure 1-5, the *receiver* is represented by *Bob*.

- An *adversary (attacker, or sometimes for simplifying the examples it is referred as Oscar or Eve*[1]*)* represents an entity in a two-party communication. It is neither the sender nor the receiver. The adversary tries to break the information security service that serves as a service provided between the sender and receiver. Other names for the adversary found in the literature are enemy, attacker, opponent, eavesdropper, intruder, and interloper. Often, the adversary will play the role of either the rightful sender or the rightful receiver.

---

[1] Alice and Bob, `https://en.wikipedia.org/wiki/Alice_and_Bob`

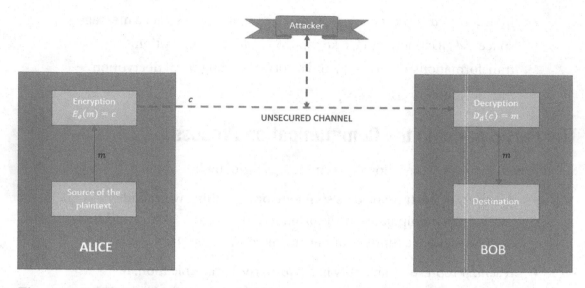

Figure 1-5. *Two-party communication process using encryption*

Digital Signatures

In this book, we will deal with digital signatures as well. A *digital signature* represents a cryptographic primitive that is fundamental in the process of authentication, authorization, and non-repudiation. The goal of a digital signature is to offer a way for an entity to map its identity with a piece of information. The process of *signing implies* the transforming of the message and a part known as secret information that is held by the entity into a *tag* known as the *signature*.

A general description is as follows:

- $\mathcal{M}$ represents the set of messages that have the possibility to be signed.

- $\mathcal{S}$ represents the set of elements known as *signatures.* The signatures can be binary strings with a fixed length.

- $\mathcal{S}_A$ is defined as a transformation from the set of messages $\mathcal{M}$ to the set of signatures $\mathcal{S}$, known as a *signing transformation* for entity A (Alice). The $\mathcal{S}_A$ is stored as a secret by A and is used to create signatures for the messages from $\mathcal{M}$.

- V_A represents a transformation from the set $\mathcal{M} \times \mathcal{S}$ to the set {*true, false*}. $\mathcal{M} \times \mathcal{S}$ consists of all pairs (m, s) where $m \in \mathcal{M}$ and $s \in \mathcal{S}$, known as the Cartesian product of $\mathcal{M}$ and $\mathcal{S}$. V_A is a transformation that can be used as a verification process for the signatures of A, is known as public, and is used by different entities in order to verify the signatures created by A.

Signing Procedure

We will use an entity A, which we will name as the signer. We will create a signature for a specific message $m \in \mathcal{M}$ by applying the following messages:

- Calculate $s = S_A(m)$.

- Send the pair (m, s), where s represents the signature for the message m.

Verification Procedure

In order to verify that a signature s for a message m is created by A, another entity B (known as Bob), who plays the verifier role, performs the following steps:

- Get the function of verification for V_A of A.

- Calculate $u = V_A(m, s)$.

- Agree on the signature that has been created by A if $u = true$ and deny the signature if $u = false$.

Public-Key Cryptography

Public-key cryptography plays an important role in .NET and when we need to implement related algorithms. There are several important commercial libraries that implement public-key cryptography solutions for developers, such as [21-30].

To understand better how public-key cryptography works, let's consider a of encryption transformations defined as $\{E_e : e \in \mathcal{K}\}$ and a set of matching decryption transformations defined as $\{D_d : d \in \mathcal{K}\}$, where $\mathcal{K}$ represents the key space. Take into consideration the following pair association of encryption/decryption transformations (E_e, D_d) and let's suppose that each pair has the property of knowing E_e that is computationally unrealizable, having a random ciphertext $c \in \mathcal{C}$ to manage to identify the message $m \in \mathcal{M}$ in such way that $E_e(m) = c$. The property defined involves that for any given e it is unrealizable to determine the corresponding decryption key d.

Having the assumptions made above, let's consider a two-party communication between Alice and Bob as illustrated in Figure 1-6.

- Bob will select a key pair (e, d).

- Bob will send the encryption key e, known as the public key, to Alice over any channel and will keep the decryption key, d, known as the private key, secure and secret.

- Alice, afterwards, will send a message m to Bob by applying the encryption transformation that is computed and determined by Bob's public key in order to get $c = E_e(m)$. Bob will decrypt the ciphertext c by using the inverse transformation D_d which is determined uniquely by d.

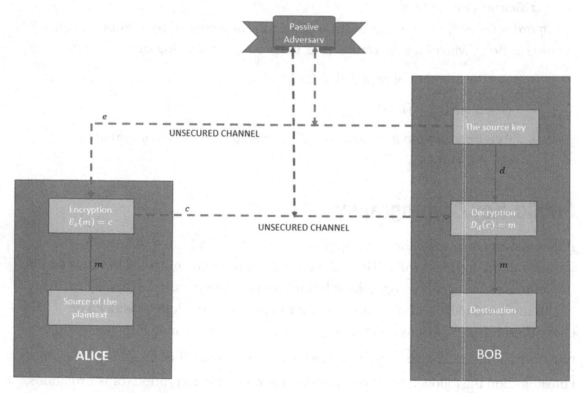

Figure 1-6. *The process of encryption using public-key mechanism*

The encryption key e does not need to be kept secret. It may be made public. Any entity can send encrypted messages to Bob, and only Bob has the ability to decrypt them. Figure 1-7 illustrates the idea where A_1, A_2, and A_3 represent different entities. Remember if A_1 destroys message m_1 after encrypting it to c_1, then even A_1 is found in the position of not being able to recover m_1 from c_1.

To make it clear, let's consider as an example a box with the cover secured by a lock with a specific combination. Bob is the only one who knows the combination. If the lock remains unlocked for any reason and is thus publicly available, anyone can get inside the box and leave a message inside and lock the lock.

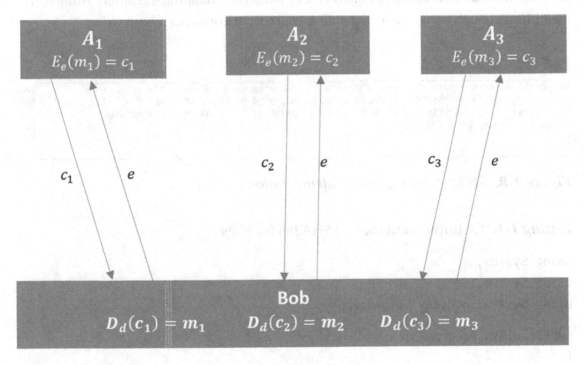

Figure 1-7. *How public-key encryption is used*

Hash Functions

.NET offers the HashAlgorithm class, which is part of the namespace System.Security. Cryptography [19]. The class represents the base class that needs to be used when all implementations of cryptographic hash algorithms must derive.

As an example (see Figure 1-8 and Listing 1-1), the following C# code example will compute the SHA1CryptoServiceProvider hash for a specific array. This example is based on the assumption that we have already a predefined byte array dataArray[]. SHA1CryptoServiceProvider represents a class that is derived from HashAlgorithm:

```
HashAlgorithm sha = new SHA1CryptoServiceProvider();
byte[] result = sha.ComputeHash(dataArray);
```

Hash functions represent one of the most important primitives in modern cryptography. A hash function is also known as a one-way hash function. A hash function represents a computationally efficient function mapping the binary string with an arbitrary length to binary strings with a fixed length known as a *hash value*.

Figure 1-8. *SHA256 example of implementation*

Listing 1-1. C# Implementation of SHA256 for Files

```
using System;
using System.IO;
using System.Security.Cryptography;

public class Program
{
    public static void Main(String[] args)
    {
        ApplyingHashOverADirectory obj = new ApplyingHashOverADirectory();
        obj.Compute();
    }
}
```

```
public class ApplyingHashOverADirectory
{
    public void Compute()
    {
        //if (args.Length < 1)
        //{
        //    Console.WriteLine("There is no directory selected to hash.");
        //    return;
        //}

        Console.Write("Enter the directory path: ");

        //string directory = args[0]; //D:\Apps C#\Chapter 1 - Cryptography
        Fundamentals
        string directory = Console.ReadLine();
        if (Directory.Exists(directory))
        {
            //** creating an object as DirectoryInfo
            //** which will represent the
            //** directory selected for hash
            var directories = new DirectoryInfo(directory);

            //** Obtaing the informations of the files from
            //** the directory select as FileInfo objects
            FileInfo[] files_from_directory = directories.GetFiles();

            //** create and SHA256 object and initialize it
            using (SHA256 mySHA256Object = SHA256.Create())
            {
                //** find the hash value for each
                //** of the file from the directory
                foreach (FileInfo file_information in files_from_directory)
                {
                    try
                    {
                        //** for each of the file
                        //** create a file stram
```

```
                        FileStream file_stream = file_information.
                        Open(FileMode.Open);

                        //** put the position at
                        //** the beginning of the stream
                        file_stream.Position = 0;

                        //** find the hash of the
                        //** fileStream object
                        byte[] hash_value = mySHA256Object.ComputeHash
                        (file_stream);

                        //** show the name and hash
                        //** value of the file in the console
                        Console.Write($"{file_information.Name}: ");
                        PrintByteArray(hash_value);

                        //** make sure that you close the file
                        file_stream.Close();
                    }
                    catch (IOException e)
                    {
                        Console.WriteLine($"I/O Exception: { e.Message}");
                    }
                    catch (UnauthorizedAccessException e)
                    {
                        Console.WriteLine($"There is an error with
                        accessing the file: { e.Message}");
                    }
                }
            }
        }
        else
        {
            Console.WriteLine("The directory selected couldn't be located
            or found. Please, select another one.");
        }
    }
```

```
//** Show the byte array for the
//** user under a readable structure
public static void PrintByteArray(byte[] array)
{
    for (int i = 0; i < array.Length; i++)
    {
        Console.Write($"{array[i]:X2}");
        if ((i % 4) == 3) Console.Write(" ");
    }
    Console.WriteLine();
}
}
```

Hash functions are widely used with digital signatures and also within the data integrity. When we are dealing with digital signatures, a long message is usually hashed and only the hash value is signed. The party that will receive the message then will hash the received message, and they will verify that the received signature is correct for this hash value. This will save time and space by signing the message directly, which consists of splitting the message into appropriate-sized blocks and individually signing each block.

Table 1-2 provides a classification of keyed cryptographic hash functions, and Table 1-3 provides unkeyed cryptographic hash functions. Most of the functions are already implemented in .NET within the System.Security.Cryptography namespace and the HashAlgorithm class.

Table 1-2. *Keyed Cryptographic Hash Functions*

Name	Length of the tag	Type	Bibliography
BLAKE2	Arbitrary	Keyed hash function with prefix-MAC	[31][42]
BLAKE3	Arbitrary	Keyed hash function with supplied initializing vector (IV)	[32]
HMAC	-	-	[33]
KMAC	Arbitrary	Based on Keccak	[34][35]
MD6	512 bits	Merkle tree with NLFSR	[37]
PMAC	-	-	[38]
UMAC	-	-	[39]

Table 1-3. *Unkeyed Cryptographic Hash Functions*

Name	Length	Type	Bibliography
BLAKE-256	256 bits	HAIFA structure [41]	[40]
BLAKE-512	512 bits	HAIFA structure [41]	[40]
GOST	256 bits	Hash	[43]
MD2	128 bits	Hash	
MD4	128 bits	Hash	[44]
MD5	128 bits	Merkle-Damgard construction [36]	[45]
MD6	Up to 512 bits	Merkle-tree NLFSR	[37]
RIPEMD	128 bits	Hash	[46]
RIPEMD-128	128 bits	Hash	[46][47][48]
RIPEMD-256	-	Hash	
RIPEMD-160	160 bits	Hash	
RIPEMD-320	320 bits	Hash	
SHA-1	160 bits	Merkle-Damgard construction [36]	[61]
SHA-256	256 bits	Merkle-Damgard construction	[50][51][54]
SHA-384	384 bits		[52][54]
SHA-512	512 bits		[53][54]
SHA-224	224 bits	Merkle-Damgard construction	[55]
SHA-3 (Keccak)	Arbitrary	Sponge function [50]	[56][57]
Whirlpool	512 bits	Hash	[58][59][60]

Case Studies

Caesar Cipher Implementation in C#

In this section, we will give an implementation in C# of a Caesar cipher. The purpose of this section is to illustrate how the mathematical foundations listed above can be useful during the implementation process and the advantages of understanding the basic math mechanisms behind the algorithms. We will NOT focus on the mathematical background of the algorithms in this book. If you want to go deeply into the mathematical background, it is recommended to follow the following references [6-18].

The encryption process used by a Caesar cipher can be represented as modular arithmetic by first transforming the letters into numbers. For this, we will use the following *alphabet* $\mathcal{A} = \{A,\ldots,Z\} = 25$ in such way that $A = 0$, $B = 1$, ..., $Z = 25$. The encryption of a letter x is done by a shift n and mathematically can be described as

$$E_n(x) = (x+n) \bmod 26$$

The decryption is done in a similar way:

$$D_n(x) = (x-n) \bmod 26$$

Let's start the implementation of the algorithm. In Solution Explorer we have only one single file, StartCaesar.cs (see Figure 1-9).

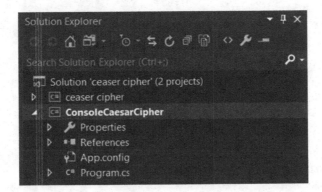

Figure 1-9. *The structure of the Caesar cipher project (main form, Program.cs)*

The application (see Figure 1-10 and Listing 1-2) is very simple and easy to interact with.

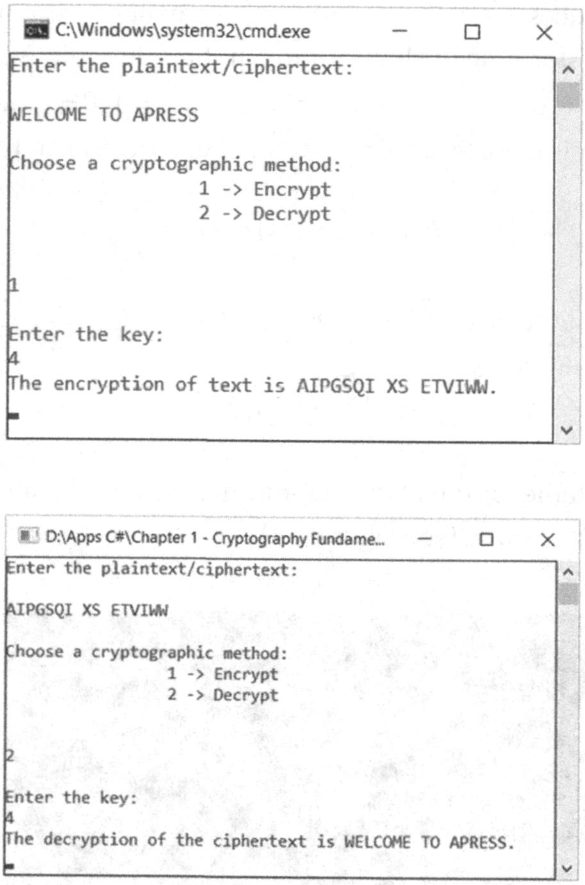

Figure 1-10.   *Caesar Cipher (encoding and decoding)*

Listing 1-2.   Caesar Cipher Implementation

```
using System;
using System.Collections.Generic;
using System.Linq;
using System.Text;
using System.Threading.Tasks;

namespace ConsoleCaesarCipher
{
    class Program
    {
        static void Main(string[] args)
```

```csharp
    {
        Console.WriteLine("Enter the plaintext/ciphertext: \n");
        string text = Convert.ToString(Console.ReadLine());

        Console.WriteLine("\nChoose a cryptographic method:");
        Console.WriteLine("\t\t 1 -> Encrypt");
        Console.WriteLine("\t\t 2 -> Decrypt\n\n");
        int option = Convert.ToInt32(Console.ReadLine());

        if (option == 1)
        {
            Console.WriteLine("\nEnter the key: ");
            int key = Convert.ToInt32(Console.ReadLine());
            Console.WriteLine("The encryption of text is {0}. ",
            Encode(text, key));
        }
        if (option == 2)
        {
            Console.WriteLine("\nEnter the key: ");
            int key = Convert.ToInt32(Console.ReadLine());
            Console.WriteLine("The decryption of the ciphertext is {0}.
            ", Decode(text, key));
        }

        Console.ReadKey();
    }

    private static string Encode(string plaintext, int key)
    {
        string alphabets = "ABCDEFGHIJKLMNOPQRSTUVWXYZ";
        string final = "";

        int indexOfChar = 0;
        char encryptedChar;

        //Convert/encrypt each and every character of the text
        foreach (char c in plaintext)
```

31

```
        {
            //Get the index of the character from alphabets variable
            indexOfChar = alphabets.IndexOf(c);

            //if encounters an white space
            if (c == ' ')
            {
                final = final + c;
            }

            //if encounters a new line
            else if (c == '\n')
            {
                final += c;
            }

            //if the character is at the end of the string "alphabets"
            else if ((indexOfChar + key) > 25)
            {
                //encrypt the character
                encryptedChar = alphabets[(indexOfChar + key) - 26];

                //add the encrypted character to a string every time to
                get an encrypted string
                final += encryptedChar;
            }
            else
            {
                //encrypt the character
                //add the encrypted character to a string every time to
                get an encrypted string
                encryptedChar = alphabets[indexOfChar + key];
                final += encryptedChar;
            }
        }

        return final;
    }
```

```csharp
private static string Decode(string ciphertext, int key)
{
    string alphabets = "ABCDEFGHIJKLMNOPQRSTUVWXYZ";
    string final = "";

    int indexOfChar = 0;
    char decryptedChar;

    //Convert/decrypt each and every character of the text
    foreach (char c in ciphertext)
    {
        //Get the index of the character from alphabets variable
        indexOfChar = alphabets.IndexOf(c);

        //if encounters a white space
        if (c == ' ')
        {
            final = final + c;
        }

        //if encounters a new line
        else if (c == '\n')
        {
            final = final + c;
        }

        //if the character is at the start of the string
        "alphabets"
        else if ((indexOfChar - key) < 0)
        {
            //decrypt the character
            //add the decrypted character to a string every time to
            get a decrypted string
            decryptedChar = alphabets[(indexOfChar - key) + 26];
            final = final + decryptedChar;
        }
        else
```

```
        {
                //decrypt the character
                //add the decrypted character to a string every time to
                get a decrypted string
                decryptedChar = alphabets[indexOfChar - key];
                final = final + decryptedChar;
        }
    }

    //Display decrypted text
    return final;
    }
  }
}
```

Vigenére Cipher Implementation in C#

The Vigenére cipher (see Figure 1-11 and Listing 1-3) represents one of the classic methods of encrypting the alphabetical text by using a series of different Caesar ciphers that are based on the letters of a keyword. Some documentation shows it as a form of polyalphabetic substitution.

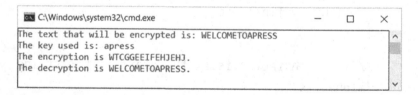

Figure 1-11. *Vigenére Cipher, encryption and decryption operations*

A short algebraic description of the cipher is as follows. The numbers will be taken as numbers ($A = 0, B = 1, etc$) and an addition operation is performed as *modulo* 26. The Vigenére encryption E using K as the key can be written as

$$C_i = E_K(M_i) = (M_i + K_i) \bmod 26$$

and decryption D using the key K as

$$M_i = D_K\left(C_i\right) = \left(C_i - K_i\right) \bmod 26$$

in which $M = M_1...M_n$ is the message, $C = C_1...C_n$ represents the ciphertext, and $K = K_1...K_n$ represents the key obtained by repeating the keyword $[n/m]$ times in which m represents the keyword length.

Our implementation has two important files. The file Program.cs contains the functions for encryption and decryption operations. See Figure 1-12.

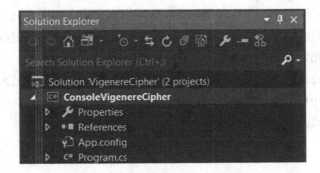

Figure 1-12. *The structure of the Vigenére cipher project*

The source code for Program.cs is shown in Listing 1-3.

Listing 1-3. Vigenére Implementation

```
using System;
using System.Collections.Generic;
using System.Linq;
using System.Text;
using System.Threading.Tasks;

namespace ConsoleVigenereCipher
{
    class Program
    {
        static void Main(string[] args)
        {
            VigenereCipher vigenere_engine = new VigenereCipher();
```

```csharp
            //the key used for encryption or decryption
            string key = "apress";

            //the text that will encrypted
            //encrypted value is "WTCGGEEIFEHJEHJ"
            string text_for_encryption = "WELCOMETOAPRESS";
            string ciphertext = "WTCGGEEIFEHJEHJ";

            //You can use also Decrypt
            Console.WriteLine("The text that will be encrypted is: {0}",
            text_for_encryption);
            Console.WriteLine("The key used is: {0}", key);
            Console.WriteLine("The encryption is {0}. ", vigenere_engine.
            Encrypt(key, text_for_encryption));
            Console.WriteLine("The decryption is {0}. ", vigenere_engine.
            Decrypt(key, ciphertext));
            Console.ReadKey();
        }
    }
    class VigenereCipher
    {
        Dictionary<sbyte, char> TheAlphabet = new Dictionary<sbyte,
        char>();

        public VigenereCipher()
        {
            //Me from the future: wtf lol
            TheAlphabet.Add(0, 'A');
            TheAlphabet.Add(1, 'B');
            TheAlphabet.Add(2, 'C');
            TheAlphabet.Add(3, 'D');
            TheAlphabet.Add(4, 'E');
            TheAlphabet.Add(5, 'F');
            TheAlphabet.Add(6, 'G');
            TheAlphabet.Add(7, 'H');
            TheAlphabet.Add(8, 'I');
            TheAlphabet.Add(9, 'J');
```

```csharp
        TheAlphabet.Add(10, 'K');
        TheAlphabet.Add(11, 'L');
        TheAlphabet.Add(12, 'M');
        TheAlphabet.Add(13, 'N');
        TheAlphabet.Add(14, 'O');
        TheAlphabet.Add(15, 'P');
        TheAlphabet.Add(16, 'Q');
        TheAlphabet.Add(17, 'R');
        TheAlphabet.Add(18, 'S');
        TheAlphabet.Add(19, 'T');
        TheAlphabet.Add(20, 'U');
        TheAlphabet.Add(21, 'V');
        TheAlphabet.Add(22, 'W');
        TheAlphabet.Add(23, 'X');
        TheAlphabet.Add(24, 'Y');
        TheAlphabet.Add(25, 'Z');
    }

    private bool CheckIfEmptyString(string Key, string Text)
    {
        if (string.IsNullOrEmpty(Key)
            || string.IsNullOrWhiteSpace(Key))
        {
            return true;
        }
        if (string.IsNullOrEmpty(Text)
            || string.IsNullOrWhiteSpace(Text))
        {
            return true;
        }
        return false;
    }
```

```
public string Encrypt(string Key, string Text)
{
    try
    {
        Key = Key.ToUpper();
        Text = Text.ToUpper();

        if (CheckIfEmptyString(Key, Text))
            { return "Enter a valid string"; }

        string ciphertext = "";

        int i = 0;

        foreach (char element in Text)
        {
            //** if we are having a character
            //** that is not in the alphabet
            if (!Char.IsLetter(element))
                { ciphertext += element; }
            else
            {
                //Obtain from the dictionary TKey by the TValue
                sbyte T_Order = TheAlphabet.FirstOrDefault
                    (x => x.Value == element).Key;
                sbyte K_Order = TheAlphabet.FirstOrDefault
                    (x => x.Value == Key[i]).Key;

                sbyte Final = (sbyte)(T_Order + K_Order);
                if (Final > 25) { Final -= 26; }
                ciphertext += TheAlphabet[Final];
                i++;
            }
            if (i == Key.Length) { i = 0; }
        }

        return ciphertext;
    }
```

```
    catch (Exception E)
    {
        return "Error: " + E.Message;
    }
}

public string Decrypt(string Key, string Text)
{
    try
    {
        Key = Key.ToUpper();
        Text = Text.ToUpper();

        if (CheckIfEmptyString(Key, Text)) { return "Enter a valid
        string value!"; }

        string plaintext = "";

        int i = 0;

        foreach (char element in Text)
        {
            //if the character is not an alphabetical value
            if (!Char.IsLetter(element)) { plaintext += element; }
            else
            {
                sbyte TOrder = TheAlphabet.FirstOrDefault
                    (x => x.Value == element).Key;
                sbyte KOrder = TheAlphabet.FirstOrDefault
                    (x => x.Value == Key[i]).Key;
                sbyte Final = (sbyte)(TOrder - KOrder);
                if (Final < 0) { Final += 26; }
                plaintext += TheAlphabet[Final];
                i++;
            }
            if (i == Key.Length) { i = 0; }
        }
```

```
            return plaintext;
        }
        catch (Exception E)
        {
            return "Error: " + E.Message;
        }
    }
  }
}
```

We will continue with the source code analysis as follows. Let's examine the source code from `Program.cs`, more precisely the source code behind the two operations that represents the main operations, `Encrypt` and `Decrypt`.

The source code for the `Encrypt` method is show in Listing 1-4.

Listing 1-4. Source Code for the Encryption Method

```
public string Encrypt(string Key, string Text)
    {
        try
        {
            Key = Key.ToUpper();
            Text = Text.ToUpper();

            if (CheckIfEmptyString(Key, Text))
                { return "Enter a valid string"; }

            string ciphertext = "";

            int i = 0;

            foreach (char element in Text)
            {
                //** if we are having a character
                //** that is not in the alphabet
                if (!Char.IsLetter(element))
                    { ciphertext += element; }
```

```
    else
    {
        //Obtain from the dictionary TKey by the TValue
        sbyte T_Order = TheAlphabet.FirstOrDefault
            (x => x.Value == element).Key;
        sbyte K_Order = TheAlphabet.FirstOrDefault
            (x => x.Value == Key[i]).Key;

        sbyte Final = (sbyte)(T_Order + K_Order);
        if (Final > 25) { Final -= 26; }
        ciphertext += TheAlphabet[Final];
        i++;
    }
    if (i == Key.Length) { i = 0; }
}

return ciphertext;
}
catch (Exception E)
{
    return "Error: " + E.Message;
}
}
```

The source code for the Decrypt method is shown in Listing 1-5.

Listing 1-5. Souce Code for the Decryption Method

```
public string Decrypt(string Key, string Text)
{
    try
    {
        Key = Key.ToUpper();
        Text = Text.ToUpper();

        if (CheckIfEmptyString(Key, Text)) { return "Enter a valid
        string value!"; }

        string plaintext = "";
```

```csharp
                int i = 0;

                foreach (char element in Text)
                {
                    //if the character is not an alphabetical value
                    if (!Char.IsLetter(element)) { plaintext += element; }
                    else
                    {
                        sbyte TOrder = TheAlphabet.FirstOrDefault
                            (x => x.Value == element).Key;
                        sbyte KOrder = TheAlphabet.FirstOrDefault
                            (x => x.Value == Key[i]).Key;
                        sbyte Final = (sbyte)(TOrder - KOrder);
                        if (Final < 0) { Final += 26; }
                        plaintext += TheAlphabet[Final];
                        i++;
                    }
                    if (i == Key.Length) { i = 0; }
                }

                return plaintext;
            }
            catch (Exception E)
            {
                return "Error: " + E.Message;
            }
        }
```

Conclusion

In this chapter, we provided a short introduction to the fundamentals of the cryptographic primitives and mechanisms. The chapter covered the following:

- Security and information security objectives

- The importance of the 1-1, one-way and trapdoor one-way functions in designing and implementing cryptographic functions

- Digital signatures and how they work

- Public-key cryptography and how it impacts developing applications

- Hash functions

- Case studies for illustrating the basic notions that the reader needs to know before advancing to high-level cryptographic concepts

In the next chapter, we will go through the basics of probability theory, information theory, number theory, and finite fields. We will discuss their importance and how they are related during the implementation already existing in .NET and how they are useful for developers.

Bibliography

[1]   Kahn, David. *The Codebreakers: The Story of Secret Writing*, 1967.

[2]   W. Diffie and M. Hellman, "New directions in cryptography." IEEE Trans. Information Theory. 22, 6 (September 2006), 644–654. DOI: https://doi.org/10.1109/TIT.1976.1055638.

[3]   R. L. Rivest, A. Shamir, and L. Adleman, "A method for obtaining digital signatures and public-key cryptosystems," Communications ACM, vol. 21, no. 2, pp. 120–126, 1978.

[4]   T. ElGamal, "A Public Key Cryptosystem and a Signature Scheme Based on Discrete Logarithms." In: Blakley G.R., Chaum D. (eds) *Advances in Cryptology*. CRYPTO 1984. Lecture Notes in Computer Science, vol 196. Springer, Berlin, Heidelberg.

[5]   ISO/IEC 9796-2:2010 – Information Technology – Security Techniques – Digital Signature schemes giving message recovery. Available: www.iso.org/standard/54788.html.

[6]   Bruce Schneier and Phil Sutherland, *Applied Cryptography: Protocols, Algorithms, and Source Code in C (Second Edition)*, ISBN: 978-0-471-12845-8. John Wiley & Sons, Inc., USA. 1995.

[7]   William Stallings, *Cryptography and Network Security: Principles and Practice*. Upper Saddle River, N.J: Prentice Hall, 1999.

[8]   Douglas R. Stinson, *Cryptography: Theory and Practice (First Edition.)*, ISBN: 978-0-8493-8521-6, CRC Press, Inc., USA. 1995

[9]   Neal Koblitz, *A Course in Number Theory and Cryptography.* New York: Springer-Verlag, 1994.

[10]   Neal Koblitz and A J. Menezes, *Algebraic Aspects of Cryptography*, 1999.

[11]   Oded Goldreich, *Foundations of Cryptography: Basic Tools.* Cambridge: Cambridge University Press, 2001. Print.

[12]   Oded Goldreich, *Modern Cryptography, Probabilistic Proofs and Pseudorandomness.* Berlin: Springer, 1999. Print.

[13]   Michael G. Luby, *Pseudorandomness and Cryptographic Applications.* Princeton, NJ: Princeton University Press, 1996. Print.

[14]   Bruce Schneier, *Secrets and Lies: Digital Security in a Networked World.* New York: John Wiley, 2000.

[15]   Peter Thorsteinson and Arun Ganesh, *.NET Security and Cryptography.* Prentice Hall Professional Technical Reference, 2003.

[16]   Adrian Atanasiu, *Criptografie (Cryptography) – Volume 1*, InfoData, 2007, ISBN: 978-973-1803-29-6, 978-973-1803-16-6. Available in Romanian language.

[17]   Adrian Atanasiu, *Protocoale de Securitate (Security Protocols) – Volume 2*, InfoData, 2007, ISBN: 978-973-1803-29-6, 978-973-1803-16-6. Available in Romanian language.

[18]   Alfred J. Menezes, Scott A. Vanstone, and Paul C. Van Oorschot, *Handbook of Applied Cryptography (First Edition).* CRC Press, Inc., USA, ISBN: 978-0-8493-8523-0. 1996.

[19]   Namespace System.Security.Cryptography, `https://docs.microsoft.com/en-us/dotnet/api/system.security.cryptography?view=netframework-4.8`.

[20] Henri Cohen, Gerhard Frey, Roberto Avanzi, Christophe Doche, Tanja Lange, Kim Nguyen, and Frederik Vercauteren, *Handbook of Elliptic and Hyperelliptic Curve Cryptography, Second Edition (Second Edition)*. Chapman & Hall/CRC. 2012.

[21] OpenPGP Library for .NET. Available: `www.didisoft.com/net-openpgp/`.

[22] Bouncy Castle .NET. Available: `www.bouncycastle.org/csharp/`.

[23] Nethereum. Availble: `https://github.com/Nethereum`.

[24] Botan. Available: `https://botan.randombit.net/`.

[25] Cryptlib. Available: `www.cs.auckland.ac.nz/~pgut001/cryptlib/`.

[26] Crypto++. Available: `www.cryptopp.com/`.

[27] Libgcrypt. Available: `https://gnupg.org/software/libgcrypt/`.

[28] Libsodium. Available: `https://nacl.cr.yp.to/`.

[29] Nettle. Available: www.lysator.liu.se/~nisse/nettle/.

[30] OpenSSL. Available: `www.openssl.org/`.

[31] J. Guo, P. Karpman, I. Nikolić, L. Wang, S. Wu, Analysis of BLAKE2. In: Benaloh J. (eds) "Topics in Cryptology – CT-RSA 2014." CT-RSA 2014. Lecture Notes in Computer Science, vol 8366. Springer, Cham.

[32] Blake3. Available: `https://github.com/BLAKE3-team/BLAKE3/`.

[33] H. Krawczyk, M. Bellare, R. Canetti, "HMAC: Keyed-Hashing for Message Authentication," RFC 2104, 1997.

[34] .API KMAC. Available: `www.cryptosys.net/manapi/api_kmac.html`.

[35] John Kelsey, Shu-jen Chang, Ray Perlner, *SHA-3 Derived Functions: cSHAKE, KMAC, TupleHash and ParallelHash*, NIST Special Publication 800-185, National Institute of Standards and Technology, December 2016.

[36]   I.B. Damgard, "A design principle for hash functions," LNCS 435 (1990), pp. 516-527.

[37]   Ronal L. Rivest, "The MD6 hash function. A proposal to NIST for SHA-3." Available: http://groups.csail.mit.edu/cis/md6/submitted-2008-10-27/Supporting_Documentation/md6_report.pdf.

[38]   PMAC. Available: https://web.cs.ucdavis.edu/~rogaway/ocb/pmac.htm.

[39]   UMAC. Available: http://fastcrypto.org/umac/.

[40]   BLAKE-256. Available: https://docs.decred.org/research/blake-256-hash-function/.

[41]   Eli Biham and Orr Dunkelman, "A Framework for Iterative Hash Functions - HAIFA." Second NIST Cryptographic Hash Workshop – via Cryptology ePrint Archive: Report 2007/278. 24. 2006.

[42]   BLAKE2 Official Implementation. Available: https://github.com/BLAKE2/BLAKE2.

[43]   GOST. Available: https://tools.ietf.org/html/rfc5830.

[44]   Roland L. Rivest, "The MD4 message digest algorithm," LNCS, 537, 1991, pp. 303-311.

[45]   Roland L. Rivest, "The MD5 message digest algorithm," RFC 1321, 1992.

[46]   RIPEMD-128. Available: https://homes.esat.kuleuven.be/~bosselae/ripemd/rmd128.txt.

[47]   RIPEMD-160. Available: https://homes.esat.kuleuven.be/~bosselae/ripemd160.html.

[48]   RIPEMD-160. Available: https://ehash.iaik.tugraz.at/wiki/RIPEMD-160.

[49]   The Sponge and Duplex Construction. Available: https://keccak.team/sponge_duplex.html.

[50] Henri Gilbert, Helena Handschuh. "Security Analysis of SHA-256 and Sisters." Selected Areas in Cryptography 2003: pp175–193.

[51] SHA256 .NET Class. Available: `https://docs.microsoft.com/en-us/dotnet/api/system.security.cryptography.sha256?view=netframework-4.8`.

[52] SHA384 .NET Class. Available: `https://docs.microsoft.com/en-us/dotnet/api/system.security.cryptography.sha384?view=netframework-4.8`.

[53] SHA512 .NET Class. Available: `https://docs.microsoft.com/en-us/dotnet/api/system.security.cryptography.sha512?view=netframework-4.8`.

[54] Descriptions of SHA-256, SHA-384, and SHA-512. Available: `www.iwar.org.uk/comsec/resources/cipher/sha256-384-512.pdf`.

[55] A 224-bit One-way Hash Function : SHA 224. Available: `www.iwar.org.uk/comsec/resources/cipher/sha256-384-512.pdf`.

[56] Paul Hernandez, "NIST Releases SHA-3 Cryptographic Hash Standard," 2015.

[57] Morris J. Dworkin, "SHA-3 Standard: Permutation-Based Hash and Extendable-Output Functions". Federal Inf. Process. STDS. (NIST FIPS) – 202. 2015.

[58] Paulo S. L. M. Barreto "The WHIRLPOOL Hash Function". 2008. Archived from the original on 2017-11-29. Retrieved 2018-08-09.

[59] Paulo S. L. M. Barreto and Vincent Rijmen, "The WHIRLPOOL Hashing Function." 2003. Archived from the original (ZIP) on 2017-10-26. Retrieved 2018-08-09.

[60] Whirlpool C# Implementation. Available: `http://csharptest.net/browse/src/Library/Crypto/WhirlpoolManaged.cs`.

[61] Xiaoyun Wang, Yiqun Lisa Yin, and Hongbo Yu, Finding Collisions in the Full SHA-1, Crypto 2005.

[62] Shor's Algorithm. Available online: `https://en.wikipedia.org/wiki/Shor%27s_algorithm`.

CHAPTER 2

Mathematical Background and Its Applicability in Cryptography

Probability Theory

Foundations

The chapter will discuss the concepts of *experiments, probability distribution, events, complementary events,* and *mutually exclusiveness.* These concepts will help the reader to understand the basic notions of what cryptographic and cryptanalysis mechanisms stand for and how they are designed in terms of probabilities [1].

Definition 2.1. An *experiment* represents a procedure that yields one of a given set of outcomes. The outcomes are individual. The possible ones are called *simple events.* The entire set of possible outcomes is known as *sample space.*

In this chapter, we will talk about discrete sample spaces, which are sample spaces that have limited possible outcomes. We will denote the simple events of a sample space as G labeled as $g_1, g_2, ..., g_n$.

Definition 2.2. A probability distribution O over G is represented by a sequence of numbers $o_1, o_2, ..., o_n$ that are non-negative and their sum is equal to 1. The number o_i has an interpretation as the *probability* of g_i, which represents the outcome of the experiment.

Definition 2.3. An *event* E represents a subset of the sample space G. In this case, the *probability* that the event E will take place, noted as $P(E)$, represents the sum of the probabilities o_i of all the simple events g_i which belong to E. If $g_i \in S$, $P(\{s_i\})$ is simply noted as $P(s_i)$.

© Marius Iulian Mihailescu and Stefania Loredana Nita 2021
M. I. Mihailescu and S. L. Nita, *Pro Cryptography and Cryptanalysis,*
https://doi.org/10.1007/978-1-4842-6367-9_2

Definition 2.4. Let's consider E an event, so the *complementary event* represents the set of simple events that don't belong to E, noted as $\overline{E}$.

Demonstration 2.1. If $E \subseteq S$ represents an event, consider the following:

- $0 \leq P(E) \leq 1$. In addition, $P(S) = 1$ and $P(\phi) = 0$, where ϕ represents an empty set.

- $P(\overline{E}) = 1 - P(E)$.

- If the results in S are just as likely, we can consider $P(E) = \dfrac{|E|}{|S|}$.

Definition 2.5. Let's consider two *mutually exclusive* events, E_1 and E_2. They are mutually exclusive if the following expression is equal to 0, $P(E_1 \cap E_2) = 0$. The appearance of one or two events will exclude the chance that others will take place.

Definition 2.6. Let's consider the following two events, E_1 and E_2.

- $P(E_1) \leq P(E_2)$ will be if $E_1 \subseteq P(E_2)$.

- $P(E_1 \cup E_2) + P(E_1 \cap E_2) = P(E_1) + P(E_2)$. Accordingly, if E_1 and E_2 are considered mutually exclusive, then the following expression takes place: $P(E_1 \cup E_2) = P(E_1) + P(E_2)$.

Conditional Probability

Definition 2.7. We will consider the following two events, E_1 and E_2, with $P(E_2) > 0$. The *conditional probability* for E_1 to give E_2 is written as $P(E_1|E_2)$ and it is expressed as

$$P(E_1|E_2) = \frac{P(E_1 \cap E_2)}{P(E_2)}$$

$P(E_1|E_2)$ measures the probability of occurring event E_1, given that E_2 has taken place.

Definition 2.8. Let's consider the following two events, E_1 and E_2. It is said that they are *independent* if $P(E1 \cap E_2) = P(E_1)P(E_2)$.

Definition 2.9. *(Bayes' Theorem)* If we have two events, E_1 and E_2, with $P(E_2) > 0$, then

$$P(E_1|E_2) = \frac{P(E_1)P(E_2|E_1)}{P(E_2)}$$

Random Variables

Let's start defining a sample space S with the distribution probability of P.

Definition 2.10. Let's consider X, *random variable,* with a function applied on S for the set of real numbers. For each event, $s_i \in S$, X will assign a real number $X(s_i)$.

Definition 2.11. Let X be the random variable on S. The *mean* or *expected value* of X is

$$E(X) = \sum_{s_i \in S} X(s_i) P(s_i).$$

For the C# implementation of a mean or expected value, refer to Case Study 3: Computing the Mean of Probability Distribution.

Demonstration 2.12. Consider X a random variable on S. In this situation,

$$E(X) = \sum_{x \in \mathbb{R}} x \cdot P(X = x)$$

Demonstration 2.13. Let's consider the following random variables on S: $X_1, X_2, ..., X_m$. The following are real numbers: $a_1, a_2, ..., a_m$. Then we will have

$$E\left(\sum_{i=1}^{m} a_i X_i\right) = \sum_{i=1}^{m} a_i E(X_i)$$

Definition 2.14. Let's consider X the random variable. The *variance* of X of mean μ is represented by the non-negative number that is defined by

$$Var(X) = E\left((X - \mu)^2\right)$$

For the C# implementation of the mean or expected value, refer to *Case Study 4: Computing the Variance.*

The *standard deviation* of X is represented by the non-negative square root of $Var(X)$.

For the C# implementation of the mean or expected value, refer to *Case Study 5: Computing the Standard Deviation.*

Birthday Problem

Definition 2.15.1. Let's consider two positive integers a, b with $a \geq b$, where the number $m^{(n)}$ is defined as follows:

$$m^{(n)} = m(m-1)(m-2)\ldots(m-n+1)$$

Definition 2.15.2. Let's consider two non-negative integers a, b with $a \geq b$. The *Stirling number of the second kind*, noted as $\begin{Bmatrix} a \\ b \end{Bmatrix}$, is

$$\begin{Bmatrix} a \\ b \end{Bmatrix} = \frac{1}{b!} \sum_{i=0}^{n} (-1)^{b-i} \binom{b}{i} i^a$$

The case of $\begin{Bmatrix} 0 \\ 0 \end{Bmatrix} = 1$ is considered an exception.

Demonstration 2.16. We will examine the classic occupancy problem via the example of an urn that has a balls numbered from 1 to m. Let's assume that b balls are extracted from the urn one at a time and then replaced, and with their numbers listed. The probability that l different balls have been drawn is

$$P_1(a,b,l) = \begin{Bmatrix} b \\ l \end{Bmatrix} \frac{a^{(l)}}{a^b}, 1 \leq l \leq b$$

The birthday problem represents one of the most special cases of the occupancy problem.

Demonstration 2.17. Let's consider the birthday problem where we have an urn with a balls that are numbered from 1 to a. Assume that a specific number of balls, h, are extracted from the urn one at a time and then replaced, with their numbers listed.

Case 2.17.1. We have the probability of at least one coincidence, for example a ball that is drawn at least twice from the urn, is

$$P_2(a,h) = 1 - P_1(a,h,h) = 1 - \frac{a^{(h)}}{a^h}, 1 \leq h \leq m$$

Case 2.17.2. Let's consider h the specific number of balls extracted from the urn. If $h = O\left(\sqrt{a}\right)$ and $a \to \infty$, then

$$P_2\left(a,h\right) \to 1 - \exp\left(-\frac{h\left(h-1\right)}{2a} + O\left(\frac{1}{\sqrt{a}}\right)\right) \approx 1 - \exp\left(-\frac{h^2}{2a}\right).$$

The demonstration provided will explain why probability distribution is referred to as the *birthday surprise* or *birthday paradox*. The probability that at least 2 people in a room with 23 people have the same birthday is $P_2(365, 23) \approx 0.507$, which is surprisingly large. The quantity $P_2(365, h)$ increases as well quite fast as h increases. As an example, $P_2(365, 30) \approx 0.706$.

For the C# implementation of the birthday paradox, refer to *Case Study 4: Birthday Paradox*.

Information Theory

Entropy

Let's consider X a random variable that takes on a finite set of value $x_1, x_2, ..., x_m$, which has the probability $P(X = x_i) = p_i$, where $0 \leq p_i \leq 1$ for each i, $1 \leq i \leq n$, in which

$$\sum_{i=1}^{n} p_i = 1.$$

Also, let's consider Y and Z random variables that will take a finite set of values [1].

The entropy of X represents a mathematical measure of the amount of information that is provided by an observation x.

Definition 2.18. Let's consider X as a random variable, the *entropy* or uncertainty of X is defined as

$$H\left(X\right) = -\sum_{i=1}^{n} p_i \lg p_i = \sum_{i=1}^{n} p_i \lg\left(\frac{1}{p_i}\right)$$

where, through convention,

$$p_i \cdot \lg p_i = p_i \cdot \lg\left(\frac{1}{p_i}\right) = 0, \text{ if } p_i = 0.$$

Definition 2.19 [1][5]. Let's consider X and Y, two random variables. The *joint entropy* is defined as

$$H(X,Y) = \sum_{x,y} P(X = x, Y = y) \lg \big(P(X = x, Y = y) \big),$$

where x and y range over all values of the random variables, X and Y.

Definition 2.20. Let's consider the random variables X and Y, and then consider the *conditional entropy* of X given $Y = y$ is

$$H(X|Y = y) = -\sum_{x} P(X = x|Y = y) \lg \big(P(X = x|Y = y) \big),$$

where x will range over all the values of the random variable X. In this situation, the *conditional entropy* of X given Y, also called the *equivocation* of Y about X, as

$$H(X|Y) = \sum_{y} P(Y = y) H(X|Y = y),$$

where the index y will range over all values of Y.

Number Theory

Integers

We will start from the idea that a set of integers $\{..., -3, -2, -1, 0, 1, 2, 3, ...\}$ is represented by the symbol $\mathbb{Z}$.

Definition 2.21. Let's consider two integers, a and b. Let's say that a *divides* b if there exist an integer c in such way that $b = a \cdot c$. If we are in the case that a divides b, then we can say that $a \mid b$.

Definition 2.22 (Division algorithm for integers). Let's consider two integers, a and b with $b \geq 1$, then we have a ordinary long division of a by b yields integers q (*quotient*) and r (*remainder*) in such way that

$a = q \cdot b + r$, where $0 \leq r < b$

Definition 2.23. Let's consider c as integer. The *common divisor* of a and b if $c \mid a$ and $c \mid b$.

Definition 2.24. We will consider a non-negative integer d, known as the *greatest common divisor (gcd)* of the integers a and b. We will note it as $d = \gcd(a, b)$, if

   a. d is a common divisor a and b

   b. $c \mid a$ and $c \mid b$, then $c \mid d$

Definition 2.25. We will consider a non-negative integer d, the *least common multiple (lcm)* of integers a and b, denoted $d = lcm(a, b)$, if

   a. $a \mid d$ and $b \mid d$

   b. $a \mid c$ and $b \mid c$, then $d \mid c$

Algorithms in $\mathbb{Z}$

We will consider two non-negative integers, a and b, each less than n or equal to n. Remember that the number of bits in a binary representation of n is $\lfloor lg\, n \rfloor + 1$, and this number will be approximated by $lg\,n$. The number of bit operations related to the four basic operations for integers using the classical algorithms as are concluded in Table 2-1.

Table 2-1. *The Bit Complexity of the Basic Operations in $\mathbb{Z}$*

Operation	Bit complexity
Addition $a + b$	$O(lg\,a + lg\,b) = O(lg\,n)$
Subtraction $a - b$	$O(lg\,a + lg\,b) = O(lg\,n)$
Multiplication $a \cdot b$	$O((lg\,a)(lg\,b)) = O((lg\,n)^2)$
Division $a = q \cdot b + r$	$O((lg\,q)(lg\,b)) = O((lg\,n)^2)$

Demonstration 2.26. The integers a and b are positive numbers with $a > b$, then we will have $\gcd(a, b) = \gcd(b, a \bmod b)$.

Algorithm 2.27 [1]. The Euclidean algorithm for calculating the *gcd* of the two integers

   INPUT :   a and b, two non − negative integers with respect for $a \ge b$

$OUTPUT$:   *The gcd*

1. *While* $b \neq 0$ *then*

    1.1. *Set* $r \leftarrow a \mod b$, $a \leftarrow b, b \leftarrow r$

2. *Return* (a)

The Euclidean algorithm has the possibility of being extended so that it will not only yield the gcd d of two integers a and b, but also integers x and y, which will satisfy $ax + by = d$.

Algorithm 2.28 [1]. Extended Euclidean algorithm

$INPUT$:   *a and b, two non − negative integers with respect for* $a \geq b$

$OUTPUT$: $d = \gcd(a,b)$ *and integers x, y which satisfy* $ax + by = d$

1.   *If* $b = 0$, *then set*

$$d \leftarrow a$$

$$x \leftarrow 1$$

$$y \leftarrow 0$$

$$return(d,x,y)$$

2.   *Set* $x_2 \leftarrow 1$, $x_1 \leftarrow 0$, $y_2 \leftarrow 0$, $y_1 \leftarrow 1$

3.   *While b > 0 then*

$$3.1. q \leftarrow \left\lfloor \frac{a}{b} \right\rfloor$$

$r \leftarrow a - qb$

$x \leftarrow x_2 - qx_1$

$y \leftarrow y_2 - qy_1$

$$3.2. a \leftarrow b$$

$$b \leftarrow r$$

$$x_2 \leftarrow x_1$$

$$x_1 \leftarrow x$$

$$y_2 \leftarrow y_1$$

$$y_1 \leftarrow y$$

4.   Set $d \leftarrow a, x \leftarrow x_2, y \leftarrow y_2$

$$Return\left(d, x, y\right)$$

In *Section Case Study 7: (Extended) Euclidean Algorithm,* there is an implementation in C# for both types, Euclidean and Extended Euclidean Algorithm.

Example 2.29. Example of Extended Euclidean algorithm. In Table 2-2 we show the steps of the above algorithm (Algorithm 2.28). As for inputs, we have the following: $a = 4864$ and $b = 3458$. Since the gcd$(4864, 3458) = 38$ and $(4864)(32) + (3458)(-45) = 38$.

Table 2-2. *Extended Euclidean Algorithm*

q	r	x	y	a	b	x_2	x_1	y_2	y_1
N/A	N/A	N/A	N/A	4864	3458	1	0	0	1
1	1406	1	-1	3458	1406	0	1	1	-1
2	646	-2	3	1406	646	1	-2	-1	3
2	114	5	-7	646	114	-2	5	3	-7
5	76	-27	38	114	76	5	-27	-7	38
1	38	32	-45	76	38	-27	32	38	-45
2	0	-91	128	38	0	32	-91	-45	128

The Integers Modulo n

We will consider p a positive integer.

Definition 2.30. Let's consider x and y as two integers. We say that *x is congruent to y modulo p*. The notation used is

$$x \equiv y \, (mod \, p), \text{ if } p \text{ will divide } (x - y)$$

The p is called the *modulus* of the congruence.

Definition 2.31. Let's consider $m \in Z_p$. The definition of the *multiplicative inverse* of m modulo p is an integer $y \in Z_p$ in such way that $m \, y \equiv 1 \, (mod \, p)$. If we have such m that exists, then that m is unique and m is said to be *invertible* or a *unit*. The inverse of m is noted as m^{-1}.

Refer to *Case Study 8: Computing the Multiplicative Inverse under Modulo m* for the C# implementation of the multiplicative inverse under modulo m.

Definition 2.32. Chinese Remainder Theorem (CRT). Let's consider the following integers $n_1, n_2, ..., n_k$, a pairwise that is relatively prime. Then we have the following system of simultaneous congruences

$$y \equiv a_1 \, (mod \, n_1)$$

$$y \equiv a_2 \; (mod \; n_2)$$

$$\vdots$$

$$x \equiv a_k \; (mod \; n_k)$$

that have a unique solution modulo, $n = n_1 \, n_2 \cdots n_k$.

Refer to *Case Study 9: Chinese Remainder Theorem* for the C# implementation of the multiplicative inverse under modulo m.

Definition 2.33. Gauss's Algorithm. In the Chinese Remainder Theorem, the solution x for simultaneous congruences may be calculated as $x = \sum_{i=1}^{k} a_i \cdot N_i \cdot M_i \; mod \; n$, where $N_i = n/n_i$ and $M_i = N_i^{-1} \; mod \; n_i$. The listed operations can be done in $O((lgn)^2)$ bit operations.

Algorithms $\mathbb{Z}_n$

Let's consider a positive integer n. As we observed, the elements of $\mathbb{Z}_n$, then

$$(a+b) \, mod \;\; n = \begin{cases} a+b, & if \; a+b < n, \\ a+b-n, & if \; a+b \geq n \end{cases}$$

Algorithm 2.34 [1]. Computing multiplicative inverses in $\mathbb{Z}_n$

$$INPUT: \qquad a \in \mathbb{Z}_n$$

$$OUTPUT: \quad a^{-1} \; mod \; n$$

1. *Apply an extended Euclidean algorithm in order to find integers x and ys such that $ax + ny = d$, where $d = \gcd(a,n)$*

$2. If\ d > 1, we\ will\ have\ a^{-1}\ mod\ n\ that\ does\ not\ exist. Else, return(x).$

Algorithm 2.35 [1]. Repeated square-and-multiply algorithm for exponentiation in $\mathbb{Z}_n$

$INPUT:$ $a \in \mathbb{Z}_n, and\ integer\ 0 \le k < n\ whose\ binary\ representation\ is\ k = \sum_{i=0}^{t} k_i 2^i.$

$OUTPUT:$ $a^k\ mod\ n$

1. $Set\ b \leftarrow 1.\ If\ k = 0,\ then\ return(b)$

2. $Set\ A \leftarrow a.$

3. $If\ k_0 = 1,\ then\ set\ b \leftarrow a,$

4. $For\ i\ from\ 1\ to\ t,\ do\ the\ following:$

    4.1. $4.1.\ Set\ A \leftarrow A^2\ mod\ n.$

    4.2. $If\ k_i = 1,\ then\ set\ b \leftarrow A \cdot b\ mod\ n.$

5. $Return(b).$

The Legendre and Jacobi Symbols

The Legendre symbol is one of the most useful tools for monitoring if an integer a is a quadratic residue module a prime .

Definition 2.36 [1]. Let's consider p an odd prime and a an integer. The *Legendre Symbol,* noted as $\left(\dfrac{a}{p}\right)$, is defined as follows:

$$\left(\frac{a}{p}\right) = \begin{cases} 0, & if\ p \mid a \\ 1, & if\ a \in Q_p \\ -1, & if\ a \in \overline{Q_p} \end{cases}.$$

Properties 2.37. Properties of Legendre Symbol [1]. Let's consider the following properties, known as the Properties of Legendre Symbol. We consider p to be an odd prime. Two integers $a, b \in \mathbb{Z}$. In this case, the following properties of the Legendre symbol are considered:

1. $\left(\dfrac{a}{p}\right) \equiv a^{\frac{p-1}{2}} \pmod{p}$. In this particular case, $\left(\dfrac{1}{p}\right) = 1$ and

   $\left(\dfrac{-1}{p}\right) = (-1)^{\frac{p-1}{2}}$. Since $-1 \in Q_p$ if $p \equiv 1 \pmod{4}$ and $-1 \in \overline{Q_p}$

   if $p \equiv 3 \pmod{4}$.

2. $\left(\dfrac{ab}{p}\right) = \left(\dfrac{a}{p}\right)\left(\dfrac{b}{p}\right)$. Since if $a \in \mathbb{Z}_p^*$, then $\left(\dfrac{a^2}{p}\right) = 1$.

3. If $a \equiv b \pmod{p}$, then $\left(\dfrac{a}{p}\right) = \left(\dfrac{b}{p}\right)$.

4. $\left(\dfrac{2}{p}\right) = (-1)^{\frac{(p^2-1)}{8}}$. Since $\left(\dfrac{2}{p}\right) = 1$ if $p \equiv 1$ or $7 \pmod{8}$, and $\left(\dfrac{2}{p}\right) = -1$

   if $p \equiv 3$ or $5 \pmod{8}$.

5. If q represent an odd prime distinct from p, we have

$$\left(\dfrac{p}{q}\right) = \left(\dfrac{q}{p}\right)(-1)^{\frac{(p-1)(q-1)}{4}}.$$

The Jacoby symbol represents a generalization of the Legendre Symbol for integers n that are not odd and also are not necessarily prime.

Definition 2.38. Jacobi Definition [1]. Consider an integer $n \geq 3$ to be odd with a prime factorization as

$$n = p_1^{e_1} p_2^{e_2} \ldots p_k^{e_k}.$$

The Jacobi symbol $\left(\dfrac{a}{n}\right)$ is defined to be as follows:

$$\left(\dfrac{a}{n}\right) = \left(\dfrac{a}{p_1}\right)^{e_1}\left(\dfrac{a}{p_2}\right)^{e_2} \ldots \left(\dfrac{a}{p_k}\right)^{e_k}.$$

Note the fact that if n is prime, the Jacobi symbol is just the Legendre symbol.

Properties 2.39. Properties for Jacobi Symbol [1]. Consider $m \geq 3$ and $n \geq 3$ to be odd integers and $a, b \in \mathbb{Z}$. The Jacobi symbol has the following properties:

1. $\left(\dfrac{a}{n} \right) = 0, 1, or -1$. More than this, $\left(\dfrac{a}{n} \right) = 0$ if and only if $\gcd(a, n) \neq 1$.

2. $\left(\dfrac{ab}{n} \right) = \left(\dfrac{a}{n} \right)\left(\dfrac{b}{n} \right)$. Hence if $a \in \mathbb{Z}_n^*$, then $\left(\dfrac{a^2}{n} \right) = 1$.

3. $\left(\dfrac{a}{nm} \right) = \left(\dfrac{a}{n} \right)\left(\dfrac{a}{m} \right)$.

4. If $a \equiv b\ (mod\ n)$, then $\left(\dfrac{a}{n} \right) = \left(\dfrac{b}{n} \right)$.

5. $\left(\dfrac{1}{n} \right) = 1$.

6. $\left(\dfrac{-1}{n} \right) = (-1)^{\frac{(n-1)}{2}}$. Hence $\left(\dfrac{-1}{n} \right) = 1$ if $n \equiv 1\ (mod\ 4)$, and $\left(\dfrac{-1}{n} \right) = -1$ if $n \equiv (3\ mod\ 4)$.

7. $\left(\dfrac{2}{n} \right) = (-1)^{\frac{n^2-1}{8}}$. Hence $\left(\dfrac{2}{n} \right) = 1$ if $n \equiv 1$ or $7\ (mod\ 8)$, and $\left(\dfrac{2}{n} \right) = -1$ if $n \equiv 3$ or $5\ (mod\ 8)$.

8. $\left(\dfrac{m}{n} \right) = \left(\dfrac{n}{m} \right)(-1)^{\frac{(m-1)(n-1)}{4}}$. In other words, $\left(\dfrac{m}{n} \right) = \left(\dfrac{n}{m} \right)$ unless both m and n are congruent to 3 modulo 4, in which case $\left(\dfrac{m}{n} \right) = -\left(\dfrac{n}{m} \right)$.

Algorithm 2.40. Jacobi Symbol (and Legendre symbol) calculating [1]

$JACOBI\,(a,n)$

$INPUT:$ *An odd integer* $n \geq 3$ *and an integer* $a, 0 \leq a < n$

$OUTPUT:$ *The Jacobi symbol* $\left(\dfrac{a}{n} \right)$

1. *If $a = 0$, then return 0.*

2. *If $a = 1$, then return 1.*

3. *Write $a = 2^e a_1$, where a_1 is odd.*

4. *If e is even, then set $s \leftarrow 1$. Else set $s \leftarrow 1$ if $n \equiv 1$ or $7 \pmod 8$,*
    or set $s \leftarrow -1$ if $n \equiv 3$ or $5 \pmod 8$.

5. *If $n \equiv 3 \pmod 4$ and $a_1 \equiv 3 \pmod 4$, then set $s \leftarrow -s$.*

6. *Set $n_1 \leftarrow n \bmod a_1$.*

7. *If $a_1 = 1$, then return(s); else return $(s \cdot JACOBI(n_1, a_1))$.*

Finite Fields

Foundations

Definition 2.41. Let's consider F to be a *finite field* that contains a finite number of elements. The *order of F* represents the number of elements in F.

   Definition 2.42. The uniqueness and existence of finite fields.

1. Let's suppose if F is a finite field, then F will have p^m elements for a prime p and integer $m \geq 1$.

2. For each prime power order p^m, we have a unique finite field of order p^m. The field is noted as $\mathbb{F}_{p_m}$ or in some other literature references it's $GF(p^m)$.

   Definition 2.43. Let's say if a F_q represents a finite field of order $q = p^m$, p is a prime, then the characteristic of $\mathbb{F}_q$ is p. More than this, $\mathbb{F}_q$ will have a copy of $\mathbb{Z}_p$ as a subfield since $\mathbb{F}_q$ can be viewed as an extension field of $\mathbb{Z}_p$ of degree m.

Polynomials and the Euclidean Algorithm

The following two algorithms are necessary to understand how we can obtain the *gcd* for two polynomials, $g(x)$ and $h(x)$, both being in $\mathbb{Z}_p[x]$:

   Algorithm 2.43. Euclidean Algorithm for $\mathbb{Z}_p[x]$ [1]

   INPUT :   *Two polynomials $g(x), h(x) \in \mathbb{Z}_p[x]$*

OUTPUT :   gcd *of* $g(x)$ *and* $h(x)$

1. *While $h(x) \neq 0$, then*

   a. *Set $r(x) \leftarrow g(x)$ mod $h(x)$, $g(x) \leftarrow h(x)$, $h(x) \leftarrow r(x)$*

2. *Return $g(x)$.*

Algorithm 2.44. Extended Euclidean Algorithm for $\mathbb{Z}_p[x]$ [1]

INPUT :   *Two polynomials* $g(x), h(x) \in \mathbb{Z}_p[x]$

OUTPUT : $d(x) = \gcd(g(x), h(x))$ *and polynomials* $s(x), t(x) \in \mathbb{Z}_p[x]$
which will satisfy $s(x)g(x) + t(x)h(x) = d(x)$.

1. If $h(x) = 0$, *then set $d(x) \leftarrow g(x)$, $s(x) \leftarrow 1$, $t(x) \leftarrow 0$.*

   a. *Return $(d(x), s(x), t(x))$.*

2. Set $s_2(x) \leftarrow 1$, $s_1(x) \leftarrow 0$, $t_2(x) \leftarrow 0$, $t_1(x) \leftarrow 1$.

3. While $h(x) \neq 0$, *then*

   a. $g(x) \leftarrow g(x)$ *div* $h(x)$, $r(x) \leftarrow g(x) - h(x)q(x)$

   b. $s(x) \leftarrow s_2(x) - q(x)s_1(x)$, $t(x) \leftarrow t_2(x) - q(x)t_1(x)$

   c. $g(x) \leftarrow h(x)$, $h(x) \leftarrow r(x)$

   d. $s_{2(x)} \leftarrow s_1(x)$, $s_1(x) \leftarrow s(x)$, $t_2(x) \leftarrow t_1(x)$, *and* $t_1(x) \leftarrow t(x)$

4. Set $d(x) \leftarrow g(x)$, $s(x) \leftarrow s_2(x)$, $t(x) \leftarrow t_2(x)$.

5. Return $d(x)$, $s(x)$, $t(x)$.

Case Study 1: Computing the Probability of an Event to Take Place Using a Number of Trials

The following application deals with computing the probability of an event occurring in a certain number of trials. The application presented below explains the fact that an event has the probability of occurring at each trial, and after N trials we have the probability for which one single trial resulted in the event to be $1 - (1 - P)^N$. See Figure 2-1 and Listing 2-1.

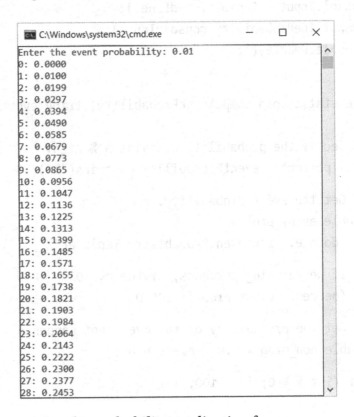

Figure 2-1. *Computing the probability application form*

Listing 2-1. Code for Computing the Probability of an Event

```
using System;
using System.Collections.Generic;
using System.Linq;
using System.Text;
using System.Threading.Tasks;
```

```csharp
namespace CompProb
{
    class Program
    {
        static void Main(string[] args)
        {
            string consoleInput;
            Console.Write("Enter the event probability: ");
            consoleInput = Console.ReadLine();
            ComputeTheProbability(consoleInput);
            Console.ReadKey();
        }

        private static void ComputeTheProbability(string eventProbability)
        {
            // See if the probability contains a % sign.
            bool percent = eventProbability.Contains("%");

            // Get the event probability.
            double event_prob =
                double.Parse(eventProbability.Replace("%", ""));

            // If we're using percents, divide by 100.
            if (percent) event_prob /= 100.0;

            // Get the probability of the event not happening.
            double non_prob = 1.0 - event_prob;

            for (int i = 0; i <= 100; i++)
            {
                double prob = 1.0 - Math.Pow(non_prob, i);

                if (percent)
                {
                    prob *= 100.0;
                    Console.WriteLine(i.ToString() + ": " + prob.
                    ToString("0.0000") + "%");
                }
```

```
            else
            {
                Console.WriteLine(i.ToString() + ": " + prob.
                ToString("0.0000"));
            }
        }
    }
}
}
```

Case Study 2: Computing the Probability Distribution

In this section, we show how to compute the probability distribution. The code is presented in Listing 2-2 and the result can be seen in Figure 2-2.

Listing 2-2. Code for Probability Distribution

```
using System;
using System.Collections.Generic;
using System.Linq;
using System.Text;
using System.Threading.Tasks;

namespace ProbDistribution
{
    class Program
    {
        static List<Distribution> values = new List<Distribution>();
        static void Main(string[] args)
        {
            Console.WriteLine("Press ESC key to exit the process...");

            string X, pOfX;
            Console.Write("X = ");
            X = Console.ReadLine();
```

```
        Console.Write("P(X) = ");
        pOfX = Console.ReadLine();
        AddValues(X, pOfX);

        while (Console.ReadKey().Key != ConsoleKey.Escape)
        {
            Console.Write("X = ");
            X = Console.ReadLine();
            Console.Write("P(X) = ");
            pOfX = Console.ReadLine();
            AddValues(X, pOfX);
        }
    }

    static void AddValues(string txtX, string txtPOfTheX)
    {
        int x = 0;
        double p = 0.00, sum = 0.00;
        Distribution dist = null;

        // Check that the user entered a value for x
        if (txtX.Length == 0)
        {
            Console.WriteLine("You must enter the x value.",
                        "Probability Distribution");
            Console.WriteLine();
            return;
        }

        // Test that the user entered a value for P(x)
        if (txtPOfTheX.Length == 0)
        {
            Console.WriteLine("You must enter the P(x) value.",
                        "Probability Distribution");
            Console.WriteLine();
            return;
        }
```

```csharp
// Get the value for x
try
{
    x = int.Parse(txtX);
}
catch (FormatException)
{
    Console.WriteLine("The value you entered is invalid.",
                "Probability Distribution");
    Console.WriteLine();
}

// Get the value for P(x)
try
{
    p = double.Parse(txtPOfTheX);
}
catch (FormatException)
{
    Console.WriteLine("The value you entered is invalid.",
                "Probability Distribution");
    Console.WriteLine();
}

// Create a Distribution value
dist = new Distribution(x, p);
// Add the value to the list
values.Add(dist);

ShowValues();

// Calculate the sum of the P(x) values
foreach (Distribution d in values)
    sum += d.PofX;
Console.WriteLine("The sum is: " + sum.ToString("F"));
```

```csharp
        // Test the first requirement
        if (sum != 1) // The first rule is not respected
        {
            Console.WriteLine("The first rule is not respected",
                            "Probability Distribution");
            Console.WriteLine("Press ENTER to continue or ESC to exit
            the process..." + "\n");
            return;
        }

        // Test the second requirement
        foreach (Distribution d in values)
        {
            if ((d.PofX < 0.00) || (d.PofX > 1)) // The second rule is
                                                    not respected
            {
                Console.WriteLine("The second rule is not respected",
                                "Probability Distribution");
                Console.WriteLine("Press ENTER to continue or ESC to
                exit the process..." + "\n");
                return;
            }
        }
    }

    static void ShowValues()
    {
        double sum = 0.00;

        foreach (Distribution dist in values)
        {
            Console.WriteLine("X=" + dist.X.ToString() + "\t" +
            "P(X)=" + dist.PofX.ToString());
        }
```

```
// Calculate the sum of the P(x) values
foreach (Distribution d in values)
    sum += d.PofX;

Console.WriteLine("No. of values: " + values.Count.ToString() +
"\t" + "Sum of P(X): " + sum.ToString());
    }
}

public class Distribution
{
    public int X { get; set; }
    public double PofX { get; set; }

    public Distribution(int x, double p)
    {
        X = x;
        PofX = p;
    }
}
}
```

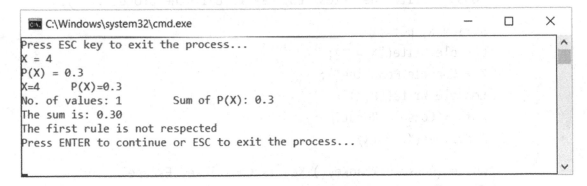

Figure 2-2. *Probability distribution application form*

Case Study 3: Computing the Mean of Probability Distribution

In this section, we show how to compute the mean of the probability distribution. The code is presented in Listing 2-3 and the result can be seen in Figure 2-3.

Listing 2-3. Code for Computing the Mean of the Probability

```csharp
using System;
using System.Collections.Generic;
using System.Linq;
using System.Text;
using System.Threading.Tasks;

namespace CalcMeanProbDistrib
{
    class Program
    {
        static List<Distribution> values = new List<Distribution>();
        static void Main(string[] args)
        {
            Console.WriteLine("Press ESC key to exit the process...");

            string X, pOfX;
            Console.Write("X = ");
            X = Console.ReadLine();
            Console.Write("P(X) = ");
            pOfX = Console.ReadLine();
            AddValues(X, pOfX);

            while (Console.ReadKey().Key != ConsoleKey.Escape)
            {
                Console.Write("X = ");
                X = Console.ReadLine();
                Console.Write("P(X) = ");
                pOfX = Console.ReadLine();
```

```csharp
        AddValues(X, pOfX);
    }
}

static void ShowValues()
{
    double sum = 0.00;
    double mean = 0.00;

    foreach (Distribution dist in values)
    {
        mean += dist.X * dist.PofX;
        Console.WriteLine(dist.X.ToString() + " * " +
                        dist.PofX.ToString() + " = " +
                        mean.ToString());
    }

    foreach (Distribution d in values)
        sum += d.PofX;

    Console.WriteLine("Number of values: " + values.Count.
    ToString() + "\t" + "Sum of P(X): " + sum.ToString() + "\t" +
    "Mean of probability distribution: " + mean.ToString());
}

static void AddValues(string txtValueOfX, string txtValueOfPX)
{
    int x = 0;
    double p = 0.00, sum = 0.00;
    Distribution dist = null;

    // Check that the user entered a value for x
    if (txtValueOfX.Length == 0)
    {
        Console.WriteLine("You must enter the x value.",
                    "Probability Distribution");
        return;
    }
```

```csharp
// Test that the user entered a value for P(x)
if (txtValueOfPX.Length == 0)
{
    Console.WriteLine("You must enter the P(x) value.",
                    "Probability Distribution");
    return;
}

// Get the value for x
try
{
    x = int.Parse(txtValueOfX);
}
catch (FormatException)
{
    Console.WriteLine("The value you entered is invalid.",
                    "Probability Distribution");
}

// Get the value for P(x)
try
{
    p = double.Parse(txtValueOfPX);
}
catch (FormatException)
{
    Console.WriteLine("The value you entered is invalid.",
                    "Probability Distribution");
}

// Create a Distribution value
dist = new Distribution(x, p);
// Add the value to the list
values.Add(dist);

ShowValues();
```

```
        // Calculate the sum of the P(x) values
        foreach (Distribution d in values)
            sum += d.PofX;
        Console.WriteLine("Sum of P(X): " + sum.ToString("F"));

        // Test the first requirement
        if (sum != 1) // The first rule is not respected
        {
            Console.WriteLine("The first rule is not respected",
                        "Probability Distribution");
            Console.WriteLine("Press ENTER to continue or ESC to exit
            the process..." + "\n");
            return;
        }

        // Test the second requirement
        foreach (Distribution d in values)
        {
            if ((d.PofX < 0.00) || (d.PofX > 1)) // The second rule is
            not respected
            {
                Console.WriteLine("The second rule is not respected",
                            "Probability Distribution");
                Console.WriteLine("Press ENTER to continue or ESC to
                exit the process..." + "\n");
                return;
            }
        }
    }
}

public class Distribution
{
    public int X { get; set; }
    public double PofX { get; set; }
```

```csharp
        public Distribution(int x, double p)
        {
            X = x;
            PofX = p;
        }
    }
}
```

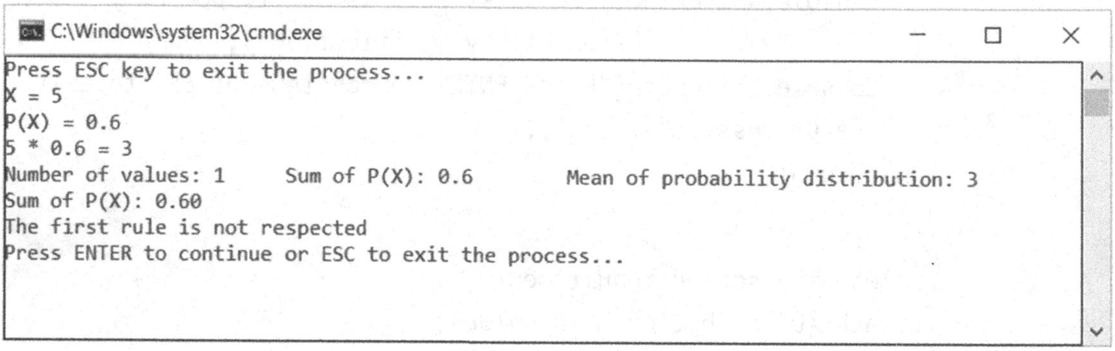

Figure 2-3. *Computing the mean of probability distribution*

Case Study 4: Computing the Variance

In this section, we show how to compute the variance. The code is presented in Listing 2-4 and the result can be seen in Figure 2-4.

Listing 2-4. Code for Computing the Variance

```csharp
using System;
using System.Collections.Generic;
using System.Linq;
using System.Text;
using System.Threading.Tasks;

namespace ConsoleComputingVariance
{
    class Program
    {
        static void Main(string[] args)
```

```
    {
        List<double> dataValues =
            new List<double> { 1, 2, 3, 4, 5, 6 };

        double variance =
            dataValues.ComputingVariance();

        Console.WriteLine("Variance is = {0}",
                variance);

        Console.ReadKey();
    }
}

public static class MyListExtensions
{
    public static double ComputingMean(this List<double> values)
    {
        return values.Count == 0 ? 0 : values.ComputingMean(0, values.
        Count);
    }

    public static double ComputingMean(this List<double> values, int
    start, int end)
    {
        double s = 0;

        for (int i = start; i < end; i++)
        {
            s += values[i];
        }

        return s / (end - start);
    }

    public static double ComputingVariance(this List<double> values)
    {
        return values.ComputingVariance(values.ComputingMean(), 0,
        values.Count);
    }
```

```
public static double ComputingVariance(this List<double> values,
double mean)
{
    return values.ComputingVariance(mean, 0, values.Count);
}

public static double ComputingVariance(this List<double> values,
double mean, int start, int end)
{
    double variance = 0;

    for (int i = start; i < end; i++)
    {
        variance += Math.Pow((values[i] - mean), 2);
    }

    int n = end - start;
    if (start > 0) n -= 1;

    return variance / (n);
}

}
}
```

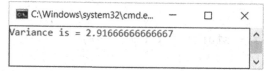

Figure 2-4. *Calculating the variance*

Case Study 5: Computing the Standard Deviation

In this section, we show how to compute the standard deviation. The code is presented in Listing 2-5 and the result can be seen in Figure 2-5.

Listing 2-5. Code for Computing Standard Deviation

```
using System;
using System.Collections.Generic;
using System.Linq;
using System.Text;
using System.Threading.Tasks;

namespace ConsoleComputingVariance
{
    class Program
    {
        static void Main(string[] args)
        {
            List<double> dataValues =
                new List<double> { 1, 2, 3, 4, 5, 6 };

            double mean = dataValues.ComputingMean();
            double variance = dataValues.ComputingVariance();
            double standard_deviation =
                dataValues.ComputingStandardDeviation();

            Console.WriteLine("Mean is = {0}," +
                "Variance is = {1}, " +
                "Standard Deviation is = {2}",
                    mean,
                    variance,
                    standard_deviation);

            Console.ReadKey();
        }
    }

    public static class MyListExtensions
    {
        public static double ComputingMean(this List<double> values)
        {
```

```
        return values.Count == 0 ? 0 : values.ComputingMean
        (0, values.Count);
    }

    public static double ComputingMean(this List<double> values,
    int start, int end)
    {
        double s = 0;

        for (int i = start; i < end; i++)
        {
            s += values[i];
        }

        return s / (end - start);
    }

    public static double ComputingVariance(this List<double> values)
    {
        return values.ComputingVariance(values.ComputingMean(), 0,
        values.Count);
    }

    public static double ComputingVariance(this List<double> values,
    double mean)
    {
        return values.ComputingVariance(mean, 0, values.Count);
    }

    public static double ComputingVariance(this List<double> values,
    double mean, int start, int end)
    {
        double variance = 0;

        for (int i = start; i < end; i++)
        {
            variance += Math.Pow((values[i] - mean), 2);
        }
```

```
    int n = end - start;
    if (start > 0) n -= 1;

    return variance / (n);
}

public static double ComputingStandardDeviation(this List<double>
values)
{
    return values.Count == 0 ? 0 : values.ComputingStandard
    Deviation(0, values.Count);
}

public static double ComputingStandardDeviation(this List<double>
values, int start, int end)
{
    double mean = values.ComputingMean(start, end);
    double variance = values.ComputingVariance(mean, start, end);

    return Math.Sqrt(variance);
}
  }
}
```

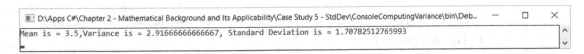

Figure 2-5. *Computing the standard deviation*

Case Study 6: Birthday Paradox

In this section, we show how to apply the birthday paradox for a given number of people. The code is presented in Listing 2-6 and the result can be seen in Figure 2-6.

Listing 2-6. Code for Birthday Paradox Application

```csharp
using System;
using System.Collections.Generic;
using System.Linq;
using System.Text;
using System.Threading.Tasks;

namespace ConsoleBirthdayParadox
{
    class Program
    {
        static void Main(string[] args)
        {
            Console.WriteLine("Enter the number of people: ");
            int people_number = Convert.ToInt32(Console.ReadLine());

            const double number_of_trials = 100000.0;

            int number_of_birthday_matches = 0;
            double sum_of_unique_birthday = 0;

            List<int> personBirthdays;
            Random rnd = new Random();

            for (int trial_number = 1; trial_number <= number_of_trials;
            trial_number++)
            {
                //** we will generate birthdays
                personBirthdays = new List<int>(people_number);
                for (int personNum = 1; personNum <= people_number;
                personNum++)
                    personBirthdays.Add(rnd.Next(1, 366));

                if (personBirthdays.Count != personBirthdays.Distinct().
                Count())
                    number_of_birthday_matches++;
```

```
        sum_of_unique_birthday += personBirthdays.Distinct().
        Count();
    }

    double percentage_matched =
        number_of_birthday_matches / number_of_trials * 100.0;

    double uniqueness_per_trial = sum_of_unique_birthday / number_
    of_trials;

    Console.WriteLine("There are {0} people. " +
        "There is at least one matching birthday {1}% " +
        "of the time. Average number of " +
        "unique birthdays is {2}.",
            people_number.ToString(),
            percentage_matched.ToString(),
            uniqueness_per_trial.ToString());

    Console.ReadKey();
        }
    }
}
```

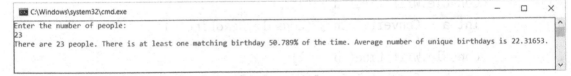

Figure 2-6. *Birthday paradox application*

Case Study 7: (Extended) Euclidean Algorithm

There are two versions of the Euclidean Algorithm, *the regular version* (see Figure 2-7 and Listing 2-7) and the *extended version* (see Figure 2-8 and Listing 2-8). The difference between the two versions of the Euclidean Algorithm is that the regular one computes the GCD between two numbers based on successive subtractions operations, while the extended version is applied to polynomials (see Algorithm 2.43 and Algorithm 2.44).

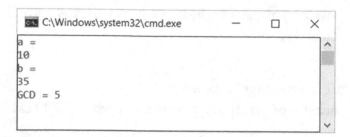

Figure 2-7. *Euclidean Algorithm application form*

Listing 2-7. Code for Computing the Euclidean Algorithm

```
using System;
using System.Collections.Generic;
using System.Linq;
using System.Text;
using System.Threading.Tasks;

namespace ConsoleEuclideanAlgorithm
{
    class Program
    {
        static void Main(string[] args)
        {
            Console.WriteLine("a = ");
            int a = Convert.ToInt32(Console.ReadLine());

            Console.WriteLine("b = ");
            int b = Convert.ToInt32(Console.ReadLine());

            int g = gcd(a, b);

            Console.WriteLine("GCD = {0}", g.ToString());
            Console.ReadKey();
        }

        public static int gcd(int x, int y)
        {
            if (x == 0)
                return y;
```

```
            return gcd(y % x, x);
        }
    }
}
```

Listing 2-8. Code for Extended Euclidean Algorithm

```csharp
using System;
using System.Collections.Generic;
using System.Linq;
using System.Text;
using System.Threading.Tasks;

namespace ConsoleExtendedEuclidean
{
    class Program
    {
        static void Main(string[] args)
        {
            Console.WriteLine("a = ");
            int a = Convert.ToInt32(Console.ReadLine());

            Console.WriteLine("b = ");
            int b = Convert.ToInt32(Console.ReadLine());

            Console.WriteLine("X = ");
            int x = Convert.ToInt32(Console.ReadLine());

            Console.WriteLine("Y = ");
            int y = Convert.ToInt32(Console.ReadLine());

            int g;

            g = gcdExtended(a, b, x, y);

            Console.WriteLine("Extended Euclidean Algorithm = {0}.",
            g.ToString());
            Console.ReadKey();
        }
```

```java
public static int gcdExtended(int a, int b, int x, int y)
{
    // Base Case
    if (a == 0)
    {
        x = 0;
        y = 1;
        return b;
    }

    // To store results of
    // recursive call
    int x1 = 1, y1 = 1;
    int gcd = gcdExtended(b % a, a, x1, y1);

    // Update x and y using
    // results of recursive call
    x = y1 - (b / a) * x1;
    y = x1;

    return gcd;
}
}
}
```

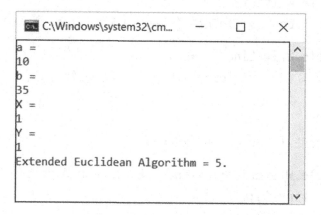

Figure 2-8. *Extended Euclidean Algorithm application form*

Case Study 8: Computing the Multiplicative Inverse Under Modulo *m*

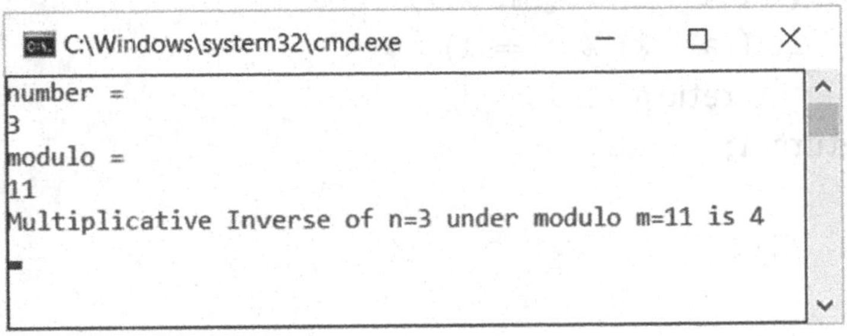

Figure 2-9. *Modular multiplicative inverse application*

Listing 2-9. Code for Computing the Modular Multiplicative Inverse

```
using System;
using System.Collections.Generic;
using System.Linq;
using System.Text;
using System.Threading.Tasks;

namespace ConsoleMultiInverse
{
    class Program
    {
        static void Main(string[] args)
        {
            Console.WriteLine("number = ");
            int n = Convert.ToInt32(Console.ReadLine());

            Console.WriteLine("modulo = ");
            int m = Convert.ToInt32(Console.ReadLine());

            Console.WriteLine("Multiplicative Inverse of n={0} " +
                "under modulo m={1} is {2}",
                n, m, Convert.ToString(modInverse(n, m)));

            Console.ReadKey();
        }
```

```
        static int modInverse(int a, int m)
        {
            a = a % m;
            for (int x = 1; x < m; x++)
                if ((a * x) % m == 1)
                    return x;
            return 1;
        }
    }
}
```

Case Study 9: Chinese Remainder Theorem

In this section, we show how to apply the Chinese Remainder Theorem. The code is presented in Listing 2-10 and the result can be seen in Figure 2-10.

Listing 2-10. Code for the Chinese Remainder Theorem

```
using System;
using System.Collections.Generic;
using System.Linq;
using System.Text;
using System.Threading.Tasks;

namespace ConsoleChineseRemainder
{
    class Program
    {
        static void Main(string[] args)
        {
            int[] num = { 3, 4, 5 };
            int[] rem = { 2, 3, 1 };
            int k = num.Length;

            Console.WriteLine("numbers = {0}",
                "{ " + num[0].ToString() + ", " +
```

```
                    num[1].ToString() + ", " +
                    num[2].ToString() + " }");

        Console.WriteLine("remainders = {0}",
            "{ " + rem[0].ToString() + ", " +
                    rem[1].ToString() + ", " +
                    rem[2].ToString() + " }");

        Console.WriteLine("Applying Chinese Remainder " +
            "Theorem is = {0}",
            findMinX(num, rem, k).ToString());

        Console.ReadKey();
    }

    static int inv(int a, int m)
    {
        int m0 = m, t, q;
        int x0 = 0, x1 = 1;

        if (m == 1)
            return 0;

        // Apply extended
        // Euclid Algorithm
        while (a > 1)
        {
            // q is quotient
            q = a / m;

            t = m;

            // m is remainder now,
            // process same as
            // euclid's algo
            m = a % m; a = t;

            t = x0;

            x0 = x1 - q * x0;
```

```
        x1 = t;
    }

    // Make x1 positive
    if (x1 < 0)
        x1 += m0;

    return x1;
}

static int findMinX(int[] num, int[] rem, int k)
{
    // Compute product of all numbers
    int prod = 1;
    for (int i = 0; i < k; i++)
        prod *= num[i];

    // Initialize result
    int result = 0;

    // Apply above formula
    for (int i = 0; i < k; i++)
    {
        int pp = prod / num[i];
        result += rem[i] *
                    inv(pp, num[i]) * pp;
    }

    return result % prod;
    }
  }
}
```

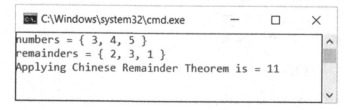

Figure 2-10. *Chinese Remainder Theorem application*

Case Study 10: The Legendre Symbol

In this section, we show how to compute the Legendre symbol. The code is presented in Listing 2-11 and the result can be seen in Figure 2-11.

Listing 2-11. Code for Computing the Legendre Symbol

```
using System;
using System.Collections.Generic;
using System.Linq;
using System.Text;
using System.Threading.Tasks;

namespace ConsoleLegendreSymbol
{
    class Program
    {
        static void Main(string[] args)
        {
            Console.WriteLine("a = ");
            int a = Convert.ToInt32(Console.ReadLine());

            Console.WriteLine("b = ");
            int b = Convert.ToInt32(Console.ReadLine());

            int result = Legendre(a, b);

            Console.WriteLine("Legendre Symbol is = {0}", result.ToString());
            Console.ReadKey();
        }

        public static int Legendre(int a, int p)
        {
            if (p < 2)  // prime test is expensive.
                throw new ArgumentOutOfRangeException("p", "p must
                not be < 2");
            if (a == 0)
            {
                return 0;
            }
```

```
    if (a == 1)
    {
        return 1;
    }
    int result;
    if (a % 2 == 0)
    {
        result = Legendre(a / 2, p);
        if (((p * p - 1) & 8) != 0) // instead of dividing by 8,
        shift the mask bit
        {
            result = -result;
        }
    }
    else
    {
        result = Legendre(p % a, a);
        if (((a - 1) * (p - 1) & 4) != 0) // instead of dividing
                                        by 4, shift the mask bit
        {
            result = -result;
        }
    }
    return result;
        }
    }
}
```

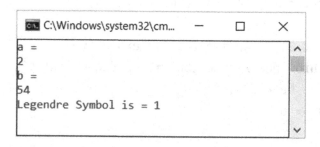

Figure 2-11. *Computation of the Legendre Symbol*

Conclusions

In this chapter, we discussed the importance of mathematical tools used in most of the modern cryptography algorithms and how they can be implemented. We covered four important aspects of the mathematical foundations that can be helpful during the implementation of the cryptographic algorithms: probability theory, information theory, number theory, and finite fields.

For each mathematical foundation, we presented the necessary equations and mathematical expressions that are used in the implementation of the algorithms. Each equation or mathematical expression was demonstrated through code implemented in C#, entitled as a case study. Each case study showed and demonstrated the skills and knowledge required by the reader in order to develop secure and reliable code. The case studies were counted from 1 to 10. At the end of the chapter, the reader should have an important amount of knowledge, both theoretical and practical, and should have learned how to move from theory to practice in a very short time.

Bibliography

[1]   Alfred J. Menezes, Paul van Oorschot, Scott A. Vanstone. *Handbook of Applied Cryptography*. CRC Press. 1996. ISBN 0-8493-8523-7.

[2]   R. Meijer, *Algebra for Cryptologists, First Edition.* New York, NY: Springer, 2016.

[3]   J. Hoffstein, J. Pipher, and J. H. Silverman, *An Introduction to Mathematical Cryptography, Second Edition*. New York: Springer, 2014.

[4]   S. Rubinstein-Salzedo, *Cryptography, First Edition*. New York, NY: Springer, 2018.

[5]   W. Stallings, *Cryptography and Network Security: Principles and Practice, 6th ed*. USA: Prentice Hall Press, 2013.

[6]   K. Academy, *Cryptography: Data and Application Security*. Independently published, 2017.

[7]   C. T. Rivers, *Cryptography: Decoding Cryptography! From Ancient To New Age Times*. JR Kindle Publishing, 2014.

[8]   D. Stinson, *Cryptography: Theory and Practice, Second Edition.* CRC/C&H, 2002.

[9]   H. Delfs and H. Knebl, *Introduction to Cryptography: Principles and Applications, Third Edition.* New York, NY: Springer, 2015.

[10] J. Katz and Y. Lindell, *Introduction to Modern Cryptography, Second Edition.* Boca Raton: Chapman and Hall/CRC, 2014.

[11] X. Wang, G. Xu, M. Wang, and X. Meng, *Mathematical Foundations of Public Key Cryptography, First Edition.* Boca Raton: CRC Press, 2015.

[12] T. R. Shemanske, *Modern Cryptography and Elliptic Curves.* Providence, Rhode Island: American Mathematical Society, 2017.

[13] S. Y. Yan, Primality *Testing and Integer Factorization in Public-Key Cryptography, First Edition.* Springer, 2013.

[14] L. M. Batten, *Public Key Cryptography: Applications and Attacks.* Hoboken, N.J: Wiley-Blackwell, 2013.

[15] J.-P. Aumasson, *Serious Cryptography.* San Francisco: No Starch Press, 2017.

[16] S. Khare, *The World of Cryptography: incl. cryptosystems, ciphers, public key encryption, data integration, message authentication, digital signatures.*

[17] Adrian Atanasiu. *Securitatea Informației (Information Security) - Criptografie (Cryptography) - volume 1*, InfoData Publisher, 2007. ISBN: 978-973-1803-29-6, 978-973-1803-16-6. [Romanian language]

[18] Adrian Atanasiu. *Securitatea Informației (Information Security) – Protocoale de Securitate (Security Protocols) - volume 2*, InfoData Publisher, 2007. ISBN: 978-973-1803-29-6, 978-973-1803-18-0. [Romanian language]

[19] Vasile Preda, Emil Simion, Adrian Popescu. *Criptanaliza. Rezultate și Tehnici Matematice (Cryptanalysis. Results and Mathematical Techniques)*, Universitatea Bucuresti Publisher, 2004. ISBN: 973-575-975-6. [Romanian language]

CHAPTER 3

Large Integer Arithmetic

During the complex implementation of complex cryptographic algorithms, operations based on large integers are difficult tasks to be achieved. Most of the limitations are due to hardware equipment (e.g. processor, RAM memory) or programming languages.

In C#, an integer value is represented as 32 bits. From those 32 bits, only 31 are used to represent positive integer arithmetic. In cryptography, it's recommended that we deal with numbers up to two billion, $2 \cdot 10^9$.

Most compilers, such as GCC, offer the `long long` type. This provides the ability to have integers around 9 quintillion, $9 \cdot 10^{18}$.

The following example shows the RSA (Rivest-Shamir-Adleman) public-key encryption cryptosystem, which requires around 300 digits. When dealing with real events and their probabilities, in most cases the computation will involve numbers that are very large. Achieving the main result might be accurate for C#, but compared to other difficult computations, we will have very large numbers.

Consider the following well-known example: compute the chances of winning a jackpot from a lottery having a single ticket. The number of combinations is 50 taken 6 at a time, "50 choose 6" is $\dfrac{50!}{\left((50-6)! \cdot 6!\right)}$. The resulting number from the computation process is 15.890.700, so in this case, the chances of winning are 1/15,890,700. If we use the C# programming language for implementation, the number 15,890,700 can be represented very easily. That could be tricky, and then we could fall for naivety during the implementation of 50! (computed using Calculator from Windows), which is 3.041409320171e+64 or

30,414,093,201,713,378,043,612,608,166,064,768,844,377,641,568,960,512,000, 000,000,000

It's almost impossible to use C # to represent that number, even if we're using a 64-bit platform.

© Marius Iulian Mihailescu and Stefania Loredana Nita 2021
M. I. Mihailescu and S. L. Nita, *Pro Cryptography and Cryptanalysis*,
https://doi.org/10.1007/978-1-4842-6367-9_3

In the following sections, we will discuss a number of algorithms that can be used with large integers for arithmetic operations. Note that as we're working with cryptography algorithms and authentication protocols, it can be very difficult to implement because we are dealing with large integers. Below we'll show a step-by-step approach on how to deal with big numbers.

Figure 3-1 and Listing 3-1 show a full implementation of BigInteger functionalities.

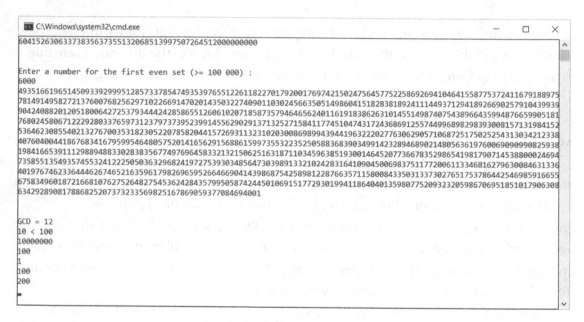

Figure 3-1. *BigInteger example for computing GCD*

Listing 3-1. BigInteger Implementation

```
using System;
using System.Collections.Generic;
using System.Linq;
using System.Text;
using System.Numerics;

namespace BigIntExample
{
    class Program
    {
        static void Main(string[] args)
```

```csharp
{
    //** compute bigger factorials
    Console.Write("Enter a factorial to be computed (>100) :  ");
    int factorial = Convert.ToInt32(Console.ReadLine());
    ComputeBigFactorial(factorial);

    Console.WriteLine(Environment.NewLine);

    //** compute sum of the first
    //** even number to get Fibonacci Series
    Console.WriteLine("Enter a number for the " +
        "first even set (>= 100 000) : ");
    int evenNumberFib = Convert.ToInt32(Console.ReadLine());
    SumOfFirstOneLacEvenFibonacciSeries(evenNumberFib);
    Console.WriteLine(Environment.NewLine);

    //** computing greatest common divisor
    Console.WriteLine("GCD = " +
            BigInteger.GreatestCommonDivisor(12, 24));

    //** comparing purpose
    BigInteger value1 = 10;
    BigInteger value2 = 100;

    switch (BigInteger.Compare(value1, value2))
    {
        case -1:
            Console.WriteLine("{0} < {1}", value1, value2);
            break;
        case 0:
            Console.WriteLine("{0} = {1}", value1, value2);
            break;
        case 1:
            Console.WriteLine("{0} > {1}", value1, value2);
            break;
    }

    //** parsing
    Console.WriteLine(BigInteger.Parse("10000000"));
```

```
    //** obtaining negation
    Console.WriteLine(BigInteger.Negate(-100));

    //** returning the sign
    Console.WriteLine(BigInteger.Negate(-1).Sign);

    //** returning conversion (int to BigInterger)
    int i = 100;
    BigInteger bI = (BigInteger)i;
    Console.WriteLine(bI);

    //** returning conversion (BigInteger to int)
    BigInteger BI = 200;
    int j = (int)BI;
    Console.WriteLine(j);
    Console.Read();
}

//** computing the factorials
private static void ComputeBigFactorial(int factorial)
{
    BigInteger number = factorial;
    BigInteger fact = 1;
    for (; number-- > 0; ) fact *= number+1;
    Console.WriteLine(fact);
}

//** computing the first even fibonacci series
private static void SumOfFirstOneLacEvenFibonacciSeries(
                int evenNumberFib)
{
    int limit = evenNumberFib;

    BigInteger value1 = 1;
    BigInteger value2 = 2;
    BigInteger theSum = 0;
    BigInteger even_sum = value1 + value2;
```

```
    for (int i = 2; i < limit; i++)
    {
        theSum = value1 + value2;
        if (theSum % 2 == 0) even_sum += theSum;
        value1 = value2;
        value2 = theSum;
    }

    Console.WriteLine(even_sum);
    }
  }
}
```

Firstly, we need to transform a standard integer using different computations in a big integer. To get this done, we write a function entitled transformIntToBigInt(A, 123). The purpose of the function is to initialize A as A[0]=3, A[1]=2, A[2]=1, and zeroes for the remaining positions as A[3,...N-1]. Listing 3-2 shows how to accomplish the statement from above by using a simple implementation in C#. In this example, the *BASE* represents the bit sign.

Listing 3-2. Transforming a Standard Integer Using Different Computations in a Big Integer

```
public void TransformIntToBigInt(int BigNo[], int number)
{
    Int   k;

    //** start indexing with 0 position
    k = 0;

    // if we still have something left
    // within the number, continue
    while (number) {
        // insert the digit that is least significant
        // into BigNo[k] number
        BigNo[k++] = number % bitSign;

        // we don't need the least significant bit
        number /= BASE;
    }
```

```
        // complete the remain of the array with zeroes
        while (k < N)
            BigNo[k++] = 0;
}
```

The algorithm from Listing 3-2 has $O(N)$ space and time.

Let's continue our trip, seeing the possibility of adding one to a large int. This procedure is quite useful and is very frequently used in cryptography. The function from Listing 3-3 is much simpler than a total addition.

Listing 3-3. Adding One to a Big Int

```
public void increment (int BigNo [])
{
    Int i;

    // start indexing with least significant digit
    i = 0;
    while (i < N)
    {

        // increment the digit
        BigNo[i]++;

        // if it overflows
        if (BigNo[i] == BASE)
        {
            // make it zero and move the index to next
            BigNo[i] = 0;
            i++;
        }
        else
            // else, we are done!
            break;
    }
}
```

The algorithm depicted in Listing 3-2 has $O(n)$ for the worst case possible (just imagine something like 99999999999999999999999....) and $\Omega(1)$ for the best case. The best case happens when we don't have any overflow on the least significant digit.

Continuing, let's take a closer look at the method for adding two big integers. In this case, we want to add two big integers in two different arrays, BigNo1[0,..., N-1] and BigNo2[0,...,N-1]. The result will be saved in another array, BigNo3[0,...,N-1]. The algorithm is very basic and there is nothing fancy about it. See Listing 3-4.

Listing 3-4. Addition Algorithm

```
public void addition(int BigNo1[], int BigNo2[], int BigNo3[])
{
        Int j, overflowCarry, sum;

        //** there is no necessary to carry at this moment
        carry = 0;
        //** move from the least to the most significant digit
        for (j=0; j<N; j++)
        {
                // the digit placed on j'th position of BigNo3[]
                // is the sum of j'th digits of
                // BigNo1[] and BigNo2[] and including the
                // overvflow carry
                sum = BigNo1[j] + BigNo2[j] + overflowCarry;

                // if the sum will go out of the base then
                // we will find ourself in an overflow situation
                if (sum >= BASE)
                {
                        carry = 1;

                        //** making adjustment in such way that
                        //** the sum will fit within a digit
                        sum -= BASE;
                }
```

```
            else
                //otherwise no carryOverflow
                carry = 0;

        // use the same sum variable to add the
        BigNo3[j] = sum;
    }

    // once we reached to the end
    // we can expect an overflow
    if (carry)
            printf ("There is an overflow in the addition!\n");
}
```

Next, we will focus on multiplication. We will use a basic method that will multiply two big numbers, *X* and *Y*, multiplying each *X* digit with each *Y* digit, so the ouputs becomes a component element. The performance result for each new digit is shifted to the left. The function that we implemented, `multiplyingOneDigit`, will multiply an entire big integer with a single digit. The result will be placed in a new large integer. We will also present another function, `left_shifting`, which will shift the number to the left with a certain number of spaces. It will be multiplied using b^i, where *b* is base and *i* represents the numbers of spaces. Listing 3-5 presents the multiplication algorithm.

Listing 3-5. Multiplication Algorithim

```
public void multiply (int BigInt1[], int BigInt2[],
                                    int BigInt3[])
{
    Int x, y, P[integer_length];

    // BigInt3 will store the sum of
    // partial products.  The value is set to 0.
    buildInteger (BigInt3, 0);

    // for each digit in BigInt1
    for (x=0; x<length_of_integer; x++)
    {
        // multiply BigInt2 with digit [x]
        multiplyOneDigit(BigInt2, P, BigInt1[x]);
```

```
        // left shifting the partial product with i bytes
        leftShifting(P, x);

        // add the output result to the current sum
        addResult(BigInt3, P, BigInt3);
    }
}
```

In Listing 3-6, we will examine a function that multiplies by a single digit.

Listing 3-6. Multiplying Using a Single Digit

```
public void multiplyUsingOneDigit (int BigOne1[], int
                                BigOne2[], int number)
{
    Int k, carryOverflow;

    // we don't need extraflow for the moment
    carryOverflow = 0;

    // for each digit, starting with least significant...
    for (k=0; k<N; k++)
    {
        // multiply the digit with the number,
        // save the result in BigOne2
        BigOne2[k] = number * BigOne1[k];

        // set extra overflow that is taking
        // place starting with the last digit
        BigOne2[k] += carryOverflow;

        // product is too big to fit in a digit
        if (BigOne2[k] >= BASE)
        {
            //** handle the overflow
            carryOverflow = B[k] / BASE;
            BigOne2[k] %= BASE;
        }
```

```
        else
                // no overflow
                carryOverflow = 0;
    }
    if (carryOverflow)
        printf ("During the multiplication
                        we experienced an overflow!\n");
}
```

Listing 3-7 shows a functional operation that will shift to the left a specific number of spaces.

Listing 3-7. Shifting to Left a Specific Number of Spaces

```
public void leftShifting (int BigInt1[], int number) {
    int i;

    //start from left to right,
    // everything with left n spaces
    for (i=N-1; i>= number; i--)
        BigInt1[i] = BigInt1[i- number];

    // complete the last n digits with zeros
    while (i >= 0) BigInt1[i--] = 0;
}
```

Working with Big Integers in C#

.NET Framework 4.0 offers the System.Numerics.BigInteger class, which is based on Microsoft.SolverFoundation.Common.BigInteger.

Working with BigInteger is very useful when designing and developing cryptography algorithms. BigInteger represents an immutable type that is used for large numbers that are characterized by having no upper or lower limits. The members that characterize the BigInteger class are Byte, Int (all three representations: 16, 32, and 64), SByte, and UInt (16, 32, and 64) types.

How to Use the BigInteger Class

There are several ways to create a BigInteger object:

- Using the new keyword and providing any floating value as a parameter to the constructor of the class. See Listing 3-8.

Listing 3-8. Using the new Keyword with BigInteger

```
BigInteger publicCryptographyKeyFromDouble
                        = new BigInteger(131312.3454354353);
Console.WriteLine(publicCryptographyKeyFromDouble);

BigInteger publicCryptographyKeyFromInt64
                        = new BigInteger(7587643562354635);
Console.WriteLine(publicCryptographyKeyFromInt64);
```

- By declaring a BigInteger variable with a value assigned. See Listing 3-9.

Listing 3-9. Using a Variable with a Value Assigned

```
long publicCryptographyKey = 87432541632312;
BigInteger cryptoPubKey = publicCryptographyKey;
Console.WriteLine(cryptoPubKey);
```

- By assign a decimal or floating value to a BigInteger object. Before the assignment will happen, first the value needs to be cast accordingly to BigInteger. See Listing 3-10.

Listing 3-10. Casting to BigIntegers

```
BigInteger publicCryptographyKeyFromDoubleValue
                        = (BigInteger) 423412.3423;
Console.WriteLine(publicCryptographyKeyFromDoubleValue);

BigInteger publicCryptographyFromDecimal
                        = (BigInteger) 23452.34m;
Console.WriteLine(publicCryptographyFromDecimal);
```

Large Integers Libraries for .NET

When we play with big integers in cryptography, 64 bits is not sufficient for numbers. This section will cover an example of a complex cryptosystem entitled RSA, and we will show some statistical tests regarding the comparison of the .NET `BigInteger` class and other .NET libraries.

As shown in the above section, `System.Numerics.BigIntegers` was introduced starting with .NET Framework 4.0, and the simple example in Listing 3-11 shows how it can be used in a different way from the rest of the examples from above.

Listing 3-11. Using System.Numerics.BigIntegers

```
var publicCryptoKey = BigInteger.Par
se("5845829436572843562734865972843659784564");
```

```
var privateCryptoKey = BigInteger.Par
se("2452454523452523424355435273625243223455");
```

Any operations (adding, multiplication, dividing, difference, etc.) using `publicCryptoKey` and `privateCryptoKey` are possible.

GMP

GMP [2] is a namespace that is also known as Emil, after Emil Stefanov. It combines the power of BigInt from F#. The disadvantage of this library is that it can be implemented only on 32-bit systems. The examples in C# look quite identical to the ones that use `BigInteger`. See Listing 3-12.

Listing 3-12. Using GMP

```
var publicCryptoKey = BigInt ("5845829436572843562734865972843659784564");
var privateCryptoKey = BigInt ("2452454523452523424355435273625243223455");
```

MPIR

MPIR [3] can be seen as a fork of GMP [2]. The purpose of MPIR is to give to the compilation process on Windows a flavor and painless process that any professional developer will want to have in their toolkit.

In order to use MPIR in .NET, some wrappers are necessary, such as DLLImports or GetProcAddress assignments. A very good wrapper that can be used is X-MPIR, proposed and developed by Sergey Bochkanov from ALGLIB [4].

The code in Listing 3-13 shows how MPIR can be used in developing complex cryptosystems.

Listing 3-13. Using MPIR

```
var publicKey = mpir.mpz_init_set_str("4657334563546345", 10);
var sessionKey = mpir.mpz_init_set_str("784567354634564", 10);
var exampleOfOperation = mpir.mpz_init();

//** random operations
mpir.mpz_mul(exampleOfOperation, publicKey, sessionKey);

//** Implement the cryptosystem operations as you like **//

//** it is recommended to invoke clear
//** method in order to avoid any memory leakage
mpir.mpz_clear(publicKey);
mpir.mpz_clear(sessionKey);
mpir.mpz_clear(exampleOfOperation);
```

Conclusions

In this chapter, we presented the most important aspects of representing big integers and how they are designed and implemented.

- We analyzed the technical aspects of implementations of the basic methods that work with big numbers.

- We presented the BigInteger class from the .NET Framework 4.0 and showed how to work with BigInteger objects.

- We included other libraries for working with big integers, such as GMP and MPIR.

Bibliography

[1]   BigInteger Class. Available online: https://docs.microsoft.com/
en-us/dotnet/api/system.numerics.biginteger?redirectedfrom=
MSDN&view=netcore-3.1.

[2]   GMP Arithmetic without Limitations. Available online:
https://gm.plib.org/.

[3]   Mpir.NET. Available online: http://wezeku.github.io/
Mpir.NET/.

[4]   ALGLIB. Available online: www.alglib.net/.

CHAPTER 4

Floating-Point Arithmetic

Working with big integers can be seen as an abstract art, and if the cryptosystems are not implemented properly, the entire cryptographic algorithm or scheme can lead to a real disaster. This chapter focuses on floating-point arithmetic and its importance for cryptography.

Why floating-point arithmetic?

Floating-point arithmetic represents a special form of arithmetic on which we need to focus because of how it is applicable in the field of cryptography, such as chaos-based cryptography, homomorphic encryption, quantum cryptography, and so on. This type of arithmetic can be observed in chaos-based cryptography or homomorphic encryption, which is presented later in Chapters 14 and 16.

In systems that use small and very large real numbers, computations using floating-point numbers can be found too. During their computations the process must be very fast.

A floating point variable is a particular category of variables that can hold real numbers, such as 4534.0, -5.232, or 0.005443. The floating part means the decimal point will "float."

C# offers different floating point data types, such as `float`, `double`, and `SByte`. As you know from C++ or other programming language with integer cases, the language does not define any size for these types. With modern architectures, most of the floating point representations are with respect for the IEEE 754 standard for binary representation format. According to this standard, a `float` type has 4 bytes, a `double` has 8 bytes, and a `long double` has 8 bytes (same as the `double`), also 80 bits (by padding we have 12 bytes or 16 bytes).

© Marius Iulian Mihailescu and Stefania Loredana Nita 2021
M. I. Mihailescu and S. L. Nita, *Pro Cryptography and Cryptanalysis*,
https://doi.org/10.1007/978-1-4842-6367-9_4

When you deal with floating values, make sure you always have at least one decimal. This helps the compiler to differentiate between a floating number and an integer. The following examples of declarations show how variables are declared and initialized:

```
int a = 4;        //** 4 is an integer
double b = 3.0    //** 3.0 represents a floating point (with no
                  //** suffix – double type by default)
```

Displaying Floating Point Numbers

Let's consider the example in Listing 4-1.

Listing 4-1. Displaying Common Float Numbers

```
using System;
using System.Collections.Generic;
using System.Linq;
using System.Text;
using System.Threading.Tasks;

namespace CommonFloatNumbers
{
    class Program
    {
        static void Main(string[] args)
        {
            float cryptoKey1 = 5.0f;
            float cryptoKey2 = 6.7f;

            Console.WriteLine(cryptoKey1);
            Console.WriteLine(cryptoKey2);

            Console.ReadKey();

        }
    }
}
```

The output is shown in Figure 4-1.

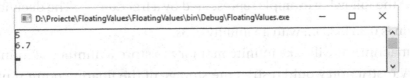

Figure 4-1. *The output of common float numbers*

By looking on the output of the program you can observe that in the first case, the output is 5 bytes and but the source code shows 5.0. This happens because the fractional part is equal to 0. In the second case, the number is printed identically to the one from the source code. In the third case, the number is displayed using scientific notation, an important asset for cryptography algorithms.

The Range of Floating Point

Let's have a look at the IEEE 754 representation and consider the following sizes with their range and precision. See Table 4-1.

Table 4-1. *IEEE 754 Standard Representation*

Size	Range	Precision
4 bytes	$\pm 1.18 \times 10^{-38}$ *to* $\pm 3.4 \times 10^{38}$	6-9 most important digits. Usually around 7 digits.
8 bytes	$\pm 2.23 \times 10^{-308}$ *to* $\pm 1.80 \times 10^{308}$	15-18 most important digits. Usually around 16 digits.
80 bits (usually using 12 or 16 bytes)	$\pm 3.36 \times 10^{-4932}$ *to* $\pm 1.18 \times 10^{4932}$	18-21 most important digits
16 bytes	$\pm 3.36 \times 10^{-4932}$ *to* $\pm 1.18 \times 10^{4932}$	33-36 most important digits

The 80-bit floating point is implemented using 12 or 16 bytes on today's processors. It's common for processors to be able to manage this size.

Floating Point Precision

Let's consider the following example represented by a fraction: $\dfrac{1}{3}$. The decimal representation is 0.3333333... with an infinity of 3s.

Using a machine, it will take infinite memory to store a number of infinite length. This memory restriction would restrict the storage of the floating point number to a certain number of significant digits. The number of the floating point and its precision will determine how many significant digits can be expressed without any loss of knowledge. If we do produce a floating point number in cryptography, the example in Listing 4-2 shows how to truncate the values to six digits. See Figure 4-2 for the output.

Listing 4-2. Representation of Floating Point Precision

```
using System;
using System.Collections.Generic;
using System.Linq;
using System.Text;
using System.Threading.Tasks;

namespace FloatingValues
{
    class Program
    {
        static void Main(string[] args)
        {
            float cryptoKey1 = 7.56756767f;
            float cryptoKey2 = 765.657667f;
            float cryptoKey3 = 345543.564f;
            float cryptoKey4 = 9976544.43f;
            float cryptoKey5 = 0.00043534345f;

            Console.WriteLine("cryptoKey1 = " + cryptoKey1);
            Console.WriteLine("cryptoKey2 = " + cryptoKey2);
            Console.WriteLine("cryptoKey3 = " + cryptoKey3);
            Console.WriteLine("cryptoKey4 = " + cryptoKey4);
            Console.WriteLine("cryptoKey5 = " + cryptoKey5);
```

```
        }
    }
}
```

```
D:\Proiecte\FloatingValues\FloatingValues\bin\Debug\FloatingValues.exe          —    □    ×

cryptoKey2 = 765.6577
cryptoKey3 = 345543.6
cryptoKey4 = 9976544
cryptoKey5 = 0.0004353434
```

Figure 4-2. *Output of floating point precision*

Note that each of the cases from above will have only six important digits.

Normally the exponent will be padded within a minimum number of digits according to the compiler used. The number of digits shown for the exponent is dependent on the compilers used, so for example Visual Studio uses 3 and other compilers use 2 (which are implemented with instructions and standards in compliance with C99). The number of digits representing the number of floating points and their accuracy depends on both the size and the particular value that is stored. The `float` values are defined with a precision of 6 and 9 digits, with a minimum of 7 significant digits for most values. The `double` values are expressed as precision with 15 and 18 digits. Long `double` values are represented with at least 15 or 33 essential digits of precision, which depends on how the bytes are occupied.

Next Level for Floating-Point Arithmetic

In Chapter 14, we will introduce a complex type of encryption. *Homomorphic encryption* represents a special type of encryption that is used as a professional technology for privacy preserving. The technology outsources storage and computation. This manner of encryption allows data to be encrypted and outsourced to commercial (or public) environments with the goal of processing them. All of these processes occur while the data are encrypted. Homomorphic encryption is derived from Ring Learning with Errors (see Chapter 15) and related to private set intersection [1].

Continuing our journey with complex cryptosystems, floating-point representation represents the hot point of the encryption/decryption mechanisms, by finding the proper way to approximate a real number in such way as to support a compromise between range and precision.

As stated, the floating term represents that a number's decimal point can float. In conclusion, it can be set anywhere within the important digits of the number. To be more specific, when we focus on complex cryptographic cryptosystems, such as homomorphic encryption, a floating-point number a can be represented as four integers, so in

$$a = \pm d \cdot n^{f-j}$$

n is the base, f is the exponent, j is the precision, and d is the important or significand. The importance or significand d has to satisfy the following relation:

$$0 \leq d \leq n^f - 1$$

Beginning with.NET Framework 4.0, there is a huge set of routines for floating-point manipulation [8]. Starting with C# 8.0, these basic functions are used for working and achieving tasks based on simple mathematical computations that are related to floating point numbers, necessary for common programming and as well for cryptography (low and simple concepts). For advanced cryptography algorithms, the function's capabilities and requirements for big floating-point numbers are quite limited and they don't provide the proper equipment for a cryptographer.

Below we will examine the IEEE standardization and implementation functions for dealing with floating points. The application is a little more complex compared with the ones already presented above. This being said, the structure of the applications contains three classes: `IEEEStandardization.cs` (see Listing 4-3), `FloatingPoint.cs` (see Listing 4-4), and `Program.cs` (see Listing 4-5). The following application is developed with respect for IEEE standardization and shows how main operations can be implemented with less effort.

In Listing 4-3, we can see the main types of values that are returned when dealing with floating point values. These values are represented as enum types and contain values from normalized to denormalized values, characters that are not numbers and sign values. In Listing 4-4, we implemented methods for obtaining parts for double binary representation, implementation of IEEE-754 standard operations, and methods for bit conversion with single precision. In Listing 4-5, we combine all of the methods into a main program and we put it to work, showing how we can use different ways of computing floating values, multiplying results and subtractions. See Figure 4-3.

```
C:\Windows\system32\cmd.exe                                             —   □   ×

FLOATING POINT ARITHMETIC by Marius Iulian MIHAILESCU and Stefania Loredana NITA

          Different ways of computing 1/105.
          Multiply the output with 105 and subtract 1
          We will get an error.
                Using double: 0.00952380952380952 * 105 - 1 = 0 < 0!
                Using single: 0.00952381 * 105 - 1 = 3.81842255592346E-08 > 0!

          Computing a chaos-based value for cryptography purpose.
                The chaotic value is 84.82999.

          Another example of chaotic value for which we need the integer part.
                Another chaotic value is 90.

          For cryptography is important to have an implementation for IEEE-754
                IEEE-754 Value Type(0) = Value_Positive_Zero
                      4.94065646E-324    -4.94065646E-324            -∞              0
                IEEE-754 Value Type(0) = Value_Negative_Zero
                      4.94065646E-324    -4.94065646E-324            -∞              0
                IEEE-754 Value Type(1) = Normalization_Positive_Normalized
                      2.22044605E-016    -1.11022302E-016             0              0
                IEEE-754 Value Type(-1) = Normalization_Negative_Normalized
                      1.11022302E-016    -2.22044605E-016             0              0
```

Figure 4-3. *Complex floating point operations based on IEEE standardization*

Listing 4-3. IEEE Standardization Implementation

```
using System;
using System.Collections.Generic;
using System.Linq;
using System.Text;
using System.Threading.Tasks;

namespace FloatingPointArithmetic
{
    public enum IEEEStandardization
    {
        // the value is a signaling NaN - not a number
        Signaling_Not_a_Number,
```

```
        // the value is represented by a quiet
        // NaN - not a number and non-signaling
        Quiet_Not_a_Number,

        // the value represents a positive infinity
        Value_Positive_Infinity,

        // the value represents a negative infinity
        Value_Negative_Infinity,

        // The value represents a normal and positive number
        Normalization_Positive_Normalized,

        // The value represents a normal and negative number
        Normalization_Negative_Normalized,

        // A denormalized positive number
        Denormalization_Positive_Denormalized,

        // The value is a denormalized negative number
        Denormalization_Negative_Denormalized,

        // The value represents a positive zero
        Value_Positive_Zero,

        // the value represents a negative zero
        Value_Negative_Zero
    }
}
```

Listing 4-4. Floating Point Implementation

```
using System;
using System.Collections.Generic;
using System.Linq;
using System.Text;
using System.Threading.Tasks;

namespace FloatingPointArithmetic
{
    public sealed class FloatingPoint
```

```
{
    #region variable and instances
        // the constructor of the class
        private FloatingPoint() { }

        // the value for conversion is 2^60
        // 2^60 = 1,152,921,504,606,846,976 (decimal base)
        // 2^60 = 10 00 00 00 00 00 00 00 (hex bytes)
        // 8 * 2^60 = 2 * 1,152,921,504,606,846,976 =
        //          = 2,305,843,009,213,693,952
        // we will use "unchecked" for supressing overflow-checking
        // for integral-type arithmetic operations and conversions
        private static readonly double UnfavorableNegativeValue
            = BitConverter.Int64BitsToDouble(unchecked(8 *
              0x1000000000000000));

        // constants
        private const Double minimum_double = 4.94065645841247e-324;

        // 0x7FFFFFFFFFFFFFFF = 9,223,372,036,854,775,807 (decimal)
        private const long mask_sign_value = -1 - 0x7FFFFFFFFFFFFFFF;
        private const long clear_mask_sign = 0x7FFFFFFFFFFFFFFF;

        private const long signficand_mask = 0xFFFFFFFFFFFFF;
        private const long clearing_significand_mask = mask_sign_value
        | significand_exponent_mask;

        private const long significand_exponent_mask =
        0x7FF0000000000000;
        private const long clearing_exponent_mask = mask_sign_value |
        signficand_mask;

        private const int deviation = 1023;
    private const int significant_bits = 52;
    #endregion

    #region Methods for getting parts of a double's binary
    representation.
```

```
// the method return the significand of double value
public static long ReuturnSignificantMantissa(double value)
{
    return BitConverter.DoubleToInt64Bits(value)
            & signficand_mask;
}

// the method will return the signicand
// for a floating-point number
public static double ReturnSignficantForFloatingPoint
(double value)
{
    if (Double.IsNaN(value)) return value;

    if (Double.IsInfinity(value)) return value;

    // computing the exponent using the deviation
    int exponentValue = ComputeDeviationExponent(value);
    long significand = ReuturnSignificantMantissa(value);

    // number 0 and denormalization
    // values has to be treated separetely
    if (exponentValue == 0)
    {
        // if the significand is equal
        // with we will return 0
        if (significand == 0)
            return 0.0;

        // otherwise we will shit the significand to the left
        // until significand will be 53 bits long
        while (significand < signficand_mask)
            significand <<= 1;
            // truncate the leading bit
            significand &= signficand_mask;
    }
```

```
        return BitConverter.Int64BitsToDouble
            ((deviation << 52) + significand);
    }

    // The function will return a non-deviation
    // exponent for a floating-point value.
    // The non-deviation is computed through
    // substracting the deviation from deviated exponent.
    public static int NonDeviationExponent(double value)
    {
        return (int)((BitConverter.DoubleToInt64Bits(value)
            & significand_exponent_mask) >> 52) - deviation;
    }

    // The function will return the
    // deviation exponnent for a
    // floating-point value.
    // The returned value is obtained
    // and computed directly from
    // and within binary representation of "value"
    public static int ComputeDeviationExponent(double value)
    {
       · return (int)((BitConverter.DoubleToInt64Bits(value)
            & significand_exponent_mask) >> 52);
    }

    // The function returns the bit sign
    // of a value. The bit sign is obtained
    // directly from the binary representation
    // of the value
    public static int SignBit(double value)
    {
        return ((BitConverter.DoubleToInt64Bits(value)
            & mask_sign_value) != 0) ? 1 : 0;
    }
#endregion

#region Below contains the implementation of the IEEE-754
```

```
// The class represents the implementation
// of IEEE-754 floating-point
// References:
// https://www.geeksforgeeks.org/ieee-standard-754-floating-
   point-numbers/
public static IEEEStandardization Class
    (double value)
{
    long bits_value_representation =
        BitConverter.DoubleToInt64Bits(value);

    bool positive_value = (bits_value_representation >= 0);

    bits_value_representation =
        bits_value_representation & clear_mask_sign;

    // case when we have a overflow
    // for Not-A-Number
    if (bits_value_representation
        >= 0x7ff0000000000000)
    {
        // this is case of infinity
        if ((bits_value_representation
            & signficand_mask) == 0)
        {
            if (positive_value)
                return IEEEStandardization.
                    Value_Positive_Infinity;
            else
                return IEEEStandardization.
                    Value_Negative_Infinity;
        }
        else
        {
            if ((bits_value_representation
                & signficand_mask)
                < 0x8000000000000)
```

```
                return IEEEStandardization.
                    Quiet_Not_a_Number;
            else
                return IEEEStandardization.
                    Signaling_Not_a_Number;
    }
}
// this is happening when we have
// 0 or a denormalization value
else if (bits_value_representation
    < 0x0010000000000000)
{
    if (bits_value_representation == 0)
    {
        if (positive_value)
            return IEEEStandardization.
                Value_Positive_Zero;
        else
            return IEEEStandardization.
                Value_Negative_Zero;
    }
    else
    {
        if (positive_value)
            return IEEEStandardization.
                Denormalization_Positive_Denormalized;
        else
            return IEEEStandardization.
                Denormalization_Negative_Denormalized;
    }
}
else
{
    if (positive_value)
        return IEEEStandardization.
            Normalization_Positive_Normalized;
```

121

```
            else
                return IEEEStandardization.
                    Normalization_Negative_Normalized;
        }
    }

    // The function copy the
    // sign of the number.
    // theSizeOfTheValue parameter
    //        the number for
    //        which we copy the sign
    // theValueOfTheSign parameter
    //        the value of the number
    //        for which we do the copy
    public static double CopyProcedureForSign
            (double theSizeOfTheValue,
             double theValueOfTheSign)
    {
        // we do a bit manipulation
        // do the copying process for
        //* the first bit for theSizeOfTheValue
        // and theValueOfTheSign
        return BitConverter.Int64BitsToDouble(
            (BitConverter.DoubleToInt64Bits
                (theSizeOfTheValue) &
                    clear_mask_sign)
            | (BitConverter.DoubleToInt64Bits
                (theValueOfTheSign) &
                    mask_sign_value));
    }

    // a boolean function to
    // check if the value is
    // finite or not
    public bool CheckIfIsFinite(double value)
```

```csharp
{
// Verify the part represented by the exponent.
// if all the bits are 1, then we
// are dealing with a infinity (not-a-number).
    long bits = BitConverter.
        DoubleToInt64Bits(value);
    return ((bits & significand_exponent_mask)
        == significand_exponent_mask);
}

// The function will return the
// non-biased exponent for a value.
public static double ComputingLogB(double value)
{
    // Let's deal with the
    // important situations.
    if (double.IsNaN(value))
        return value;
    if (double.IsInfinity(value))
        return double.PositiveInfinity;
    if (value == 0)
        return double.NegativeInfinity;

    int exponentDeviationValue =
        ComputeDeviationExponent(value);

    // if we dealing with a denormalization value
    // we need to take the right action
    if (exponentDeviationValue == 0)
    {
        exponentDeviationValue = -1074;

        // compute the signficand with no sign
        long bits = BitConverter.
            DoubleToInt64Bits(value) & clear_mask_sign;

        // we move on if we finish dealing with situations
        // when bits = 0
```

```
            do
            {
                bits >>= 1;
                exponentDeviationValue++;
            }
            while (bits > 0);
            return exponentDeviationValue;
        }

    // exponentDeviationValue was significand,
    // proceed with subtraction the deviation
    // to obtain and compute the non-deviation exponent
    return exponentDeviationValue - deviation;
}

// Compute the floating-point
// number for the next number.
// 'from' parameter
//          - represent the starting point
// 'to' parameter
//          - represent a value that shows
//            the direction in which we will
//            move in order to identity
//            the next value
public static double
    ComputerNextValue(double from, double to)
{
    // If 'to' is equal with from
    // there is no direction to move in,
    // so we will compute and get 'from' value
    if (from == to)
        return from;

    // if not-a-number occur will
    // be returned by themselves
    if (double.IsNaN(from))
        return from;
```

```
if (double.IsNaN(to))
    return to;

// an infinity will be an infinity all time
if (double.IsInfinity(from))
    return from;

// deal with 0 situation
if (from == 0)
    return (to > 0) ?
        minimum_double : -minimum_double;

// For the rest of the
// situation we are dealing.
// With incrementation or
// decrementation the bits value.
// Values for transitions to infinity,
// denormalized values, and to zero are
// managed in this way.
long bits_value = BitConverter.DoubleToInt64Bits(from);

// A xor here avoids nesting conditionals. We have to
    increment if
// fromValue lies between 0 and toValue.

// XOR operation will help us to
// not taken into consideration
// conditionals.
if ((from > 0) ^ (from > to))
    bits_value++;
else
    bits_value--;
return BitConverter.
    Int64BitsToDouble(bits_value);
}
```

```csharp
// the function compute and return
// a value that is powered with 2
public static double Scalb(double number,
                          int exponent)
{
    // Treat special cases first.
    if (number == 0 ||
            double.IsInfinity(number) ||
            double.IsNaN(number))
        return number;

    if (exponent == 0)
        return number;

    int computedExponentValue = ComputeDeviationExponent
    (number);
    long significand = ReuturnSignificantMantissa(number);
    long getting_sign = ((number > 0) ? 0 : mask_sign_value);

    // check if 'number' is denormalized
    if (computedExponentValue == 0)
    {
        if (exponent < 0)
        {
            // an exponent that is negative
            // we will shift the significand
            // -exponent bits to the right
            significand >>= -exponent;
            return BitConverter.
                Int64BitsToDouble(getting_sign | significand);
        }
        else
        {
            // a number that is positive is
            // necessary to be shifted on left
            // and this will be done until a
            // normalized number is obtained
```

```
    while (significand <= signficand_mask
        && exponent > 0)
    {
        significand <<= 1;
        exponent--;
    }

    if (significand > signficand_mask)
        exponent++;

    // test if we have a overflow
    if (exponent > 2 * deviation)
        return (number > 0) ?
            double.PositiveInfinity
            : double.NegativeInfinity;

    // the number represents the
    // significand exponent for the result
    return BitConverter.Int64BitsToDouble(getting_sign
        | ((long)exponent << 52) |
            (significand & signficand_mask));

    }
}

// Once we are reaching here,
// we are aware that 'exoponent'
// is normalized.
// Proceeding with scaling. 'exponent'
// will be the significand exponent for the result
computedExponentValue =
    computedExponentValue + exponent;

// verify if we have 0 or denormalization
if (computedExponentValue < 0)
{
    significand = ((1L << 52) +
        significand) >> (1 -
            computedExponentValue);
```

```
            return BitConverter.
                Int64BitsToDouble(getting_sign | significand);
        }

        // Veirfy if we have an overflow
        if (computedExponentValue >
            2 * deviation)
            return (number > 0) ?
                double.PositiveInfinity :
                double.NegativeInfinity;

        // If we're here, the result is normalized.
        long bits = getting_sign |
            ((long)computedExponentValue << 52) | significand;

        return BitConverter.Int64BitsToDouble(bits);
    }

    // the function computes a value
    // wich will point out if the two
    // values are unordered
    public static bool Unordered(double value1, double value2)
    {
        return double.IsNaN(value1) || double.IsNaN(value2);
    }
#endregion

#region Methods for conversion bit with single-precision
    public static unsafe int ConversionSingleToInt32Bits(float val)
    {
        return *((int*)&val);
    }

    public static unsafe float ConversionInt32BitsToSingle(int val)
    {
        return *((float*)&val);
    }
```

```
        #endregion
    }
}
```

Listing 4-5. Main Program Implementation

```csharp
using System;
using System.Collections.Generic;
using System.Linq;
using System.Text;
using System.Threading.Tasks;

namespace FloatingPointArithmetic
{
    class Program
    {
        static void Main(string[] args)
        {
            Console.WriteLine("FLOATING POINT ARITHMETIC " +
                "by Marius Iulian MIHAILESCU " +
                "and Stefania Loredana NITA \n");

            Console.WriteLine("\t\tDifferent ways of computing 1/105.");
            Console.WriteLine("\t\tMultiply the output with 105 and
            subtract 1");
            Console.WriteLine("\t\tWe will get an error.");

            double d = 1 / 105.0;
            float s = 1 / 105.0F;

            Console.WriteLine("\t\t\tUsing double: {0} * " +
                "105 - 1 = {1} < 0!", d, d * 105.0 - 1.0);
            Console.WriteLine("\t\t\tUsing single: {0} * " +
                "105 - 1 = {1} > 0!", s, s * 105.0 - 1.0);
            Console.WriteLine();

            Console.WriteLine("\t\tComputing a chaos-based " +
                "value for cryptography purpose.");
            float chaotic_value = 4.99F * 17;
```

```
Console.WriteLine("\t\t\tThe chaotic value is " +
    "{0}.", chaotic_value);
Console.WriteLine();

Console.WriteLine("\t\tAnother example of chaotic " +
    "value for which we need the integer part.");
int another_chaotic_value = (int)(100 * (1 - 0.1F));
Console.WriteLine("\t\t\tAnother chaotic value is {0}.",
    another_chaotic_value);
Console.WriteLine();

Console.WriteLine("\t\tFor cryptography is " +
    "important to have an implementation " +
    "for IEEE-754");
double[] double_values = new double[] { 0, -1 /
    Double.PositiveInfinity, 1, -1,
    //Math.PI,
    //Math.Exp(20),
    //Math.Exp(-20),
    //Double.PositiveInfinity,
    //Double.NegativeInfinity,
    //Double.NaN,
    //Double.Epsilon,
    // -Double.Epsilon,
    //10 / Double.MaxValue
};

for (int i = 0; i < double_values.Length; i++)
{
    Console.WriteLine("\t\t\tIEEE-754 Value Type({0}) = {1}",
        double_values[i],
        FloatingPoint.Class(double_values[i]));

    Console.WriteLine("\t\t\t{0,19:E8}{1,19:E8}{2,19}{3,19}",
        FloatingPoint.ComputerNextValue(double_values[i],
            Double.PositiveInfinity) - double_values[i],
```

```
    FloatingPoint.ComputerNextValue(double_values[i],
    Double.NegativeInfinity) - double_values[i],

    FloatingPoint.ComputingLogB(double_values[i]),
    FloatingPoint.ReuturnSignificantMantissa
    (double_values[i]));
        }
    Console.ReadLine();
    }
  }
}
```

Conclusions

In this chapter, we discussed the general representations of floating point numbers and how they can be implemented in complex cryptosystems. We did an analysis of the most important terms and basic foundation notions that a professional should be aware of when they are planning to set up an environment for developing complex cryptosystems.

We also justified the importance of floating-point arithmetic within complex cryptosystems, such as homomorphic encryption, chaos-based cryptography, lattice-based cryptography, or ring learning with errors.

Bibliography

[1]   H. Chen, K. Laine, and P. Rindal, "Fast Private Set Intersection from Homomorphic Encryption." *CCS '17 Proceedings of the 2017 ACM SIGSAC Conference on Computer and Communication Security*, 2017.

[2]   L. Ducas and D. Micciancio, "FHEW: Bootstrapping homo-morphic encryption in less than a second," In *Advances in Cryptology–Eurocrypt 2015*, pp. 617–640, Springer, Berlin, Germany, 2015.

[3]   S. Halevi and V. Shoup, "Algorithms in HElib," in *Crypto '14*, vol. 8616, Springer, Heidelberg, Germany, 2014.

[4]   J. Campos, P. Sharma, E. Jantunen, D. Baglee, and L. Fumagalli, "The Challenges of Cybersecurity Frameworks to Protect Data Required for the Development of Advanced Maintenance," In *Procedia CIRP*, vol. 47, p. 227, 2016.

[5]   C. Burnikel and J. Ziegler, "Fast Recursive Division," In *ResearchReport Max-Planck-Institut fuer Informatik Research ReportMPI-I-98-1-022*, Max–Planck–Institut für Informatik, Saarbr ¨ucken, Germany, 1998.

[6]   N. Dowlin, R. Gilad-Bachrach, K. Lainc, K. Lautcr, M. Nachrig, and J. Wernsing, "Manual for Using Homomorphic Encryption for Bioinformatics," In *Proceedings of the IEEE*, vol. 105, no. 3, 2017.

[7]   J. H. Cheon, A. Kim, M. Kim, and Y. Song, "Homomorphicencryption for Arithmetic of Approximate Numbers," In *Proceedings of the International Conference on the Theory and Application of Cryptology and Information Security (ASIA-CRYPT'17)*, pp. 409–437, Hong Kong, China, December 2017.

[8]   Floating Point Support. Available online: `https://docs.microsoft.com/en-us/cpp/c-runtime-library/floating-point-support?view=vs-2019`.

CHAPTER 5

What's New in C# 8.0

This chapter will cover the most important features of C# 8.0 for professionals in the fields of cryptography and cryptanalysis. For more details about which version of C# is used with different versions of .NET Framework and .NET Core, we recommend the resource from [3].

C# 8.0 offers many improvements and enhancements to the C# language, and several of them can be used with success to improve the performance of the implementation process of cryptography and cryptanalysis algorithms and security schemes. There is support for C# 8.0 on .NET Core 3.X and .NET Standard 2.1. More details about C# language versioning can be found here [1]. The enhancements are

- Readonly members

- Default interface methods

- Improvements for pattern matching: switch expressions, property patterns, tuple patterns, positional patterns

- Using declarations

- Static local functions

- Disposable ref structs

- Nullable reference types

- Asynchronous streams

- Asynchronous disposable

- Indices and ranges

- Null-coalescing assignment

- Unmanaged constructed types

- Stackalloc in nested expressions

- Enhancement of interpolated verbatim strings

As mentioned, this chapter will describe the features that will help professionals to improve the quality and performance of cryptographic solutions. To explore more details about the features provided by C# 8.0 within the environment, it is recommended to use the dotnet try tool. To explore the features in depth, the following solution and steps can be used with success:

- Visit https://github.com/dotnet/try/blob/master/README. md#setup, and download and install the dotnet try tool.

- Clone the dotnet/try-samples repository. It can be accessed at https://github.com/dotnet/try-samples.

- Configure and set the path for the current directory to the csharp8 subdirectory for the try-samples repository.

- Invoke and run dotnet try.

The following sections will cover the enhancements that significantly improve the quality and performance of cryptographic applications.

Readonly Members

The new readonly modifier can be applied to the members of a struct. The readonly is used when we don't want the state of a member to be modified. We will show a more granular representation by applying readonly to the members instead of struct declaration.

Let's consider the following example from Listing 5-1 where we implement a struct that deals with a RSA cryptosystem.

Listing 5-1. Applying Readonly for a Cryptographic Purpose

```
using System;
using System.Collections.Generic;
using System.Linq;
using System.Text;
using System.Threading.Tasks;
```

```csharp
namespace Listing_5_1___ReadOnlyMembers
{
    class Program
    {
        public int cryptoKey1;

        //** initializing and dealing with
        public readonly int cryptoKey2 = 25;
        public readonly int cryptoKey3;

        public Program()
        {
            // Initialize a readonly instance field
            cryptoKey3 = 24;
        }
        public Program(int value1, int value2, int value3)
        {
            cryptoKey1 = value1;
            cryptoKey2 = value2;
            cryptoKey3 = value3;
        }
        public static void Main()
        {
            Program cryptoProgram1 = new Program(13, 27, 39);
            Console.WriteLine($"Crypto Program 1: crypto_key
            1={cryptoProgram1.cryptoKey1}, crypto_key 2={cryptoProgram1.
            cryptoKey2}, crypto_key 3={cryptoProgram1.cryptoKey3}");

            Program cryptoProgram2 = new Program();
            cryptoProgram2.cryptoKey1 = 55;
            Console.WriteLine($"Crypto Program 2: crypto_key
            1={cryptoProgram2.cryptoKey1}, crypto_key 2={cryptoProgram2.
            cryptoKey2}, crypto_key 3={cryptoProgram2.cryptoKey3}");

            Console.ReadKey();
        }
    }
}
```

As with most structs, the `ToString()` method will not update or modify the state. We can specify for this to happen by putting `readonly` in front of the `override` keyword (see Figure 5-1).

```
C:\Windows\system32\cmd.exe                                    —    □    ×
Crypto Program 1: crypto_key 1=13, crypto_key 2=27, crypto_key 3=39
Crypto Program 2: crypto_key 1=55, crypto_key 2=25, crypto_key 3=24
Press any key to continue . . . ▪
```

Figure 5-1. Example of output using the readonly keyword

Patterns Matching

In cryptography pattern matching, techniques can be used in different places, such as resolving passwords requirements, strings, and cryptographic key expectations.

Starting with C# 8.0, more pattern expressions can be used and implemented in different places within the code. Another important enhancement of C# 8.0 is *recursive patterns*, a pattern expression that can be used over the output of another pattern expression result. Let's consider the example from Listing 5-2 where we use an `enum` struct with the goal of listing the cryptographic algorithms.

Listing 5-2. Using an enum struct

```
public enum CryptoType
{
    RSA,
    AES,
    TripleDES,
}
```

If the application that is being developed contains a definition of the `CryptographicAlgorithm` type, it is being constructed from cryptography components (e.g. encryption, decryption, compute private key, compute public key, etc.), so we can convert a `CryptographicAlgorithm` value to the `CryptoType` values by using the example from Listing 5-3 with a `switch` instruction.

Listing 5-3. Using a switch Expression

```
public static CryptographicAlgorithm
    GetCryptoAlgorithm(CryptographicAlgorithm crypto)
{
   return crypto.cryptosystemType switch
   {
     CryptoType.RSA => new RSA(),
     CryptoType.AES => new AES(),
     CryptoType.TripleDES => new TripleDES(),
     _ => throw new ArgumentException(message: "There is no
              such cryptographic algorithm ",
              paramName: nameof(crypto.cryptosystemType))
   };
}
```

An entire example is presented in Listing 5-4. The result of this listing is provided in Figure 5-2.

Listing 5-4. Chosing an Encryption System Based on switch Expressions

```
using System;

namespace PatternsMatching
{
    class Program
    {
        static void Main(string[] args)
        {
            CryptographicAlgorithm cryptoAlg =
                    new CryptographicAlgorithm();
            Console.WriteLine("Pick a cryptosystem [1=RSA,
                            2=AES, 3=TripleDES]");

            string type = Console.ReadLine();
            CryptoType ct = type switch
            {
                "1" => CryptoType.RSA,
```

```
        "2" => CryptoType.AES,
        "3" => CryptoType.TripleDES,
        _ => throw new ArgumentException(message:
                "There is no such option ",
                paramName: nameof(type))
    };

    try
    {
        cryptoAlg.cryptosystemType = ct;
        GetCryptoAlgorithm(cryptoAlg);

        Console.ReadKey();
    }
    catch(Exception ex)
    {
        Console.WriteLine(ex.Message);
    }
}

public static CryptographicAlgorithm
    GetCryptoAlgorithm(
            CryptographicAlgorithm crypto)
{
    return crypto.cryptosystemType switch
    {
        CryptoType.RSA => new RSA(),
        CryptoType.AES => new AES(),
        CryptoType.TripleDES => new TripleDES(),
        _ => throw new ArgumentException(message:
                "There is no such cryptographic algorithm ",
                paramName: nameof(crypto.cryptosystemType))
    };
}
}
```

```csharp
public enum CryptoType
{
    RSA,
    AES,
    TripleDES,
}

public class CryptographicAlgorithm
{
    internal CryptoType cryptosystemType;
    public CryptographicAlgorithm()
    {

    }
}

class RSA : CryptographicAlgorithm
{
    public RSA()
    {
        Console.WriteLine("RSA chosen!");
    }
}

class AES : CryptographicAlgorithm
{
    public AES()
    {
        Console.WriteLine("AES chosen!");
    }
}
```

```
class TripleDES : CryptographicAlgorithm
{
    public TripleDES()
    {
        Console.WriteLine("TripleDES chosen!");
    }
}
}
```

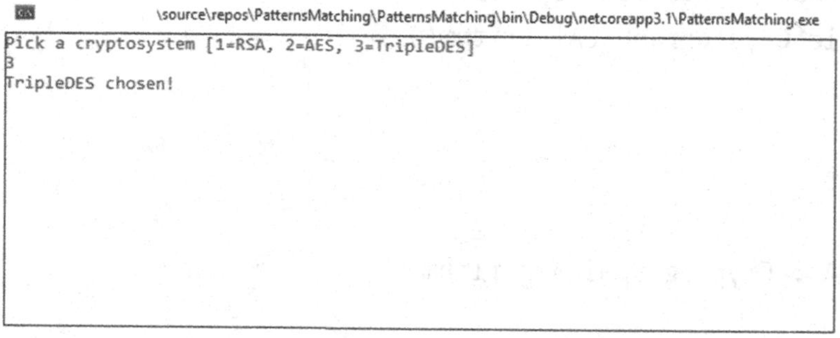

```
                    \source\repos\PatternsMatching\PatternsMatching\bin\Debug\netcoreapp3.1\PatternsMatching.exe
Pick a cryptosystem [1=RSA, 2=AES, 3=TripleDES]
3
TripleDES chosen!
```

Figure 5-2. *The result of the code in Listing 5-4*

Patterns

Property Patterns

The new feature using *property patterns* gives professionals the ability to match on the properties that belong to the object. Let's consider an e-learning platform as an example (see Listing 5-5). We need to encrypt the message using a specific cryptographic algorithm, based in the `cryptosystemType` property of the `CryptographicAlgorithm` object. Note that the examples in these sections are for demonstration only.

Listing 5-5. Using Property Patterns

```
public static int Encrypt(CryptographicAlgorithm crypto, Parameters
parameters, int message)
{
    return crypto switch
    {
      { cryptosystemType: CryptoType.RSA } => (new RSA()).
```

```
Encrypt(parameters.n, parameters.e, message),
    { cryptosystemType: CryptoType.AES } => (new AES()).
            Encrypt(parameters.key, message),
    { cryptosystemType: CryptoType.TripleDES } => (new
        TripleDES().Encrypt(parameters.k1, parameters.k2,
                    parameters.k3, message)),
    _ => throw new ArgumentException(message: "There is no
                    such cryptographic algorithm ",
                    paramName:
                        nameof(crypto.cryptosystemType))
    };
}
```

The entire code is presented in Listing 5-6 and the output is shown in Figure 5-3.

Listing 5-6. Demonstration of Using Property Patterns

```
using System;
namespace PropertyPatterns
{
    class Program
    {
        static void Main(string[] args)
        {
            CryptographicAlgorithm cryptoAlg = new
                        CryptographicAlgorithm();
            Console.WriteLine("Pick a cryptosystem [1=RSA,
                        2=AES, 3=TripleDES]");

            string type = Console.ReadLine();
            CryptoType ct = type switch
            {
                "1" => CryptoType.RSA,
                "2" => CryptoType.AES,
                "3" => CryptoType.TripleDES,
```

```
            _ => throw new ArgumentException(message:
                "There is no such option ",
                paramName: nameof(type))
        };

        //** the parameters should be initialized
        Parameters parameters = new Parameters();
        //** the message that needs to be encrypted
        int message = 0;
        try
        {
            cryptoAlg.cryptosystemType = ct;
            Encrypt(cryptoAlg, parameters, message);
            Console.ReadKey();
        }
        catch (Exception ex)
        {
            Console.WriteLine(ex.Message);
        }
    }

    public static int Encrypt(
                CryptographicAlgorithm   crypto,
                Parameters parameters,
                int message)
    {
        return crypto switch
        {
            { cryptosystemType: CryptoType.RSA } => (new
                    RSA()).Encrypt(parameters.n,
                                    parameters.e,
                                    message),
            { cryptosystemType: CryptoType.AES } => (new
                    AES()).Encrypt(parameters.key,
                                    message),
            { cryptosystemType: CryptoType.TripleDES } =>
```

```
                    (new TripleDES().Encrypt(parameters.k1,
                                        parameters.k2,
                                        parameters.k3,
                                        message)),
            _ => throw new ArgumentException(message:
                    "There is no such cryptographic
                    algorithm ",
                    paramName:
                        nameof(crypto.cryptosystemType))
        };
    }
}
public enum CryptoType
{ RSA, AES, TripleDES, }

public class Parameters
{
    public Parameters() { }
    internal int n, e, k1, k2, k3;
    internal int[,] key;
}

public class CryptographicAlgorithm
{
    internal CryptoType cryptosystemType;
    public CryptographicAlgorithm() { }
    public int Encrypt()
    {
        return 0;
    }
}

class RSA : CryptographicAlgorithm
{
    public RSA()
    {
        Console.WriteLine("RSA chosen!");
    }
```

```csharp
    public int Encrypt(int n, int e, int message)
    {
        Console.WriteLine("Here goes the implementation of
                    the RSA encryption algorithm.");
        return 0;
    }

}

class AES : CryptographicAlgorithm
{
    public AES()
    {
        Console.WriteLine("AES chosen!");
    }
    public int Encrypt(int[,] key, int message)
    {
        Console.WriteLine("Here goes the implementation of
                        the AES encryption algorithm.");
        return 0;
    }
}

class TripleDES : CryptographicAlgorithm
{
    public TripleDES()
    {
        Console.WriteLine("TripleDES chosen!");
    }
    public int Encrypt(int k1, int k2, int k3,
                    int message)
```

```
    {
        Console.WriteLine("Here goes the implementation of
                the TripleDES encryption algorithm.");
        return 0;
    }
  }
}
```

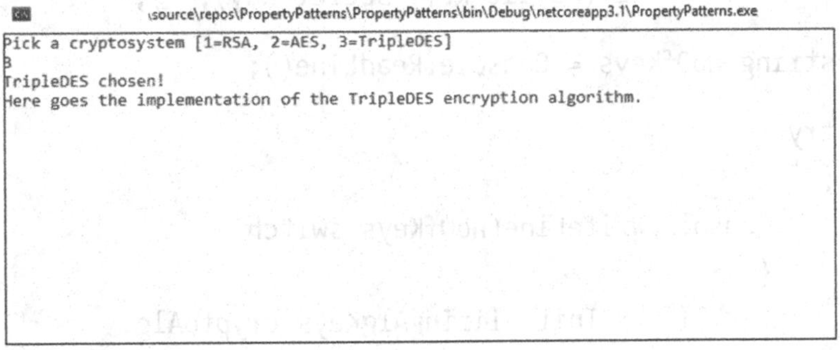

Figure 5-3. *The result of the code in Listing 5-6*

Tupple Patterns

Some of the cryptographic algorithms (e.g. RSA or a searchable encryption scheme)
depend on a variety of inputs. Using *tuple patterns* gives us the possibility of switching
between multiple values that are represented as tuples. The code in Listing 5-7
illustrates how a switch expression can be used to swap between different cryptographic
algorithms.

In this example, you may choose an encryption system based on the number of
keys: one secret key for both encryption and decryption or a pair of keys (the public key
for encryption and the secret key for decryption). The result of Listing 5-7 is shown in
Figure 5-4.

Listing 5-7. Using Tupple Patterns

```
using System;

namespace TuplePatterns
{
```

```csharp
class Program
{
    static void Main(string[] args)
    {
        CryptographicAlgorithm cryptoAlg =
                    new CryptographicAlgorithm();
        Console.WriteLine("Enter the number of keys:
                    1=(secret key);
                    2=(public key, secret key); ");

        string noOfKeys = Console.ReadLine();

        try
        {
            Console.WriteLine(noOfKeys switch
            {
                "1" => InitializingAlgKeys(cryptoAlg,
                                            false, true),
                "2" => InitializingAlgKeys(cryptoAlg,
                                            true, true),
                _ => throw new ArgumentException(message:
                            "There is no such option ")
            });

        }
        catch (Exception ex)
        {
            Console.WriteLine(ex.Message);
        }
    }

    public static string InitializingAlgKeys
            (CryptographicAlgorithm crypto,
                bool publicKey,
                bool secretKey)
    {
        return (publicKey, secretKey) switch
```

```
        {
            (true, true) => (new RSA()).InitializeKeys(),
            (false, true) => (new AES()).InitializeKeys(),
            _ => throw new ArgumentException(message:
                            "There is no such option. ")
        };
    }
}

public class CryptographicAlgorithm
{
    public CryptographicAlgorithm() { }
    public string InitializeKeys()
    {
        return "";
    }
}

class RSA : CryptographicAlgorithm
{
    public string InitializeKeys(int publicKey = -1,
                                 int secretKey = -1)
    {
        return "RSA uses a public key and a secret key.
                Initializing the keys for RSA...";
    }
}

class AES : CryptographicAlgorithm
{
    public string InitializeKeys(int secretKey = -1)
    {
        return "AES uses a secret key.
                Initializing the  key for AES...";
    }
}
}
```

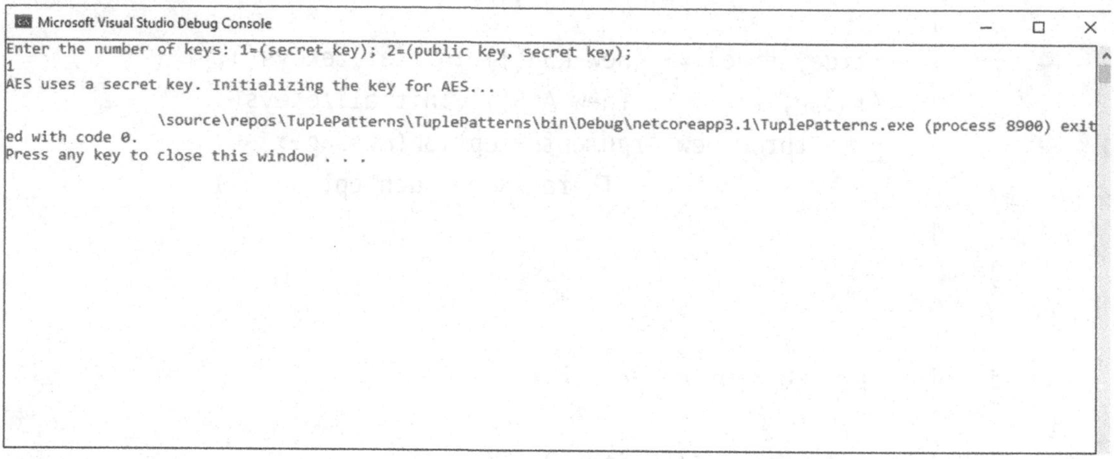

Figure 5-4. *The result of Listing 5-7*

Positional Patterns

Some applications and implementations use the Deconstruct method. The purpose of this method is to deconstruct the properties into discrete variables. To use the positional patterns, the Deconstruct method should be accessible and in this way we will be able to look over the properties that characterize the object and use these properties to generate a pattern. Listing 5-8 shows the CryptoAlgorithms class, which includes a Deconstruct method in order to create a discrete variable for prvKey (private key) and pubKey (public key). The code in Listing 5-8 shows how positional patterns can be used in the field of cryptography. The results are shown in Figure 5-5.

Listing 5-8. Positional Patterns

```
using System;

namespace PositionalPattern
{
    class Program
    {
        static void Main(string[] args)
        {
            KeysAdministration k1 = new
                KeysAdministration("This is the private key",
                            "This is the public key");
```

```csharp
        KeysAdministration k2 = new
            KeysAdministration("This is the private key", null);
        KeysAdministration k3 = new
            KeysAdministration(null, "This is the public key");

        CryptographicAlgorithm cryptoAlg;

        cryptoAlg = GetAlgorithmType(k1);
        Console.WriteLine("public and private keys: " +
                            cryptoAlg.ToString());
        cryptoAlg = GetAlgorithmType(k2);
        Console.WriteLine("just the private key: " +
                            cryptoAlg.ToString());
        cryptoAlg = GetAlgorithmType(k3);
        Console.WriteLine("no matching keys: " +
                            cryptoAlg.ToString());

        Console.ReadKey();

    }
    static CryptographicAlgorithm
        GetAlgorithmType(KeysAdministration keys)
        => keys switch
    {
        var (privKey, pubKey) when
            !string.IsNullOrEmpty(privKey) &&
            !string.IsNullOrEmpty(pubKey)
                => CryptographicAlgorithm.RSA,
        var (privKey, pubKey) when
            !string.IsNullOrEmpty(privKey) &&
            string.IsNullOrEmpty(pubKey)
                => CryptographicAlgorithm.AES,
        _ => CryptographicAlgorithm.Unknown
    };
}
public enum CryptographicAlgorithm
{
```

```
        Unknown,
        RSA,
        AES,
    }

    public class KeysAdministration
    {
        public string prvKey { get; }
        public string pubKey { get; }

        public KeysAdministration(string PrivateKey,
                                  string PublicKey)
            => (prvKey, pubKey) = (PrivateKey, PublicKey);
        public void Deconstruct(out string PrivateKey,
                                out string PublicKey)
            => (PrivateKey, PublicKey) = (prvKey, pubKey);
    }
}
```

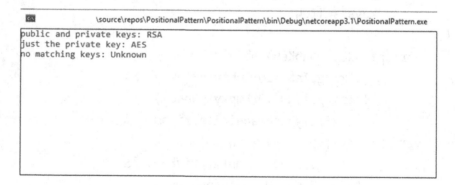

\source\repos\PositionalPattern\PositionalPattern\bin\Debug\netcoreapp3.1\PositionalPattern.exe

```
public and private keys: RSA
just the private key: AES
no matching keys: Unknown
```

Figure 5-5. The result of Listing 5-8

Using Declarations

Using a declaration represents a type of variable declaration that has the using keyword in front of the variable (or its type). For example, let's consider the example in Listing 5-9, which writes the encryption of a message to a file. The output is shown in Figure 5-6.

Listing 5-9. Using Declarations

```
using System;
using System.Collections.Generic;
using System.Linq;

namespace Declarations
{
    class Program
    {
        static void Main(string[] args)
        {
            List<string> encryptedMessageLines = new
                                List<string>();

            encryptedMessageLines.Add("Option 1 key:
                            sdkjegiorjgvldmgkA64");
            encryptedMessageLines.Add("This is the message to
                    be encrypted: This is an example of using
                    declarations in C# 8.0.");
            encryptedMessageLines.Add("Option 2 key:
                            l$klj4grg565j");

            Console.Write("The number of lines skipped: ");
            Console.WriteLine(WriteEncryptedMessages(
                encryptedMessageLines.AsEnumerable<string>())
                                .ToString());

            Console.ReadKey();
        }

        static int WriteEncryptedMessages(IEnumerable<string>
                                    encryptedMessageLines)
        {
            using var fileWithEncryption = new
             System.IO.StreamWriter("Message.txt");

            //** A note to be done on how we will declare
            //** lines_to_be_skipped after the using
            //** statement.
```

151

```csharp
        int lines_to_be_skipped = 0;

        foreach (string lineMessage in
                encryptedMessageLines)
        {
            if (!lineMessage.Contains("key"))
            {
                fileWithEncryption.WriteLine(lineMessage);
            }
            else
            {
                lines_to_be_skipped++;
            }
        }
        //** Notice how the skipped lines
        //** are the main subject here

        return lines_to_be_skipped;

        //** the file will be disposed once
        //** the compiler reached here
    }
  }
}
```

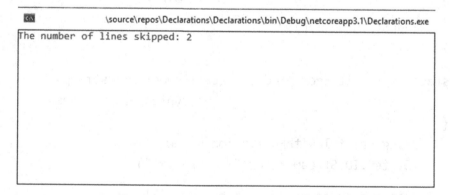

Figure 5-6. *The result of Listing 5-9*

In Figure 5-6, we obtain two lines because the list `encryptedMessageLines` has two lines that contain the string key that was mentioned in this line of code:

`if (!lineMessage.Contains("key"))` from the `WriteEncryptedMessages` method

To check if indeed the two lines from `encryptedMessageLines` were skipped, take a look at Figure 5-7, which shows the content of the `Message.txt` file where the text was written. If a full path is not specified, then the file can be found in the `bin > Debug > netcoreapp3.1` folder of the project (if the project is using .Net Core 3.1; otherwise the path is similar).

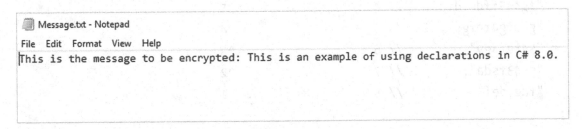

Figure 5-7. *The content of the file used in Listing 5-9*

Indices and Ranges

Indices and *ranges* offer a short and precise syntax for accessing single elements or ranges within the sequence.

- C# 8.0 offers support for two new types and operators, such as `System.Index` is defined as the index within a sequence.

- The index at the end of the operator ^ specifies that an index is relative within the end of the sequence.

- `System.Range` defines a sub range if a declared sequence.

- The operator used for ranges, …, specifies the start and the end within a range within the operands.

In Listing 5-10, we consider an array that is noted with the index from the start and end.

Listing 5-10. Working with Indexes

```
var cryptograms = new string[]
{
                        // beginning index        ending index
    "ghdghdg",          // 0                       ^9
    "gfhdgfhdgfh",      // 1                       ^8
    "hsfgd",            // 2                       ^7
    "dg545ghfd44",      // 3                       ^6
    "fg435ffdgsdfg",    // 4                       ^5
    "gdsfg4refgs",      // 5                       ^4
    "54tgt4gv",         // 6                       ^3
    "ge43fsda",         // 7                       ^2
    "fdgsdef"           // 8                       ^1
};
```

As you can see, you can return the ^1 index, as shown in the next example, Listing 5-11.

Listing 5-11. Returning ^1 Index

```
//** this will return the cryptogram value "fdgsdef"
Console.WriteLine($"The last cryptogram (encrypted message) has
                    the following value {cryptograms[^1]}");
```

In Listing 5-12, we create a subrange with the cryptograms "gfhdgfhdgfh," "hsfgd," and "dg545ghfd44." This includes cryptograms[1] through cryptograms[3]. As a note, the element cryptograms[4] is not situated within the range.

Listing 5-12. Creating Subranges

```
var encryptedTexts = cryptograms[1..4];
```

In Listing 5-13, we create a subrange using the cryptograms "ge43fsda" and "fdgsdef." This will included cryptograms[^2] and cryptograms[^1]. As a note, the index is cryptograms[^0].

Listing 5-13. Another Subrange

```
var encryptedTexts = cryptograms[^2..^0];
```

In Listing 5-14, we create a range that is open at the end for the start, end, or in some cases, both.

Listing 5-14. Open Range

```
//** contains "ghdghdg" through "fdgsdef".
var encryptedTexts = cryptograms[..];

//** contains "ghdghdg" through "dg545ghfd44"
var firstEncryptedText = cryptograms[..4];

//** contains "ghdghdg", "ge43fsda" and "fdgsdef"
var lastEncryptedText = cryptograms[6..];
```

Putting it all together, we have the code in Listing 5-15 and the result is presented in Figure 5-8.

Listing 5-15. Example of Functional Indices and Ranges

```
using System;

namespace IndicesRanges
{
    class Program
    {
        static void Main(string[] args)
        {
            var cryptograms = new string[]
            {
                                         // beginning index      ending index
                "ghdghdg",               // 0                    ^9
                "gfhdgfhdgfh",           // 1                    ^8
                "hsfgd",                 // 2                    ^7
                "dg545ghfd44",           // 3                    ^6
                "fg435ffdgsdfg",         // 4                    ^5
                "gdsfg4refgs",           // 5                    ^4
                "54tgt4gv",              // 6                    ^3
```

```
        "ge43fsda",              // 7                        ^2
        "fdgsdef"                // 8                        ^1
};

//** this will return the cryptogram value "fdgsdef"
Console.WriteLine($"The last cryptogram (encrypted message) has
the following value { cryptograms[^1]}");

Console.Write("\n\n" + "Example 1 ~encryptedTexts~: ");
var encryptedTexts = cryptograms[1..4];
for (int i=0;i<encryptedTexts.Length;i++)
{
    Console.Write(encryptedTexts[i] + " ");
}

Console.Write("\n\n" + "Example 2 ~encryptedTexts~: ");
encryptedTexts = cryptograms[^2..^0];
for (int i = 0; i < encryptedTexts.Length; i++)
{
    Console.Write(encryptedTexts[i] + " ");
}

//** contains "ghdghdg" through "fdgsdef".
Console.Write("\n\n" + "Example 3 ~encryptedTexts~: ");
encryptedTexts = cryptograms[..];
for (int i = 0; i < encryptedTexts.Length; i++)
{
    Console.Write(encryptedTexts[i] + " ");
}

//** contains "ghdghdg" through "dg545ghfd44"
Console.Write("\n\n" + "Example 4 ~firstEncryptedText~: ");
var firstEncryptedText = cryptograms[..4];
for (int i = 0; i < firstEncryptedText.Length; i++)
{
    Console.Write(firstEncryptedText[i] + " ");
}
```

```
        //** contains "ghdghdg", "ge43fsda" and "fdgsdef"
        Console.Write("\n\n" + "Example 5 ~lastEncryptedText~: ");
        var lastEncryptedText = cryptograms[6..];
        for (int i = 0; i < lastEncryptedText.Length; i++)
        {
            Console.Write(lastEncryptedText[i] + " ");
        }

        Console.ReadKey();
    }
  }
}
```

```
GN        \source\repos\IndicesRanges\IndicesRanges\bin\Debug\netcoreapp3.1\IndicesRanges.exe      –  □  ×
The last cryptogram (encrypted message) has the following value fdgsdef

Example 1 ~encryptedTexts~: gfhdgfhdgfh hsfgd dg545ghfd44

Example 2 ~encryptedTexts~: ge43fsda fdgsdef

Example 3 ~encryptedTexts~: ghdghdg gfhdgfhdgfh hsfgd dg545ghfd44 fg435ffdgsdfg gdsfg4refgs 54tgt4gv ge43fsda fdgsdef

Example 4 ~firstEncryptedText~: ghdghdg gfhdgfhdgfh hsfgd dg545ghfd44

Example 5 ~lastEncryptedText~: 54tgt4gv ge43fsda fdgsdef
```

Figure 5-8. *Indices and ranges output*

Null-Coalescing Assignment

C# 8.0 offers a new feature that can significantly improve the quality and performance of code that represents cryptographic algorithms. The operator ??= (see Listing 5-16) can be used to assign the value of a right-hand operand with the left-hand operand only if the returned output of the left-hand operand is evaluated as null.

Below, we will put everything together and show how to use a null-coalescing assignment with an application of cryptography. See Listing 5-16 and Figure 5-9.

Listing 5-16. Operator ??=

```
using System;
using System.Collections.Generic;

namespace NullCoalescingAssignment
{
    class Program
    {
        static void Main(string[] args)
        {
            List<string> cryptograms = null;
            string val = null;

            cryptograms ??= new List<string>();
            cryptograms.Add(val ??= "fdsfasdf");
            cryptograms.Add(val ??= "dsfasdfads4234");

            //** output: "fdsfasdf" and "fdsfasdf"
            Console.WriteLine(string.Join(" ", cryptograms));

            //** output: "fdsfasdf"
            Console.WriteLine(val);

            Console.ReadKey();
        }
    }
}
```

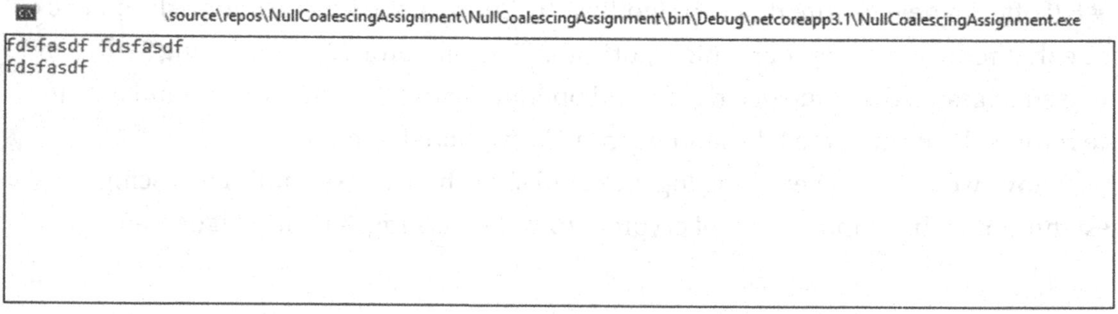

| ⬛ | \source\repos\NullCoalescingAssignment\NullCoalescingAssignment\bin\Debug\netcoreapp3.1\NullCoalescingAssignment.exe |

```
fdsfasdf fdsfasdf
fdsfasdf
```

Figure 5-9. *The result of Listing 5-16*

158

Unmanaged Constructed Types

Unmanaged constructed types can be a very interesting topic in terms of the implementation of cryptographic algorithms and security solutions. With C# 7.3, a constructed type cannot be an unmanaged type (see Listing 5-17). This is very useful when we work with variables and different types for implementing cryptographic algorithms, especially when the size plays a major role in their representation. See Listing 5-17 and Figure 5-10.

Listing 5-17. Unmanaged Type Example (According to C# 7.3)

```
using System;

namespace TheUnmanagedTypes
{
    class Program
  {
        static void Main(string[] args)
     {
       ShowTypeVariableSize<CryptographicAlgorithms<int>>();
       ShowTypeVariableSize<CryptographicAlgorithms<double>>();
       Console.ReadKey();
     }
        public struct CryptographicAlgorithms<T>
        {
            public T prvEncKey;
            public T pubEncKey;
        }

private unsafe static void ShowTypeVariableSize<T>()
where T : unmanaged
        {
            Console.WriteLine($"{typeof(T)} represents an
                        unmanaged type and the size is
                        { sizeof(T) } bytes");
        }
    }
```

```
//** The resulted outputed is:
//** CryptographicAlgorithms`1[System.Int32] is unmanaged.
//** The size is 8 bytes
//** CryptographicAlgorithms`1[System.Double] is
//** unmanaged.
//** The size is 16 bytes
}
```

```
\source\repos\TheUnmanagedTypes\TheUnmanagedTypes\bin\Debug\netcoreapp3.1\TheUnmanagedTypes.exe                    —  □  ×

TheUnmanagedTypes.Program+CryptographicAlgorithms`1[System.Int32] represents an unmanaged type and the size is 8 bytes
TheUnmanagedTypes.Program+CryptographicAlgorithms`1[System.Double] represents an unmanaged type and the size is 16 bytes
```

Figure 5-10. *The result of Listing 5-17*

If we are dealing with generic structures, we can deal with unmanaged and not unmanaged constructed types. The example in Listing 5-17 defines a generic structure `CryptographicAlgorithms<T>` and shows an example of unmanaged constructed types. If we want an example of unmanaged type, it is `CryptographicAlgorithms<object>`. This is not unmanaged because it has fields that are characterized by the object type, which is the perfect example of not being unmanaged. If we wish to have all of the constructed types to be unmanaged types, then we need to use the unmanaged constraint (see Listing 5-18).

Listing 5-18. Using an Unmanaged Constraint (According to C# 7.3)

```
public struct CryptographicAlgorithms<T> where T : unmanaged
{
    public T prvEncKey;
    public T pubEncKey;
}
```

Based on the example from Listing 5-18, the CryptographicAlgorithms<T> type is an unmanaged type starting with C# 8.0 and later. As you saw, for some of the unmanaged types, we are able to declare a pointer to a variable declared of this type or make the proper allocation of a memory block on the stack (see Listing 5-19). For this we will need to focus on System.Span [2]. See Figure 5-11 for the output.

Listing 5-19. Allocation of a Memory Block on the Stack

```
using System;

namespace MemoryAllocation
{
    class Program
    {
        static void Main(string[] args)
        {
            Random r = new Random();
            int k1 = r.Next(0, 255), k2 = r.Next(0, 255),
                k3 = r.Next(0, 255), k4 = r.Next(0, 255),
                k5 = r.Next(0, 255);

            Span<int> keys = stackalloc[] { k1, k2, k3, k4, k5 };
            Console.Write("The keys are: ");
            for (int i = 0; i < keys.Length; i++)
                Console.Write(keys[i] + " ");
            var ind = keys.IndexOfAny(stackalloc[] { k3, k5});
            Console.WriteLine("\n \n" + ind);  // output: 1

            Console.ReadKey();
        }
    }
}
```

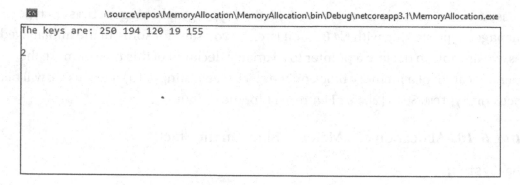

Figure 5-11. *The result from Listing 5-19*

Conclusions

In this chapter, we covered the most important new features of C# 8.0 that can be used during the implementation of cryptographic algorithms and security schemes. The new features that we covered focus on two main aspects of a cryptographic solution, which are

- **Code quality:** Moving from classic source code to a modern perspective of writing the source code

- **Improving the performance of source code by using advanced programming concepts:** Classic vs. modern code, using elegant and disciplined source code for rewriting most of the cryptographic primitives (e.g. RSA, AES, DES, Blowfish, Twofish, etc.) focusing on lambda expressions and the LINQ language

- **Size of the variables used during the implementation and making sure that the proper size is allocated:** Allocation of the memory size and using the proper sizes and types are very important, especially when attacks occur over the application (software obfuscation, buffer overflow, etc.). This kind of attack is very tricky and, once exploited, can create serious breaches into software applications.

Bibliography

[1]   C# language versioning. Available online: `https://docs.`
`microsoft.com/en-us/dotnet/csharp/language-reference/`
`configure-language-version`.

[2]   Span<T> Struct. Available online: `https://docs.microsoft.com/`
`en-us/dotnet/api/system.span-1?view=netcore-3.1`.

[3]   C# Language Versioning. Available online: `https://docs.`
`microsoft.com/en-us/dotnet/csharp/language-reference/`
`configure-language-version`.

CHAPTER 6

Secure Coding Guidelines

Introduction

When software applications have vulnerabilities, it means high costs for the application maker. Some organizations pay more than $500,000 per security incident. The efforts used for the elimination of vulnerabilities in a software application should focus on secure coding, avoiding deploying any vulnerabilities in the production phase.

Writing secure source code is a difficult task. It is very important to understand the implications of the code that is being written and to have a checklist of things that need to be checked. The checklist will help the developers pursue a fast verification of their code for well-known security problems. Usually, the verification is done by a security team and not by software developers or engineers. A software developer cannot be objective with their own code.

The idea of a checklist should start from the following idea: verifying the source code that will process data outside of its domain and take into consideration the user input, the network communication, the process of the binary files, receiving output from database management systems or servers, and so on.

When we work with a software application (doesn't matter whether the application is a desktop, web, or mobile one), the idea that the application is secure because it was developed by a well-known company is just a myth. Don't trust this notion. Companies that rely on this idea end up spending a huge amount of the budget on security incidents, maintenance, consultancy, and audit sessions.

There are two environments in which a software application works, and its behavior is different in each environment. The software application that is in the analysis and development process within a company represents its circle of trust (at least, most companies think in this way and they enjoy considering their infrastructure very resistant to security attacks). The behavior of the software application in that circle of

165

trust represents the most critical environment in which an application can be developed and tested. No developer, IT security officer, or software analyst will hack his own code. For this purpose, some companies such as Microsoft used to have software development engineers in test (SDETs) who were tasked with breaking or attempting to break the code written by the software development engineers (SDEs). This environment is the comfort one. Once the application leaves that comfort zone and enters the real environment, the issues start happening. The trust boundary is hard and easy at the same time to be drawn and to create a delimitation between the comfort zone and the real zone. It's not an easy task to achieve, especially if those applications are running in a virtualized infrastructure, cloud, or big data environments.

In the comfort zone, a security threat is represented by the malicious end users. The malicious end user will attack the confidentiality and/or the integrity of the software application. One of the interesting methods and concepts proposed is *software obfuscation*.

Secure Coding Checklist

In this section, we will discuss and propose a secure coding checklist (it can be seen as a procedure as well). Table 6-1 shows an example of such checklist, and it can be developed as much as you want. The checklist contains minimal examples of items that can be checked when code is written in C#, no matter if it is on a Windows or Linux operating system. A frequently used practice among developers is that they suppress the warnings, which is not beneficial.

In later sections, we will discuss the most important rules to apply to the process of developing cryptographic algorithms. Each rule is well explained within the guide.

Table 6-1. *Example of a Secure Coding Checklist*

No. #	Item to be checked	Description	Yes/No	Notes
1	***Compiler warnings***			

Make sure that the GCC compiler will output and that a flag is raised for receiving notifications for the potential errors listed for the following items.
For more flags with their definitions and actions, the compiler options to Request or Suppress Warnings section is recommended to be followed [1]. This is very useful if complex cryptographic algorithms and security schemes are being implemented.

| 2 | ***Allocate enough memory for buffer memory when working with strings.*** | | | |

Check the following functions to see if there is an upper limit for the destination buffer when a copy process is done until NULL is met. In order to avoid this situation, the recommendation is to allocate enough memory space for the destination buffer before the data is copied there.

| 3 | ***Check for direct breaks of system security.*** | | | |

Checking for untrusted input will lead to a direct breach of the application's security. With this step, you will protect the application against malicious users and attackers trying to exploit the program using metachars.

| 4 | ***Check for wrong size of parameters and getting unexpected results.*** | | | |

When complex programs are written, such as the implementation of SHA-256 from Listing 2-9 in Chapter 2, assigning a wrong size of one of the parameters or doing a wrong arithmetic operation can cause a serious pitfall and a fix should be provided immediately. Make sure that the size allocated for the parameters is the same on the destination side. As a best practice, especially in implementing cryptography algorithms, it is better to work with returning sizes for types. Be type-safe and don't create overflows.

(continued)

Table 6-1. (*continued*)

No. #	Item to be checked	Description	Yes/No	Notes
5	**Check if too much memory is allocated.**			

Allocating too much memory and external parameters represents a certain part of the size. This means dealing with a wrong memory allocation and you will experience the *denial-of-service* result. To avoid this happening, it is better to follow the below criteria.

| 6 | *Avoid wrong casts.* | | | |

Avoid coding like below. The compiler will think that memory allocation will return an `int`, which is totally incorrect. It will create a bug, which easily can be exploited by hackers.

| 7 | *Avoid variable parameter lists.* | | | |

When you are implementing security schemes based on strings, you can get a new type of problem, which security analysts or ethical hackers enjoy playing with when performing tests. A simple test that is commonly used by ethical hackers to check untrusted data is to check if a function allows a variable as a list of parameters or arguments, such as `Console.WriteLine()` or `MessageBox.Show()`. The untrusted data (created by an ethical hacker) is directly used as a string format and not as an argument. Follow the below logic for any similar situations.

| 8 | *Operations with files* | | | |

When handling files during cryptographic operations, use `mkstemp()`.

| 9 | *File permissions* | | | |

Not everyone should have the ability to read or write from or to a file. In order to avoid files assigned the wrong permissions, make a habit of using the `FileIOPermission` class.

(continued)

Table 6-1. (*continued*)

No. #	Item to be checked	Description	Yes/No	Notes

10   *Avoid using Code Access Security (CAS)*

CAS uses resources that can be exploited during the running process of the main program. Examples of such resources are XML files, database, images, settings and configuration files, etc. Because of the fact that is not recommended to use CAS, it is not support in .NET Core, .NET 5, or later versions. Generally speaking, CAS is not supported by versions of C# later than 7.0.

11   *Avoid using partially trusted code.*

The assemblies represent a vulnerable point in an application and they can be easily exploited and overridden in order to gain access to the core of the functions and methods, as well to the main code.

12   *Avoid using the* AllowPartiallyTrustedCaller *attribute.*

Starting with .NET Framework 4, new security rules affect the behavior of the AllowPartiallyTrustedCallersAttribute attribute. Starting with .NET Core, partially trusted code is no longer supported. The recommendation is to use a .NET 4 library and to stick with the .NET 4 security model and use the appropriate SecurityCritical, SecuritySafeCritical, and Security Transparent attributes where needed.

13   *Avoid using .NET Remoting.*

.NET Remoting is the technology that makes it possible to make an object, called a *remotable object*, available across different remoting boundaries, which are based on different application domains (AppDomain), processes, or different computers that are connected within or by a network. Because of this fact, the processes or the computers (networks) can be exploited and the object (remotable object) can be overridden in order to get malicious access to the application and resources of the application. Such a situation is presented in [21].

(*continued*)

Table 6-1. (*continued*)

No. #	Item to be checked	Description	Yes/No	Notes
14	Avoid using DCOM (Distributed Component Object Model).			

DCOM represents a programming construction that allows a computer to execute programs over networks on a different computer as if the program was running locally. Through a man-in-the-middle attack, an attacker can take control of the communication channel and hack the communications between the applications and their computers.

| 15 | Avoid using binary formatters. | | | |

The `BinaryFormatter` type from .NET Framework is very dangerous and is not recommended when data processing is done. Applications should stop using `BinaryFormatter` immediately, even if the developers believe that the data they're processing can be trustworthy. Indeed, `BinaryFormatter` is insecure but some aspects can be made secure. However, it is recommended to avoid it completely [20].

CERT Coding Standards

The CERT Coding Standard was developed only for versions of the C++ programming language that are defined by the ISO/IEC 14882-2014 standard, but some of the coding standards can be used with success for other programming languages, such as C#, Java, or Python.

The coding standard is very well organized and it follows this structure: identifiers, noncompliant code examples and compliant solutions, exceptions, risk assessment, automated detection, related vulnerabilities, and related guidelines [7].

In the following sections, we will examine each item of the structure and we will explain the main objective and purpose.

Identifiers

Each identifier has three parts:

- A three-letter mnemonic that represents the section within the standard.

- A numeric value of two digits situated in the range 00 and 99.

- The language that it is associated with, which is represented as a suffix (-CPP, -C, -J, -PL).
    - –CPP: SEI CERT C# Coding Standard [7]
    - –C: SEI CERT C Coding Standard [8]
    - –J: SEI CERT Oracle Coding Standard for Java [9]
    - –PL: SEI CERT Perl Coding Standard [10]

The three letter mnemonic is used for grouping related coding practices and to point out which category a related coding belongs to.

Noncompliant Code Examples and Compliant Solutions

The examples of noncompliant code show the code that is violating the guideline. It is very important to keep in mind that these are only examples. The removing process of all appearances of the example does not mean that the code we are analyzing is compliant with the SEI CERT standard.

Exceptions to the Rules

Exceptions have an informative character and are not required to be followed. Any of the rules can have a set of exceptions, which give details about the circumstances in which the guideline is not necessary to be followed for ensuring the safety, security, or reliability of the software.

As with any type of exception, the programming language doesn't matter, the principle is the same. It is necessary to pay extra attention to the exceptions and to catch any possible exception and to learn from it. Don't ignore them. Don't think that a programming language is perfect and that it doesn't have any bugs or certain doors that can be exploited.

Risk Assessment

For each guideline from the CERT C++ Coding Standard, there is a risk assessment section assigned. The purpose of the risk assessment section is to provide software developers with potential consequences for not following or addressing a specific rule or recommendation. The risk assessment looks like a metric and its main purpose is to help the remediation process of the software applications and complex projects.

Each rule and recommendation has a *priority*. In order to assign a priority, it is recommended to understand IEC 60812 [11]. The priority is evaluated and assigned using a metric that is characterized by three types of analysis: failure mode, effects, and criticality. Each rule will also have a value that is assigned on a scale between 1 and 3, such as severity, likelihood, and remediation cost (see Table 6-2).

Table 6-2. *Assigning Values for Each Rule [7]*

Severity – What are the consequences if the rule is ignored?		
Value	**Meaning**	**Examples of different vulnerabilities**
1	Low	Denial-of-service attack, unexpected termination
2	Medium	Violation of the data integrity, information disclosure without any intention
3	High	Run random code

Likelihood – Statistically speaking, what is the probability a flaw has been introduced in the code by avoiding and ignoring the rule specifications, leading to a vulnerability that could be exploited by a malicious user?

Value	Definition
1	Unlikely
2	Probable
3	Likely

Remediation cost – What are the costs to follow and comply with the rule?

Value	Definition	Detection	Correction
1	High	Manual	Manual
2	Medium	Automatic	Manual
3	Low	Automatic	Automatic

For each of the rules, the values are multiplied together. The metric in Table 6-3 gives you a measure that can be useful for prioritizing the rules within the application. The values are from 1 to 27. From all 27 values, only 10 different values occurs and are available in most of the cases: 1, 2, 3, 4, 6, 8, 9, 12, 18, and 27. Table 6-3 shows the possible interpretations and meanings of the priorities and levels.

Table 6-3. *Levels and Priorities [7]*

Level	Priorities	Possible Interpretation
L1	12, 18, 27	High severity, likely, inexpensive to fix
L2	6, 8, 9	Medium severity, portable, medium cost to fix
L3	1, 2, 3, 4	Low severity, unlikely, expensive to repair

Automated Detection

The rules and recommendations have sections that describe the automated detection process. The mentioned sections have sets of tools which can be used as analyzers to automatically diagnose the violations. The Secure Coding Validation Suite [12] can be used to perform tests on the ability of analyzers to provide diagnosis information on violations of the rules specified with ISO/IEC TS 17961:2013 [14], which is related to the rules of the SEI CERT C Coding Standard [13].

Related Guidelines

This section has a special slot when software applications are developed, according to the standard. It also contains links, technical specifications, and guideline collections such as *"Information Technology – Programming Languages, Their Environments and System Software Interfaces – C Secure Coding Rules [14]; Information Technology – Programming Languages – Guidance to Avoiding Vulnerabilities in Programming Languages through Language Selection and Use [15]; MISRA C# 2008: Guidelines for the Use of the C# Language in Critical Systems [16];and CWE IDs in MITRE's Common Weakness Enumeration (CWE) [17]."* [18]

Rules

In the following sections, we will give a short overview of the main rules that strongly apply to implementing cryptographic algorithms and security schemes using C#. Especially with the new version of it, it is best to know the following rules. Note that we will examine only 6 of the 10 rules. All the explanations and examples are provided within the guide [19].

For some rules, there are also rules from the C programming language that apply to C#. The following rules can be used within the procedure explained in Table 6-1.

The duty of any information security officer, security analyst, ethical hacker, etc. is to improve code by designing such a checklist. Further, the checklist can also be used by developers as a guide when they are developing critical cryptographic algorithms. It is recommended to make a code review of the sections of the algorithms that are quite vulnerable and to make sure that the rules (Rule 01, Rule 02, Rule 03, Rule 05, Rule 06, and Rule 07) are followed as much as possible.

Following these rules will give you as a security analyst or ethical hacker a certain level of trust that the security mechanisms (cryptographic algorithms, security protocols, security schemes, and other cryptographic primitives) are implemented properly and that common vulnerabilities have been eliminated. See Tables 6-4 through 6-9.

Rule 01. Declarations and Initializations (DCL)

Table 6-4. *Rule 01 – Declarations and Initializations [19]*

Rule	Apply in C#	Title
DCL51-CPP	Y	Do not declare or define a reserved identifier.
DCL52-CPP	Y	Never qualify a reference type with const or volatile.
DCL53-CPP	Y	Do not write syntactically ambiguous declarations.
DCL54-CPP	Y	Overload allocation and deallocation functions as a pair in the same scope.
DCL55-CPP	Y	Avoid information leakage when passing a class object across a trust boundary.
DCL56-CPP	Y	Avoid cycles during initialization of static objects.
DCL57-CPP	Y	Do not let exceptions escape from destructors or deallocation functions.
DCL58-CPP	Y	Do not modify the standard namespaces.

(continued)

Table 6-4. (*continued*)

Rule	Apply in C#	Title
DCL59-CPP	Y	Do not define an unnamed namespace in a header file.
DCL60-CPP	Y	Obey the one-definition rule.
DCL30-C	Y	Declare objects with appropriate storage durations.
DCL39-C	Y	Avoid information leakage when passing a structure across a trust boundary.
DCL40-C	Y	Do not create incompatible declarations of the same function or object.

Rule 02. Expressions (EXP)

Table 6-5. *Rule 02 – Expressions [19]*

Rule	Apply in C#	Title
EXP50-CPP	Y	Do not depend on the order of evaluation for side effects.
EXP51-CPP	Y	Do not delete an array through a pointer of the incorrect type.
EXP52-CPP	Y	Do not rely on side effects in unevaluated operands.
EXP53-CPP	Y	Do not read uninitialized memory.
EXP54-CPP	Y	Do not access an object outside of its lifetime.
EXP56-CPP	Y	Do not call a function with a mismatched language linkage.
EXP57-CPP	Y	Do not cast or delete pointers to incomplete classes.
EXP60-CPP	Y	Do not pass a nonstandard-layout type object across execution boundaries.
EXP61-CPP	Y	A lambda object must not outlive any of its reference captured objects.
EXP62-CPP	Y	Do not access the bits of an object representation that are not part of the object's value representation.
EXP63-CPP	Y	Do not rely on the value of a moved-from object.

Rule 03. Integers (INT)

Table 6-6. *Rule 03 – Integers [19]*

Rule	Apply in C#	Title
INT50-CPP	Y	Do not cast to an out-of-range enumeration value.
INT30-C	Y	Ensure that unsigned integer operations do not wrap.
INT31-C	Y	Ensure that integer conversions do not result in lost or misinterpreted data.
INT32-C	Y	Ensure that operations on signed integers do not result in overflow.
INT33-C	Y	Ensure that division and remainder operations do not result in divide-by-zero errors.
INT34-C	Y	Do not shift an expression by a negative number of bits or by greater than or equal to the number of bits that exist in the operand.
INT35-C	Y	Do not call a function with a mismatched language linkage.

Rule 05. Characters and Strings (STR)

Table 6-7. *Rule 05 – Characters and Strings [19]*

Rule	Apply in C#	Title
STR50-CPP	Y	Guarantee that storage for strings has sufficient space for character data and the null terminator.
STR52-CPP	N	Use valid references, pointers, and iterators to reference elements of a `basic_string`.
STR53-CPP	Y	Range check element access.
STR30-C	Y	Do not attempt to modify string literals.
STR31-C	Y	Guarantee that storage for strings has sufficient space for character data and the null terminator.
STR32-C	Y	Do not pass a non-null-terminated character sequence to a library function that expects a string.
STR34-C	Y	Cast characters to unsigned char before converting to larger integer sizes.
STR37-C	Y	Arguments to character-handling functions must be representable as an unsigned char.
STR38-C	Y	Do not confuse narrow and wide character strings and functions.

Rule 06. Memory Management (MEM)

Table 6-8. *Rule 06 – Memory Management [19]*

Rule	Apply in C#	Title
MEM50-CPP	Y	Do not access freed memory.
MEM51-CPP	Y	Properly deallocate dynamically allocated resources.
MEM52-CPP	Y	Detect and handle memory allocation errors.
MEM53-CPP	Y	Explicitly construct and destruct objects when manually managing object lifetime.
MEM54-CPP	Y	Provide placement new with properly aligned pointers to sufficient storage capacity.
MEM55-CPP	Y	Honor replacement dynamic storage management requirements.
MEM56-CPP	Y	Do not store an already-owned pointer value in an unrelated smart pointer.
MEM57-CPP	Y	Avoid using default operator new for over-aligned types.
MEM30-C	Y	Do not access freed memory.
MEM31-C	Y	Free dynamically allocated memory when no longer needed.
MEM34-C	Y	Only free memory allocated dynamically.
MEM35-C	Y	Allocate sufficient memory for an object.
MEM36-C	N	Do not modify the alignment of objects by calling `realloc()`.

Rule 07. Input/Output (FIO)

Table 6-9. *Rule 07 – Input/Output [19]*

Rule	Apply in C#	Title
FIO50-CPP	Y	Do not alternately input and output from a file stream without an intervening positioning call.
FIO51-CPP	Y	Close files when they are no longer needed.
FIO30-C	Y	Exclude user input from format strings.
FIO32-C	Y	Do not perform operations on devices that are only appropriate for files.
FIO34-C	Y	Distinguish between characters read from a file and EOF or WEOF.
FIO38-C	N	Do not copy a FILE object.
FIO39-C	Y	Do not alternately input and output from a stream without an intervening flush or positioning call.
FIO42-C	Y	Close files when they are no longer needed.
FIO44-C	N	Only use values for `fsetpos()` that are returned from `fgetpos()`.
FIO45-C	N	Avoid TOCTOU race conditions while accessing files.
FIO46-C	Y	Do not access a closed file.
FIO47-C	Y	Use valid format strings.

Conclusions

In this chapter, you learned about *rules* and *recommendations*. You went on a journey of the most important security aspects that need to be taken into consideration in the process of developing cryptographic algorithms and security schemes.

It is very important to understand the difference between a *rule* and a *recommendation*. The general idea is that a rule has to follow a specific amount of criteria compared with a recommendation, which represents a suggestion for improving the code quality.

You have acquired a significant amount of knowledge. At the end of this chapter, you are now capable of performing a security analysis of source code, creating a secure coding checklist, filtering those aspects that are vital for your application, and instructing developers on how to proceed when they are implementing cryptographic algorithms and writing related source code.

Bibliography

[1]   GCC Options to Request or Suppress Warnings. Available online:
      `https://gcc.gnu.org/onlinedocs/gcc/Warning-Options.`
      `html#Warning-Options`.

[2]   HXprox_*, libHX – Get Things Done. Available online: `http://`
      `libhx.sourceforge.net/`.

[3]   [ISO/IEC TR 24772:2013] ISO/IEC. *Information Technology—*
      Programming Languages—Guidance to Avoiding Vulnerabilities in
      Programming Languages through Language Selection and Use. TR
      24772-2013. ISO. March 2013.

[4]   [ISO/IEC TS 17961:2012] ISO/IEC TS 17961. *Information*
      Technology—Programming Languages, Their Environments and
      System Software Interfaces—C Secure Coding Rules. ISO. 2012.

[5]   [ISO/IEC 14882-2014] ISO/IEC 14882-2014. *Programming*
      Languages — C#, Fourth Edition. 2014.

[6]   Ballman, A., 2016. *SEI CERT C# Coding Standard (2016 Edition)* 435.

[7]   SEI CERT C# Coding Standard: Available online: `https://`
      `wiki.sei.cmu.edu/confluence/pages/viewpage.`
      `action?pageId=88046682` (accessed 4.9.20).

[8]   SEI CERT C Coding Standard. Available online: `https://wiki.`
      `sei.cmu.edu/confluence/display/c` (accessed 4.9.20).

[9]   SEI CERT Oracle Coding Standard for Java. Available online:
      `https://wiki.sei.cmu.edu/confluence/display/java`
      (accessed 4.9.20).

[10] SEI CERT Perl Coding Standard. Available online: `https://wiki.`
      `sei.cmu.edu/confluence/display/perl` (accessed 4.9.20).

[11] [IEC 60812 2006] IEC (International Electrotechnical
      Commission). *Analysis Techniques for System Reliability—*
      Procedure for Failure Mode and Effects Analysis (FMEA), 2nd ed.
      (IEC 60812). Geneva, Switzerland: IEC, 2006.

[12]   Secure Coding Validation Suite. Available online: `https://github.com/SEI-CERT/scvs`.

[13]   SEI CERT C Coding Standard: *Rules for Developing Safe, Reliable, and Secure Systems (2016 Edition)*, n.d. 534.

[14]   [ISO/IEC TS 17961:2012] ISO/IEC TS 17961. *Information Technology—Programming Languages, Their Environments and System Software Interfaces—C Secure Coding Rules*. ISO. 2012.

[15]   [ISO/IEC TR 24772:2013] ISO/IEC. *Information Technology—Programming Languages—Guidance to Avoiding Vulnerabilities in Programming Languages through Language Selection and Use*. TR 24772-2013. ISO. March 2013.

[16]   [MISRA 2008] MISRA Limited. *MISRA C# 2008 Guidelines for the Use of the C# Language in Critical Systems*. ISBN 978-906400-03-3 (paperback); ISBN 978-906400-04-0 (PDF). June 2008.

[17]   [MITRE] MITRE. *Common Weakness Enumeration, Version 1.8*. February 2010. Available online: `http://cwe.mitre.org/`.

[18]   "How this Coding Standard is Organized." Available online: `https://wiki.sei.cmu.edu/confluence/display/cplusplus/How+this+Coding+Standard+Is+Organized`.

[19]   "Rules." Available online: `https://wiki.sei.cmu.edu/confluence/pages/viewpage.action?pageId=88046322`.

[20]   BinaryFormatter Class. Available online: `https://docs.microsoft.com/en-us/dotnet/standard/serialization/binaryformatter-security-guide`.

[21]   "Finding and Exploiting .NET Remoting over HTTP using Deserialization." Available online: `www.nccgroup.com/uk/about-us/newsroom-and-events/blogs/2019/march/finding-and-exploiting-.net-remoting-over-http-using-deserialisation/`.

CHAPTER 7

.NET Cryptography Services

In this chapter, we will discuss the main services and cryptographic primitives that
.NET Framework and .NET Core offer to professionals. Knowing what services and
cryptographic primitives a development technology has to offer is very important,
especially if you don't want to develop the cryptographic algorithms and security
schemes from scratch.

The following topics will be covered:

- Cryptographic primitives

- Encryption using a secret key

- Encryption using a public key

- Digital signatures

- Hash values

- Random number generation

- Support for Suite B

- Cryptography Next Generation (CHG) classes

Communication through the Internet is not inherently secure, and in this case
encryption needs to be used with the goal of guaranteeing the security of such
communication. The communication between these network entities is likely to be
read by unauthorized third parties, or even altered. As you have seen before, the
purpose of cryptography is to protect the data from being viewed or modified by
parties who are not authorized to do so. With the help of the .NET Framework, we

© Marius Iulian Mihailescu and Stefania Loredana Nita 2021
M. I. Mihailescu and S. L. Nita, *Pro Cryptography and Cryptanalysis*,
https://doi.org/10.1007/978-1-4842-6367-9_7

have cryptographic classes that are designed to be used within `System.Security.Cryptography` (see Chapter 9), a namespace that handles cryptography functions and their operations. Also, we are dealing with wrappers for the unmanaged CryptoAPI (Microsoft Cryptography API). Meanwhile, others are fully implemented and tested accordingly. The nice thing is that once we create a new instance of a specific encryption algorithm class, the keys are automatically generated in order to be used as easy as possible, using default properties that are very secure.

This being said, in the following sections we will provide a quick synopsis of the most important encryption algorithms that are supported by the .NET Framework (ClickOnce, Suite B, and CNG), features that were introduced starting with .NET Framework 3.5.

Encryption Using a Secret Key

The encryption algorithms based on a secret key use a single secret key for the encryption and decryption processes. It is very important to guarantee the security of the key from unauthorized parties or services. Any unauthorized party that has access to the key can use it to decrypt data or encrypt other data, claiming and impersonating the real authorized party.

Encryption using a secret key is also known as symmetric encryption because the same key is used for both processes: encryption and decryption operations (see Figure 7-1). The encryption algorithms based on the secret key are very fast compared to the algorithms based on a public key. At the same time, they are most suitable for doing cryptographic encoding for large data streams. On the other hand, we have algorithms that are based on asymmetric encryption such as RSA, and their mathematical limitation is based on how much data has to be encrypted.

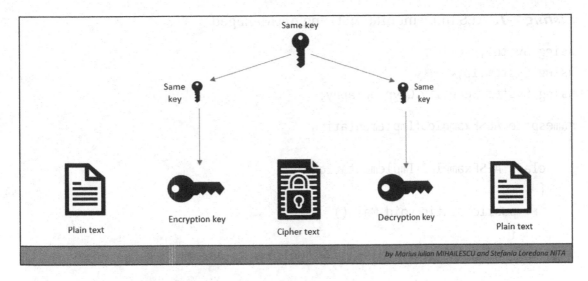

Figure 7-1. *Symmetric encryption*

The .NET Framework contains the following classes for helping professionals implement encryption and decryption operations using the same secret key:

- `AesManaged` [38] (starting with .NET Framework 3.5). See an implementation in Listing 7-1 and Figure 7-2.

- `RijndaelManaged` [41]. See an implementation in Listing 7-2.

- `DESCryptoServiceProvider` [39]. See an implementation in Listing 7-3.

- `RC2CryptoServiceProvider` [40]. The implementation is similar with the one from Listing 7-3.

- `TripleDESCryptoServiceProvider` [42].

```
D:\Apps\Chapter 7 - Cryptographic Services in .NET\AesCrypto\AesCrypto\bin\Debug\AesCrypto.exe           —     □     ×
The original message is: Welcome to Apress!

The trip round is: Welcome to Apress!
The encrypted message is (byte-byt-byte view): new byte[] { 99 176 232 171 42 188 104 107 114 131 224 63 243 152 173 124
 118 32 161 170 61 2 161 28 254 246 120 167 155 224 10 197 }

The encrypted message is (default view): c°è«*%hkrƒà?ó~-|v ¡ª=◘¡◙_öx◙>à
Å

The encrypted message is (UTF8 view): c??*?hkr????|v ??=◘?◙??x???
?

The encrypted message is (UTF32 view): ????????
▪
```

Figure 7-2. *AES execution*

183

Listing 7-1. AES Implementation Using AesManaged

```csharp
using System;
using System.IO;
using System.Security.Cryptography;

namespace AESExampleOfImplementation
{
    class AESExampleOfImplementation
    {
        public static void Main()
        {
            string genuineMessage = "Welcome to Apress!";

            //** Declare a new instance
            //** of the class AESManaged.
            //** With its help a new key
            //** and initialization vector is generated
            using (AesManaged aes_encryption =
new AesManaged())
            {
                //** the string is encrypted and
                //** stored as an array of bytes
                byte[] message_encrypted =
EncryptStringToBytes_Aes(genuineMessage,
aes_encryption.Key,
aes_encryption.IV);

                //** the decryption will take place as
                //** decrypting the bytes into a string
                string tripRound =
DecryptStringFromBytes_Aes(
message_encrypted,
aes_encryption.Key,
aes_encryption.IV);

                //** Shows in the console the original
                //** message and the data decrypted
```

```
Console.WriteLine("The original message is:
{0}", genuineMessage);

Console.WriteLine("The trip round is: {0}",
tripRound);

Console.WriteLine("The encrypted message is
(byte-by-byte view): {0}", PrintByteArray(message_encrypted));

            Console.WriteLine("The encrypted message is
(default view): {0}", Encoding.Default.GetString
(message_encrypted));

            Console.WriteLine("The encrypted message is
(UTF8 view): {0}", Encoding.UTF8.GetString(message_encrypted));

            Console.WriteLine("The encrypted message is
(UTF32 view): {0}",
Encoding.UTF32.GetString
(message_encrypted));
            Console.ReadKey();

        }
      }

    //** processing byte values to display them
    static string PrintByteArray(byte[] encrypted_message)
      {
          var build_string =
new StringBuilder("new byte[] { ");
          foreach (var each_byte in encrypted_message)
          {
              build_string.Append(each_byte + " ");
          }
          build_string.Append("}");
          return build_string.ToString();
      }

    static byte[] EncryptStringToBytes_Aes
```

```
(string genuineText,
 byte[] crypto_key,
 byte[] initializationVector)
        {
            //** verify the arguments
            if (genuineText == null ||
genuineText.Length <= 0)
                throw new ArgumentNullException("genuineText");

            if (crypto_key == null || crypto_key.Length <= 0)
                throw new ArgumentNullException("crypto_key");

  if (initializationVector == null ||
initializationVector.Length <= 0)
                throw new ArgumentNullException("IV");

            byte[] encryptionRepresentation;

            //** declare an AesManaged instance
            //** Create an AesManaged object
           //** the declaration should include the specified
           //** key and initialization vector.
            using (Aes aes_algorithm = Aes.Create())
            {
                aes_algorithm.Key = crypto_key;
                aes_algorithm.IV = initializationVector;

                //** do the stream transformation
                //** for this declare an ecnryptor
               //** using ICryptoTransform
                ICryptoTransform crypto_transformation =
aes_algorithm.CreateEncryptor
(aes_algorithm.Key, aes_algorithm.IV);

                //** use the streams and work with the
                //** encryption Create the streams
                //** used for encryption
                using (MemoryStream memoryStreamForEncryption
```

```
= new MemoryStream())
                {
                    using (CryptoStream cryptoStreamEncryption
 = new CryptoStream(memoryStreamForEncryption,
 crypto_transformation, CryptoStreamMode.Write))
                    {
                        using (StreamWriter
  streamWriterForEncryption = new
                        StreamWriter(cryptoStreamEncryption))
                        {
                            //** write the entire volume of
                            //** data with the stream
streamWriterForEncryption.
Write(genuineText);
                        }
                        encryptionRepresentation =
   memoryStreamForEncryption.ToArray();
                    }
                }
            }

            //** Return the encrypted bytes from
 //** the memory stream.
            return encryptionRepresentation;
        }

        static string DecryptStringToBytes_Aes
(byte[] encryptedText,
 byte[] encryption_key,
 byte[] initialization_vector)
        {
            //** verify the arguments
            if (encryptedText == null ||
encryptedText.Length <= 0)
                throw new
ArgumentNullException("encryptedText");
```

```csharp
            if (encryption_key == null ||
encryption_key.Length <= 0)
                throw new ArgumentNullException("Key");

 if (initialization_vector == null ||
initialization_vector.Length <= 0)
                throw new ArgumentNullException("IV");

            //** the string used to store
            //** the original decrypted text
            string original_text = null;

            //** declare an AesManaged instance
            //** using the encryption key
            //** and initialization vector
            using (Aes aes_algorithm = Aes.Create())
            {
                aes_algorithm.Key = encryption_key;
                aes_algorithm.IV = initialization_vector;

                //** do the stream transformation
                //** for this declare an
                //** encryptor using ICryptoTransform
                ICryptoTransform decrypt_transformation =
aes_algorithm.CreateDecryptor(
aes_algorithm.Key,
aes_algorithm.IV);

                //** use the streams and work
                //** with the encryption
                //** Create the streams used for encryption
                using (MemoryStream memoryStreamDecryption =
                        new MemoryStream(encryptedText))
                {
                    using (CryptoStream cryptoStreamDecryption
= new CryptoStream(
memoryStreamDecryption,
decrypt_transformation,   CryptoStreamMode.Read))
```

```
                      {
                          using (StreamReader
streamReaderDecryption =
                          new StreamReader(
cryptoStreamDecryption))
                              {
                //** read the decrypted bytes from
                //** the stream reader
                //** and save it in
                //** original_text variable
                              original_text =
streamReaderDecryption.
ReadToEnd();
                          }
                      }
                  }
              }
          return original_text;
      }
  }
}
```

In Listing 7-2 and Figure 7-3 you can observe how Rijndael can be implemented.

Listing 7-2. RijndaelManaged Implementation

```
using System;
using System.IO;
using System.Security.Cryptography;
using System.Text;

namespace RijndaelManagedImplementationExample
{
    class RijndaelManagedImplementationExample
    {
        public static void Main()
        {
```

```
try
{
    string genuineMessage = "Folks, Welcome to Apress!";

    //** declare a new instance of the
    //** RijndaelManaged class with this
    //** instance a new key and
    //** initialization vector (IV)
    using (RijndaelManaged rijndeal_crypto = new
    RijndaelManaged())
    {
        rijndeal_crypto.GenerateKey();
        rijndeal_crypto.GenerateIV();

        //** encrypt the message (string)
        //** and store the content to an
        //** array of bytes
        byte[] encrypted = EncryptStringToBytes(genuineMessage,
        rijndeal_crypto.Key, rijndeal_crypto.IV);

        //** Decrypt the bytes to a string
        string tripRound = DecryptStringFromBytes(encrypted,
        rijndeal_crypto.Key, rijndeal_crypto.IV);

        //** Display the original data
        //** and the decrypted data
        Console.WriteLine("Original Message:{0}",
        genuineMessage);
        Console.WriteLine("Round Trip: {0}",tripRound);

        Console.WriteLine("\nThe encrypted message is (byte -
        byt - byte view): {0}", PrintByteArray(encrypted));
        Console.WriteLine("\nThe encrypted message is (default
        view): {0}", Encoding.Default.GetString(encrypted));
        Console.WriteLine("\nThe encrypted message is (UTF8
        view): {0}", Encoding.UTF8.GetString(encrypted));
        Console.WriteLine("\nThe encrypted message is (UTF32
        view): {0}", Encoding.UTF32.GetString(encrypted));
```

```
            Console.ReadKey();
        }
    }
    catch (Exception e)
    {
        Console.WriteLine("There is an error:{0}", e.Message);
    }
}

//** processing byte values to display them
static string PrintByteArray(byte[] encrypted_message)
{
    var build_string = new StringBuilder("new byte[] { ");
    foreach (var each_byte in encrypted_message)
    {
        build_string.Append(each_byte + " ");
    }
    build_string.Append("}");
    return build_string.ToString();
}

static byte[] EncryptStringToBytes(string genuineText, byte[]
encryption_key, byte[] initialization_vector)
{
    //** verify the arguments
    if (genuineText == null ||
    genuineText.Length <= 0)
        throw new ArgumentNullException("genuineText");

    if (encryption_key == null ||
        encryption_key.Length <= 0)
        throw new ArgumentNullException("encryption_key");

    if (initialization_vector == null ||
        initialization_vector.Length <= 0)
        throw new ArgumentNullException("IV");
```

```
byte[] encryption_content;

//** Create an RijndaelManaged object
//**  with the specified key and IV.
using (RijndaelManaged rijndaelAlgorithm = new
RijndaelManaged())
{
    rijndaelAlgorithm.Key = encryption_key;

    rijndaelAlgorithm.IV = initialization_vector;

    //** Create an encryptor to perform
    //** the stream transform.
    ICryptoTransform encryptorTransformation = rijndael
    Algorithm.CreateEncryptor(rijndaelAlgorithm.Key,
    rijndaelAlgorithm.IV);

    //** Create the streams used for encryption
    using (MemoryStream memoryStreamEncrypt = new
    MemoryStream())
    {
        using (CryptoStream cryptoStreamEncrypt = new Crypto
        Stream(memoryStreamEncrypt, encryptorTransformation,
        CryptoStreamMode.Write))
        {
            using (StreamWriter streamWriterEncrypt = new Strea
            mWriter(cryptoStreamEncrypt))
            {
                //** write the entire volume of
                //** data to the stream
                streamWriterEncrypt.Write(genuineText);
            }
            encryption_content = memoryStreamEncrypt.ToArray();
        }
    }
}
```

```
    //** get the encrypted bytes
    //** from the memory stream.
    return encryption_content;
}

static string DecryptStringFromBytes(byte[] encrypted_text, byte[]
encryption_key, byte[] initialization_vector)
{
    //** verify the arguments
    if (encrypted_text == null ||
        encrypted_text.Length <= 0)
        throw new ArgumentNullException("encrypted_text");

    if (encryption_key == null ||
        encryption_key.Length <= 0)
        throw new ArgumentNullException("encryption_key");

    if (initialization_vector == null ||
        initialization_vector.Length <= 0)
        throw new ArgumentNullException("initialization_vector");

    //** Declare the string used to hold
    //** the decrypted text.
    string original_text = null;

    //** Create an RijndaelManaged object
    //** with the specified key and IV.
    using (RijndaelManaged rijndael_algorithm = new
    RijndaelManaged())
    {
        rijndael_algorithm.Key = encryption_key;

        rijndael_algorithm.IV = initialization_vector;

        //** Create a decryptor to
        //** perform the stream transform.
        ICryptoTransform decryptionTransformation = rijndael_
        algorithm.CreateDecryptor(rijndael_algorithm.Key,
        rijndael_algorithm.IV);
```

```
//** Create the streams used for decryption.
using (MemoryStream memoryStreamDecryption = new
MemoryStream(encrypted_text))
{
    using (CryptoStream cryptoStreamDecrypt = new CryptoSt
    ream(memoryStreamDecryption, decryptionTransformation,
    CryptoStreamMode.Read))
    {
        using (StreamReader streamReaderDecryption = new St
        reamReader(cryptoStreamDecrypt))
        {
            //** Read the decrypted bytes
            //** from the decrypting stream
            //** and place them in a string.
            original_text = streamReaderDecryption.
            ReadToEnd();
        }
    }
}

return original_text;
        }
    }
}
```

Figure 7-3. *Example of RijndaelManaged*

- In the following example, we will do two cases of implementation for
  the DES algorithm. Despite the fact that is overcomed, it is a good
  example of how cryptographic algorithms and primitives should be
  treated practically. What makes these two implementations different
  from the rest of the implementations that exist in real practice is
  that the first example (see Figure 7-4, Figure 7-5, and Listing 7-3)
  is doing the encryption/decryption within a file and the second
  example (see Figure 7-6 and Listing 7-4) is doing the encryption/
  decryption in memory. When we are dealing with complex systems
  that use files (such as clear JSON files for Hadoop systems or big data
  environments), one of the solutions is to design the cryptographic
  primitives in such way that we are doing the encryption/decryption
  properly of the files or in the memory without exposing something
  that could impact the business.

Listing 7-3. Example of Implementation of the DES Algorithm Using
DESCryptoServiceProvider

```
using System;
using System.Security.Cryptography;
using System.Text;
using System.IO;

class DESSample
{
    static void Main()
    {
        try
        {
            //** instance of the DES algorithm and
            //** with help of Create() method
            //** an initialization vector is generated
            DES des_algorithm = DES.Create();

            //** declare a string for being encrypted
            string plaintext = "Welcome to Apress. Enjoy reading.";
            string file_name = "encrypted_file.txt";
```

```
            //** do the encryption to the file based on
            //** the file name, key, and initialization vector
            DesEncryptionToFile(plaintext, file_name, des_algorithm.Key,
            des_algorithm.IV);

            //** Decrypt the text from a file using the file name,
                key, and IV.
            string ciphertext = DesDecryptionFromFile(file_name, des_
            algorithm.Key, des_algorithm.IV);

            //** Show in the console the results
            Console.WriteLine("The message for encryption is: {0}",
            plaintext);
            Console.WriteLine("The message has been encrypted with
            success.");
            Console.WriteLine("\tCheck your file \"{0}\" at the following
            location: {1}", file_name, Path.GetFullPath("encrypted_file.
            txt"));
            Console.ReadKey();
        }
        catch (Exception exception)
        {
            Console.WriteLine(exception.Message);
        }
    }

    public static void DesEncryptionToFile(String text_to_encrypt, String
    file_name, byte[] encryption_key, byte[] initialization_vector)
    {
        try
        {
            //** create the file or open the file if exist
            FileStream file_stream = File.Open(file_name, FileMode.
            OpenOrCreate);

            //** declare a DES object
            DES des_algorithm = DES.Create();
```

```
        //** use the key and initialization vector.
        //** pass them to the CryptoStream together with the file stream
        CryptoStream crypto_stream = new CryptoStream(file_stream,
            des_algorithm.CreateEncryptor(encryption_key,
            initialization_vector),
            CryptoStreamMode.Write);

        //** based on a crypto_stream create an instance of stream
            writer
        StreamWriter stream_writer = new StreamWriter(crypto_stream);

        //** take data and write it within the stream writer
        stream_writer.WriteLine(text_to_encrypt);

        //** make sure that the file stream, crypto stream and stream
            writer are closed
        stream_writer.Close();
        crypto_stream.Close();
        file_stream.Close();
    }
    catch (CryptographicException exception){
        Console.WriteLine("There is an error regarding your encryption
        cryptographic process: {0}", exception.Message);
    }
    catch (UnauthorizedAccessException exception){
        Console.WriteLine("There is an error regarding creating/
        accessing the file: {0}", exception.Message);
    }
}

public static string DesDecryptionFromFile(String file_name, byte[]
decryption_key, byte[] initialization_vector)
{
    try
    {
        //** create the file or open the file if exist
        FileStream file_stream = File.Open(file_name, FileMode.
        OpenOrCreate);
```

```
        //** declare a DES object
        DES des_algorithm = DES.Create();

        //** use the key and initialization vector.
        //** pass them to the CryptoStream together with the file
            stream
        CryptoStream crypto_stream = new CryptoStream(file_stream,
            des_algorithm.CreateDecryptor(decryption_key,
            initialization_vector),
            CryptoStreamMode.Read);

        //** based on a crypto_stream create an instance of stream
            reader
        StreamReader stream_reader = new StreamReader(crypto_stream);

        //** before decryption take place
        //** we need to read the data from the stream
        string val = stream_reader.ReadLine();

        //** make sure that the file stream, crypto stream and stream
            writer are closed
        stream_reader.Close();
        crypto_stream.Close();
        file_stream.Close();

        //** return the decryption value
        return val;
    }
    catch (CryptographicException cryptoException)
    {
        Console.WriteLine("There was a cryptographic error. Please
        see: {0}. Correct the error and try again.", cryptoException.
        Message);
        return null;
    }
    catch (UnauthorizedAccessException unauthorizedException)
    {
```

```
Console.WriteLine("There was an error with the file
(unauthorized/existance). Please, check: {0}",
unauthorizedException.Message);
        return null;
    }
  }
}
```

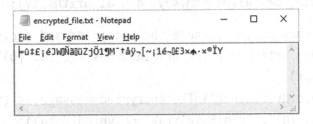

The message for encryption is: Welcome to Apress. Enjoy reading.
The message has been encrypted with success.
        Check your file "encrypted_file.txt" at the following location: D:\Apps\Chapter 7 - Cryptographic Services in .N
ET\DesCrypto\DesCrypto\bin\Debug\encrypted_file.txt

Figure 7-4. *DES algorithm with encryption/decryption in a file*

encrypted_file.txt - Notepad

File Edit Format View Help

├─û‡£¡éJWﬠÑaﬠûZjÖ19M¯†åÿ¬[~¡1é¬ﬡ£3×♠·×®ÏY

Figure 7-5. *DES encryption result*

Listing 7-4. Implementation of DES Encryption and Decryption in Memory

```
using System;
using System.Security.Cryptography;
using System.Text;
using System.IO;

class DESMemoryImplementationExample
{
    static void Main()
    {
        try
```

```csharp
    {
        //** declare a DES instance and with Create()
        //** generate the key and initialization vector
        DES des_algorithm = DES.Create();

        //** declare a variable that contains the string to encrypt
        string data_to_encrypt = "Welcome to Apress. Enjoy your
        adventure.";

        //** use a memory buffer and proceed encrypting the text
        byte[] encrypted_data = EncryptionOfTextInMemory(data_to_
        encrypt, des_algorithm.Key, des_algorithm.IV);

        //** use the buffer and proceed with decryption and obtain the
            plaintext
        string decrypted_data = DecryptionOfTheTextFromMemory(encrypt
        ed_data, des_algorithm.Key, des_algorithm.IV);

        //** show in the console the encrypted and decrypted values
        Console.WriteLine("The original message is: {0}", data_to_
        encrypt);
        Console.WriteLine("\nThe encrypted message is (byte-by-byte
        view): {0}", PrintByteArray(encrypted_data));
        Console.WriteLine("\nThe encrypted message is (default view):
        {0}", Encoding.Default.GetString(encrypted_data));
        Console.WriteLine("\nThe encrypted message is (UTF8 view):
        {0}", Encoding.UTF8.GetString(encrypted_data));
        Console.WriteLine("\nThe encrypted message is (UTF32 view):
        {0}", Encoding.UTF32.GetString(encrypted_data));
        Console.WriteLine("\nThe original text is: {0}.", decrypted_data);

        Console.ReadKey();
    }
    catch (Exception general_exception)
    {
        Console.WriteLine(general_exception.Message);
    }
}
```

```
static string PrintByteArray(byte[] encrypted_message)
{
    var build_string = new StringBuilder("new byte[] { ");
    foreach (var each_byte in encrypted_message)
    {
        build_string.Append(each_byte + " ");
    }
    build_string.Append("}");
    return build_string.ToString();
}

public static byte[] EncryptionOfTextInMemory(string data_to_encrypt,
byte[] key_for_encryption, byte[] initialization_vector)
{
    try
    {
        //** declare an instance for the memory buffer
        MemoryStream memory_stream = new MemoryStream();

        //** declare an instance of DES
        DES DESalg = DES.Create();

        //** declare an crypto stream instance and use
        //** the key used for encryption and the initialization vector
        CryptoStream crypto_stream = new CryptoStream(memory_stream,
            DESalg.CreateEncryptor(key_for_encryption, initialization_
            vector),
            CryptoStreamMode.Write);

        //** the string that has been passed will be converted to a
            byte array
        byte[] for_encryption = new ASCIIEncoding().GetBytes(data_to_
        encrypt);

        //** take the byte array and write it in the crypto stream
        crypto_stream.Write(for_encryption, 0, for_encryption.Length);
```

```csharp
        //** don't forget to flush it
        crypto_stream.FlushFinalBlock();

        //** take the memory stream and write
        //** it as an array of bytes and store it accordingly
        byte[] stream_content_byteArray = memory_stream.ToArray();

        //** make sure to have the streams closed
        crypto_stream.Close();
        memory_stream.Close();

        //** the buffer with the encrypted content
        return stream_content_byteArray;
    }
    catch (CryptographicException cryptoException)
    {
        Console.WriteLine("There was an cryptographic error expected.
        Please see: {0}", cryptoException.Message);
        return null;
    }
}

public static string DecryptionOfTheTextFromMemory(byte[] data_for_
decryption, byte[] decryption_key, byte[] initialization_vector)
{
    try
    {
        //** declare an memory stream instance used for decryption
        //** and as parameter pass the encrypted data
        MemoryStream memory_stream_decryption = new MemoryStream(data_
        for_decryption);

        //** create an instance of DES object
        DES DESalg = DES.Create();

        //** declare an crypto stream instance based on
        //** the memory stream instance and pass as
        //** parameters the decryption and initialization vector
```

```
      CryptoStream crypto_stream_decryption = new CryptoStream
      (memory_stream_decryption,
          DESalg.CreateDecryptor(decryption_key, initialization_vector),
          CryptoStreamMode.Read);

      //** declare a buffer and we will use it
      //** to store the decrypted data
      byte[] from_encryption = new byte[data_for_decryption.Length];

      //** proceed reading the decrypted data from the crypto stream
      //** and store its content in a temporary buffer
      crypto_stream_decryption.Read(from_encryption, 0, from_
      encryption.Length);

      //** do the conversion of the buffer in a string
      //** and return its value
      return new ASCIIEncoding().GetString(from_encryption);
  }
  catch (CryptographicException cryptoException)
  {

      Console.WriteLine("There was an cryptographic error. Please
      see: {0}", cryptoException.Message);
      return null;

  }
 }
}
```

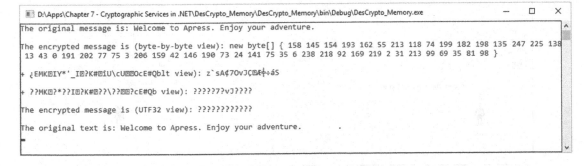

Figure 7-6. DES encryption and decryption in memory

Encryption Using a Public Key

Public key encryption uses a private key that must be stored secretly in such way that unauthorized parties or malicious users cannot access it. Also, it is uses a public key which can be made available to anyone. The relation between the *public key* and the *private key* is mathematically based. The data that is encrypted using the public key can only be decrypted using the private key. In this situation, the data that has been signed using the private key can be verified using only the public key.

Let's consider two parties (classical noted as Alice and Bob, as shown in Figure 7-7) who will use a public-key encryption as described: Alice will generate a pair formed of a public key and private key. When Bob decides to send Alice an encrypted message, he will need the public key from Alice, so he will ask for it. Alice will send Bob her public key over a nonsecure network communication channel. Bob will use it to encrypt the message. Bob will send the encrypted message to Alice, who will decrypt it using her private key.

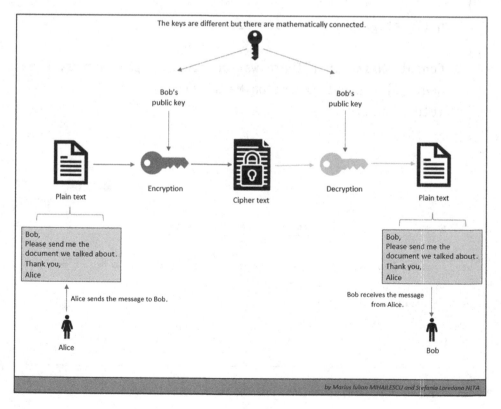

Figure 7-7. *Public-key encryption*

The following list shows a comparison between public-key and private-key algorithms:

- Algorithms based on a public key use a fixed buffer size. It is very important to mention that the secret key and algorithms based on it use a buffer that is represented as a variable and the size varies.

- Regarding the chain of data, there is a difference between public-key algorithms and symmetric-key algorithms. Symmetric-key algorithms chain data together into streams, and public-key algorithms don't have this ability. The streaming model is not the same for the asymmetric operations as for symmetric operations.

- Encryption using a public key uses a larger space for the key representation. The space used by symmetric-key encryptions is much smaller compared with the public key encryptions.

- Public keys are very easy to distribute because there is no need to have a security mechanism. If necessary, there are mechanisms to verify and check the identity of the sender.

- To create a digital signature with the goal of verifying and checking the identity of the sender, public-key algorithms such as RSA and DSA can be used with success.

- Regarding speed, public-key algorithms are very slow if we compare them with symmetric algorithms. They are designed in such way that no large amount of data can be encrypted. Thus, public-key algorithms are recommended only for a small amount of data.

The .NET Framework contains the following classes, which already contain implementations for algorithms and operations for public-key encryption:

- DSACryptoServiceProvider [1]. The implementations are similar and they can be done in the same way as the ones from Listing 7-1, 7-2, or 7-3.

- RSACryptoServiceProvider [2]. For an example of an implementation, see Listing 7-5 and Figure 7-8.

- ECDiffieHellman [3]. The implementations are similar and they can be done in the same way as the ones from Listing 7-1, 7-2, or 7-3.

- ECDiffieHellmanCng [4]. The implementations are similar and they can be done in the same way as the ones from Listing 7-1, 7-2, or 7-3.

- ECDiffieHellamnCngPublicKey [5]. The implementations are similar and they can be done in the same way as the ones from Listing 7-1, 7-2, or 7-3.

- ECDiffieHellmanKeyDerivationFunction [6]. The implementations are similar and they can be done in the same way as the ones from Listing 7-1, 7-2, or 7-3.

- ECDsaCng [7]. For an example of an implementation of ECDSA (Elliptic Curve Digital Signature Algorithm), see Listing 7-5.

Listing 7-5. Implementation of RSA Using RSACryptoServiceProvider

```
using System;
using System.ComponentModel;
using System.Security.Cryptography;
using System.Text;

class RSAExampleOfImplementation
{
    static void Main()
    {
        try
        {
            //** the object will be used for
            //** conversion between the bytes
            //** of the array and string
            UnicodeEncoding byte_converter = new UnicodeEncoding();

            //** Create byte arrays to hold original,
            //** encrypted, and decrypted data.
            string plaintext = "Hi, Apress!";
            byte[] data_to_be_encrypted = byte_converter.
            GetBytes(plaintext);
            byte[] encrypted_data;
            byte[] decrypted_data;
```

```
//** declare a new object of
//** RSACryptoServiceProvider
//** to generate the public
//** and private key data.
using (RSACryptoServiceProvider rsa_algorithm = new
RSACryptoServiceProvider())
{
    //** the data to be encrypted
    //** will be passed
    //** to EncryptionWithRSA along with the
    //** informations related to public key
    encrypted_data = EncryptionWithRSA(data_to_be_encrypted,
    rsa_algorithm.ExportParameters(false), false);
    //** the data to be encrypted
    //** will be passed to DecryptionWithRSA
    //** along with the informations related //** to public key
    decrypted_data = DecryptionWithRSA(encrypted_data, rsa_
    algorithm.ExportParameters(true), false);

    //** shows in the console the
    //** decryption of the plaintext
    Console.WriteLine("The plaintext for encryption is: {0}",
    plaintext);
    Console.WriteLine("\nPlaintext for encryption is: {0}",
    PrintByteArray(data_to_be_encrypted));
    Console.WriteLine("\nDecrypted plaintext: {0}", byte_
    converter.GetString(decrypted_data));

    Console.ReadKey();
}
}
catch (ArgumentNullException)
{
    //** in case that something is going wrong with
    //** the encryption, catch the exception
    Console.WriteLine("Encryption has failed.");
```

```csharp
        }
    }

    static string PrintByteArray(byte[] encrypted_message)
    {
        var build_string = new StringBuilder("new byte[] { ");
        foreach (var each_byte in encrypted_message)
        {
            build_string.Append(each_byte + " ");
        }
        build_string.Append("}");
        return build_string.ToString();
    }

    public static byte[] EncryptionWithRSA(byte[] data_to_be_encrypted,
    RSAParameters rsa_key_info, bool oaep_padding)
    {
        try
        {
            byte[] encrypted_data;

            //** declare a new instance of
            //** RSACryptoServiceProvider.
            using (RSACryptoServiceProvider rsa_csp = new
            RSACryptoServiceProvider())
            {
                //** do the import for RSA Key information
                rsa_csp.ImportParameters(rsa_key_info);

                //** the byte passed array
                //** will be encrypted
                //** and mention OAEP padding
                encrypted_data = rsa_csp.Encrypt(data_to_be_encrypted,
                oaep_padding);
            }
            return encrypted_data;
        }
```

```
    //** in case that something is going wrong with
    //** the encryption, catch the exception
    catch (CryptographicException exception)
    {
        Console.WriteLine(exception.Message);

        return null;
    }
}

public static byte[] DecryptionWithRSA(
    byte[] data_to_be_decrypted,
    RSAParameters rsa_key_info,
    bool oaep_padding)
{

    try
    {
        byte[] decrypted_data;

        //** declare a new instance of
        //** RSACryptoServiceProvider.
        using (RSACryptoServiceProvider rsa_csp = new
        RSACryptoServiceProvider())
        {
            //** do the import for RSA Key information
            rsa_csp.ImportParameters(rsa_key_info);

            //** the byte passed array will be decrypted
            //** and mention OAEP padding
            decrypted_data = rsa_csp.Decrypt(data_to_be_
            decrypted,     oaep_padding);
        }
        return decrypted_data;
    }

    //** in case that something is going wrong with
    //** the encryption, catch the exception
    catch (CryptographicException exception)
```

```
        {
            Console.WriteLine(exception.ToString());

            return null;
        }
    }
}
```

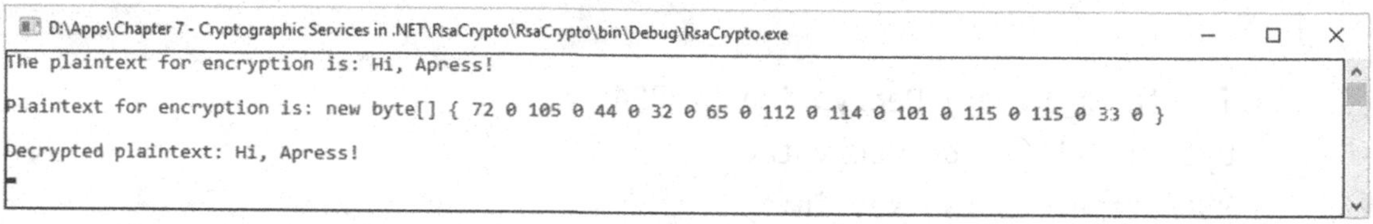

```
 D:\Apps\Chapter 7 - Cryptographic Services in .NET\RsaCrypto\RsaCrypto\bin\Debug\RsaCrypto.exe          —    □    ×
The plaintext for encryption is: Hi, Apress!

Plaintext for encryption is: new byte[] { 72 0 105 0 44 0 32 0 65 0 112 0 114 0 101 0 115 0 115 0 33 0 }

Decrypted plaintext: Hi, Apress!
```

Figure 7-8. *RSA example encryption*

Digital Signature

Public-key algorithms are used to form digital signatures. The role of digital signatures is to authenticate the real identity of the sender and to offer protection regarding the integrity of the data. See Figure 7-9 for the digital signature path.

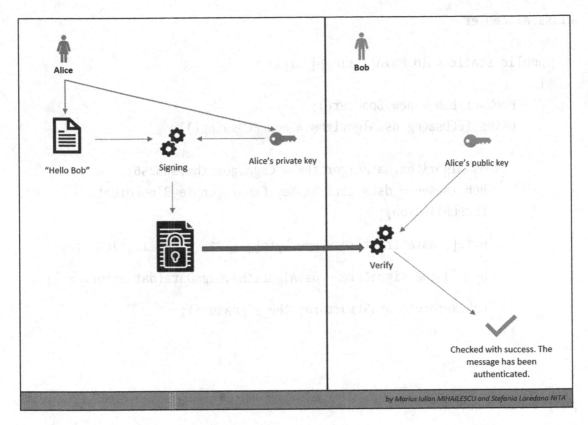

by Marius Iulian MIHAILESCU and Stefania Loredana NITA

Figure 7-9. *ECDsaCng example*

.NET Framework offers the following classes for implementing digital signature algorithms:

- DSACryptoServiceProvider [8]
- RSACryptoServiceProvider [9]
- ECDsa [10]. See Listing 7-6 and Figure 7-10 for details about implementation.
- ECDsaCng [11]. See Listing 7-6 and Figure 7-10 for details about implementation.

Listing 7-6. Implementation of ECDsaCng

```
using System;
using System.IO;
using System.Security.Cryptography;
using System.Text;
```

211

```csharp
class AliceUser
{
    public static void Main(string[] args)
    {
        BobUser bob = new BobUser();
        using (ECDsaCng dsaAlgorithm = new ECDsaCng())
        {
            dsaAlgorithm.HashAlgorithm = CngAlgorithm.Sha256;
            bob.theKey = dsaAlgorithm.Key.Export(CngKeyBlobFormat.
            EccPublicBlob);

            byte[] dataStructure = new byte[] { 21, 5, 8, 12, 207 };

            byte[] the_signature = dsaAlgorithm.SignData(dataStructure);

            bob.Receive(dataStructure, the_signature);
        }
    }
}

public class BobUser
{
    public byte[] theKey;

    public void Receive(byte[] data, byte[] the_signature)
    {
        using (ECDsaCng ecsdKey = new ECDsaCng(CngKey.Import(theKey,
        CngKeyBlobFormat.EccPublicBlob)))
        {
            if (ecsdKey.VerifyData(data, the_signature))
                Console.WriteLine("Data is good");
            else
                Console.WriteLine("Data is bad");
        }
    }
}
```

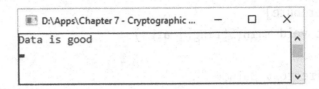

Figure 7-10. *Digital signature*

Hash Values

The purpose of a hash algorithm is to map binary values that are represented as having an arbitrary length to smaller binary values that have a fixed length. A hash value is represented as a numerical value that represents a specific piece of data.

The .NET Framework has the following classes already implemented, which help us to get a quick implementation of the hashing algorithms:

- HMACSHA1 [12]

- MACTripleDES [13]

- MD5CryptoServiceProvider [14]

- RIPEMD160 [15]

- SHA1Managed [16]

- SHA256Managed [17]

- SHA384Managed [18]

- SHA512Managed [19]

For examples of implementations, let's look at RIPEMD160 (see Listing 7-7 and Figure 7-11) and SHA256Managed (see Listing 7-8 and Figure 7-12).

Listing 7-7. RIPEMD160 Implementation

```
using System;
using System.IO;
using System.Security.Cryptography;
using System.Windows.Forms;

public class RIPEMD160Example
{
```

```
[STAThreadAttribute]
public static void Main(String[] args)
{
    string directory_path = "";
    if (args.Length < 1)
    {
        FolderBrowserDialog folder_browser_dialog = new
        FolderBrowserDialog();
        DialogResult dialog_result = folder_browser_dialog.
        ShowDialog();
        if (dialog_result == DialogResult.OK)
        {
            directory_path = folder_browser_dialog.SelectedPath;
        }
        else
        {
            Console.WriteLine("There is no directory selected.");
            return;
        }
    }
    else
    {
        directory_path = args[0];
    }

    try
    {
        //** store the selected directory
        DirectoryInfo directoryInfo = new DirectoryInfo(directory_path);

        //** select the informations of
        //** each file from the folder
        FileInfo[] files = directoryInfo.GetFiles();

        //** declare a RIPEMD160 object
        RIPEMD160 myRIPEMD160 = RIPEMD160Managed.Create();
        byte[] hash_value;
```

```
        //** get the hash value of each file
        //** from the selected directory
        foreach (FileInfo infoOfTheFile in files)
        {
            //** declare a file stream for the file
            FileStream stream_file = infoOfTheFile.Open(FileMode.Open);

            //** put its position at the
            //** beginning of the stream
            stream_file.Position = 0;

            //** for the declared stream
            //** calculate the hash value
            hash_value = myRIPEMD160.ComputeHash(stream_file);

            //** show the name of the value in the console
            Console.Write(infoOfTheFile.Name + ": ");

            //** show the hash value in the console
            ShowReadableByteArray(hash_value);

            //** make sure that the file will
            //** closed properly
            stream_file.Close();
        }
        return;
        Console.ReadKey();
    }
    catch (DirectoryNotFoundException)
    {
        Console.WriteLine("Error: The selected directory could not be
        found.Try again!.");
    }

    catch (IOException)
    {
        Console.WriteLine("Error: There is a problem with the access of
        the file.");
    }
```

```
    }

    //** show the byte array in a possible readable format
    public static void ShowReadableByteArray(byte[] byteArray)
    {
        for (int k = 0; k < byteArray.Length; k++)
        {
            Console.Write(String.Format("{0:X2}",byteArray[k]));
            if ((k % 4) == 3)
                Console.Write(" ");
        }
        Console.WriteLine();
    }
}
```

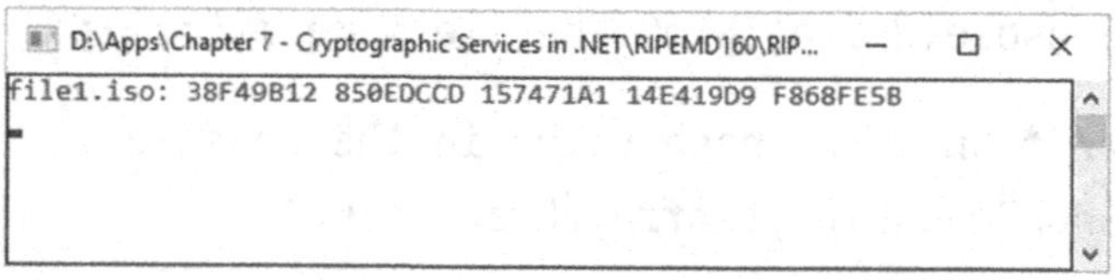

```
D:\Apps\Chapter 7 - Cryptographic Services in .NET\RIPEMD160\RIP...   —   □   ×
file1.iso: 38F49B12 850EDCCD 157471A1 14E419D9 F868FE5B
```

Figure 7-11. *RIPEMD160 example with a hash value for an *.iso file*

Listing 7-8. SHA256Managed Implementation

```
using System;
using System.IO;
using System.Security.Cryptography;

public class HASH256ManagedImplementation
{
    public static void Main(String[] args)
    {
        string path_to_folder = @"D:\SHA256FileExample";
        //if (args.Length < 1)
        //{
        //    Console.WriteLine("There is no directory selected.");
        //    return;
        //}
```

```csharp
string directoryPathSelected = path_to_folder;
if (Directory.Exists(directoryPathSelected))
{
    //** the directory that has been selected
    var theDirectory = new DirectoryInfo(directoryPathSelected);

    //** get details about every file
    //**in the directory
    FileInfo[] theFiles = theDirectory.GetFiles();

    //** declare an instance of SHA256
    using (SHA256 theSha256 = SHA256.Create())
    {
        //** calculate the hash value
        //** of each of the files
        foreach (FileInfo informationOfTheFile in theFiles)
        {
            try
            {
                //** declare a stream for the file
                FileStream file_stream = informationOfTheFile.
                Open(FileMode.Open);

                //** set the cursor at the
                //** beginning of the stream
                file_stream.Position = 0;

                //** get the hash of the stream
                byte[] the_hash_value =
                theSha256.ComputeHash(file_stream);

                //** show in the console the
                //** name and hash of the file
                Console.Write($"{informationOfTheFile.Name}: ");

                ShowReadableByteArray(the_hash_value);

                //** make sure that once is
                //** done the file is closed
```

```
                    file_stream.Close();
                }
                catch (IOException e)
                {
                    Console.WriteLine($"There is an Input / Output
                    Exception:{ e.Message}");
                }
                catch (UnauthorizedAccessException e)
                {
                    Console.WriteLine($"There is an error with the
                    access: { e.Message}");
                }
            }
        }
    }
    else
    {
        Console.WriteLine("The directory cannot be found. Select
        another one.");
    }
}

//** show the byte array in a
//** possible readable format
public static void ShowReadableByteArray(byte[] byteArray)
{

    for (int k = 0; k < byteArray.Length; k++)
    {
        Console.Write($"{byteArray[k]:X2}");
        if ((k % 4) == 3) Console.Write(" ");
    }
    Console.WriteLine();
}
}
```

Figure 7-12. *Example of SHA256 implementation*

Random Number Generation

Many cryptographic operations are based on the generation of random numbers. As an example, let's consider cryptographic keys that are required to be random as much as possible in such way that it will impossible to reproduce them.

The RNGCryptoServiceProvider class [20] provides a professional implementation of a cryptographic random number generation (RNG) based on the implementation that is provided by the cryptographic service provided (CSP).

ClickOnce Manifests

ClickOnce [21] is a deployment technology that provides the ability to create a self-updating windows-based application. It offers a minimal user interaction and it is as easy as possible to use.

ClickOnce technology is still used within small and medium businesses. There are challenges due to the security of the signatures and the collection of signatures. Consumer applications are largely developed in UWP or Win32 and use different technologies for the deployment process. Some internal business applications use different deployment technologies these days.

.NET Framework 3.5 offers cryptography classes that allow professionals to get and verify the information of the signatures assigned to the ClickOnce manifests that are deployed. The classes are as follows:

- ManifestSignatureInformation class [22]. Used to obtain information related to the manifest signature. This can be achieved with the help of the VerifyMethod method. An example method for verifying the signature of a manifest can be seen in Listing 7-9.

- ManifestKinds enumeration [23]. This enumeration is used to mention which manifests should be checked. The output of the checking process is represented by an enumeration value within SignatureVerificationResult enum type [24].

- ManifestSignatureInformationCollection class [25]. The class provides guidance related to the read-only collection of the objects of the ManifestSignatureInformation class [26] for verifying the signatures.

Listing 7-9. Verifying the Signature with X509

```
public static System.Security.Cryptography.
    ManifestSignatureInformationCollection
    VerifyingTheSignature
        (ActivationContext nameOfApplication,
        System.Security.ManifestKinds listOfManifests,
        System.Security.Cryptography.X509Certificates.
                X509RevocationFlag theRevocationFlag,
        System.Security.Cryptography.X509Certificates.
                X509RevocationMode theRevocationMode);
```

The following classes provide information about signatures:

- StrongNameSignatureInformation class [27]. The class holds the (strong) name of the signature and its information for a specific manifest.

- AuthenticodeSignatureInformation class [28]. Represents a special type of signature, called authenticode, which is contained together with the signature information for a specific manifest.

- TimestampInformation class [29]. Gets the time stamp on an authenticode signature.

- TrustStatus enum. Checks if an authenticode signature can be trusted or not.

Suite B Support

.NET Framework 3.5 offers support for Suite B, an important set of cryptographic algorithms published by the National Security Agency (NSA). In 2018, NSA replaced Suite B with the Commercial National Security Algorithm Suite (CNSA) [31].

Here are some of algorithms that are included and recognized:

- Advanced Encryption Standard (AES) algorithm. Support for key sizes 128, 192, and 256.

- Secure Hash Algorithm SHA-1, SHA-256, SHA-384, and SHA-512

- Elliptic Curve Digital Signature Algorithm (ECDSA). There is support for 256-bit, 384-bit, and 521-bit curves.

- Elliptic Curve Diffie-Hellman (ECDH) algorithm. There is support for 256-bit, 384-bit, and 521-bit curves. This is used for key exchanges and secret agreements.

Cryptography Next Generation Classes

The CNG classes offer support for managed wrappers related to native CNG operations and functions. It is very important to mention that CNG is the replacement for CryptoAPI. All of the classes contain "CNG" as part of their name. The main class or CNG wrapper is CngKey [32], which is a container class that contains an abstraction of the storage and the way the CNG keys will be used.

With the help of this class, we can store a public key or key pair in a secure way and have the possibility of referring to it based on a string name. Classes related to elliptic curves, such as ECDsaCng for signatures and ECDiffieHellmanCng [33] for encryption operations, can use CngKey instances [34].

.NET Framework 3.5 supports different CNG classes, such as

- CngProvider class [35]. Deals with the provider for key storage.

- CngAlgorithm class [36]. Deals with the CNG algorithm.

- CngProperty class [37]. Contains key properties that are quite frequently used.

Conclusion

The chapter covered the most important cryptographic services from the .NET Framework, starting with version 3.5. Professionals can perform complex implementation tasks of different cryptographic algorithms and providers.

The chapter provided a short and comprehensive guide on how to implement cryptographic services and providers available in .NET without having to implement them from scratch. The cryptographic services and providers covered were

- Symmetric encryption key algorithms

- Asymmetric encryption key algorithms

- Digital signatures

- Hash algorithms and working with their values

- Random number generation

- ClickOnce manifests and solutions for checking their identities

- Suite B support and its main role

Bibliography

[1]   DSACryptoServiceProvider Class. Available online: `https://docs.microsoft.com/en-us/dotnet/api/system.security.cryptography.dsacryptoserviceprovider?view=netcore-3.1`.

[2]   RSACryptoServiceProvider Class. Available online: `https://docs.microsoft.com/en-us/dotnet/api/system.security.cryptography.rsacryptoserviceprovider?view=netcore-3.1`.

[3]   ECDiffieHellman Class. Available online: `https://docs.microsoft.com/en-us/dotnet/api/system.security.cryptography.ecdiffiehellman?view=netcore-3.1`.

[4]   ECDiffieHellmanCng Class. Available online: `https://docs.microsoft.com/en-us/dotnet/api/system.security.cryptography.ecdiffiehellmancng?view=dotnet-plat-ext-3.1`.

[5]   ECDiffieHellmanCngPublicKey Class. Available online: https://docs.microsoft.com/en-us/dotnet/api/system.security.cryptography.ecdiffiehellmancngpublickey?view=dotnet-plat-ext-3.1.

[6]   ECDiffieHellmanKeyDerivation Function Enum. Available online: https://docs.microsoft.com/en-us/dotnet/api/system.security.cryptography.ecdiffiehellmankeyderivatio nfunction?view=dotnet-plat-ext-3.1.

[7]   ECDsaCng Class. Available online: https://docs.microsoft.com/en-us/dotnet/api/system.security.cryptography.ecdsacng?view=dotnet-plat-ext-3.1.

[8]   DSACryptoServiceProvider Class. Available online: https://docs.microsoft.com/en-us/dotnet/api/system.security.cryptography.dsacryptoserviceprovider?view=netcore-3.1.

[9]   RSACryptoServiceProvider Class. Available online: https://docs.microsoft.com/en-us/dotnet/api/system.security.cryptography.rsacryptoserviceprovider?view=netcore-3.1.

[10] ECDsa Class. Available online: https://docs.microsoft.com/en-us/dotnet/api/system.security.cryptography.ecdsa?view=netcore-3.1.

[11] ECDsaCng Class. Available online: https://docs.microsoft.com/en-us/dotnet/api/system.security.cryptography.ecdsacng?view=dotnet-plat-ext-3.1.

[12] HMACSHA1 Class. Available online: https://docs.microsoft.com/en-us/dotnet/api/system.security.cryptography.hmacsha1?view=netcore-3.1.

[13] MACTripleDES Class. Available online: https://docs.microsoft.com/en-us/dotnet/api/system.security.cryptography.mactripledes?view=netframework-4.8.

[14] MD5CryptoServiceProvider Class. Available online: https://docs.microsoft.com/en-us/dotnet/api/system.security.cryptography.md5cryptoserviceprovider?view=netcore-3.1.

[15] RIPEMD160 Class. Available online: https://docs.microsoft.
com/en-us/dotnet/api/system.security.cryptography.ripemd
160?view=netframework-4.8.

[16] SHA1Managed Class. Available online: https://docs.microsoft.
com/en-us/dotnet/api/system.security.cryptography.sha1ma
naged?view=netcore-3.1.

[17] SHA256ManagedClass. Available online: https://docs.
microsoft.com/en-us/dotnet/api/system.security.
cryptography.sha256managed?view=netcore-3.1.

[18] SHA384Managed Class. Available online: https://docs.microsoft.
com/en-us/dotnet/api/system.security.cryptography.sha384
managed?view=netcore-3.1.

[19] SHA512Managed Class. Available online: https://docs.microsoft.
com/en-us/dotnet/api/system.security.cryptography.sha512
managed?view=netcore-3.1.

[20] RNGCryptoServiceProvider Class. Available online: https://
docs.microsoft.com/en-us/dotnet/api/system.security.
cryptography.rngcryptoserviceprovider?view=netcore-3.1.

[21] ClickOnce Security and Deployment. Available online: https://
docs.microsoft.com/en-us/visualstudio/deployment/
clickonce-security-and-deployment?view=vs-2019.

[22] ManifestSignatureInformation Class. Available online:
https://docs.microsoft.com/en-us/dotnet/api/system.
security.cryptography.manifestsignatureinformation?view=
netframework-4.8.

[23] ManifestKinds Enum. Available online: https://docs.
microsoft.com/en-us/dotnet/api/system.security.manifestk
inds?view=netframework-4.8.

[24] SignatureVerificationResult Enum. Available online: https://
docs.microsoft.com/en-us/dotnet/api/system.security.
cryptography.signatureverificationresult?view=netframewo
rk-4.8.

[25] ManifestSignatureInformationCollection Class. Available online: https://docs.microsoft.com/en-us/dotnet/api/system.security.cryptography.manifestsignatureinformationcollection?view=netframework-4.8.

[26] ManifestSignatureInformation Class. Available online: https://docs.microsoft.com/en-us/dotnet/api/system.security.cryptography.manifestsignatureinformation?view=netframework-4.8.

[27] StrongNameSignaureInformation Class. Available online: https://docs.microsoft.com/en-us/dotnet/api/system.security.cryptography.strongnamesignatureinformation?view=netframework-4.8.

[28] AuthenticodeSignatureInformation Class. Available online: https://docs.microsoft.com/en-us/dotnet/api/system.security.cryptography.x509certificates.authenticodesignatureinformation?view=netframework-4.8.

[29] TimestampInformation Class. Available online: https://docs.microsoft.com/en-us/dotnet/api/system.security.cryptography.x509certificates.timestampinformation?view=netframework-4.8.

[30] TrustStatus Enum. Available online: https://docs.microsoft.com/en-us/dotnet/api/system.security.cryptography.x509certificates.truststatus?view=netframework-4.8.

[31] Commercial National Security Algorithm. Available online: https://apps.nsa.gov/iaarchive/programs/iad-initiatives/cnsa-suite.cfm.

[32] CngKey Class. Available online: https://docs.microsoft.com/en-us/dotnet/api/system.security.cryptography.cngkey?view=dotnet-plat-ext-3.1.

[33] ECDiffieHellmanCng Class. Available online: https://docs.microsoft.com/en-us/dotnet/api/system.security.cryptography.ecdiffiehellmancng?view=dotnet-plat-ext-3.1.

[34] CngKey Class. Available online: `https://docs.microsoft.com/en-us/dotnet/api/system.security.cryptography.cngkey?view=dotnet-plat-ext-3.1.`

[35] CngProvider Class. Available online: `https://docs.microsoft.com/en-us/dotnet/api/system.security.cryptography.cngprovider?view=dotnet-plat-ext-3.1.`

[36] CngAlgorithm Class. Available online: `https://docs.microsoft.com/en-us/dotnet/api/system.security.cryptography.cngalgorithm?view=dotnet-plat-ext-3.1.`

[37] CngProperty Struct. Available online: `https://docs.microsoft.com/en-us/dotnet/api/system.security.cryptography.cngproperty?view=dotnet-plat-ext-3.1.`

[38] AesManaged Class. Available online: `https://docs.microsoft.com/en-us/dotnet/api/system.security.cryptography.aesmanaged?view=netcore-3.1.`

[39] DesCryptoServiceProvider Class. Available online: `https://docs.microsoft.com/en-us/dotnet/api/system.security.cryptography.aesmanaged?view=netcore-3.1.`

[40] RC2CryptoServiceProvider Class. Available online: `https://docs.microsoft.com/en-us/dotnet/api/system.security.cryptography.aesmanaged?view=netcore-3.1.`

[41] RijndelManaged Class. Available online: `https://docs.microsoft.com/en-us/dotnet/api/system.security.cryptography.rijndaelmanaged?view=netcore-3.1.`

[42] TripleDESCryptoService Provider Class. Available online: `https://docs.microsoft.com/en-us/dotnet/api/system.security.cryptography.tripledescryptoserviceprovider?view=netcore-3.1.`

CHAPTER 8

Overview of the Security. Cryptography Namespace

This chapter offers a quick overview of the main classes, structs, and enums of the System.Security.Cryptography namespace, including cryptographic services, secure encoding and decoding process of the data, and many other operations, such as hashing, generation of random numbers, and message authentication. More details about cryptographic services and their implementations can be seen in *Chapter 7*.

The goal of this chapter is to provide a comprehensive roadmap for professionals, offering a clear overview of the cryptographic services in the.NET Framework.

Classes

Table 8-1 lists the main classes that deal with the implementation and encapsulation process of cryptographic algorithms, which are in Cryptography Next Generation (CNG).

Table 8-1. *System.Security.Cryptography Namespace*

Class	Description
AesCng	Implements support for CNG for the Advanced Encryption (AES) algorithm
CngAlgorithm	Encapsulates the name of an encryption algorithm
CngAlgorithmGroup	The same as CngAlgorithm, but the encapsulation is done for a group of encryption algorithms
CngKey	Defining the functionalities of the cryptographic keys used with CNG

(continued)

Table 8-1. (*continued*)

Class	Description
CngKeyBlobFormat	The key is declared as the BLOB format and is used with CNG objects.
CngKeyCreationParameters	Advanced support for properties regarding the key creation
CngPropertyCollection	Provides strong support for a typed collection related to CNG properties
CngProvider	The name of the key storage provider (KSP) is encapsulated in order to be used further with CNG objects.
CngUIPolicy	An optional configuration parameter for the user interface (UI) CNG displays when a protected key is being accessed. It also provides encapsulation for the configuration.
DSACng	Support for the CNG implementation of the Digital Signature Algorithm (DSA)
DSAOpenSsl	Offers implementation for DSA with OpenSSL support
ECDiffieHellmanCng	Offers support for the CNG implementation of the Elliptic Curve Diffie-Hellman (ECDH) algorithm. The class' purpose is to perform cryptographic operations.
ECDiffieHellmanCngPublicKey	Creates a public key for ECDH which can be used with the ECDiffieHellmanCng class
ECDiffieHellmanOpenSsl	Offers support for the implementation of the Elliptic Curve Diffie-Hellman (ECDH) algorithm supported by OpenSSL
ECDsaCng	Offers CNG support and implementation for ECDSA
ECDsaOpenSsl	Offers support for the implementation of the Elliptic Curve Digital Signature Algorithm (ECDSA) based on OpenSSL

(*continued*)

Table 8-1. (*continued*)

Class	Description
ProtectedData	Offers methods for encrypting and decrypting data. The class cannot be inherited.
RSACng	Offers CNG support and implementation for the RSA algorithm
RSAOpenSsl	Offers support and implementations for RSA with OpenSSL support
SafeEvpPKeyHandle	Represents a special pointer (EVP_PKEY*) for OpenSSL
TripleDESCng	Offers CNG support and implementation for the Triple Data Encryption Standard (3DES) algorithm

Structs

Table 8-2 shows one of the most important structs that deal with the encapsulation of the properties of CNG key providers.

Table 8-2. *Structs within the System.Security.Cryptography Namespace*

Struct	Description
CngProperty	It provides encapsulation for the property of a CNG key or provider.

Enums

.NET Framework, starting with 3.5 and related to cryptography and security mechanisms, has a set of enums that offer important options for dealing with policies, key creation, and handling cryptographic operations. Table 8-3 mentions the main important enums that can be found within the System.Security.Cryptography namespace.

Table 8-3. *Enums within the System.Security.Cryptography Namespace*

Enum	Description
CngExportPolicies	Key export policies for a cryptographic key
CngKeyCreationOptions	Options for key creations
CngKeyHandleOpenOptions	Options for opening key handles
CngKeyOpenOptions	Options for opening a key
CngKeyUsages	Cryptographic operations for CNG keys that are used with it
CngPropertyOptions	CNG key property options
CngUIProtectionLevels	Protection level related to the key used in a user interface and its scenarios
DataProtectionScope	Gets the scope of the data protection that can be applied using the Protect(Byte[], Byte[], DataProtectionScope) method
ECKeyXmlFormat	Defines and offers support for XML serialization formats for elliptic curve keys

Security Model in .NET Framework

Figure 8-1 shows a general security model that offers a quick overview on how role-based security plays an important role in the authentication process. The authentication process plays a vital role due to the spread of the most important components of the security architecture, such as the *application domain*, the *verification process*, and *code access security*.

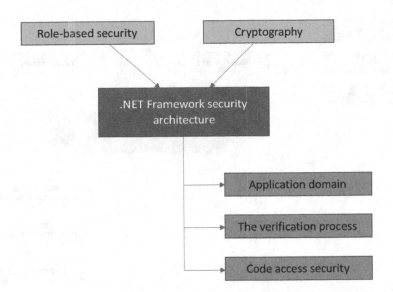

Figure 8-1. *.NET Framework security architecture with role-based security*

Looking at the components that form the security architecture during the process of implementing cryptographic mechanisms, it's important to understand the definitions and borders of each of the components. The *application domain* provides a certain level of isolating processes and is necessary to make sure that the code running in the application cannot be affected by an adversary. Based on this aspect, the isolation boundary within the application domain provides an isolation boundary for security, reliability, and versioning. Most of the application domains are created during the runtime hosts.

In Figure 8-2, you can see the main components on which the role-based security is focused, such as *authentication, authorization* and, *principal and identity*.

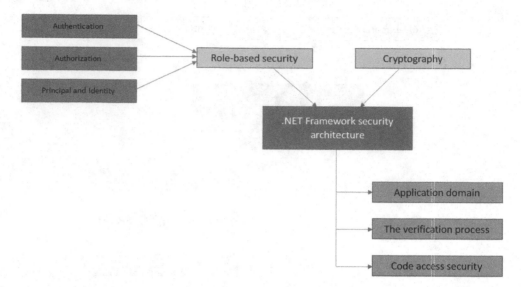

Figure 8-2. *.NET Framework security architecture with role-based security*

In Figure 8-3, the components of the *application domain* should be treated with maximum responsibility during the implementation process. During the implementation, there is a Boolean property called IsFullyTrusted.

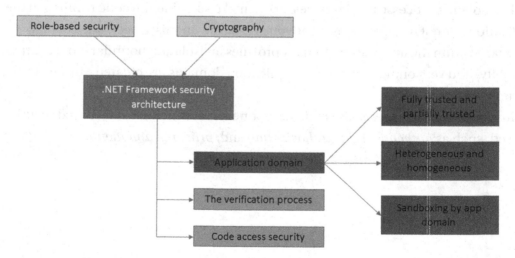

Figure 8-3. *.NET Framework security architecture with application domain components*

Achieving the goal of the first components, *fully trusted* and *partially trusted*, Listing 8-1 shows how such a process can be implemented and transposed in a real case. The same method and procedure can be used to prove if it is *heterogeneous, homogeneous,* or *sandboxing by application domain.* See Figure 8-4 for the output.

Listing 8-1. Fully Trusted or Partially Trusted Example

```
using System;
using System.Collections.Generic;
using System.Linq;
using System.Text;
using System.Threading.Tasks;

namespace FullyOrPartiallyTrustedExample
{
    class Program
    {
        public class InstanceWorker : MarshalByRefObject
        {
            static void Main()
            {
                InstanceWorker iw = new InstanceWorker();
                iw.RunningTestIfItIsFullyTrusted();

                AppDomain adSandbox = GetInternetSandbox();
                iw = (InstanceWorker)
                        adSandbox.CreateInstanceAndUnwrap(
                        typeof(InstanceWorker).Assembly.FullName,
                        typeof(InstanceWorker).FullName);
                iw.RunningTestIfItIsFullyTrusted();
            }

            public void RunningTestIfItIsFullyTrusted()
            {
                AppDomain app_domain = AppDomain.CurrentDomain;
                Console.WriteLine("\r\nApplication domain '{0}':
                IsFullyTrusted = {1}", app_domain.FriendlyName, app_domain.
                IsFullyTrusted);
```

```
        Console.WriteLine("IsFullyTrusted = {0} for the current
        assembly", typeof(InstanceWorker).Assembly.IsFullyTrusted);

        Console.WriteLine("IsFullyTrusted = {0} for mscorlib",
        typeof(int).Assembly.IsFullyTrusted);
    }

    static AppDomain GetInternetSandbox()
    {
        System.Security.Policy.Evidence theEvidenceOfHost = new
        System.Security.Policy.Evidence();

        theEvidenceOfHost.AddHostEvidence(new System.Security.
        Policy.Zone(System.Security.SecurityZone.Internet));

        System.Security.PermissionSet thePermissionSet = System.
        Security.SecurityManager.GetStandardSandbox(theEvidence
        OfHost);

        AppDomainSetup appDomainSetup = new AppDomainSetup
        {
            ApplicationBase = System.IO.Directory.
            GetCurrentDirectory()
        };

        return AppDomain.CreateDomain("Sandbox", theEvidenceOfHost,
        appDomainSetup, thePermissionSet, null);
    }
}
}
}
```

```
C:\Windows\system32\cmd.exe                                          —    □    ×

Application domain 'FullyOrPartiallyTrustedExample.exe': IsFullyTrusted = True
IsFullyTrusted = True for the current assembly
IsFullyTrusted = True for mscorlib

Application domain 'Sandbox': IsFullyTrusted = False
IsFullyTrusted = False for the current assembly
IsFullyTrusted = True for mscorlib
Press any key to continue . . . _
```

Figure 8-4. *The output of the application domain*

In Figure 8-5, you can see which components and modules are involved the verification process. You can see that the verification process looks like a collection of steps, *C# compilation, JIT compilation, Native Image Generator* and *PEVerify Tool*. In the following sections, we will analyze the most important components listed above.

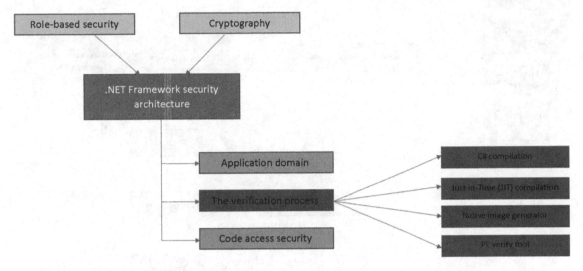

Figure 8-5.   *.NET Framework security architecture with the verification process components*

The *JIT compilation* (see Figure 8-6) is a complex process with vital points that can be exploited to gain access to different parts of the application. The goal of the JIT compilation is to speed up the execution of the code and to provide support for multiple platforms. The support is tricky since it can expose and create security breaches into the system.

Many security specialists and professionals consider this a gap in the process of assuring the security of the application because of the multiple points that can be exploited by an attacker, such as dissembling .exe or .dll files with the proper tools and proceeding with software obfuscation attacks.

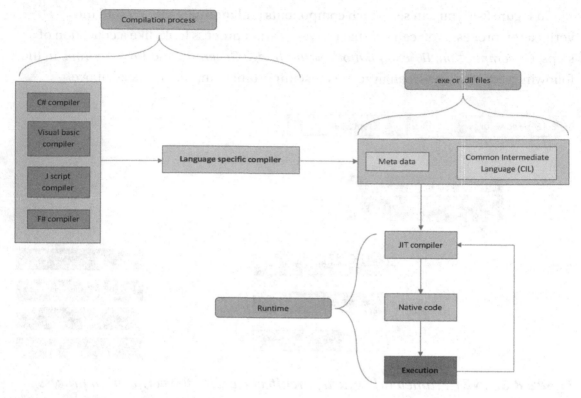

Figure 8-6. *JIT compilation process*

Once the JIT process is completed, we can move further to the *native generator image (NGEN)*. NGEN is a powerful tool that improves the performance of managed applications. NGEN, which can be found as `Ngen.exe,` creates (compiles) native images (for example, ISO files), which contain files that are compiled in a manner specific for processors as machine code, and deploys them on the native image cache of the end user's local computer. This is a dangerous point due to the fact that we never know who and what the users will have on their computers and if a malicious user is waiting for the proper moment to exploit in order to find their vulnerability point.

The last step is based on the PE Verify Tool or `Peverify.exe.` It's a very useful tool that offers an a significant amount of help to developers who are generating Microsoft Intermediate Language (MSIL), such as compiler writers, with the goal of determining if the safety requirements are met and expected with their MSIL code.

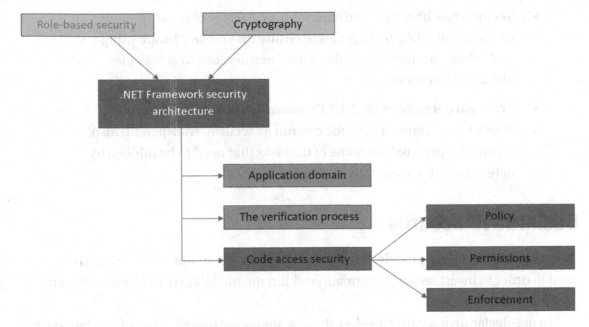

Figure 8-7. *The .NET Framework security architecture with the code access security components*

Figure 8-7 shows that we are on the last component of the .NET Framework security architecture, entitled *code access security*. All of its components are important and every professional developer should include them in their application in the developing process and in security analysis and design.

Policy, permissions, and *enforcement* should be seen as a whole unit, as a "heart" that beats for each level of trust on different code that is running in the same application.

Getting familiarized with the following code access security concepts and mechanisms will give professionals a strong background of deep knowledge on the internal mechanisms of code access security (CAS). This being said, for writing effective applications with the purpose of targeting a common language runtime, we have the following:

- **Type-safe code**: A special type of code that accesses only those types that are well-defined

- **Imperative and declarative syntax**: The code that targets a common language runtime has the ability to have an interaction with the security system. The interaction is to request permissions and override certain security settings.

- **Secure class libraries**: The libraries have a usage of security demands and their main goal is to ensure that those who are using and calling the library have the proper permissions to access the library and its resources.

- **Transparent code**: With .NET Framework 4 professionals have the ability to determine if the code can run as security-transparent. Also, identifying permissions is one of the tasks that need to be fulfilled by determining the transparence allowance.

Declarative Security

The syntax that is used by the declarative security is based on the attributes that are used in order to insert security information within the metadata of the code written by professional developers.

To use declarative security invokes, the first step is the initialization of the data state within the permission object. Listing 8-2 shows an example of a declarative syntax. The example is very suggestive and you can provide the code invoker if you have a permission entitled UserPermission.

Listing 8-2. Example of Declarative Security

```
using System.Security.Permissions;
[UserPermission(SecurityAction.Demand, Unrestricted = true)]
public class Example
{
   public Example()
   {
     //** is beging protected by the security call
   }

   public void SomeMethodForUserA()
   {
     //** is beging protected by the security call
   }
```

```
public void SomeOtherMethodForUserB()
{
    //** is beging protected by the security call
}
}
```

The SecurityAction.Demand specifies that the invokers need that permission for running the code.

Imperative Security

The syntax provided by imperative security invokes a security call to create a new instance of the object that holds the permission. The imperative security can be used to invoke demand and to override. It is very important that no requests are done. This is impossible to fulfill within imperative security.

Listing 8-3 shows an example of how the imperative syntax works for requesting the code's caller to have a certain permission called UserPermission.

Listing 8-3. Example of Imperative Security

```
public class Example
{
    public Example()
    {
        //** the constructor of the class
    }

    public void SomeMethodForUserA()
    {
        //** UserPermission has been demanded
        //** to use imperative syntax.
        UserPermission user_permission = new UserPermission();
        user_permission.Demand();
        //** here is being protected by the security call
    }
```

```
public void SomeOtherMethodForUserB()
{
    //** is not being protected by the security call
}
}
```

Conclusion

In this chapter, we discussed the System.Security.Cryptography namespace and we gave an overview of its classes, structs, and enums by pointing out their main designation. We continued our journey by explaining why professionals should work based on the .NET Framework security model, respecting their components and following the workflow as a necessary guideline.

At the end of this chapter, you will have

- A big picture of the System.Security.Cryptography namespace

- An understanding of the main designations of the classes, structs, and enums

- An understanding of the vital points of the security model within .NET Framework which can lead to a security disaster

- A clear image of how the main components work and communicate, such as the application domain, verification process, and code access security

- An in-depth understanding of JIT compilation and its process

- An understanding of how the verification process can expose security breaches

- An understanding of how, when, and why to use declarative and imperative security and an overview of their importance during the implementation process

Bibliography

[1]   Sarcar Vaskaran. *Interactive C#: Fundamentals, Core Concepts and Patterns*. Apress, 2018.

[2]   Andrew Troelsen and Philip Japikse. *Pro C# 7 with .NET and .NET Core*. Apress, 2017.

[3]   Joshi Bipin. *Beginning XML with C# 7: XML Processing and Data Access for C# Developers*. Apress, 2017.

CHAPTER 9

Cryptography Libraries in C# and .NET

In this chapter, we will cover some of the most important cryptography libraries that can be used within .NET and C# applications. Choosing a cryptography library, especially one that is open source, represents a sensitive task compared to the .NET Framework itself. You need to be sure of what you are doing and know what kind of data you are using. Relying upon an open source project for a security aspect could lead to significant security incidents if there are bugs in the open source project that can be used by an attacker.

In the following sections, we will cover these libraries: NSec [1], Bouncy Castle [2], Inferno [3], and SecureBlackbox [4].

NSec

NSec [1] is one of the most modern and easy to use cryptographic libraries for .NET Core. The library is based on Libsodium [5].

Some of the features of NSec are as follows:

- **Modern approach**. Libsodium offers a small set of cryptographic algorithms and primitives. The nice thing about NSec and Libsodium compared to other libraries is the support of features such as X25519, Ed25519, and ChaCha-Poly1305. The performance and how the features are implemented within NSec are based on a modern .NET API which is developed based on types Span<T> and ReadOnlySpan<T>.

243

© Marius Iulian Mihailescu and Stefania Loredana Nita 2021
M. I. Mihailescu and S. L. Nita, *Pro Cryptography and Cryptanalysis*,
https://doi.org/10.1007/978-1-4842-6367-9_9

- **Extremely easy to use**. It is very useful and easy to use. The elegance and reliability of NSec means it's easy to implement. It offers support for the type data model, which is designed with respect for keys and shared secrets, based on dedicated classes instead of empty byte arrays. This helps developers avoid using a key within a wrong algorithm.

- **Secure**. The mission of NSec is to make the cryptographic primitives as easy as possible.

- **Fast**. NSec and Libsodium are very fast during their cryptographic processes. There is no allocation memory for the heaps. NSec is designed to avoid any kind of memory allocations or non-useful copies.

- **Agile**. Most of the algorithms implemented in NSec are derived from a tiny set of base classes. The purpose is to provide a productive way of writing code against the algorithm interfaces instead of a specific algorithm.

In the following examples, you'll see how NSec works and how easy it is to use. The NSec uses with success some features from C# 8.0 and they are very easy to spot and understand.

Listing 9-1 shows how to work with the Ed25519 signature algorithm and sign messages. Figure 9-1 shows the output.

Listing 9-1. Ed25519 Signature

```
using System;
using System.Collections.Generic;
using System.Linq;
using System.Text;
using System.Threading.Tasks;
using NSec.Cryptography;

namespace NSecLibrary
{
    class Program
    {
        static void Main(string[] args)
```

```
    {
        Console.WriteLine("NSec Library");

        //** select the Ed25519 signature algorithm
        var algorithm = SignatureAlgorithm.Ed25519;

        //** create a new key pair
        var key = Key.Create(algorithm);

        //** generate some data to be signed
        var data = Encoding.UTF8.GetBytes("Use the Force, Luke!");

        //** sign the data using the private key
        var signature = algorithm.Sign(key, data);

        //** verify the data using the signature and the public key
        if (algorithm.Verify(key.PublicKey, data, signature))
        {
            Console.WriteLine("The message ");

            for (int i = 0; i < data.Length; i++)
            {
                Console.Write(data[i].ToString() + " ");
            }

            Console.WriteLine("\n has been verified with success.");
        }
        else
        {
            Console.WriteLine("The message: {0} has not been
            verified.", data.ToString());
        }
    }
  }
}
```

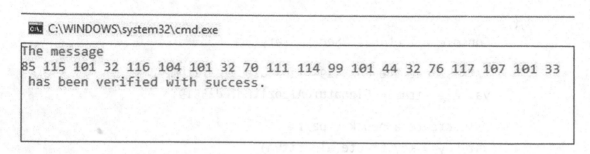

Figure 9-1. *NSec output*

NSec Installation

NSec can be found and installed using the NuGet package [6] and it contains all the details necessary for the installation process (see Figure 9-2).

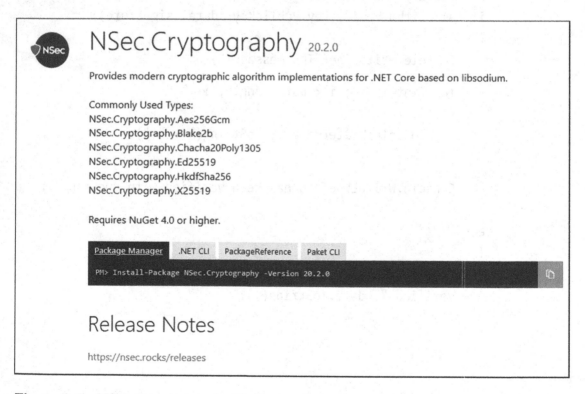

Figure 9-2. *NSec.Cryptography NuGet package*

NSec can also be added to a project using the following different ways:

- Using **dotnet CLI**:

  ```
  $ dotnet add package NSec.Cryptography --version XX.X.X
  ```

- Using **Visual Studio**:

  ```
  PM> Install-Package NSec.Cryptography -Version XX.X.X
  ```

- Using a reference in the ***.csproj file**:

  ```
  <PackageReference Include="NSec.Cryptography"
  Version="XX.X.X"/>
  ```

Bouncy Castle

Bouncy Castle is one of the most important and well-known libraries. It contains an implementation in C# of cryptographic algorithms and protocols.

It has a significant number of useful features. The list of the most important features is [7] as follows:

- "Support for parsing and generate PKCS-12 files" [7].

- "**X.509**: Support for V1 and V3 certificates (generating and parsing). Also, V2 CRLs and certificates based on the attributes" [7].

- "**PBE algorithms supported by PbeUtilities**" [7].

- "**Signature algorithms supported by SignerUtilities**" [7].

- "**Symmetric key algorithms**: AES, Blowfish, Camellia, CAST5, CAST6, ChaCha, DES, DESede, GOST28147, HC-128, HC-256, IDEA, ISAAC, Noekeon, RC2, RC4, RC5-32, RC5-64, RC6, Rijndael, Salsa20, SEED, Serpent, Skipjack, TEA/XTEA, Threefish, Tnepres, Twofish, VMPC and XSalsa20" [7].

- "**Symmetric key modes**: CBC, CFB, CTS, GOFB, OFB, OpenPGPCFB, and SIC (or CTR)" [7].

- "**Symmetric key paddings**: ISO10126d2, ISO7816d4, PKCS-5/7, TBC, X.923, and Zero Byte" [7].

- **"Asymmetric key algorithms**: ElGamal, DSA, ECDSA, NaccacheStern and RSA (with blinding)" [7].

- **"Asymmetric key paddings/encoding**s: ISO9796d1, OAEP, and PKCS-1" [7].

- **"AEAD block cipher modes**: CCM, EAX, GCM and OCB" [7].

- **"Digests**: GOST3411, Keccak, MD2, MD4, MD5, RIPEMD128, RIPEMD160, RIPEMD256, RIPEMD320, SHA-1, SHA-224, SHA-256, SHA-384, SHA-512, SHA3, Tiger, and Whirlpool" [7].

- **"XOFs**: SHAKE" [7].

- **"Signer mechanisms**: DSA, ECDSA, ECGOST3410, ECNR, GOST3410, ISO9796d2, PSS, RSA, X9.31-1998" [7].

- **"Key agreement**: Diffie-Hellman, EC-DH, EC-MQV, J-PAKE, SRP-6a" [7].

- **"MACs**: CBCBlockCipher, CFBBlockCipher, CMAC, GMAC, GOST28147, HMac, ISO9797 Alg. 3, Poly1305, SipHash, SkeinMac, VMPCMAC" [7].

- **"PBE generators**: PKCS-12, and PKCS-5 - schemes 1 and 2" [7].

- "OpenPGP (RFC 4880)" [7].

- "Cryptographic Message Syntax (CMS, RFC 3852), including streaming API" [7].

- "Online Certificate Status Protocol (OCSP, RFC 2560)" [7].

- "Time Stamp Protocol (TSP, RFC 3161)" [7].

- "TLS/DTLS client/server up to version 1.2, with support for the most common ciphersuites and extensions, and many less common ones. Non-blocking API available" [7].

- **Elliptic curve cryptography**.

Bouncy Castle Examples

Listing 9-2 shows an example of using Bouncy Castle to generate cryptographic keys. In Figure 9-3 you can see the output for a key size set to 256.

Listing 9-2. AES – Encryption with CBC Mode and PKCS5/7 Padding

```
using System;
using System.Collections.Generic;
using System.IO;
using System.Linq;
using System.Text;
using System.Threading.Tasks;
using Org.BouncyCastle.Crypto;
using Org.BouncyCastle.Crypto.Generators;
using Org.BouncyCastle.Crypto.Parameters;
using Org.BouncyCastle.OpenSsl;
using Org.BouncyCastle.Security;

namespace BouncyCastleLibrary
{
    class Program
    {
        public static string Xvalue;
        public static string Yvalue;
        public static int Dvalue;

        static void Main(string[] args)
        {
            Console.WriteLine("Using BouncyCastle Library to show how we
            can generate cryptography keys (private and public).\n");
            Console.WriteLine("Please, choose the size of the keys
            (128 or 256)");
            int key_size = Convert.ToInt32(Console.ReadLine());

            if (key_size == 128)
                KeyGeneration(128);
```

```
    else if (key_size == 256)
        KeyGeneration(256);
}

public static AsymmetricCipherKeyPair GenerateKeys(int keySize)
{
    //** choosing ECDSA for key generation
    var key_generation = new ECKeyPairGenerator("ECDSA");

    //** for creating randomly values
    var randomly_secure_value = new SecureRandom();

    //** generating the parameters based on the random value and
        size of the key
    var key_generation_parameters = new KeyGenerationParameters(ran
    domly_secure_value, keySize);

    //** proceed with the initialization of the generation
        algorithm with parameters
    key_generation.Init(key_generation_parameters);

    //** the key pair generation
    return key_generation.GenerateKeyPair();
}

public static void KeyGeneration(int key_size)
{
    //** generating process
    var key_pair = GenerateKeys(key_size);
    TextWriter text_writer = new StringWriter();
    PemWriter pem_writer = new PemWriter(text_writer);

    pem_writer.WriteObject(key_pair.Private);
    pem_writer.Writer.Flush();

    string privateKey = text_writer.ToString();
    Console.WriteLine("The private key is: {0}", privateKey);

    ECPrivateKeyParameters privateKeyParam = (ECPrivate
    KeyParameters)key_pair.Private;
```

```
Console.WriteLine("D value is: {0}", privateKeyParam.D.
ToString());
text_writer = new StringWriter();
pem_writer = new PemWriter(text_writer);
pem_writer.WriteObject(key_pair.Public);
pem_writer.Writer.Flush();

ECPublicKeyParameters publicKeyParam = (ECPublicKeyParameters)
key_pair.Public;
string publickey = text_writer.ToString();
Console.WriteLine("The public key is: {0}", publickey);
Console.ReadKey();

Xvalue = publicKeyParam.Q.XCoord.ToBigInteger().ToString();
Yvalue = publicKeyParam.Q.YCoord.ToBigInteger().ToString();
        }
    }
}
```

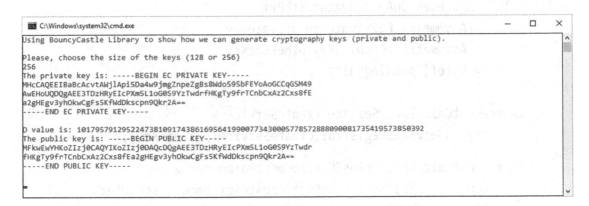

Figure 9-3. *Generating cryptography keys using BouncyCastle*

The next three examples (see Listing 9-3, Listing 9-4 and Listing 9-5) show how to deal with key agreement and exchange algorithms.

If you are working with a basic agreement (see Listing 9-3) that uses a cofactor with an agreed value, the following example should be quite explanatory.

Listing 9-3. Basic Agreement with an Agreed Value

```
public byte[] AgreementOnAgreedValue
                    (AsymmetricECPrivateKey privateKey,
                     AsymmetricECPublicKey otherEncKey)
{
    IAgreementCalculatorService createService =
        CryptoServicesRegistrar.CreateService(privateKey);

    IAgreementCalculator<FipsEC.AgreementParameters>
        contract_agreement =
        createService.CreateAgreementCalculator(FipsEC.Cdh);

    return contract_agreement.Calculate(otherEncKey);
}
```

In Listing 9-4, you can see how to work with a SHA256 function and with a PRF (Pseudo Random Function) function in order to compute on the agreed value.

Listing 9-4. Agreement Using PRF

```
public byte[] AgreementOnAgreedValueWithPrf
            (AsymmetricECPrivateKey privateKey,
             AsymmetricECPublicKey otherEncKey,
             byte[] paddingSalt)
{
    IAgreementCalculatorService createService =
        CryptoServicesRegistrar.CreateService(privateKey);

    IAgreementCalculator<FipsEC.AgreementParameters>
        contract_agreement = dhFact.CreateAgreementCalculator
        (FipsEC.Cdh.WithKeyMaterialGenerator
        (new FipsPrfKmg
                    (FipsPrfAlgorithm.Sha256HMac,
    paddingSalt));

    return contract_agreement.Calculate(otherEncKey);
}
```

Listing 9-5 shows another type of agreement with X9.63 KDF (Key Derivation Function).

Listing 9-5. Working with an Agreement Based on X9.63 KDF

```
public byte[] AgreementWithCofactorAndKdf
    (AsymmetricECPrivateKey privateKey,
     AsymmetricECPublicKey otherEncKey,
     byte[] paddingSalt)
{
    IAgreementCalculatorService createService =
        CryptoServicesRegistrar.CreateService(privateKey);

    IAgreementCalculator<FipsEC.AgreementParameters>
        contract_agreement =
            dhFact.CreateAgreementCalculator
            (FipsEC.Cdh.WithKeyMaterialGenerator
            (new FipsKdfKmg(FipsKdf.X963,
                    paddingSalt, 32));

    return agreement.Calculate(otherEncKey);
}
```

Bouncy Castle Installation

Bouncy Castle can be found and installed using the NuGet package [8] and it contains all the details necessary for the installation process (see Figure 9-4).

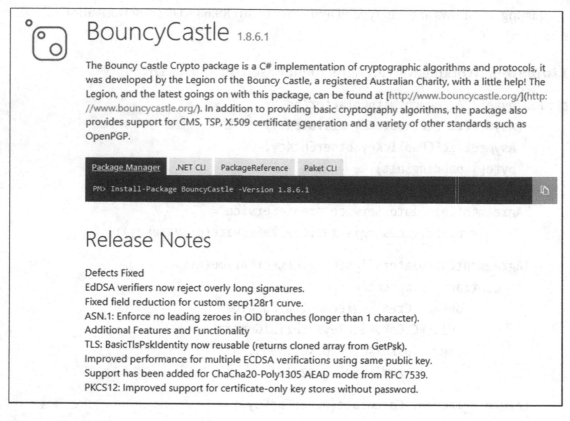

Figure 9-4. Bouncy Castle NuGet package

Bouncy Castle can also be added to a project in the following ways:

- Using **dotnet CLI**:

  $ dotnet add package BouncyCastle --version XX.X.X

- Using **Visual Studio**:

  PM> Install-Package BouncyCastle -Version XX.X.X

- Using a reference in the ***.csproj file**:

  <PackageReference Include="BouncyCastle" Version="XX.X.X"/>

Inferno

Inferno is another interesting cryptographic library for .NET developed using C#. It offers a unique elegance in writing the code and the performances obtained during processing the code are quite promising.

The following list represents the features [9] of Inferno:

- "[random]: CryptoRandom (.NET Random done right)" [9]

- "[ciphers]: AES-256 only (fast, constant-time, side-channel-resistant AES-NI)" [9]

- "[hi-level]: AEAD (AES-CTR-HMAC). Streaming AEAD (EtM Transforms)" [9]

- " [ciphers-misc]: AES-CTR implementation (CryptoTransform) " [9]

- "[ciphers-misc]: AEAD (AES-CBC-HMAC)" [9]

- "[hash]: SHA2 hash factories (256, 384, 512). SHA-384 is recommended (default)" [9]

- "[hash]: SHA1 hash factory (mostly for legacy integration)" [9]

- "[mac]: HMAC2 (.NET HMAC done right)" [9]

- "[mac]: HMAC-SHA1, HMAC-SHA2 factories" [9]

- "[kdf]: HKDF, PBKDF2, SP800_108_Ctr. Any HMAC factory is supported" [9]

- "[otp]: TOTP" [9]

- "[helpers]" [9]

  - "Constant-time byte and string comparison" [9]

  - "Safe UTF8" [9]

  - "Fast 64-bit byte-array Xor" [9]

Inferno Examples

The following examples show case studies of how the library should be used. In Listing 9-6, you can see the basic declaration of functions that deal with encryption, decryption, and authentication. Note the flexibility and the suggestive declaration of the functions.

Listing 9-6. Encryption, Decryption, and Authentication Functions

```
//** The namespace that has to be used when working with
//** Inferno is: SecurityDrive.Inferno
//** If SecurityDrive.Inferno is not visible it means that is
//** not properly installed and it is necessary to check the
//** section "Inferno Installation"

public static class BasicOperations
{
    public static byte[] Encrypt(byte[] master_crypto_key,
        ArraySegment<byte> clearText,
        ArraySegment<byte>? saltPadding = null);

    public static byte[] Decrypt(byte[] master_crypto_key,
        ArraySegment<byte> cryptotext,
        ArraySegment<byte>? saltPadding = null);

    public static bool Authenticate(byte[] master_crypto_key,
        ArraySegment<byte> cryptotext,
        ArraySegment<byte>? saltPadding = null);
}
```

Working with hash functions (see Listing 9-7) is quite interesting and easy. It is very important once you reached at the end of the process and application to invoke dispose.

Listing 9-7. Working with Hash

```
public static Func<SHA384> HashFactory
```

Listing 9-8 shows how to use a HMAC.

Listing 9-8. Using HMAC

```
var dataForHmac = Utils.SafeUTF8.GetBytes("Welcome To Apress!");

//** this is for HMACSHA384
using (var theHmac = SuiteB.HmacFactory())
{
    theHmac.Key = new byte[] { 6, 5, 4, 3, 2 };
    theHmac.ComputeHash(dataForHmac).ToBase16().Dump();
}
```

Listing 9-9 shows a case of DSA (Digital Signature Algorithm) usage. Figure 9-5 shows the output.

Listing 9-9. Dealing with a DSA

```
using SecurityDriven.Inferno.Extensions;
using System;
using System.Collections.Generic;
using System.Linq;
using System.Security.Cryptography;
using System.Text;
using System.Threading.Tasks;

namespace InfernoLibrary
{
    class Program
    {
        static void Main(string[] args)
        {
            //** generate the DSA keys
            CngKey thePrivateKey = CngKeyExtensions.CreateNewDsaKey();
            //** generate the cryptographic keys
            //** that will be used with DSA
            byte[] dsa_private_key_blob = thePrivateKey.GetPrivateBlob();
```

```csharp
//** convert and store private key as bytes
byte[] dsa_public_key_blob = thePrivateKey.GetPublicBlob();

//** convert and store public key as bytes
CngKey dsa_public_key = dsa_public_key_blob.
ToPublicKeyFromBlob();

//** some data (sample)
byte[] data_sample = Guid.NewGuid().ToByteArray();
byte[] theSignature = null;

//** using the private key, generate the
//** DSA signature and store it properly
using (var ecdsaAlgorithm = new ECDsaCng(thePrivateKey) {
HashAlgorithm = CngAlgorithm.Sha384 })
{
    theSignature = ecdsaAlgorithm.SignData(data_sample);
}

//** play with the data
data_sample[5] ^= 1;

Console.WriteLine("Private key is: {0}", BitConverter.
ToString(dsa_private_key_blob));
Console.WriteLine("\nPublic key is: {0}", BitConverter.
ToString(dsa_public_key_blob));
Console.WriteLine("\nSample data: {0}", BitConverter.
ToString(data_sample));
Console.WriteLine("\nThe signature is: {0}", BitConverter.
ToString(theSignature));

//** using the public key, verify the DSA signature
using (var ecdsaAlgorithm = new ECDsaCng(dsa_public_key){
HashAlgorithm = CngAlgorithm.Sha384})
{
    if (ecdsaAlgorithm.VerifyData(data_sample, theSignature))
```

```
            {
                Console.WriteLine("\nOups! Something went wrong.
                Signature was unable to be verified properly.");
            }
            else
            {
                Console.WriteLine("\nThe signature has been verified
                with success.");
            }

            Console.ReadKey();
        }
    }
}
}
```

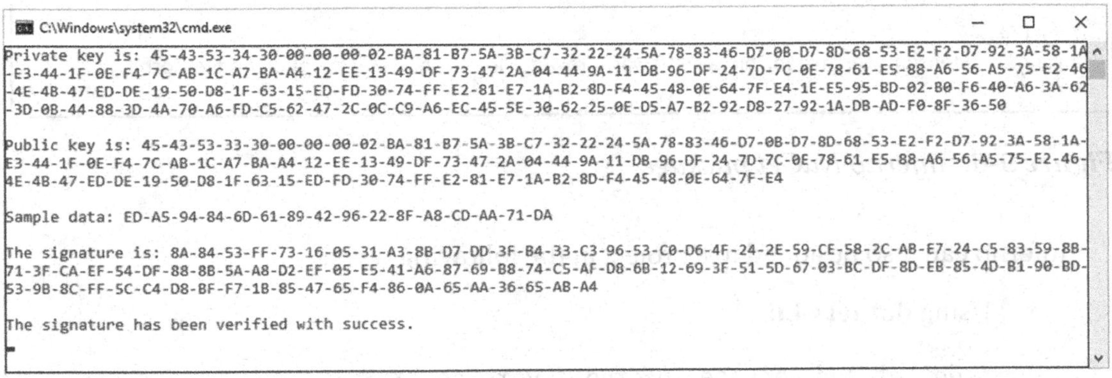

Figure 9-5. *The output*

Inferno Installation

Inferno can be found and installed using the NuGet package [10] and it contains all the details necessary for the installation process (see Figure 9-6).

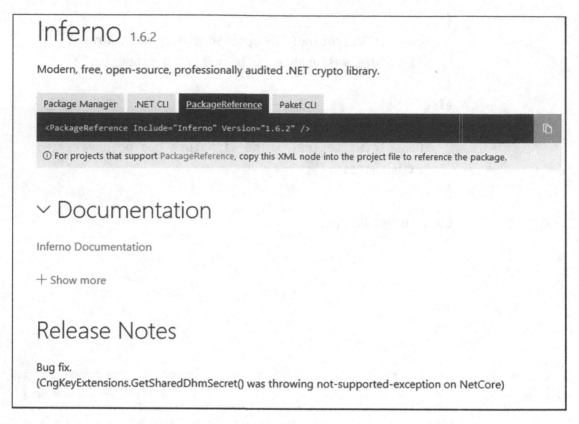

Figure 9-6. Inferno NuGet package

Inferno can also be added to a project in the following ways:

- Using **dotnet CLI**:

  $ dotnet add package Inferno --version XX.X.X

- Using **Visual Studio**:

  PM> Install-Package Inferno -Version XX.X.X

- Using a reference in the ***.csproj file**:

  <PackageReference Include="Inferno" Version="XX.X.X"/>

SecureBlackbox

SecureBlackbox is one of the most comprehensive sets of tools and classes for dealing with digital security and security for a network.

Developing security solutions is done in the same way as in NSec or Inferno. The methods and functions are similar to the ones from NSec and Inferno. The differences are very few and are specific to the allocation of buffer arrays.

The library is not free. To run the example in Listing 9-10, you need a license. Once you run the application, the message from Figure 9-7 will be shown.

For testing purposes, for the example from Listing 9-10, the owner of the library can be contacted and they will provide to you with a temporary license key.

Once the license is received (usually it is a text file, such as LicenseKey.txt), two functions can be called and the license as a key parameter to them. The two functions are void SetLicenseKey(ByteArray key) and void SetLicenseKey(string key).

If you need more key licenses at the same time, just call the function(s) several times with different file names. Each license should have a different name.

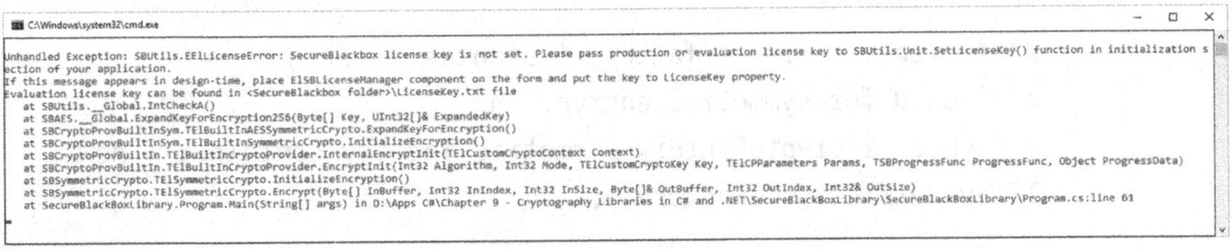

Figure 9-7. *License required to run the example*

Listing 9-10. Example of Symmetric Encryption with SecureBlackbox

```
using SBSymmetricCrypto;
using System;
using System.Collections.Generic;
using System.Linq;
using System.Security.Cryptography;
using System.Text;
using System.Threading.Tasks;
```

```csharp
namespace SecureBlackBoxLibrary
{
    class Program
    {
        static void Main(string[] args)
        {
            var key = "b14ca5898a4e4133bbce2ea2315a1916";
            byte[] encryptionKeyBuffer;
            byte[] initializationBuffer = new byte[16];

            using (Aes aes = Aes.Create())
            {
                aes.Key = Encoding.UTF8.GetBytes(key);
                aes.IV = initializationBuffer;

                encryptionKeyBuffer = aes.Key;
                initializationBuffer = aes.IV;
            }

            //** create a crypto factory instances
            //** used for symmetric encryption
            TElSymmetricCryptoFactory symmetric_factory_container = new
            TElSymmetricCryptoFactory();

            //** use the factory container to
            //** declare an appropriate algorithm
            TElSymmetricCrypto symmetric_encryption = symmetric_factory_
            container.CreateInstance (SBConstants.Unit.SB_ALGORITHM_CNT_
            AES256, TSBSymmetricCryptoMode.cmDefault);

            //** declare a key and assign the proper
            //** value for the secret key and the initialization vector
            TElSymmetricKeyMaterial km = new TElSymmetricKeyMaterial(null);
            km.Key = encryptionKeyBuffer;
            km.IV = initializationBuffer;

            //** assign the key container to the cryptographic
            //** object using the property KeyMaterial
            symmetric_encryption.KeyMaterial = km;
```

```
//** proceed further with the encryption
byte[] input_buffer = Encoding.UTF8.GetBytes("Welcome to
Apress!");

//** declare the output_buffer and output_size and initialize
//** them with 0. In this way we will point out that the first
//** invoked is getting the call.
byte[] output_buffer = null;
int output_size = 0;

//** Finding out about the output
//** length - this may be approximate
symmetric_encryption.Encrypt(input_buffer, 0, input_buffer.
Length, ref output_buffer, 0, ref output_size);

//** create an allocation as an array for the output data
output_buffer = new byte[output_size];

//** do the encryption
symmetric_encryption.Encrypt(input_buffer, 0, input_buffer.
Length, ref output_buffer, 0, ref output_size);

//**copy the data that has been encrypted to a dedicate buffer
output_buffer = SBUtils.Unit.CloneArray(output_buffer, 0,
output_size);

//** before continue with the encryption
//** invoke InitializeEncryption method
//** within the cryptographic object
symmetric_encryption.InitializeEncryption();

//** as much as it is required, pass the data as necessary
//** using invokations of EncryptUpdate()
symmetric_encryption.EncryptUpdate(input_buffer, 0, input_
buffer.Length, ref output_buffer, 0,ref output_size);
output_buffer = SBUtils.Unit.CloneArray(output_buffer, 0,
output_size);
```

```
//** Once we reach at the end of EncryptUpdate(),
//** we need to endup the encryption
//** by invoking FinalizeEncryption() method
symmetric_encryption.FinalizeEncryption(ref output_buffer, 0,
ref output_size);
output_buffer = SBUtils.Unit.CloneArray(output_buffer, 0,
output_size);

Console.WriteLine("The encryption key is: {0}", key);
Console.WriteLine("\nThe buffer for encryption key is: {0}",
BitConverter.ToString(encryptionKeyBuffer));
Console.WriteLine("\nThe initialization buffer is: {0}",
BitConverter.ToString(initializationBuffer));
Console.WriteLine("\nThe encryption is: {0}", symmetric_
encryption.ToString());
Console.ReadKey();
        }
    }
}
```

SecureBlackbox Installation

SecureBlackbox can be found and installed using the NuGet package [10] and it contains
all the details necessary for the installation process (see Figure 9-8).

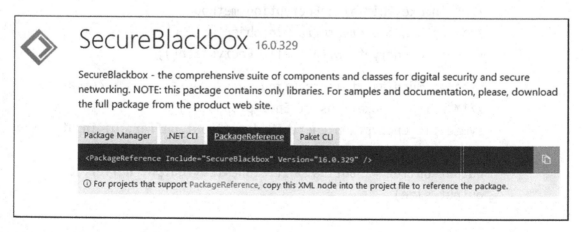

Figure 9-8. *SecureBlackbox NuGet package*

SecureBlackbox can also be added to a project in the following ways:

- Using **dotnet CLI**:

  `$ dotnet add package SecureBlackbox --version XX.X.X`

- Using **Visual Studio**:

  `PM> Install-Package SecureBlackbox -Version XX.X.X`

- Using a reference in the ***.csproj file**:

  `<PackageReference Include=" SecureBlackbox" Version="XX.X.X"/>`

Conclusion

In this chapter, we covered the most important cryptography libraries (NSec, Bouncy Castle, Inferno, and SecureBlackbox) that can serve as guidance, extra libraries, and tools for achieving the confidentiality, integrity, and authenticity of the data within applications developed by professionals. The criteria used for selecting these libraries are their recognition by other professionals in the field and FIPS and NIST standards.

The libraries can be used in parallel with the System.Security.Cryptography namespace, offering a more exhaustive coverage of the cryptographic primitives.

Bibliography

[1]   NSec. Available online: `https://nsec.rocks/`.

[2]   Bouncy Castle. Available online: `https://cryptobook.nakov.com/crypto-libraries-for-developers/c-crypto-libraries`.

[3]   Inferno. Available online: `https://nugetmusthaves.com/Package/Inferno`.

[4]   SecureBlackbox. Available online: `https://nugetmusthaves.com/Package/SecureBlackbox`.

[5]   Libsodium for .NET. Available online: `https://nugetmusthaves.com/Package/libsodium-net`.

[6]   NSec.Cryptography. Available online: `www.nuget.org/packages/NSec.Cryptography/20.2.0`.

[7]   Bouncy Castle Features. Available online: `www.bouncycastle.org/csharp/index.html`.

[8]   Bouncy Castle NuGet Package. Available online: `www.nuget.org/packages/BouncyCastle/`.

[9]   Inferno Features and Project. Available online: `https://securitydriven.net/inferno/`.

[10]   Inferno NuGet Package. Available online: `www.nuget.org/packages/Inferno/`.

[11]   SecureBlackbox NuGet Package. Available online: `www.nuget.org/packages/SecureBlackbox/`.

PART II

Cryptography

CHAPTER 10

Elliptic-Curve Cryptography

Elliptic-curve cryptography (ECC) is a public-key cryptography approach based on the algebraic structure of elliptic curves over finite fields. ECC can be used in cryptography applications and primitives, such as *key agreements, digital signatures,* and *pseudo-random generators.* They can be used for operations such as encryption, an operation that is achieved through a combination between key agreements with a symmetric encryption scheme. Some other interesting usages can be seen in several tries of integer factorization algorithms that are based on elliptic curves (EC), with applications in cryptography, such as Lenstra Elliptic-Curve Factorization (L-ECC) [1].

Microsoft .NET offers strong support for ECC, through Cryptography Next Generation (CNG) implementation for the Elliptic Curve Diffie-Hellman (ECDH) algorithm.

For extended functionalities for cryptanalysis usage, there are few open source libraries that are available for ECC in C#. One of the most used is Bouncy Castle, with support for the P-128 curve and a plan to extend support to the P-256 curve.

In this chapter, we will provide two examples. The first example (Listing 10-1) uses the `ECDiffieHellmanCng` class from Microsoft .NET, and the second example (Listing 10-2) uses the Bouncy Castle library to illustrate the functionalities.

ECDiffieHellmanCng Class

Listing 10-1 shows how the `ECDiffieHellmanCng` class can be used to set a key exchange. We will explain how the key is used further for message encryption that is sent through a public channel and decrypted by the receiver (see Figure 10-1).

269

© Marius Iulian Mihailescu and Stefania Loredana Nita 2021
M. I. Mihailescu and S. L. Nita, *Pro Cryptography and Cryptanalysis*,
https://doi.org/10.1007/978-1-4842-6367-9_10

```
Command Prompt                                                          —    □    ×

D:\Proiecte\ECDiffiedHellmanCng\ECDiffiedHellmanCng\bin\Debug>ECDiffiedHellmanCng.exe

(Encrypted) Message sended from Alice -> Bob
================================================
        Secret message is: Hello Bob, Welcome to CryptoWorld!
        EncryptedMessage is: new byte[] { 207 56 234 238 18 142 48 87 219 119 88 183 139 5 150 65 172 6 177 245 157 69 1
78 31 135 10 130 9 208 197 100 46 68 187 243 35 22 13 70 211 46 61 67 201 252 13 68 149 }
        Initialize vector is: new byte[] { 1 61 148 202 117 184 153 1 12 126 80 244 157 74 243 231 }

ALICE Side
==========
        Alice sends: Hello Bob, Welcome to CryptoWorld!
        Alice public key: new byte[] { 69 67 75 53 66 0 0 0 0 122 96 134 19 27 69 45 175 5 26 40 177 148 181 11 93 147 1
49 169 153 184 135 10 247 122 218 199 165 4 51 159 207 21 120 154 125 44 81 56 62 24 227 192 255 99 219 25 30 42 29 188
216 180 13 17 136 28 113 124 140 71 128 176 118 203 1 232 131 183 253 43 168 153 118 232 1 183 136 5 32 161 69 104 113 1
51 159 60 218 183 119 97 165 92 123 12 210 200 58 254 127 63 214 220 109 117 9 52 162 228 203 204 32 95 17 142 208 67 32
 110 178 22 61 186 187 179 145 231 64 179 219 68 }
        The initialization vector (IV): new byte[] { 1 61 148 202 117 184 153 1 12 126 80 244 157 74 243 231 }
        Length of the message: 34

BOB Side
============
The plaintext message is: Hello Bob, Welcome to CryptoWorld!
The length of the message received by Bob is : 34

D:\Proiecte\ECDiffiedHellmanCng\ECDiffiedHellmanCng\bin\Debug>_
```

Figure 10-1.   *Output of encryption using ECDiffieHellmanCng*

Below, let's take a close look at the implementation.

Listing 10-1.   Implementation of ECDiffieHellmanCng

```
using System;
using System.Collections.Generic;
using System.Linq;
using System.Text;
using System.Threading.Tasks;
using System.IO;
using System.Security.Cryptography;

namespace ECDiffiedHellmanCng
{
    class Program
    {
        //** Alice User
        class UserA
```

```csharp
{
    //** represents the public key of alice
    public static byte[] pk_alice;

    public static void Main(string[] args)
    {
        string message_send_by_alice = "Hello Bob,
                            Welcome to CryptoWorld!";

        using (ECDiffieHellmanCng user_alice = new
                            ECDiffieHellmanCng())
        {
            user_alice.KeyDerivationFunction =
            ECDiffieHellmanKeyDerivationFunction.Hash;

            user_alice.HashAlgorithm =
                CngAlgorithm.Sha256;
            pk_alice =
                    user_alice.PublicKey.ToByteArray();

            //** we send to Bob
            UserB user_bob = new UserB();
            CngKey k = CngKey.Import(user_bob.pk_bob,
                        CngKeyBlobFormat.EccPublicBlob);

            byte[] alice_key =
                    user_alice.DeriveKeyMaterial(CngKey
                .Import(user_bob.pk_bob,
                    CngKeyBlobFormat.EccPublicBlob));

            byte[] encryptionOfMessage = null;
            byte[] initialize_vector = null;

            //** sending the message
            SendMessage(alice_key,
                        message_send_by_alice,
                        out encryptionOfMessage,
                        out initialize_vector);
```

```
            Console.WriteLine("\n\nALICE Side");
            Console.WriteLine("==========\n");
            Console.WriteLine("\tAlice sends: {0}",
                                    message_send_by_alice);
        Console.WriteLine("\tAlice public key:{0}",
                PrintByteArray(pk_alice).ToString());

            Console.WriteLine("\tThe initialization
                    vector (IV): {0} ",
            PrintByteArray(initialize_vector).
                                        ToString());

    Console.WriteLine("\tLength of the message: {0}",
                message_send_by_alice.Length.ToString());

    //** receiving message
    user_bob.ReceivingMessage(encryptionOfMessage,
                                    initialize_vector);
        }
    }

    //** the function will help us
    //** to convert a byte to string.
    public static StringBuilder PrintByteArray(byte[] bytes)
    {
        var string_builder = new StringBuilder("new byte[] { ");

        foreach (var theByte in bytes)
        {
            string_builder.Append(theByte + " ");
        }

        string_builder.Append("}");
        return string_builder;
    }
```

```csharp
    private static void SendMessage(byte[] key,
                    string theSecretMessage,
                    out byte[] encryption_message,
                    out byte[] initialize_vector)
{
    //** we will use AES cryptography
    //** algorithm for encryption
using (Aes aes_crypto_alg = new
                    AesCryptoServiceProvider())
    {
        aes_crypto_alg.Key = key;
        initialize_vector = aes_crypto_alg.IV;

        //** we encrypt the message using AES
        using (MemoryStream encrypted_text = new
                MemoryStream())
        using (CryptoStream crypto_stream = new
                CryptoStream(encrypted_text,
                aes_crypto_alg.CreateEncryptor(),
                CryptoStreamMode.Write))
        {
            byte[] clear_text =
                Encoding.UTF8.GetBytes(theSecretMessage);
            crypto_stream.Write(clear_text,
                                    0, clear_text.Length);

        //** close the stream!
            crypto_stream.Close();
            encryption_message =
            encrypted_text.ToArray();
        }

        Console.WriteLine("\n\n(Encrypted) Message
                sent from Alice -> Bob");
```

```
                    Console.WriteLine("\tSecret message is: {0}",
                    theSecretMessage.ToString());

                    Console.WriteLine("\tEncryptedMessage is: {0}",
                    PrintByteArray(encryption_message).ToString());

                    Console.WriteLine("\tInitialize vector is: {0}",
                    PrintByteArray(initialize_vector).ToString());
                }
            }
        }

    //** User Bob
    public class UserB
    {
        //** the public key of bon
        public byte[] pk_bob;
        private byte[] bob_key;

        public UserB()
        {
            using (ECDiffieHellmanCng user_bob = new
            ECDiffieHellmanCng())
            {
                user_bob.KeyDerivationFunction =
                ECDiffieHellmanKeyDerivationFunction.Hash;

                user_bob.HashAlgorithm =
                                    CngAlgorithm.Sha256;

                pk_bob = user_bob.PublicKey.ToByteArray();
                bob_key =
                    user_bob.DeriveKeyMaterial(CngKey.Import
                    (UserA.pk_alice, CngKeyBlobFormat.EccPublicBlob));
            }
        }
```

```
public void ReceivingMessage(
            byte[] message_encrypted,
            byte[] initialize_vector)
{
    using (Aes aes = new
            AesCryptoServiceProvider())
    {
        aes.Key = bob_key;
        aes.IV = initialize_vector;

        //** let's decrypt the message
        using (MemoryStream plaintext = new
                            MemoryStream())
        {
            using (CryptoStream crypto_stream =
            new CryptoStream(plaintext,
            aes.CreateDecryptor(),
            CryptoStreamMode.Write))
            {
                crypto_stream.Write(
                    message_encrypted,
                    0,
                    message_encrypted.Length);

                crypto_stream.Close();
                string message = Encoding.UTF8.
                GetString(plaintext.ToArray());

Console.WriteLine("\n\nBOB Side");
Console.WriteLine("The plaintext message is: {0}", message);
Console.WriteLine("The length of the message received by Bob is : {0}",
message.Length.ToString());
Console.ReadKey();
                }
            }
        }
```

```
            }
        }
    }
}
```

Using ECC with the Bouncy Castle Library

The Bouncy Castle library [2] represents a collection of APIs that can be used in cryptography. For this example, we will use P-128 curve support, we will generate the keys for a selected curve, and we will output the result in the console.

The following example is composed of two classes, the `Program` class that represents the main class of the project and the `EllipticCurveKeyGenerator` class. For a quick overview on the project structure, see Figure 10-2. Before running the project, please install Bouncy Library from Microsoft Visual Studio or using PowerShell. In the "Bouncy Castle Installation" section, there is a guide on how to perform the installation using Microsoft Visual Studio.

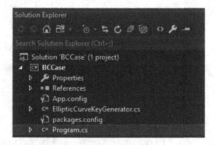

Figure 10-2. *Bouncy Castle project structure*

The `Program` class (see Listing 10-2) represents the main class of the project and contains three functions: `Main`, `GeneratePKeys()`, and `AsymmetricCipherKeyPair GenerateKeys()`. The description of each function and its purpose is as follows:

- `Main` function: The main function that will be executed first. Contains the general output message and calls the `GeneratePKeys()` function for two types of sizes, 128 and 256 bytes.

- `GeneratePKeys(int intSize)` function: The function generates a pair of keys based on the size that has been sent as a parameter in the Main function. The `TextWriter` class helps us write in sequential series the characters. It is an abstract class. The `PemWriter` class represents a general class to help us to work with OpenSSL PEM objects. The `ECPrivateKeyParameters` class is used to specify the private key parameters of the elliptic curve, as in the same way for `ECPublicKeyParameters` class.

- `AsymmetricCipherKeyPair GenerateKeys(int keySize)` function: The function uses ECDSA to generate the keys for the cipher. In order to generate the parameters, we will use the `KeyGenerationParameters` constructor class and we will send two parameters, the random secure value (`secureRandom`) and the size of the key (`keySize`). With the `Init()` function we will initialize the ECDSA algorithm, and using `GenerateKeyPair()` function the pair of keys will be generated.

The `EllipticCurveKeyGenerator` class (see Listing 10-3) overrides the functions and methods from the `IAsymmetricCipherKeyPairGenerator` interface. The class has two constructors, `EllipticCurveKeyGenerator()` and `EllipticCurveKeyGenerator(string choose_algorithm)`. Note that the first one is never used in our example. The rest of the functions and their goals are as follows:

- The `Init(KeyGenerationParameters)` function: The goal of the function is to initialize the parameters for generating the keys.

- The `AsymmetricCipherKeyPair GenerateKeyPair()` function: As the name says, the function is used to generate a pair of keys.

- The `ECMultiplier CreateBasePointMulitplier()` function: The function returns a fixed point multiplier.

- The `X9ECParameters IdentifyEllipticCurveByObjectIdentifier (DerObjectIdentifier object_identifier)` function: Based on the object identifier, the function returns the parameters of elliptic curve according with X9 format.

- The ECPublicKeyParameters GetCorrespondingPublicKey(ECPr
  ivateKeyParameters private_key) function: The function is an
  internal static one and its purpose is to obtain the corresponding
  public key based on the private key that was set for the elliptic curve
  as private parameter.

Listing 10-2. Generating Cryptographic Keys Using Bouncy Castle

```
using System;
using System.Collections.Generic;
using System.IO;
using System.Linq;
using System.Text;
using System.Threading.Tasks;
using Org.BouncyCastle.Crypto;
using Org.BouncyCastle.Crypto.Parameters;
using Org.BouncyCastle.Security;
using Org;
namespace BCCase
{
    class Program
    {
        static void Main(string[] args)
        {
            Console.WriteLine("Generate private
                          /public key pair");

            //** 1st case when the key size is 128 b
            Console.WriteLine("CASE 1 - 128 Bytes\n");
            GeneratePKeys(128);

            //** 2nd case when the key size is 256 b
            Console.WriteLine("\n\n\nCASE 2 - 256 Bytes\n");
            GeneratePKeys(256);

        }
```

```
public static void GeneratePKeys(int intSize)
{
    //Generating p-128 keys 128 specifies strength
    var keyPair = GenerateKeys(intSize);
    TextWriter textWriter = new StringWriter();

    Org.BouncyCastle.OpenSsl.PemWriter pemWriter = new
       Org.BouncyCastle.OpenSsl.PemWriter(textWriter);

    pemWriter.WriteObject(keyPair.Private);
    pemWriter.Writer.Flush();

     string privateKey = textWriter.ToString();


    Console.WriteLine("\tThe private key is:");
    Console.WriteLine("\t\t\t {0}", privateKey.ToString());

    ECPrivateKeyParameters privateKeyParam =
                      (ECPrivateKeyParameters)keyPair.Private;

    Console.WriteLine("\tD parameter: {0}",
                      privateKeyParam.D.ToString());

    textWriter = new StringWriter();

    pemWriter = new
          Org.BouncyCastle.OpenSsl.PemWriter(textWriter);

    pemWriter.WriteObject(keyPair.Public);
    pemWriter.Writer.Flush();

        ECPublicKeyParameters publicKeyParam =
                   (ECPublicKeyParameters)keyPair.Public;

    string publickey = textWriter.ToString();

    Console.WriteLine("\nThe public key is:");
    Console.WriteLine("\t\t\t{0}", publickey.ToString());
```

```
        Console.WriteLine("\nX parameter: {0}",
            publicKeyParam.Q.XCoord.ToBigInteger().ToString());

        Console.WriteLine("Y parameter: {0}",
            publicKeyParam.Q.YCoord.ToBigInteger().ToString());
    }

    public static AsymmetricCipherKeyPair GenerateKeys(int keySize)
    {
        //** we will choose ECDSA for generating the keys
        var gen = new
                    Org.BouncyCastle.Crypto.Generators.
                        EllipticCurveKeyGenerator("ECDSA");

        //** randomly generation
        var secureRandom = new SecureRandom();

        //Parameters creation using the random and keysize
        var keyGenParam = new
                            KeyGenerationParameters(secureRandom,
                                keySize);

        //** send the parameters for generating
        gen.Init(keyGenParam);

        //** generate the key pair
        return gen.GenerateKeyPair();
    }
  }
}
```

Listing 10-3. The Generating of Elliptic Curve Keys

```
using System;
using System.Collections.Generic;
using System.Linq;
using System.Text;
using System.Threading.Tasks;
```

```
using Org.BouncyCastle.Asn1;
using Org.BouncyCastle.Asn1.Nist;
using Org.BouncyCastle.Asn1.Sec;
using Org.BouncyCastle.Asn1.TeleTrust;
using Org.BouncyCastle.Asn1.X9;
using Org.BouncyCastle.Crypto;
using Org.BouncyCastle.Crypto.EC;
using Org.BouncyCastle.Crypto.Parameters;
using Org.BouncyCastle.Math;
using Org.BouncyCastle.Math.EC;
using Org.BouncyCastle.Math.EC.Multiplier;
using Org.BouncyCastle.Security;
using Org.BouncyCastle.Utilities;

namespace Org.BouncyCastle.Crypto.Generators
{
    class EllipticCurveKeyGenerator : IAsymmetricCipherKeyPairGenerator
    {
        private readonly string theAlgorithm;

        private ECDomainParameters theParameters;
        private DerObjectIdentifier publicKeyParamSet;
        private SecureRandom random;

        //** first constructor
        public EllipticCurveKeyGenerator()
            : this("EC")
        {
        }

        //** second constructor
        public EllipticCurveKeyGenerator(
            string choosen_algorithm)
        {
            this.theAlgorithm = choosen_algorithm ??
                throw new ArgumentNullException("algorithm");
        }
```

281

```
public void Init(KeyGenerationParameters theParams)
{
    if (theParams is ECKeyGenerationParameters
                                elliptic_curve_parameters)
    {
        this.publicKeyParamSet =
            elliptic_curve_parameters.PublicKeyParamSet;
        this.theParameters =
            elliptic_curve_parameters.DomainParameters;
    }
    else
    {
        DerObjectIdentifier oid;
        switch (theParams.Strength)
        {
            case 192:
                oid = X9ObjectIdentifiers.Prime192v1;
                break;
            case 224:
                oid = SecObjectIdentifiers.SecP224r1;
                break;
            case 128:
                oid = SecObjectIdentifiers.SecP128r1;
                break;
            case 239:
                oid = X9ObjectIdentifiers.Prime239v1;
                break;
            case 256:
                oid = X9ObjectIdentifiers.Prime256v1;
                break;
            case 384:
                oid = SecObjectIdentifiers.SecP384r1;
                break;
            case 521:
                oid = SecObjectIdentifiers.SecP521r1;
                break;
```

```
                default:
                    throw new
                        InvalidParameterException("The key
                        size is not
                    defined or it is unknown.");
        }

        X9ECParameters ecps =
        IdentifyEllipticCurveByObjectIdentifier (oid);

        this.publicKeyParamSet = oid;
        this.theParameters = new ECDomainParameters(
            ecps.Curve,
            ecps.G,
            ecps.N,
            ecps.H,
            ecps.GetSeed());
    }

    this.random = theParams.Random;

    if (this.random == null)
    {
        this.random = new SecureRandom();
    }
}

public AsymmetricCipherKeyPair GenerateKeyPair()
{
    BigInteger n = theParameters.N;
    BigInteger d;
    int minWeight = n.BitLength >> 2;

    for (; ; )
    {
        d = new BigInteger(n.BitLength, random);
```

```
        if (d.CompareTo(BigInteger.Two) < 0 ||
                            d.CompareTo(n) >= 0)
            continue;

        if (WNafUtilities.GetNafWeight(d) < minWeight)
            continue;

        break;
    }

    ECPoint ellipticCurvePoint =
            CreateBasePointMultiplier().
             Multiply(theParameters.G, d);

    if (publicKeyParamSet != null)
    {
        return new AsymmetricCipherKeyPair(
                new ECPublicKeyParameters(theAlgorithm,
                ellipticCurvePoint, publicKeyParamSet),
              new ECPrivateKeyParameters(theAlgorithm,
                            d,
                            publicKeyParamSet));
    }

    return new AsymmetricCipherKeyPair(
        new ECPublicKeyParameters(theAlgorithm,
                            ellipticCurvePoint,
                            theParameters),
        new ECPrivateKeyParameters(theAlgorithm,
                            d,
                            theParameters));
}

protected virtual ECMultiplier
                    CreateBasePointMultiplier()
{
    return new FixedPointCombMultiplier();
}
```

```
internal static X9ECParameters
            IdentifyEllipticCurveByObjectIdentifier
            (DerObjectIdentifier
                    object_identifier)
{
    X9ECParameters x9_elliptic_curve_parameters =
            CustomNamedCurves.GetByOid(object_identifier);
    if (x9_elliptic_curve_parameters == null)
    {
        x9_elliptic_curve_parameters =
                ECNamedCurveTable.GetByOid(
                                        object_identifier);
    }
    return x9_elliptic_curve_parameters;
}

internal static ECPublicKeyParameters
        GetCorrespondingPublicKey(
    ECPrivateKeyParameters private_key)
{
    ECDomainParameters ellipticCurve_DomainParameters
                        = private_key.Parameters;

    ECPoint ellipticCurvePoint =
            new FixedPointCombMultiplier().

        Multiply(ellipticCurve_DomainParameters.
            G, private_key.D);

    if (private_key.PublicKeyParamSet != null)
    {
        return new
            ECPublicKeyParameters(
                private_key.AlgorithmName,
                ellipticCurvePoint,
                private_key.PublicKeyParamSet);
    }
```

```
            return new
                ECPublicKeyParameters(
                        private_key.AlgorithmName,
                    ellipticCurvePoint,
                            ellipticCurve_DomainParameters);
        }
    }
}
```

The output is shown in Figure 10-3.

Figure 10-3. *The keys*

Bouncy Castle Installation

In order to run the code, you have to make sure that Bouncy Castle is installed properly on your computer. In order to achieve this, first you need to go into Microsoft Visual Studio ➤ Tools ➤ NuGet Package Manager ➤ Manage NuGet Packages for Solution, as you can see from Figure 10-4.

The next steps are to select the Bouncy Castle library, click Install (see Figure 10-5), and click OK to agree to the changes that will be made (see Figure 10-6). Figure 10-7 shows the confirmation of the installation.

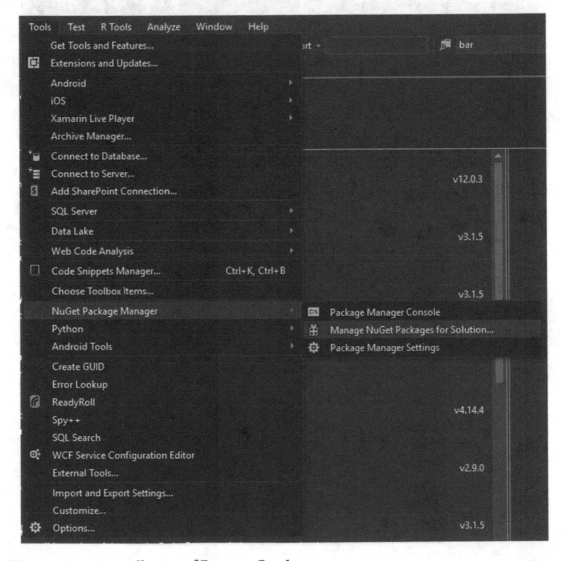

Figure 10-4. *Installation of Bouncy Castle*

Figure 10-5. *Selecting Bouncy Castle from the list for installation*

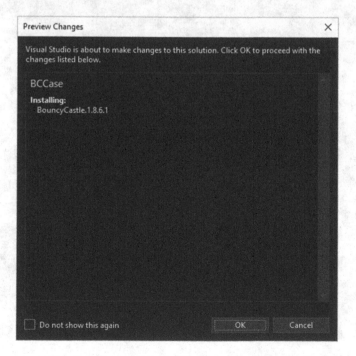

Figure 10-6. *Preview of the changes before installation*

```
Output
Show output from:  Package Manager

Attempting to gather dependency information for package 'BouncyCastle.1.8.6.1' with respect to project 'BCCase', targeting '.NETFramework,Version=v4.6.1'
Gathering dependency information took 659.93 ms
Attempting to resolve dependencies for package 'BouncyCastle.1.8.6.1' with DependencyBehavior 'Lowest'
Resolving dependency information took 0 ms
Resolving actions to install package 'BouncyCastle.1.8.6.1'
Resolved actions to install package 'BouncyCastle.1.8.6.1'
Retrieving package 'BouncyCastle 1.8.6.1' from 'nuget.org'.
  GET https://api.nuget.org/v3-flatcontainer/bouncycastle/1.8.6.1/bouncycastle.1.8.6.1.nupkg
  OK https://api.nuget.org/v3-flatcontainer/bouncycastle/1.8.6.1/bouncycastle.1.8.6.1.nupkg 509ms
Installing BouncyCastle 1.8.6.1.
Adding package 'BouncyCastle.1.8.6.1' to folder 'D:\Proiecte\BCCase\packages'
Added package 'BouncyCastle.1.8.6.1' to folder 'D:\Proiecte\BCCase\packages'
Added package 'BouncyCastle.1.8.6.1' to 'packages.config'
Successfully installed 'BouncyCastle 1.8.6.1' to BCCase
Executing nuget actions took 17.02 sec
Time Elapsed: 00:00:18.3735969
========== Finished ==========

Error List  Output
```

Figure 10-7. *Confirmation of the installation*

Conclusion

In this chapter, we discussed how to work with elliptic-curve cryptography and how to implement practical solutions for generating keys and encrypting messages.

At the end of this chapter, you now know the following:

- The difference between Microsoft .NET Elliptic Curve support and open source libraries, such as Bouncy Castle

- How to encrypt messages and generate keys using the ECDiffieHellmanCng class

- How to generate encryption key pairs using the Bouncy Castle library

Working with ECC in Microsoft .NET can be very tricky, and the performance and quality of the code can represent a major step down if you don't know the framework/libraries properly.

Bibliography

[1]   Lenstra Elliptic-Curve Cryptography. Available online: https://en.wikipedia.org/wiki/Lenstra_elliptic-curve_factorization.

[2]   Bouncy Castle. Available online: www.bouncycastle.org/.

CHAPTER 11

Lattice-Based Cryptography

In this chapter, we will discuss lattice-based cryptography, its importance in the field of cryptography together with its future challenges, and how we can design and develop practical solutions that are appropriate for cryptography applications.

The importance of lattice-based cryptography is vital as we move into a quantum era with an increasing number of quantum cryptography primitives. Currently, lattice-based construction is an important candidate for post-quantum cryptography. Cryptosystems such as RSA, Diffie-Hellman, or elliptic-curve cryptosystems are, according to theoreticians, easily attacked using quantum computers. Some of the cryptographic constructions based on lattices are getting very good results regarding their resistance to attacks from classic and quantum computers.

Applying lattices in practice as a cryptography solution is not an easy task to achieve because the mathematical background is complex and involves understanding different abstract concepts. In this chapter, we will make use of the NTRU-Sharp library [1] which is a free/open source library that contains the implementation for NTRU, the public key cryptosystem [2].

Mathematical Background

In this section, we will provide a quick overview of the basic concepts and methods that form the minimum theoretical knowledge of lattice mathematical background that you should know.

Let's consider the space R^n and a basis of it as $(b_1, ..., b_n)$, $b_1, ..., b_n \in R$. A lattice represents the set of all integers that form a linear combination with the basis, namely $\mathcal{L} = \{\sum a_i b_i \mid a_i \in \mathbb{Z}\}$. An example of lattice is Z^n, which is generated through the classic

291

© Marius Iulian Mihailescu and Stefania Loredana Nita 2021
M. I. Mihailescu and S. L. Nita, *Pro Cryptography and Cryptanalysis*,
https://doi.org/10.1007/978-1-4842-6367-9_11

basis of R. In cryptography, a common hardness assumption from a lattice apparatus is the Shortest Vector Problem (SVP). The SVP requires us to estimate the minimal value of the Euclidean distance of a non-zero lattice vector.

One of the cryptosystems that use lattices is NTRU [2], which is resistant to attacks that use Schor's algorithm. The SVP hardness assumption for NTRU consists of a factorization of specific polynomials into two polynomials that have extremely low coefficients. Note that the specific polynomials that need to be factored should be defined from a truncated polynomial ring. Further, here are the key generation, encryption and decryption algorithms for NTRU:

- **Key generation.** Choose $n \in N$ and two polynomials f and g that have a maximum degree of $n - 1$ and coefficients from the set $\{-1, 0, 1\}$. The polynomial f should have an additional property, namely f_p, and f_q should exist where $f \cdot f_p = 1 \pmod p$ and $f \cdot f_q = 1 \pmod q$. The private key is $k_{priv} = (f, f_p, g)$ and the public key is $k_{pub} = p \cdot f_q \cdot g \pmod q$.

- **Encryption.** The message that needs to be encrypted is a polynomial m whose coefficients are in $\{-1, 0, 1\}$. Choose randomly a polynomial r that has low coefficients and is kept private by the sender of the encrypted message. The encryption of m is computed as $c = r \cdot h + m \pmod q$.

- **Decryption.** To decrypt the message, the following computations need to be made:

$$a = f \cdot c \pmod q$$

$$b = a \pmod p$$

$$m = f_p \cdot b$$

Practical Implementation

As mentioned, to implement and illustrate the basic operations of encryption/
decryption, we are using the NTRU-Sharp library. The vendor of the library did an
amazing effort and made it available for free under the terms of the GNU General Public
License as published by the Free Software Foundation, version 3 of the license. NTRU-
Sharp is a very complex library (see Figure 11-1) and contains important and significant
contributions for cryptography primitives and those that are based on lattices.

Figure 11-1. *NTRU library structure*

The purpose of the practical implementation is to show how to use the library to provide encryption and decryption of messages. To achieve this, you need to get familiar with the NTRUEngine project. For this, once the project is loaded in your favorite IDE (integrated development environment), you need to navigate to the NTRU folder (see Figure 11-1). Here, you can find all the classes, structures, and methods/functions that you need, such as NTRUParameters, NTRUParamSets, NTRUKeyPair, NTRUKeyGenerator, NTRUEncrypt, and NTRUDecrypt. We will take a closer look at them and we will provide a few details (see Table 11-1 and Table 11-2) in order for you to have a quick understanding of the purpose of the classes and their functions/methods.

Table 11-1. *NTRU Classes*

Class Name	Description
NTRUParameters	Creates, reads, and writes parameter settings for NTRUEncrypt
NTRUParamSets	A set of pre-defined EES encryption parameter sets
NTRUKeyPair	An NTRU key-pair container
NTRUKeyGenerator	This class implements the key pair generation of the NTRU Public Key Crypto System
NTRUEncrypt	An NTRU asymmetric cipher implementation

Table 11-2. *NTRU Methods*

Field, Property, Constructor, Method, Function Name	Description	Type
NTRUParamSets. APR2011743FAST	This parameter set gives 256 bits of security but uses product-form polynomials and f=1+pF.	Field
NTRUKeyGenerator(new NTRUParameters())	Constructs a new instance with a set of encryption parameters	Constructor
GenerateKeyPair()	An NTRU key-pair container	Method
Initialize()	Initializes the cipher for encryption. This Initialize() method is only for encryption.	Method
Encrypt(byte[] Input)	The message to encrypt	Method
Decrypt(byte[] Input)	The message to decrypt	Method

Now let's take a look at the example and understand how it works. For the example, we have chosen a simple message to encrypt, as shown in Figure 11-2.

Figure 11-2. *NTRU lattice-based cryptography encryption example*

Listing 11-1 contains the main functions that are used for encryption and decryption. Note that to run this example, you should to the following things:

- Download the library from `https://github.com/Steppenwolfe65/NTRU-NET` [1].

- Go to the project named Test and modify the file called `Program.cs` by copying and pasting the code from Listing 11-1.

- As a second alternative, use the GitHub repository provided for this book.

Listing 11-1. Encryption/Decryption Operation Using NTRU-Sharp

```
using System;
using Test.Tests.Arith;
using Test.Tests.Encode;
using Test.Tests.Encrypt;
using Test.Tests.Polynomial;
using System.Runtime.InteropServices;
using System.Diagnostics;
```

```csharp
//** NTRU Engine libraries
using VTDev.Libraries.CEXEngine.
                    Crypto.Cipher.Asymmetric.Interfaces;
using VTDev.Libraries.CEXEngine.
                    Crypto.Cipher.Asymmetric.Encrypt.NTRU;
using VTDev.Libraries.CEXEngine.Tools;
using VTDev.Libraries.CEXEngine.Crypto.Prng;
using VTDev.Libraries.CEXEngine.Crypto;

//** The test project
using Test.Tests;

using System.Text;
using System.ComponentModel;

namespace Test
{
    static class Program
    {
        static void Main(string[] args)
        {
            //** we will use as an example the
            //** following example
            //** "Welcome to Apress and Enjoy the adventure"
            byte[] data = new byte[41] { 87, 101, 108, 99,
                                111, 109, 101, 32, 116, 111,
                                32, 65, 112, 114, 101, 115,
                                115, 32, 97, 110, 100, 32,
                                69, 110, 106, 111, 121, 32,
                                116, 104, 101, 32, 97, 100,
                                118, 101, 110, 116, 117, 114,
                                101 };
            Console.WriteLine("Text to encrypt is:
                            { Welcome to Apress
                                and Enjoy the adventure}");
```

```csharp
        Console.WriteLine("Byte representation (ASCII):
                            {0}\n\n", PrintByteArray(data));

        //** Enc() function will do the
        //** encryption and decryption
        Enc();

        Console.ReadKey();
    }

private static void Enc()
{
    //** the predefines parameters
    NTRUParameters prm = NTRUParamSets.APR2011743FAST;
    NTRUKeyPair keyPair;
    byte[] enc, dec;
    byte[] data = { 87, 101, 108, 99, 111, 109, 101,
                    32, 116, 111, 32, 65, 112, 114,
                    101, 115, 115, 32, 97, 110, 100,
                    32, 69, 110, 106, 111, 121, 32,
                    116, 104, 101, 32, 97, 100, 118,
                    101, 110, 116, 117, 114, 101 };

    //** generate and display the key pair
    using (NTRUKeyGenerator gen = new
                            NTRUKeyGenerator(prm))
    {
        keyPair = (NTRUKeyPair)gen.GenerateKeyPair();
        Console.WriteLine("\t\tKey pair is:");

        Console.WriteLine("\t\t\tPUBLIC KEY is: {0}",
            PrintByteArray(keyPair.PublicKey.ToBytes()));

        Console.WriteLine("\n\t\t\tPRIVATE KEY is:
            {0}",
            PrintByteArray(keyPair.PrivateKey.ToBytes()));
    }
```

```csharp
        // encrypt a message
        using (NTRUEncrypt ntru = new NTRUEncrypt(prm))
        {
            // initialize with public key for encryption
            ntru.Initialize(keyPair.PublicKey);
            // encrypt using public key
            enc = ntru.Encrypt(data);
            Console.WriteLine("\n\n\t\t\tTEXT ENCRYPTED:
                        {0}", PrintByteArray(enc));
        }

        // decrypt a message
        using (NTRUEncrypt ntru = new NTRUEncrypt(prm))
        {
            // initialize with both keys for decryption
            ntru.Initialize(keyPair);
            // decrypt using key pair
            dec = ntru.Decrypt(enc);

            Console.WriteLine("\n\t\t\tTEXT DECRYPTED:
                    {0}", PrintByteArray(dec));
        }
    }

    //** conversion of ascii to text
    private static string ConvertASCII_To_Text(byte[] val)
    {
        //** Instantiate an ASCII encoding object
        ASCIIEncoding ascii = new ASCIIEncoding();

        foreach (var value in val)
            Console.Write(value);
        Console.WriteLine();

        //** Decode the bytes and display
        //** the resulting Unicode string.
        String decoded = ascii.GetString(val);

        return decoded.ToString();
    }
```

```
//** perform parsing of the byte values byte by byte
public static string PrintByteArray(byte[] bytes)
{
    var string_builder = new StringBuilder
                                    ("new byte[] { ");
    foreach (var theByte in bytes)
    {
        string_builder.Append(theByte + " ");
    }
    string_builder.Append("}");
    return string_builder.ToString();
}
}
}
```

Conclusion

In this chapter, we discussed lattice-based cryptography and its importance. At the end of this chapter, you now know the following:

- The importance of lattice-based cryptography and its impact on the future of cryptography

- How to apply the NTRU-Sharp Library for business software applications

- How to implement practical functions and methods related to lattices

- How to work with byte types in complex processes

Bibliography

[1]   NTRU-Sharp. Available online : `https://github.com/Steppenwolfe65/NTRU-NET`.

[2]   J. Hoffstein, J. Pipher, and J.H. Silverman, "NTRU: A ring-based public key cryptosystem." In J. P. Buhler (ed) *Algorithmic Number Theory. ANTS 1998. Lecture Notes in Computer Science, vol. 1423.* Springer, Berlin, Heidelberg. 1998.

[3]   D. Coppersmith and A. Shamir, "Lattice Attacks on NTRU." In W. Fumy (ed) *Advances in Cryptology — EUROCRYPT '97. EUROCRYPT 1997. Lecture Notes in Computer Science, vol 1233.* Springer, Berlin, Heidelberg. 1997.

[4]   C. Gentry and M. Szydlo, "Cryptanalysis of the Revised NTRU Signature Scheme." In L. R. Knudsen (ed) *Advances in Cryptology — EUROCRYPT 2002. EUROCRYPT 2002. Lecture Notes in Computer Science, vol. 2332.* Springer, Berlin, Heidelberg. 2002.

CHAPTER 12

Searchable Encryption

Searchable encryption (SE) allows encrypted data to be outsourced to potentially untrusted third-party service providers while simultaneously offering users the ability to search directly over the encrypted data in a safe and secure way. Searchable encryption is a particular case of homomorphic encryption, which will be discussed in Chapter 13.

Consider the following situation. Data owner A has some documents they want to store on a server, but, at the same time receiver B needs to be able to access and search through the data. To accomplish this property of the data, A chooses to encrypt the documents using B's public key and then A stores them on the server. When B wants to search for documents that contain a specific keyword, let's say "programming," they generate a value called a trapdoor using the "programming" keyword and their private key. Then B submits the trapdoor to the server, which will perform the search according to an algorithm and will send the documents that meet the criteria to B.

A more practical scenario is the following: a company is developing a software solution that includes social security numbers (SSNs) obtained from its customers. The rules and good practices say that the SSNs must be encrypted when not involved in a data process. On the other hand, the employees work with the SSNs when they need to search for a user account. What if the employees don't "see" the SSNs when they work with them? Using a searchable encryption scheme would make this possible.

Having these examples, we can say that searchable encryption is a technique through which the user can search on encrypted content for particular data. There are multiple domains in which it can be applied, such as in healthcare, when doctors work with patients' medical files, in education, and so on.

© Marius Iulian Mihailescu and Stefania Loredana Nita 2021
M. I. Mihailescu and S. L. Nita, *Pro Cryptography and Cryptanalysis*,
https://doi.org/10.1007/978-1-4842-6367-9_12

Components

Searchable encryption schemes have two types of components: the entities that are involved in the searchable encryption processes and the algorithms of the schemes. We will present these components next.

Entities

When a software solution is implemented, more aspects should be clarified before the implementation itself. Who will use the application? Who will maintain it? What are the types of data and who can access them? Where will the data be stored? And so on. From the searchable encryption point of view, the following entities are involved within the whole process:

- **Data owner**. The data owner posses a set of n documents $D = \{D_1, ..., D_n\}$ that are described by keywords. Both, the documents and the keywords, will be outsourced, for example, on cloud servers. Before storing the documents on the server, the data owner will encrypt them using a specific encryption scheme. The data owner is considered a trusted entity.

- **Data user**. This is an authorized user who may trigger the search process. This user generates a trapdoor value based on a keyword that needs to be searched in the encrypted content. Also, the data user may decrypt the received documents if they possess the private key.

- **Server**. The server stores the encrypted data and performs the search algorithms based on the trapdoor value that it receives from the data user. The server is considered semi-trusted or honest-but-curious, which means that it performs the search algorithms as instructed, but can perform additional analysis of the data that was given to it.

Note that from the above description the data owner can be a data user.

Types

Searchable encryption schemes can be divided into two categories regarding cryptography types: *symmetric searchable encryption* (SSE) schemes and *public encryption with keywords search* (PEKS) schemes. In symmetric searchable encryption schemes, just a key is used to encrypt or to decrypt the content and also in other specific algorithms, as you will see later in this section. The public encryption schemes with keyword searches use two types of keys, namely a public key for encryption and a private (secret) key for decryption.

The algorithms of the SSE schemes are [1]

- **KeyGeneration**. The key generation algorithm is run by the data owner. To call it, the data owner needs as input a security parameter λ, based on which the algorithm will output one type of key, namely the secret key SK.

- **BuildIndex**. The algorithm that builds an index structure is run by the data owner. This algorithm needs as input the secret key SK and the set of documents D, and the output is an index structure I. More exactly, this algorithm starts with an empty index structure and then it takes each document of the set and for each document the algorithm adds to the index structure some keywords that describe that document. Note that the keywords are encrypted (using the secret key SK) before being added to the index structure.

- **Trapdoor**. The data user runs this algorithm. To generate a trapdoor value, the algorithm takes as input the desired keyword kw, which the search is based on, and the secret key SK, and the output is a trapdoor value T_{kw}. Note that the trapdoor algorithm does not make just a simple encryption of the kw. Instead, it adds a noise value or works with some kind of control.

- **Search**. The server performs the search algorithm. The input is the trapdoor value T_{kw} generated previously, and the index structure I results from the BuildIndex algorithm. Note that the search algorithm does not do a simple matching of T_{kw} in I. The search algorithm should know how to handle or how to work with the special value T_{kw} (do not forget that T_{kw} is not a simple encryption).

If the server finds one or more documents that meet the criteria, it will send them to the data user; otherwise, it will send a message. Note that an encryption and decryption algorithm is not mentioned above. The data owner can choose different encryption schemes for the documents themselves and for the searchable encryption scheme.

This is because the documents do not interact directly with any component of the searchable encryption scheme. All algorithms from above work only with the keywords and/or the index structure of encrypted keywords.

Further, the algorithms of the PEKS schemes are [2]

- **KeyGeneration**. Similarly to KeyGeneration from SSE, the data owner runs this algorithm, too. The input is a security parameter λ and the output is a pair of keys, the public key and the private key (PK, SK).

- **Encryption**. The encryption algorithm is run by the data owner, and the input is the public key PK and a keyword KW. The output is the encryption SW of KW.

- **Trapdoor**. This algorithm is similar to the one from SSE. The data user generates a trapdoor value using as input their secret key SK and the keyword KW to trigger the search. The output is the trapdoor value T_{KW}.

- **Test**. The server performs the test algorithm taking as input the public key PK, an encrypted text C (which encrypts the text KW') and the trapdoor value T_{KW}. The output of the test algorithm is 1 if $KW' = KW$, and 0 otherwise.

The same observations occur for the trapdoor algorithm and the test algorithm; they are not just a regular encryption and a regular matching, respectively. However, the algorithms for the SSE and PEKS schemes from above are presented as they were introduced in early works in this field, respectively in [1] and [2]. They suffered transformations over time, as more types of search possibilities were explored. For example, some works allow multiple keyword searches, others allow fuzzy searches (which allow for small typos or inconsistencies of the format) based on keywords [3, 4], and others allow semantic searches (here, the data user receives the documents that contain keywords from the semantic field of the query keyword) [5], etc. Other works are centered on the documents, namely the documents to be updated directly on the server, without needing to be retrieved from the server, decrypted, updated, encrypted, and stored again on the server or the index structure to be updated directly on the server [6]. However, the algorithms that are present in any searchable encryption scheme are the trapdoor and the search/test algorithm, and, of course, encryption and decryption.

Security Characteristics

Two of the things that searchable encryption needs to protect are the search pattern and the access pattern. The search pattern is the information that can be learned from the fact that two search results come from the same query keywords. The access pattern is the set of documents that are returned for a given keyword *KW*. In addition, the searchable encryption schemes should accomplish security requirements regarding the search queries, too. According to [7], the SE schemes should provide controlled searching (only authorized users may submit search queries), encrypted queries (the query search itself needs to be encrypted before being sent to the server), and query isolation (the server learns nothing from the queries that it receives).

The SSE schemes should ensure that the index structure is not compromised, therefore is should resist IND1-CKA and/or IND2-CKA (chosen keyword attack for indexes). In IND1-CKA, the same number of keywords is chosen for all documents, while in IND2-CKA the documents can be described by a different number of keywords. Similarly, the PEKS scheme should resist chosen keyword attacks (which consist of a challenge played between an attacker and the structure that manages the PEKS scheme).

More recent security requirements are *forward* and *backward privacy* for so-called dynamic SE schemes, which support operations of insertion, updates, or deletion for the set of documents or the keywords directly on the server, in the encrypted format. Backward and forwards privacy are related to the information that is learned in the process of insertion/deletion/update. Backward privacy deals with the information that is learned when the search is based on a keyword present in documents that were deleted before the current search, while in forward privacy the current update operation is not related to previous operations.

A Simple Example

However, even if searchable encryption has great potential, it is quite difficult to implement a scheme from zero in regular applications, due to its abstraction (a wrong implementation leads to wrong encryption and therefore to less/no security and maybe more resources consumed). One of the few libraries that provides searchable encryption facilities is developed by Crypteron[1]. On their website, they explain how to install their

---

[1]www.crypteron.com/

libraries and include them in projects [10]. After installing the desired library, all the developer needs to do is to put a flag on the field of a class that allows search queries based on keywords. Inspired by their example, Listing 12-1 shows how it works by applying it to a class called Student and searching based on their personal code (see Listing 12-1).

Listing 12-1. A Simple Example Framework for Searchable Encryption Implemention

```
public class Student
{
    public int StudentId {get; set;}

    [Secure]
    public string StudentName {get; set;}

    [Secure(Opt.Search)]
    public string StudentPersonalCode {get; set;}
}

var queryKeywod =
    SecureSearch.GetPrefix("123456789");

var resultStudent = myDatabase.Students.Where(p =>
    p.StudentPersonalCode.StartsWith(searchPrefix))
```

In this example, note the Opt.Search option that enables the searchable property for the StudentPersonalCode field. Before the search, the query keyword is processed by SecureSearch.GetPrefix.

A Complex Example

In the next example [18], you will see that searchable encryption represents an advanced and very powerful encryption technique, which gives the advantage to the user to search for keywords within encrypted documents. It is very important to know the participants in the system. For this, we have classify them as follows: the *data user*, who has a set of documents $S = \{D_1, ..., D_n\}$ and makes the system ready by generating the keys, encrypting them, and storing them on a cloud server; the *data owner*, who has the possibility and advantage of submitting search queries on the cloud server; and the *cloud server*, which stores the encrypted documents and invokes the search algorithm. A typical SE technique contains the following randomized algorithms [13]:

- **KeyGeneration**(λ) → ($\mathbf{K_p, K_s}$): The generation of the key is based on the security parameter. Based on the security parameter λ, a set consisting of a pair of public key and private key is generated, (K_p) respectively (K_s).

- **Encryption**($\mathbf{D_i, K_p}$) → $\mathbf{C_i}$: The algorithm will output the encrypted document C_i based on the encryption that takes the public key K_p and a document D_i.

- **BuildIndex**($\mathbf{D_i, w, K_p}$) → $\mathbf{I}$: A build index algorithm has as input the following parameters: the document D_i, the keyword w associated with the document, and the public key K_p. The output is represented by an index structure that is based on the association between the documents and the keywords.

- **Trapdoor**($\mathbf{w, K_s}$) → $\mathbf{t_w}$: The trapdoor algorithm has two parameters as input: the keyword on which the search is made and the secret key. The output is a trapdoor value t_w.

- **Searching**($\mathbf{t_w, K_p, I}$) → $\mathbf{C}$: The search algorithm has the following parameters: the trapdoor value and the public key. The output represents the encrypted documents $C = \left\{ C_{i_1},...,C_{i_w} \right\}$ with their keyword.

- **D**($\mathbf{C, K_s}$) → $\mathbf{D}$: The decryption algorithm has as the input parameters the C of encrypted documents and the secret key K_s. The output is represented by a set $D = \left\{ D_{i_1},...,D_{i_w} \right\} \subset S$ of decrypted documents.

Nowadays, elliptic curves (see Chapter 10) are used in important topics such as blockchain ([14], [15]) or the Internet of Things ([16], [17]).

In Figure 12-1 [18], you can see a real example of a searchable encryption scheme combined with Elliptic Curve Cryptography and a big data environment (see Chapter 16). We used the Elliptic Curve Digital Signature Algorithm (ECDSA) in order to secure the courses that are made available for the students through an e-learning platform. The private key from the ECDSA algorithm is passed to the searchable encryption scheme and is used as the security parameter (λ).

There is no implementation for searchable encryption for .NET or open source. We explored the recent research in depth and we couldn't find at this moment any real implementation as a library, module, or framework. In order to implement a searchable encryption scheme, some basic guidelines should be considered before performing the implementation. The guidelines are as follows:

- The architecture of the software application (server, database, services, etc.)

- The hardware equipment and how it is structured for the current applications that are using security and cryptographic mechanisms

- Designing the architecture in such way that the searchable encryption steps are represented as independent algorithms and they can be deployed properly between the end users of the entire network infrastructure

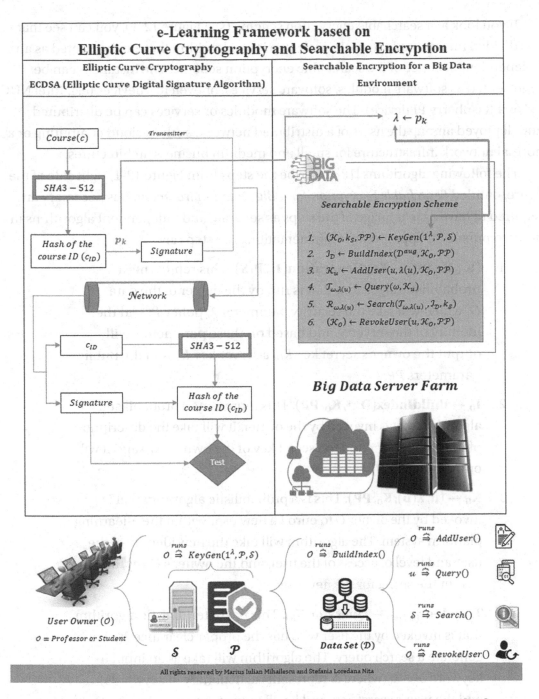

e-Learning Framework based on Elliptic Curve Cryptography and Searchable Encryption

| Elliptic Curve Cryptography | Searchable Encryption for a Big Data |
| ECDSA (Elliptic Curve Digital Signature Algorithm) | Environment |

$\lambda \leftarrow p_k$

Course(c) — *Transmitter*

SHA3 − 512

Hash of the course ID (c_{ID}) p_k Signature

Network

c_{ID} SHA3 − 512

Signature   Hash of the course ID (c_{ID})

Test

BIG DATA

Searchable Encryption Scheme

1. $(\mathcal{K}_O, k_S, \mathcal{PP}) \leftarrow KeyGen(1^\lambda, \mathcal{P}, \mathcal{S})$
2. $\mathcal{I}_D \leftarrow BuildIndex(D^{aug}, \mathcal{K}_O, \mathcal{PP})$
3. $\mathcal{K}_u \leftarrow AddUser(u, \lambda(u), \mathcal{K}_O, \mathcal{PP})$
4. $\mathcal{T}_{\omega, \lambda(u)} \leftarrow Query(\omega, \mathcal{K}_u)$
5. $\mathcal{R}_{\omega, \lambda(u)} \leftarrow Search(\mathcal{T}_{\omega, \lambda(u)}, \mathcal{I}_D, k_S)$
6. $(\mathcal{K}_O) \leftarrow RevokeUser(u, \mathcal{K}_O, \mathcal{PP})$

Big Data Server Farm

User Owner (O)

O = Professor or Student

$\mathcal{S}$ $\mathcal{P}$

runs
$O \stackrel{\cong}{} KeyGen(1^\lambda, \mathcal{P}, \mathcal{S})$

runs
$O \stackrel{\cong}{} BuildIndex()$

Data Set (D)

runs
$O \stackrel{\cong}{} AddUser()$

runs
$u \stackrel{\cong}{} Query()$

runs
$\mathcal{S} \stackrel{\cong}{} Search()$

runs
$O \stackrel{\cong}{} RevokeUser()$

Figure 12-1. *An example of a practical searchable encryption scheme [18]*

If you look at a searchable encryption scheme (see Figure 12-1), you can see that it is divided into multiple steps. In each step is an algorithm that can be treated as an independent instance of the searchable encryption scheme. The instances can be represented as software modules, software services, or even IoT devices (e.g. Intel NUC PC or a Raspberry PI device). The software modules or services can be distributed and deployed among the users of a distributed network, such as cloud computing or a normal network infrastructure for small and medium business architectures.

The following algorithms [18] describe the steps from Figure 12-1, right side of the figure, entitled *Searchable Encryption for a Big Data Environment*. It is necessary and required to have a clear image of the steps as separate and independent algorithms in order to pursue an appropriate implementation. The steps are

1. $(\mathbf{K_O}, \mathbf{K_s}, \mathbf{PP}) \leftarrow \mathbf{KeyGeneration}(\mathbf{1}^\lambda, \mathbf{P}, \mathbf{S})$. This represents a probabilistic algorithm that is run by the owner of the data O, which will take the security parameter λ, policy P, and the identity of the server S, and based on these parameters will output the owner's secret key K_O, a server key K_s, and the public parameters PP.

2. $\mathbf{I_D} \leftarrow \mathbf{BuildIndex}(\mathbf{D^{aug}}, \mathbf{K_O}, \mathbf{PP})$. This represents a probabilistic algorithm that is invoked by the owner. It will take the description of the data set D^{aug} and the secret key of the owner (K_O) and it will output an index I_D.

3. $\mathbf{K_U} \leftarrow (\mathbf{u}, \lambda(\mathbf{u}), \mathbf{K_O}, \mathbf{PP})$. This is a probabilistic algorithm that is invoked by the owner O to enroll a new user within the e-learning platform system. The algorithm will take the new identity of the user and level of access of the user, and the owner's O key, and it output the secret for the new user.

4. $\mathbf{Trapdoor}_{(\omega, \lambda(u))} \leftarrow \mathbf{Query}(\omega, \mathbf{K_u})$. This is a deterministic algorithm that is invoked by the user who has the proper clearance $\lambda(u)$ to generate a search query. The algorithm will take as an input a keyword $\omega \in \Delta$ (where Δ represents a dictionary of keywords) and the user's secret key, and it will output the query token $Trapdoor_{(\omega, \lambda(u))}$.

5. $R_{(\omega, \lambda(u))} \leftarrow$ **Searching(Trapdoor$_{(\omega, \lambda(u))}$, I$_D$, K$_s$).** The deterministic algorithm is run by the server (S) to search the index for the data items that contain the keyword ω. It will take the search query and the index, and it will return the results of the search as $R_{(\omega, \lambda(u))}$, including a set of identifiers of the data items $d_j D_{\omega, \lambda(u)}$ which contains ω such that $\lambda(d_j) \leq \lambda(u)$, where $\lambda(u_i)$ represents the access level of the user which is submitted to the search query, or a failure symbol φ.

6. $(K_0) \leftarrow$ **RevokeUser(u, K$_0$, PP).** The probabilistic algorithm is run by the owner O to revoke a specific user from the system. It will take the user's id and the secret keys of the data owner and server, and it will output the new keys for the owner and server.

The searchable encryption scheme designed for this chapter is correct if for all $k \in N$, for all K_O, K_S outputted by $KeyGen(1^\lambda, P)$, for all D^{aug}, for all I_D that is outputted by $BuildIndex(D^{aug}, K_O)$, for all $\omega \in \Delta$, for all $u \in U$ for all K_u outputted by $AddUser(K_O, u, \lambda(u), PP)$, $Search(I_D, T_{\omega, \lambda(u)}) = D_{\omega, \lambda(u)}$.

The example in Listing 12-2, which is developed using LINQ-TO-SQL, is a practical way of implementing the searchable encryption scheme proposed in Figure 12-1. It has to be mentioned that the implementation is purely indicative as the implementations (frameworks, libraries, etc.) for searchable encryption do not exist.

Listing 12-2. Implementation of Searchable Encryption Scheme

```
public class KeyGeneration
{
    //** Step 1
    //** the algorithm from KeyGeneration step (algorithm)
    //** are runned and invoked by the data owner

    //** global variables
    public string securityParameter = string.Empty();
    public string ownerID = string.Empty();
    public string policyContent = string.Empty();
    public string serverIdentity = string.Empty();
```

```
//** the function will return the policy,
//** as a content or file
public string GetPolicy(IServiceCollection policyService)
{
    policyService.AddAuthorization(policyChoices =>
    {
        policyChoices.AddPolicy("Policy content", policy
                        =>policy.Requirements.Add(new
                        UserPolicy())));
    });

    policyContent = policyChoices.ToString();
}
//** getting server identity can be tricky and it has
//** different meanings, such as the name of computer,
//** IP, active directory reference name etc...
//** For the current example we will use the hardware ID
public string GetServerIdentity()
{
    ManagementObject hardwareID = new
    ManagementObject(@"win32_logicaldisk.
    deviceid=""c:""");
    hardwareID.Get();
    string idOfTheHardware = hardwareID
    ["VolumeSerialNumber"].ToString();

    serverIdentity = ifOfTheHardware;

    return serverIdentity;
}

//** class constructor
public KeyGeneration(){}

//** let's generate the secret key, server key
//** and public parameters
//** "#" represents the separator
```

```csharp
    public string ReturnParameters()
    {
        StringBuilder sbParameters = new StringBuilder();

        sbParameters.Append(ownerSecretKey + "#" +
        serverKey + "#" +);
    publicParameters);
    }
}

public class BuildIndex
{
    //** Step 2
    //** the algorithm from BuildIndex step (algorithm)
    //** are runned and invoked by the data owner

    //** constructor of the class
    public void BuildIndex(){}

    //** the function centralize the build index parameters
    //** after their initialization and processing
    public void UseBuildIndexParameters()
    {
        LinkedList descriptionDataSet =
        new LinkedList();
        string ownerPrivateKey = string.Empty();
        string outputIndex = string.Empty();
    }

    //** simulation of getting the data set and their
    //** descriptions
    public LinkedList GetDataSet()
    {
        for(int i=0; i<dataSet.Length; i++)
        {
            LinkedList ll = new LinkedList();
            ll.Items.Add(dataSet[i],description[i]);
        }
    }
```

```csharp
        //** getting the private of the owner
        public string ownerPrivateKey()
        {
            string privateKey = string.Empty();

            //** get the private key and work with it arround

            return privateKey;
        }

        //** get the index
        public string Index()
        {
            string index = string.Empy();

            //** implement the query for getting
            //** or generating the index

            return index;
        }
    }

public class AddUser
{
    //** Step 3
    //** the algorithm from AddUser step (algorithm)
    //** are runned and invoked by the data owner
    //** constructor of the class AddUser
    public string AddUser() {}

    //** property for getting the identity of the user
    //** see below the Class Student
    public string IdentityOfTheUser()

        string identity = string.Empty();

        //** implement the way of getting
        //** the identity of the user

        return identity;
    }
```

```csharp
    //** property for getting the owners key
    public string OwnerSecretKey()
    {
        string secretKey = string.Empty();

        //** implement the way of querying
        //** for secret key

        return secretKey;
    }

public void AssignSecretKeyToUser()
{
    Student stud = new
    Student(OwnerSecretKey.ToString());
}
}

public class Query
{
    //** Step 4
    //** the algorithm from Query step (algorithm)
    //** are runned and invoked by the user

    //** constructor of the class Query
    public void Query() {}

    //** function for getting the keywords
    public string Keyword()
    {
        string kw = string.Empty();

        //** query for the keywords;

        Return kw;
    }

    //** function for getting the secret key of the users
    public string UserSecretKey()
```

```csharp
    {
        string secretKey = string.Empty();

        //** implement the way of querying
        //** for secret key

        return secretKey;
    }

    //** the generation of the output as query
    //** token for the trapdoor
    public string QueryToken()
    {
        string query_token = string.Empty();

        //** generate and build
        //** the query token for trapdoor

        return query_token
    }
}

public class Search
{
    //** Step 5
    //** the algorithm from Search step (algorithm)
    //** are runned and invoked by the server

    //** the constructor of the Search class
    public void Search() {}

    public string SearchQuery()
    {
        string query = string.Empty();

        //** take the search query

        return query;
    }
```

```
public string Index()
{
    string index = string.Empty();

    //** take the search query

    return index;
}

public string ReturnResult()
{
    string result = string.Empty();
    string setOfIdentifiers = string.Empty();

    //** based on the search query and index,
    //** get the set identifiers of the data items
    setOfIdentifier = "query for identifiers";

    //** build the result. "#" is the separator for
    //** illustration purpose only
    result = SearchQuery + "#" + Index;

    return result;
}
}

public class RevokeUser
{
    //** Step 6
    //** the algorithm from Search step (algorithm)
    //** are runned and invoked by the data owner

    //** constructor of RevokeUser class
    public void RevokeUser(){}

    //** second constructor of the class
    //** this can be implemented as a
    //** solution for revoking a user
```

```
    public void RevokeUser(string userID,
                           string secretKeyDataOwner,
                           string secretKeyServer)
    {
        //** implement the revoking process

        //** output the new key for data owner

        //** output the new key for server
    }
}

public class Course
{
    //** the db_panel represents an instance of the generated
    //** DBML file which contains classes for each of tables
    //** from the database
    DatabaseDBPanel db_panel = new DatabaseDBPanel();

    //** Class Courses it is a generated class and assigned
    //** to the table Courses from the database
    Courses c = new Courses();

    //** student ID
    string demoStudentID = "435663";

    //** select the course ID based on the student
    public string GetCourse()
    {
        //** select the courses for a
        //** specific user (student)
        var c = (from x in db_panel.Courses
        where x.StudentID ==
                demoStudentID.ToString()).Single();

        return c.ToString();
    }

}
```

```
public class Student
{
    public string secretKey {get; set;}
    public int StudentId {get; set;}
    public string CourseID {get; set;}

    [Secure]
    public string StudentName {get; set;}

    [Secure]
    public string StudentIdentity {get; set;}

    [Secure(Opt.Search)]
    public string StudentPersonalCode {get; set;}

     //** constructor of the class
     public void Student(string secret_key)
     {
          secretKey = secret_key;
     }

}

var queryKeywod =
    SecureSearch.GetPrefix("123456789");

var resultStudent = myDatabase.Students.Where(p =>
    p.StudentPersonalCode.StartsWith(searchPrefix))
```

Summary

In this chapter, the searchable encryption schemes were described and a simple example of a library that supports searchable encryption was provided.

Searchable encryption, which is a particular case of homomorphic encryption, has great potential in many domains of activity. If you are interested in more theoretical aspects of searchable encryption, any of the references provide a deeper view of SE. For some recent samples of pseudo-code, consult [11] or [12].

Bibliography

[1]   E. J. Goh, "Secure indexes." IACR Cryptology ePrint Archive, 2003, 216.

[2]   D. Boneh, G. Di Crescenzo, R. Ostrovsky, and G. Persiano, "Public key encryption with keyword search." In *International conference on the theory and applications of cryptographic techniques* (pp. 506-522). 2004. Springer, Berlin, Heidelberg.

[3]   J. Li, Q. Wang, C. Wang, N. Cao, K. Ren, and W Lou, "Fuzzy keyword search over encrypted data in cloud computing." In *2010 Proceedings IEEE INFOCOM* (pp. 1-5). 2010. IEEE.

[4]   J. Bringer, H. Chabanne, and B Kindarji, "Error-tolerant searchable encryption." In *2009 IEEE International Conference on Communications* (pp. 1-6). IEEE. 2009.

[5]   J. Lai, X. Zhou, R. H. Deng, Y. Li, and K. Chen, "Expressive search on encrypted data." *In Proceedings of the 8th ACM SIGSAC symposium on Information, computer and communications security* (pp. 243-252). 2013.

[6]   R. Bost, "$\sum$ oφoς: Forward secure searchable encryption." In *Proceedings of the 2016 ACM SIGSAC Conference on Computer and Communications Security* (pp. 1143-1154). 2016.

[7]   D. X. Song, D. Wagner, and A. Perrig, "Practical techniques for searches on encrypted data." In *Proceeding 2000 IEEE Symposium on Security and Privacy*. S&P 2000 (pp. 44-55). IEEE. 2000.

[8]   J. Ghareh Chamani, D. Papadopoulos, C. Papamanthou, and R. Jalili, "New constructions for forward and backward private symmetric searchable encryption." In *Proceedings of the 2018 ACM SIGSAC Conference on Computer and Communications Security* (pp. 1038-1055). 2018.

[9]   C. Zuo, S. Sun, J. K. Liu, J. Shao, and J. Pieprzyk, "Dynamic searchable symmetric encryption with forward and stronger backward privacy." In *European Symposium on Research in Computer Security* (pp. 283-303). Springer, Cham. 2019.

[10]   Crypteron Documentation, `www.crypteron.com/docs/`

[11]   C. Ma, Y. Gu, and H. Li. "Practical Searchable Symmetric Encryption Supporting Conjunctive Queries without Keyword Pair Result Pattern Leakage."

[12]   S. Fu, Q. Zhang, N. Jia, and M. Xu, "A Privacy-Preserving Fuzzy Search Scheme Supporting Logic Query over Encrypted Cloud Data." In *Mobile Networks and Applications*, 1-12. 2010.

[13]   Dan Boneh et al. "Public key encryption with keyword search." International conference on the theory and applications of cryptographic techniques. Springer, Berlin, Heidelberg, 2004.

[14]   Ernest Bonnah and Ju Shiguang, "Privacy Enhancement Scheme (PES) in a Blockchain-Edge Computing Environment (October 2019)." IEEE Access 2020.

[15]   Mohammad Shahriar Rahman et al, "Accountable cross-border data sharing using blockchain under relaxed trust assumption." In *IEEE Transactions on Engineering Management*, 2020.

[16]   C. Bösch, P. Hartel, W. Jonker, and A. Peter, "A Survey of Provably Secure Searchable Encryption," In *ACM Comput. Survey, vol. 47*, no. 2, pp. 1–51, 2014.

[17]   Prabhat Kumar Panda and Sudipta Chattopadhyay. "A secure mutual authentication protocol for IoT environment," In *Journal of Reliable Intelligent Environments* (pp. 1-16), 2020.

[18]   Mihailescu Marius Iulian, Nita Stefania Loredana, and Pau Valentin Corneliu. "E-Learning System Framework using Elliptic Curve Cryptography and Searchable Encryption." In *Proceedings of International Scientific Conference for e-Learning and Software for Education, Volume 1*, (pp. 545-552), 2020. DOI: 10.12753/2066-026X-20-071.

CHAPTER 13

Homomorphic Encryption

Homomorphic encryption (HE) represents an encryption technique that supports computations over encrypted data, without the need for decryption while computing. It is mandatory that the result of the computations applied on plain data be the same as the decryption of the result achieved by applying over the encrypted data corresponding computations that reflect the ones applied on the plain data. These types of encryption schemes have great potential, because third parties may compute functions (and therefore apply algorithms) over the encrypted data, without having access to the plain data. Thus, the data is processed, while its privacy and security are ensured. For example, you are on a trip and you want to search for nearby restaurants. This simple search may reveal information about you, such as which town you are in and the time of your search. If the search engine uses a homomorphic encryption scheme, then no information about you is visible to others, nor are the search results you receive. Important areas in which homomorphic encryption may be used are the financial/business sector, healthcare, and other domains that work with sensitive data.

A function $f: A \rightarrow B$ is said to be *homomorphic over an operation "*"* if it satisfies the following property:

$$f(x_1) * f(x_2) = f(x_1 * x_2), \forall x_1, x_2 \in A$$

In addition to key generation, encryption, and decryption, homomorphic encryption schemes have one more algorithm, `Eval` (called *evaluation*), which takes as input encrypted data and outputs encrypted data. In the `Eval` algorithm, a function `f` is applied over encrypted data c_1 and c_2, without having access to plain data m_1 and m_2, with the following property:

$$Dec\left(key_{priv}, Eval\left(key_{eval}, c_1, c_2\right)\right) = f\left(m_1, m_2\right)$$

© Marius Iulian Mihailescu and Stefania Loredana Nita 2021
M. I. Mihailescu and S. L. Nita, *Pro Cryptography and Cryptanalysis*,
https://doi.org/10.1007/978-1-4842-6367-9_13

In homomorphic encryption, the homomorphism is considered just for two mathematical operations, addition and multiplication, because any circuit corresponding to a function may be expressed using the gates corresponding to these two operations. The first observation of homomorphic encryption encountered in the Unpadded RSA algorithm, where the homomorphic operation is multiplication,

$$Enc(m_1) \cdot Enc(m_2) = m_1^e m_2^e \bmod n$$

$$= \left(m_1 m_2\right)^e \bmod n$$

$$= Enc\left(m_1 \quad m_2\right),$$

where m_1, m_2 are two plain messages and Enc represents the encryption function. There are three types of homomorphic encryption schemes:

- **Partial homomorphic encryption (PHE)**. Accepts a single operation for an unlimited number of times. Important PHE schemes that represent foundations for other encryption schemes are RSA [1], Goldwasser-Micali [2], and El-Gamal [3].

- **Somewhat homomorphic encryption (SWHE)**. Accepts multiple operations for a limited number of times. An example of a SWHE scheme is [4].

- **Fully homomorphic encryption (FHE)**. Accepts multiple operations for an unlimited number of times. The FHE is called "cryptography's holy grail" or "the Swiss Army Knife of cryptography" [5] because it enables any number of functions applied any number of times over encrypted data. The first FHE scheme was proposed in 2009 and it is based on ideal lattices [6]. Although this scheme had great potential and opened FHE's way, it had a few drawbacks, such as its complexity and abstraction, which made it impractical in that initial form. Further, many studies used the general framework FHE presented in [6] to create or to improve fully homomorphic schemes.

Fully Homomorphic Encryption

It is worth having a deeper view of FHE because it is such a great technique that has the potential to resolve (almost) all security, privacy, and confidentiality concerns.

The first FHE scheme was proposed in 2009, based on ideal lattices [6] and *ideal coset problem* hardness assumption, and it was followed by many other proposals, opening the way for the first generation of FHE schemes. An immediately following work is [7], in which the authors propose a simpler FHE scheme based on integer arithmetic. Still, the drawback of both schemes was the rapid noise growth, which had a great impact on practical implementation and security and limited the homomorphic capabilities. In addition, the noise growth made decryption impossible, too, at some point.

The second generation started with schemes in which the noise was manipulated more effectively [8], [9], which led to better performance and strong security under some conditions (called *hardness assumptions*). This generation resulted in *leveled schemes*, which supported the evaluation of circuits of a given polynomial depth, and *bootstrappable schemes*, from which can result FHE schemes. An encryption scheme is called bootstrappable if the encryption scheme can evaluate its own decryption circuit and, in addition, one NAND gate.

The third generation began with [10], introducing a new way of noise handling. The second-generation schemes provided better efficiency than the third generation, but those in the third generation can have weaker hardness assumptions. Many of the schemes from the third generation are based on asymmetric multiplication, which means that, for two ciphertexts c_1, c_2, the product of $c_1 \cdot c_2$ is different from the product of $c_2 \cdot c_1$, even if they encrypt the same plain text product $b_1 \cdot b_2$.

FHE has more applications in cryptography:

- **Outsourcing**. Storage and computations may be outsourced without disclosing private information. For example, a small company wants to store its data in the cloud, but it should encrypt the data such that the cloud provider does not access it. FHE would help here because the cloud provider may process the company's data in the encrypted format, without having access to the plain data. Further, the cloud provider would send the result of the computations to the data's owner in an encrypted format, too, which would be decrypted only by the private key's possessor.

- **Private information retrieval** (PIR) **or private queries**. These are important in database querying or search engines, for example, when a client wants to submit a query to a large database stored on a server, but the client does not want that the server to learn anything about the query. Therefore, the client encrypts the query and sends it to the server; then the server applies the encrypted query over encrypted data and responds with the encrypted result.

- **General computations between two entities** (two-party computations). Let's assume there are two parties, each one owning a private input, x for party A and y for party B, and an agreed function F, known by both. When party A wants to compute the function over the owned input, it will bring x and compute $r = F(x, y)$, and it will learn the result r, but will learn nothing about y. On the other side, party B will learn nothing about x and r. In a semi-honest model, this would be equivalent to B computing $Fy(x)$, where A encrypts x and sends to B because the semantic security assures the fact that B will learn nothing about the plain value corresponding to x. If homomorphic encryption is used here to evaluate the function, A will learn just the result of $F(x,y)$ and nothing else.

- **Zero-knowledge**. Zero-knowledge proof protocols may use homomorphic encryption to apply it for each language L in NP (nondeterministic polynomial time).

FHE Schemes Implemented in Microsoft SEAL

The BFV [11] and CKKS [12] encryption schemes are implemented in Microsoft's FHE library, called SEAL [13], [14].

In [11], the encryption function is defined over the set of polynomials of degree maximum n and the coefficients are computed modulo t. This set is denoted $R_t = Z_t[x]/(x^n + 1)$. On the other hand, the ciphertexts lie in the R_q set, in which the coefficients of the polynomials are modulo q. The homomorphic operations in this scheme are addition and multiplication, which preserves the ring structure of R_t. To encrypt a plain value, it should be first brought to a polynomial form accepted by the structure R_t. The algorithms of the scheme presented in [11] are SecretKeyGen (the secret key is generated based on a security parameter), `PublicKeyGen` (the public key is generated based on the secret key), `EvaluationKeyGen` (the evaluation key is generated based on the secret key), `Encrypt` (uses the public key to encrypt a plain value), `Decrypt` (uses the secret key to decrypt a ciphered value), `Add` (performs addition of two encrypted values), and `Multiply` (performs multiplication between two encrypted values). Note that the result of addition and multiplication must fall in the same structure R_q. For more details and theoretical aspects, please consult [11].

While [11] provides a way to apply modular arithmetic over integers, in [12] the authors provide ways to apply it over real numbers and complex numbers, too. Anyway, in [12] the results are approximate, but the techniques are among the best to sum up real numbers in an encrypted format, to apply machine learning algorithms on encrypted data, or to compute distance between encrypted locations.

The SEAL Library

SEAL's name comes from *Simple Encrypted Arithmetic Library* [15] and it is written in C++. The latest stable version of SEAL is 3.5 (released in May 2020) and it provides support for .NET Standard wrappers, making it easier to work with public APIs and to be used by non-experts in cryptography, too. The library has a GitHub page [16], from where it can be downloaded.

The SEAL library is independent and it does not require external libraries like other FHE scheme implementations. This makes things easier because it contains modules, which automatically select parameters for the encryption scheme, and modules for noise estimation. In [17] it is shown that SEAL v2.0 is secure against dual lattice attacks.

The easiest way to install the SEAL library is to use the NuGet Package Manager Console in Visual Studio (in this chapter, we will use Visual Studio 2019 Community on Windows 10 Education x64).

Create a new project in Visual Studio (we created a project called `SEALDemo`, whose type is `ConsoleApp(.NET Core)`) and then open select `Tools > NuGet Package Manager > Package Manager Console`, and type

```
PM> Install-Package Microsoft.Research.SEALNet -Version 3.5.6
```

If the installation is successful, a message similar to the one in Figure 13-1 should be shown in the console.

```
PM> Install-Package Microsoft.Research.SEALNet -Version 3.5.6
Restoring packages for D:\Apps C#\Chapter 13 - Homomorphic Encryption\SealDemo356\SealDemo356\SealDemo356.csproj...
  GET https://api.nuget.org/v3-flatcontainer/microsoft.research.sealnet/index.json
  OK https://api.nuget.org/v3-flatcontainer/microsoft.research.sealnet/index.json 602ms
  GET https://api.nuget.org/v3-flatcontainer/microsoft.research.sealnet/3.5.6/microsoft.research.sealnet.3.5.6.nupkg
  OK https://api.nuget.org/v3-flatcontainer/microsoft.research.sealnet/3.5.6/microsoft.research.sealnet.3.5.6.nupkg 626ms
Installing Microsoft.Research.SEALNet 3.5.6.
Installing NuGet package Microsoft.Research.SEALNet 3.5.6.
Committing restore...
Generating MSBuild file D:\Apps C#\Chapter 13 - Homomorphic Encryption\SealDemo356\SealDemo356\obj
\SealDemo356.csproj.nuget.g.targets.
Writing lock file to disk. Path: D:\Apps C#\Chapter 13 - Homomorphic Encryption\SealDemo356\SealDemo356\obj\project.assets.json
Restore completed in 6.61 sec for D:\Apps C#\Chapter 13 - Homomorphic Encryption\SealDemo356\SealDemo356\SealDemo356.csproj.
Successfully installed 'Microsoft.Research.SEALNet 3.5.6' to SealDemo356
Executing nuget actions took 1.32 sec
Time Elapsed: 00:00:08.0612948
PM> |
```

Figure 13-1. *SEAL's installation using Package Manager Console*

Before going further, we duplicate this warning from SEAL's GitHub page:

"It is impossible to use Microsoft SEAL correctly without reading all examples or by simply re-using the code from examples. Any developer attempting to do so will inevitably produce code that is vulnerable, malfunctioning, or extremely slow."

—https://github.com/microsoft/SEAL/blob/
master/README.md#getting-started

In the newly created project, add a new class called Example and inside this class add the static void method EasyExample(). The code should look like Listing 13-1.

Listing 13-1. The Initial Structure

```
using System;
using System.Collections.Generic;
using System.Text;

namespace SEALDemo
{
    class Example
    {
        public static void EasyExample()
        {
        }
    }
}
```

Note that the libraries `System`, `System.Collections.Generic`, and `System.Text` are added automatically when you create a new class. For other versions of Visual Studio, these libraries may be different or won't appear at all. Delete the three directives from above and replace them with `Microsoft.Research.SEAL;` in this way, you can use methods from the SEAL library in your class.

Further, let's add code into the `EasyExample()` method and add functionalities from the SEAL library, using BFV encryption scheme. Firstly, you need to specify the encryption parameters. They are the degree of polynomial modulus (n), the coefficient modulus for the ciphertext (q), and the modulus for the plaintext (t). To tell the application that you want to define the parameters for BFV scheme, you add the following lines of code from Listing 13-2 in `EasyExample()`.

Listing 13-2. Defining the BFV Parameters

```
EncryptionParameters parameters = new EncryptionParameters(SchemeType.BFV);
```

Next, you need to provide values for each parameter. The value of the *polynomial modulus degree* represents a power of 2, which is, in fact, the degree of a cyclotomic polynomial[1]. The recommended range for this degree is {`1024, 2048, 4096, 8192, 16384, 32768`}. The higher the value is, the more difficult computations over encrypted data are allowed, but it will become slower. A mid-ranged value is 4096, which allows a reasonable number of computations, so pick this value for your application. The next parameter, the *coefficient modulus for ciphertexts*, represents a large integer. It should have representation as a product of prime numbers, whose size in bits should be the sum of the bit-sizes of its prime factors. The higher the value is, the more encryption computations are supported. Anyway, between the polynomial modulus degree and the maximum bit-size for the coefficient modulus, there is a relationship. For example, the value of 4096 for a polynomial modulus degree corresponds the value 109 for a bit size of the coefficient modulus. The last parameter, the *modulus for plaintext*, is generally a positive integer. In this example, you will initialize it with a power of two. In other situations, the modulus should be a prime integer. The purpose of this value is to give the bit size for plain data and to set consumption limits for the multiplication operation. More information about the encryption parameters can be found in [13] and [14].

---

[1]https://en.wikipedia.org/wiki/Cyclotomic_polynomial

Another notion that we need to explain is *the noise budget*, expressed as a number of bits. Briefly, *the initial noise budgeted* is given by the encryption parameters and the rate at which it is consumed during the homomorphic operations (addition and multiplication) is given by the encryption parameters, too. The value of the coefficient modulus has an important influence on the initial noise budget; a higher value of the coefficient modulus leads to a higher value of the initial noise budget. If the noise budged of an encrypted value reaches the value 0, then the ciphertext cannot be decrypted anymore, because the quantity of noise is too high.

Coming back to the example, add the following initialization from the Listing 13-3 in the EasyExample() method:

Listing 13-3. Initialization

```
parameters.PolyModulusDegree = 4096;
parameters.CoeffModulus = CoeffModulus.BFVDefault(4096);
parameters.PlainModulus = new Modulus(1024);
```

The correctness of the encryption parameters is checked using the SEAL context:

```
SEALContext SEALctx = new SEALContext(parameters);
```

The next steps are easier. You need to instantiate the classes that provide the BFV encryption scheme's algorithms, as in Listing 13-4.

Listing 13-4. Instantiate the Classes for BFV

```
KeyGenerator keyGenerator = new KeyGenerator(SEALctx);
PublicKey pK = keyGenerator.PublicKey;
SecretKey sK = keyGenerator.SecretKey;
Encryptor encrypt = new Encryptor(SEALctx, pK);
Evaluator evaluate = new Evaluator(SEALctx);
Decryptor decrypt = new Decryptor(SEALctx, sK);
```

As a simple example, let's evaluate the polynomial $p(x) = 3x^4 + 6x^3 + 9x^2 + 12x + 6$ for the value $x = 3$.

To check that the encryption and decryption works, let's encrypt the value $x = 3$ and then decrypt the result. At the same time, you check some metrics (Listing 13-5).

Listing 13-5. Encryption of x=3 and Metrics Checking

```
int value = 3;
Plaintext plainValue = new Plaintext(value.ToString());
Console.WriteLine($"The value = {value} is expressed as a plaintext
polynomial 0x{plainValue}.");
Console.WriteLine();
Ciphertext encryptedValue = new Ciphertext();
encrypt.Encrypt(plainValue, encryptedValue);
Console.WriteLine($"- the size of the freshly encrypted value is:
{encryptedValue.Size}");
Console.WriteLine("- the initial noise budget of the encrypted value: {0} bits",
        decrypt.InvariantNoiseBudget(encryptedValue));
Plaintext decryptedValue = new Plaintext();
Console.Write("- the decryption of encrypted value: ");
decrypt.Decrypt(encryptedValue, decryptedValue);
Console.WriteLine($"0x{decryptedValue}");
```

Now you should run the application. To do this, you need to go to the `Program` class (Listing 13-6) in your solution and call the `EasyExample()` method:

Listing 13-6. The Main Method

```
public class Program
{
    static void Main(string[] args)
    {
        Example.EasyExample();
        GC.Collect();
    }
}
```

The `GC.Collect` is needed in Listing 13-6 because it shows with accuracy the usage of the memory pool. Running the application you will obtain the output shown in Listing 13-7 and Figure 13-2.

Listing 13-7. The Result of Running the Application

The value = 3 is expressed as a plaintext polynomial 0x3.

- the size of the freshly encrypted value is: 2
- the initial noise budget of the encrypted value: 55 bits
- the decryption of encrypted value: 0x3

```
The value = 3 is expressed as a plaintext polynomial 0x3.

- the size of the freshly encrypted value is: 2
- the initial noise budget of the encrypted value: 55 bits
- the decryption of encrypted value: 0x3
```

Figure 13-2. *The result of running the application*

Let's return to the encryption/decryption verification. The plain values, through the Plaintext constructor, are converted to polynomials with a lower degree than the modulus polynomial, whose coefficients are represented as hexadecimal values. The ciphertexts from using the SEAL library are expressed as two or more polynomials, which have coefficients computed as integers modulo the result of the primes' multiplication from CoeffModulus. You instantiate the Ciphertext class with the object encryptedValue, in which you put the encryption of the plainValue. You do this using the Encrypt method of the encrypt object. It is easy to observe that the Encrypt method has two parameters here: the parameter that represents the source of the plaintext value (plainValue) and the second parameter that represent the destination of the encryption of the source plain value (encryptedValue). The size of the ciphertext is given by the number of the polynomials and the size of a freshly encrypted ciphertext is always 2. This value is returned by the Size method of the encryptedValue object. Further, the InvariantNoiseBudget method of the decrypt object computes for us the initial noise budget of the encryption of plain value 3. The InvariantNoiseBudget is implemented into the Decryptor class because it shows if the decryption will work at some point in your computations. To decrypt the result, use the Decrypt method, called by the decrypt object. Finally, indeed the decryption works because the value 0x3 in hexadecimal representation means 3.

To optimize the work, it is recommended to bring the polynomial to a form with fewer multiplication operations because the multiplication is costly and will decrease the noise budget faster. Therefore, $p(x)$ may be factorized as $p(x) = 3(x^2 + 2)(x + 1)^2$, which means you will evaluate firstly $(x^2 + 2)$, then $(x + 1)^2$, and then you will multiply the result between them and with 3.

To compute $(x^2 + 2)$, proceed as shown in Listing 13-8.

Listing 13-8. Computing $(x^2 + 2)$

```
Console.WriteLine("Compute squareValuePlusTwo (x^2+2).");
Ciphertext squareValuePlusTwo = new Ciphertext();
evaluate.Square(encryptedValue, squareValuePlusTwo);
Plaintext plainTextTwo = new Plaintext("2");
evaluate.AddPlainInplace(squareValuePlusTwo, plainTextTwo);

Console.WriteLine($"- the size of squareValuePlusTwo:
    {squareValuePlusTwo.Size}");
Console.WriteLine("- the noise budget in plainTextTwo: {0} bits",
    decrypt.InvariantNoiseBudget(squareValuePlusTwo));

Plaintext decryptedResult = new Plaintext();
Console.Write("- the decryption of squareValuePlusTwo: ");
decrypt.Decrypt(squareValuePlusTwo, decryptedResult);
Console.WriteLine($"0x{decryptedResult}");
```

Listing 13-9 and Figure 13-3 shows the output after running the application.

Listing 13-9. The Result of Computing $(x^2 + 2)$

```
Compute squareValuePlusTwo (x^2+2).
- the size of squareValuePlusTwo: 3
- the noise budget in squareValuePlusTwo: 33 bits
- the decryption of squareValuePlusTwo: 0xB
```

```
Compute squareValuePlusTwo (x^2+2).
- the size of squareValuePlusTwo: 3
- the noise budget in squareValuePlusTwo: 33 bits
- the decryption of squareValuePlusTwo: 0xB
```

Figure 13-3. *The result of computing $(x^2 + 2)$*

Indeed, if you compute $3^2 + 2$, you get 11, whose hexadecimal representation is 0xB; the noise budget is greater than 0, so the decryption still works. Note that the evaluate object allows you to apply operations directly over the encrypted data. The collector variable for this example is squareValuePlusTwo. Firstly, you put in this variable the encrypted value raised at power 2, i.e. x^2, using the method Square. Next, you add a plaintext value 2, using the method AddPlainInplace, leading to $x^2 + 1$. Note that in this example, $x = 3$. In addition, the Square and AddPlainInplace methods have two parameters, a source and a destination.

Similarly, you compute $(x + 1)^2$, using as collector variable valuePlusOneSquare, as shown in Listing 13-10.

Listing 13-10. Computing $(x + 1)^2$

```
Console.WriteLine("Compute valuePlusOneSquare ((x+1)^2).");
Plaintext plainTextOne = new Plaintext("1");
Ciphertext valuePlusOneSquare = new Ciphertext();
evaluate.AddPlain(encryptedValue, plainTextOne,
        valuePlusOneSquare);
evaluate.SquareInplace(valuePlusOneSquare);
Console.WriteLine($"- the size of valuePlusOneSquare:
        {valuePlusOneSquare.Size}");
Console.WriteLine("- the noise budget in valuePlusOneSquare:
        {0} bits", decrypt.InvariantNoiseBudget(valuePlusOneSquare));
Console.Write("- decryption of valuePlusOneSquare: ");
decrypt.Decrypt(valuePlusOneSquare, decryptedResult);
Console.WriteLine($"0x{decryptedResult}");
```

Listing 13-11 and Figure 13-4 show the results of running the application.

Listing 13-11. The Result of Computing $(x + 1)^2$

```
Compute valuePlusOneSquare ((x+1)^2).
- the size of valuePlusOneSquare: 3
- the noise budget in valuePlusOneSquare: 33 bits
- decryption of valuePlusOneSquare: 0x10
```

```
Compute valuePlusOneSquare ((x+1)^2).
- the size of valuePlusOneSquare: 3
- the noise budget in valuePlusOneSquare: 33 bits
- decryption of valuePlusOneSquare: 0x10
```

Figure 13-4. *The result of computing $(x + 1)^2$*

Indeed, if you compute $(3 + 1)^2$, you get 10, whose hexadecimal representation is 0x10; the noise budget is greater than 0, so the decryption still works.

The final result of $3(x^2 + 2)(x + 1)^2$ is collected into the encryptedOutcome variable, as shown in Listing 13-12.

Listing 13-12. Computing $3(x^2 + 2)(x + 1)^2$

```
Console.WriteLine("Compute encryptedOutcome 3(x^2 + 2)(x + 1)^2 .");
Ciphertext encryptedOutcome = new Ciphertext();
Plaintext plainTextThree = new Plaintext("3");
evaluate.MultiplyPlainInplace(squareValuePlusTwo, plainTextThree);
evaluate.Multiply(squareValuePlusTwo, valuePlusOneSquare,
encryptedOutcome);
Console.WriteLine($"- size of encryptedOutcome:
    {encryptedOutcome.Size}");
Console.WriteLine("- the noise budget in encryptedOutcome:
    {0} bits", decrypt.InvariantNoiseBudget(encryptedOutcome));
decrypt.Decrypt(encryptedOutcome, decryptedResult);
Console.WriteLine("- decryption of 3(x^2+2)(x+1)^2 = 0x{0}",
decryptedResult);
```

Listing 13-13 and Figure 13-5 show the results.

Listing 13-13. The Output of Computing $3(x^2 + 2)(x + 1)^2$

```
Compute encryptedOutcome 3(x^2 + 2)(x + 1)^2 .
- size of encryptedOutcome: 5
- the noise budget in encryptedOutcome: 2 bits
- decryption of 3(x^2+2)(x+1)^2 = 0x210
```

```
Compute encryptedOutcome 3(x^2 + 2)(x + 1)^2 .
- size of encryptedOutcome: 5
- the noise budget in encryptedOutcome: 2 bits
- decryption of 3(x^2+2)(x+1)^2 = 0x210
```

Figure 13-5. *The output of computing $3(x^2 + 2)(x + 1)^2$*

Indeed, if you compute $3(3^2 + 2)(3 + 1)^2$, we get 528. Do not forget that the plaintext modulus is 1024, so 528 mod 1024 = 528, which has the 0x210 hexadecimal representation. The noise budget is greater than 0, which allowed you to decrypt the final encrypted result.

Listing 13-14 puts it all together.

Listing 13-14. The Entire Code

```
class Example
{
  public static void EasyExample()
  {
    EncryptionParameters parameters = new
    EncryptionParameters(SchemeType.BFV);

    parameters.PolyModulusDegree = 4096;
    parameters.CoeffModulus = CoeffModulus.BFVDefault(4096);
    parameters.PlainModulus = new Modulus(1024);

    SEALContext SEALctx = new SEALContext(parameters);

    KeyGenerator keyGenerator = new KeyGenerator(SEALctx);
    PublicKey pK = keyGenerator.PublicKey;
      SecretKey sK = keyGenerator.SecretKey;
      Encryptor encrypt = new Encryptor(SEALctx, pK);
      Evaluator evaluate = new Evaluator(SEALctx);
      Decryptor decrypt = new Decryptor(SEALctx, sK);

    Console.WriteLine("Evaluation of 3(x^2 + 2)(x + 1)^2");
    Console.WriteLine();
    int value = 3;
    Plaintext plainValue = new Plaintext(value.ToString());
```

```
Console.WriteLine($"The value = {value} is expressed as
      a plaintext polynomial 0x{plainValue}.");
Console.WriteLine();
Ciphertext encryptedValue = new Ciphertext();
encrypt.Encrypt(plainValue, encryptedValue);

Console.WriteLine($"- the size of the freshly encrypted
      value is: {encryptedValue.Size}");
Console.WriteLine("- the initial noise budget of the
      encrypted value: {0} bits",
decrypt.InvariantNoiseBudget(encryptedValue));

Plaintext decryptedValue = new Plaintext();
Console.Write("- the decryption of encrypted value: ");
decrypt.Decrypt(encryptedValue, decryptedValue);
Console.WriteLine($"0x{decryptedValue}");

/* Compute (x^2 + 2).*/
Console.WriteLine("Compute squareValuePlusTwo (x^2+2).");
Ciphertext squareValuePlusTwo = new Ciphertext();
evaluate.Square(encryptedValue, squareValuePlusTwo);
Plaintext plainTextTwo = new Plaintext("2");
evaluate.AddPlainInplace(squareValuePlusTwo, plainTextTwo);

Console.WriteLine($"- the size of squareValuePlusTwo:
    {squareValuePlusTwo.Size}");
Console.WriteLine("- the noise budget in
    squareValuePlusTwo: {0} bits",

decrypt.InvariantNoiseBudget(squareValuePlusTwo));

Plaintext decryptedResult = new Plaintext();
Console.Write("- the decryption of squareValuePlusTwo: ");
decrypt.Decrypt(squareValuePlusTwo, decryptedResult);
Console.WriteLine($"0x{decryptedResult}");
```

```
/*Compute (x + 1)^2.*/
Console.WriteLine("Compute valuePlusOneSquare ((x+1)^2).");
Plaintext plainTextOne = new Plaintext("1");
Ciphertext valuePlusOneSquare = new Ciphertext();
evaluate.AddPlain(encryptedValue, plainTextOne,
    valuePlusOneSquare);
evaluate.SquareInplace(valuePlusOneSquare);
Console.WriteLine($"- the size of valuePlusOneSquare:
    {valuePlusOneSquare.Size}");
Console.WriteLine("- the noise budget in
    valuePlusOneSquare: {0} bits",

decrypt.InvariantNoiseBudget(valuePlusOneSquare));
Console.Write("- decryption of valuePlusOneSquare: ");
decrypt.Decrypt(valuePlusOneSquare, decryptedResult);
Console.WriteLine($"0x{decryptedResult}");

/* Multiply (x^2 + 2) * (x + 1)^2 * 3. */

Console.WriteLine("Compute encryptedOutcome
  3(x^2 + 2)(x + 1)^2 .");
Ciphertext encryptedOutcome = new Ciphertext();
Plaintext plainTextThree = new Plaintext("3");
evaluate.MultiplyPlainInplace(squareValuePlusTwo,
    plainTextThree);
evaluate.Multiply(squareValuePlusTwo, valuePlusOneSquare,
    encryptedOutcome);
Console.WriteLine($"- size of encryptedOutcome:
        {encryptedOutcome.Size}");
Console.WriteLine("- the noise budget in encryptedOutcome:
    {0} bits", decrypt.InvariantNoiseBudget(encryptedOutcome));
decrypt.Decrypt(encryptedOutcome, decryptedResult);
Console.WriteLine("- decryption of 3(x^2+2)(x+1)^2 =
        0x{0}", decryptedResult);
    }
}
```

The entire output is shown in Figure 13-6.

```
Microsoft Visual Studio Debug Console                                        —   □   ×
Evaluation of 3(x^2 + 2)(x + 1)^2

The value = 3 is expressed as a plaintext polynomial 0x3.

- the size of the freshly encrypted value is: 2
- the initial noise budget of the encrypted value: 55 bits
- the decryption of encrypted value: 0x3
Compute squareValuePlusTwo (x^2+2).
- the size of squareValuePlusTwo: 3
- the noise budget in squareValuePlusTwo: 33 bits
- the decryption of squareValuePlusTwo: 0xB
Compute valuePlusOneSquare ((x+1)^2).
- the size of valuePlusOneSquare: 3
- the noise budget in valuePlusOneSquare: 33 bits
- decryption of valuePlusOneSquare: 0x10
Compute encryptedOutcome 3(x^2 + 2)(x + 1)^2 .
- size of encryptedOutcome: 5
- the noise budget in encryptedOutcome: 2 bits
- decryption of 3(x^2+2)(x+1)^2 = 0x210

C:\Program Files\dotnet\dotnet.exe (process 6968) exited with code 0.
To automatically close the console when debugging stops, enable Tools->Options->Debugging->Automatically close the conso
le when debugging stops.
Press any key to close this window . . .
```

Figure 13-6. *The entire output*

This polynomial evaluation represents a simple example of how the SEAL library can be used. Of course, in real-life applications, you will need to handle more complex functions or algorithms. Even this simple example may be dramatically optimized using the *relinearization technique*, which resets the size of the encrypted text to the initial value of 2. Briefly, the relinearization should be applied after each multiplication. This technique is available in the SEAL library and it is implemented in the `Evaluator` class, under `RelinearizeInplace`, which takes two arguments: the encrypted text that needs to be relinearized and the relinearization keys. The above example can be modified as follows: firstly, define the relinearization keys:

```
RelinKeys relinearizationKeys = keyGenerator.RelinKeys();
```

Then, after each multiplication, proceed with the relinearization. For example, relinearize the `squareValuePlusTwo` variable:

```
evaluate.RelinearizeInplace(squareValuePlusTwo, relinearizationKeys);
```

Note that you need to relinearize the `valuePlusOneSquare` and the `encryptedOutcome` variables in order to achieve a maximum optimization.

As you have seen with this simple example, the SEAL library is powerful and a great advantage is that it is independent of other external libraries. When the applications work with the exact values of integers, the BFV encryption scheme implemented in the SEAL library is great. If the application needs to work with real or complex numbers, the CKKS encryption scheme is the best choice, which is also implemented in the SEAL library.

Conclusion

In this chapter:

- You saw what homomorphic encryption is and the types of homomorphic encryption.

- You got a deeper view of fully homomorphic encryption and you saw why it is so important.

- You used Microsoft's SEAL library, which implements the BFV encryption scheme, in a simple example with a polynomial evaluation.

Bibliography

[1]   Ronald L. Rivest, Adi Shamir, and Leonard Adleman, "A method for obtaining digital signatures and public-key cryptosystems." Communications of the ACM 21.2 (1978): 120-126.

[2]   Shafi Goldwasser and Silvio Micali, "Probabilistic encryption and how to play mental poker keeping secret all partial information." Proceedings of the Fourteenth Annual ACM Symposium on Theory of Computing. 1982.

[3]   Taher ElGamal, "A public key cryptosystem and a signature scheme based on discrete logarithms." IEEE transactions on information theory 31.4 (1985): 469-472.

[4]   Dan Boneh, Eu-Jin Goh, and Kobbi Nissim, "Evaluating 2-DNF formulas on ciphertexts." Theory of Cryptography Conference. Springer, Berlin, Heidelberg, 2005.

[5]   B. Barak and Z. Brakerski. "The Swiss Army Knife of Cryptography," http://windowsontheory.org/2012/05/01/the-swiss-army-knife-of-cryptography/, 2012.

[6]   Craig Gentry, "Fully homomorphic encryption using ideal lattices." Proceedings of the forty-first annual ACM symposium on Theory of computing. 2009.

[7]   Marten Van Dijk et al, "Fully homomorphic encryption over the integers." Annual International Conference on the Theory and Applications of Cryptographic Techniques. Springer, Berlin, Heidelberg, 2010.

[8]   Zvika Brakerski and Vinod Vaikuntanathan, "Efficient fully homomorphic encryption from (standard) LWE." SIAM Journal on Computing 43.2 (2014): 831-871.

[9]   Craig Gentry, Z. Brakerski, and V. Vaikuntanathan, "Fully homomorphic encryption without bootstrapping." Security 111.111 (2011): 1-12.

[10] Craig Gentry, Amit Sahai, and Brent Waters, "Homomorphic encryption from learning with errors: Conceptually-simpler, asymptotically-faster, attribute-based." Annual Cryptology Conference. Springer, Berlin, Heidelberg, 2013.

[11] Junfeng Fan and Frederik Vercauteren, "Somewhat Practical Fully Homomorphic Encryption." IACR Cryptology ePrint Archive 2012 (2012): 144.

[12] Jung Hee Cheon et al, "Homomorphic encryption for arithmetic of approximate numbers." International Conference on the Theory and Application of Cryptology and Information Security. Springer, Cham, 2017.

[13] Hao Chen, Kim Laine, and Rachel Player, "Simple encrypted arithmetic library-SEAL v2.1." International Conference on Financial Cryptography and Data Security. Springer, Cham, 2017.

[14]   Kim Laine, "Simple encrypted arithmetic library 2.3. 1." Microsoft Research, www.microsoft.com/en-us/research/uploads/prod/2017/11/sealmanual-2-3-1.pdf (2017).

[15]   Microsoft SEAL, www.microsoft.com/en-us/research/project/microsoft-seal/

[16]   Microsoft/SEAL, https://github.com/Microsoft/SEAL

[17]   Martin R. Albrecht, "On dual lattice attacks against small-secret LWE and parameter choices in HElib and SEAL." Annual International Conference on the Theory and Applications of Cryptographic Techniques. Springer, Cham, 2017.

CHAPTER 14

Ring-Learning with Errors Cryptography

In this chapter, we will discuss Ring-Learning with Errors cryptography (RLWE) as one of the most powerful and challenging approaches for developing professional and complex applications and systems.

In 2005, Oded Regev introduced the Learning with Errors (LWE) [4] problem and it turned out to be an amazingly versatile basis for the future of cryptography and providing complex cryptographic constructions. If you want more information about LWE and related problems, we've listed some of the best surveys on lattice-based cryptography [5, 6, 7, 8].

LWE represents a computation problem the main purpose of which is to be used as a foundation for new cryptographic algorithms and to build new, practical cryptographic constructions. An example is *NewHope* [9], a post-quantum key encapsulation. NewHope was designed to provide protection against cryptanalysis attacks issued by quantum computers and also as a basic foundation for homomorphic encryption.

R-LWE represents a larger LWE problem that is based on specialized polynomial rings over finite fields. Based on the presumption difficulty of resolving RLWE problems even using quantum computers, RLWE cryptography is seen as the fundamental base for public-key cryptography for the future (see Figure 14-2 and Listing 14-2 for an example).

The important advantage of RLWE cryptography over LWE consists in the size of the public and private keys. The keys that are generated by RLWE represent the square root of the keys that are obtained from LWE. Let's consider the following example for the sake of discussion: we are using a 128-bit security level and a RLWE cryptographic algorithm will use public keys with size of 7000 bits.

© Marius Iulian Mihailescu and Stefania Loredana Nita 2021
M. I. Mihailescu and S. L. Nita, *Pro Cryptography and Cryptanalysis*,
https://doi.org/10.1007/978-1-4842-6367-9_14

There are three categories of RLWE cryptographic algorithms:

- **RLWE Key Exchanges (RLWE-KE):** In 2011, at the University of Cincinnati, Jintai Ding proposed an idea of LWE and RLWE with key exchange. His elementary idea [10] was born from the associativity property of the matrix multiplications. The errors in this case are used to serve for providing security. The paper was published in 2012 and the patent filled in the same year. In 2014, Chris Peikert introduced a key transport scheme based on Ding's idea [11].

- **RLWE Signature (RLWE-S):** In 2011, Lyubashevsky proposed an improved version of the Identification protocol proposed by Feige, Fiat, and Shamir [12] by converting it to a digital signature [13]. In 2012, the signature was extended by GLP (Gunesyu, Lyubashevsky, and Popplemann) [14].

- **RLWE Homomorphic Encryption (RLWE-HE):** The main goal of homomorphic encryption is to allow computations over sensitive data. In 2011, Brakeersky and Vaikuntanathan proposed a fully homomorphic encryption scheme using RLWE and achieving security using key-dependent messages [15].

In the following sections, we will go through a short mathematical background showing the minimum necessary theoretical information you know before moving further with the implementation.

Mathematical Background
Learning with Errors

With the evolution of quantum computers, many of the existing public-key cryptosystems will be easily broken. Therefore, there are necessary hardness assumptions for encryption schemes that are resistant to quantum computers. One such methods is Learning with Errors. Informally, the LWE problem is based on the hardness of discovering the values that solve the following equality:

$$b = as + e$$

In the above equality, a and b are the public keys, s represents the secret key, and e represents an error value (or noise).

The LWE problem has application in many fields of cryptography. For example, it is used to make public-key encryption secure against chosen-plaintext attacks or chosen ciphertext attacks, oblivious transfers, identity-based encryption, and fully homomorphic encryption.

In the paper [1], the equality from above is applied in linear equations and it becomes $b = A \times s + e$, where (1) A is a bidimensional matrix and b, e are one-dimensional matrices if s is a one-dimensional matrix or (2) A, b are one-dimensional matrices if s is a scalar value.

A simple encryption scheme that uses LWE can be defined as follows, considering $p \in Z$ a prime number:

- **Key generation**: Choose randomly a vector $s \in \mathbb{Z}_p^n$, choose a matrix A with m rows representing m independent vectors from a uniform distribution, and chose randomly the vector $e = (e_1, ..., e_m)$ from an error distribution defined over Z. Compute $b = As + e$. The public key is the pair (A, b) and the secret key is s.

- **Encryption**: Given the matrices, A and b and the message $m \in \{0, 1\}$ that needs to be encrypted, apply random sampling on A and b to obtain $v_A = \sum a_i$ and $v_b = \sum b_j - \frac{p}{2} m$, where a_i are samples from A and b_j are samples from b. The encryption of m is the pair (u, v).

- **Decryption**: Compute the value $val = v_b - s v_A \ (mod\ p)$. If $val \le \frac{p}{2}$, then the message is $m = 0$; otherwise, the message is $m = 1$.

The example from above is just a very simple encryption scheme to demonstrate how the LWE problem works. Important public-key encryption schemes based on the LWE problem are the Regev [2] and Lindner-Peikert encryption schemes.

There are two types of LWE problems: LWE search and LWE decision. In the following, we provide the formal definitions for these variants of the LWE problem:

Definition of LWE Search. Given the values $m, n, p \in Z$ and the distributions χ_s and χ_e defined over the integers numbers set $\mathbb{Z}$, choose $s \leftarrow \chi_s^n$, $e_i \leftarrow \chi_e$ and $a_i \leftarrow \mathcal{U}(\mathbb{Z}_p^n)$ and compute the value of $b_i := \langle a_i, s \rangle + e_i \ mod\ p$, where $i = 1, ..., m$. The *Learning with Errors Search* variant problem for the tuple $(n, m, p, \chi_s, \chi_e)$ consists in determining s knowing $\left(a_i, b_i\right)_{i=1}^m$.

Note in the above definition that s is a column-vector with n values, a_i is a row-vector with n values from $\mathbb{Z}_p$, b is a column-vector with m elements from $\mathbb{Z}_p$, and the notation $x \leftarrow S$ means that x is a random variable picked from the finite set S.

Definition of LWE Decision. Given the values $n, p \in \mathbb{Z}$ and the distributions χ_s and χ_e defined over the integers numbers set $\mathbb{Z}$, choose $s \leftarrow \chi_s^n$ and establish two oracles as below:

- $\mathcal{O}: a \leftarrow \mathcal{U}\left(\mathbb{Z}_p^n\right), e \leftarrow \chi_e$; output $(a, \langle a, s \rangle + e \bmod p)$

- $U: a \leftarrow \mathcal{U}\left(\mathbb{Z}_p^n\right), u \leftarrow \mathcal{U}\left(\mathbb{Z}_p\right)$; output (a, u)

The *Learning with Errors Decision* represents a variant problem for the tuple (n, p, χ_s, χ_e) and its purpose is to differentiate between $\mathcal{O}$ and U.

Ring-Learning with Errors

The LWE problem can be applied in the rings of polynomials that have coefficients from a finite field. In this case, the LWE problem is called *Ring-Learning with Errors* (RLWE). In cryptography, RLWE is used in topics such as key exchange, signatures, or homomorphic encryption. The principles are similar to those from simple LWE and in the first equality a, b, s, e are all of them polynomials. The two variants of the LWE problem become

Definition (RLWE Search). Given the values $n, p \in Z$ with $n = 2^k$, letting R be $R = \dfrac{\mathbb{Z}[X]}{X^n + 1}$ and $R_p = \dfrac{R}{pR}$ and the distributions χ_s and χ_e defined over the ring R_p, choose $s \leftarrow \chi_s$, $e \longleftarrow \chi_e$ and $a \leftarrow \mathcal{U}\left(R_p\right)$ and compute the value of $b := as + e$. The *Ring-Learning with Errors Search* variant problem for the tuple (n, p, χ_s, χ_e) consists in determining s knowing (a, b).

Note that in the above definition, $R_p = \dfrac{\mathbb{Z}_p[X]}{X^n + 1}$.

Definition (RLWE Decision). Given the values $n, p \in Z_+$ and the distributions χ_s and χ_e defined over the ring R_p, choose $s \leftarrow \chi_s$ and establish two oracles as below:

- $\mathcal{O}: a \leftarrow \mathcal{U}\left(R_p\right), e \leftarrow \chi_e$; output $(a, as + e)$

- $U: a \leftarrow \mathcal{U}\left(R_p\right), u \leftarrow \mathcal{U}\left(R_p\right)$; output (a, u)

The *Ring-Learning with Errors Decision* variant problem for the tuple (n, p, χ_s, χ_e) is to differentiate between $\mathcal{O}$ and U.

For an encryption scheme based on (R)LWE to be secure, it needs that the advantage of any polynomial-time algorithm $\mathcal{A}$ (called attacker) to solve the (R)LWE problem is a negligible function.

Practical Implementation

LWE represents a robust method with a quantum flavor for cryptography. When you decide to move to the practical side of LWE and to implement a simple method that deals with LWEs, you need to have in mind that you will need to create a secret key value (*sk*) and another value (*random _ value*). The next step is quite straightforward, as you will need to have a set of values (*set _ of _ values*[]) and to compute p[]=t[]×sk + e. Later, *p*[] and *set _ of _ values*[] will be the public key.

The first example (see Figure 14-1) that we will show represents an encryption method that was defined by Oded Regev in [4], known as Learning with Errors. The workflow of the algorithm is simple: *each bit of the message* (see the first line in Figure 14-1) is encrypted following the scheme of Oded Regev from [4]. The code is shown in Listing 14-1.

```
D:\Apps C#\Chapter 15 - (Ring)Learning With Errors Cryptography\LWECase1\LWECase1\bin\Debug\LWECase1.exe    —  □  ×
The message to be send: 1
The random values:
        5       8      12      16       2       6      11       3       7      10
The public key is:
       37      52      72      92      22      42      67      27      47      62       0       0       0       0
0       0       0       0       0       0       0       0       0       0       0       0       0       0       0
0       0       0       0       0       0       0       0       0       0       0       0       0       0       0
0       0       0       0       0       0       0       0       0       0       0       0       0       0       0
0       0       0       0       0       0       0       0       0       0       0       0       0       0       0
0       0       0       0       0       0       0       0       0       0       0       0       0       0       0
0       0       0       0       0       0       0       0       0       0       0       0       0       0       0
0       0       0       0       0       0       0       0       0       0       0       0       0       0       0
0       0       0       0       0       0       0       0       0       0       0       0       0       0       0
0       0       0       0       0       0       0       0       0       0       0       0       0       0       0
0       0       0       0       0       0       0       0       0       0       0       0       0       0       0
0       0       0
The selected values are:
       60      60      81      96      65      86      88      85      87      74       0      57      37      23
97      12      79      90      50      48      78       1      65      15      36       2      55      94      87
56      23      89      66      52       0      28      86      23      24      15      64      38      76      48
68      87      17      78      85      19      79      65      59      76      59      35      51      20      14
53      21      69      91      20       9      10      91      84      23      68      25      56      66      35
83      40      25      16      47      49      84      77       9      68      76      58      30      89      93
64      76      66       8      70      94      95      46      56      38      57      95      33      55      16
93      23      99      23      93      18      10      34      72      64      69      43      59      23      43
51      80       1      90      58      92      58      47      95      41      87      93      68      78      89
53      51      22      93      74      53      58       6      96      74      53      41      94      43       1
50      36      23      12      87      77      93      42      96      24      35      76       3      82       5
25      41      56      82      11      17      21      66      48      90      92      73       5      16       4
50      64       3      94      90      51      70      55      90      12      59       9      25      69      39
77      55      23      90      49      11
The sum is: 10722
The encrypted message is: 10722
The message received is 0
```

Figure 14-1. *Encryption method used by Oded Regev*

Listing 14-1. Implementation of LWE Encryption Method by Oded Regev

```
using System;
using System.Collections.Generic;
using System.Linq;
using System.Text;
using System.Threading.Tasks;

namespace LWECase1
{
    class Program
    {
        public static int[] public_key = new int[200];
        public static int[] values = new int[]
                                { 5, 8, 12, 16, 2, 6, 11, 3, 7, 10 };
        public static int s = 5;
        public static int e = 12;
        public static int message = 1;
        public static int val = 0;
        public static int sum = 0;
        public static int remainder = 0;

        static void Main(string[] args)
        {
            Random randValue = new Random();
            int[] res = new int[200];
            int k = 0;

            //**
            for (int x=0; x<values.Length; x++)
            {
                public_key[k] = values[x] * s + e;
                k++;
            }
```

```
for(int i=0; i< public_key.Length; i++)
{
    res[i] = randValue.Next(public_key[i],
                        public_key.Length / 2);
}

for(int j=0; j<res.Length; j++)
{
    sum += res[j];
}

Console.WriteLine("The message to be send: {0}", message);
Console.WriteLine("The random values:");
PrintValues(values);
Console.WriteLine("The public key is: ");
PrintValues(public_key);
Console.WriteLine("The selected values are:");
PrintValues(res);

//** compute the sum
if (message == 1)
    sum += 1;

Console.WriteLine("The sum is: {0}", sum);

Console.WriteLine("The encrypted message is: {0}", sum);
//** compute the remainder
remainder = sum % s;

if(remainder % 2 == 0)
    Console.WriteLine("The message received is 0");
else
    Console.WriteLine("The message received is 1");

Console.ReadKey();
}
```

```
//** dealing with arrays
public static void PrintValues(Object[] myArr)
{
    foreach (Object i in myArr)
    {
        Console.Write("\t{0}", i);
    }
    Console.WriteLine();
}

//** dealing with arrays
public static void PrintValues(int[] myArr)
{
    foreach (int i in myArr)
    {
        Console.Write("\t{0}", i);
    }
    Console.WriteLine();
}
}
}
```

In Listing 14-2, we will provide an example of public key encryption based on LWE. We will start by creating a secret value (s), which will represent the private key. The next step creates the public key formed from the values of the random numbers (A). We will generate another set of numbers (B) which are based on A, s, and random errors e. This example is done for a single bit, as is the previous example in Listing 14-1.

A simple workflow for this example is

- Between 0 and 100, we will select a random set of 20 values which represent the public key (A). Let's assume that those 20 values are

$$A = [80,86,19,62,2,83,25,47,20,58,45,15,30,68,4,13,8,6,42,92]$$

- Next, we will define a list (B) and each element will be as $B_i = A_i \times s + e_i(mod\ q)$, where s represents the secret key and e represents a list of small random values, called *the errors values*. As an example of the statement made, let's consider a prime number (q) equal with 97, and the error vector (e) *as*

$$e = \left[3,3,4,1,3,3,4,4,1,4,3,3,2,2,3,2,4,4,1,3\right]$$

- A and B lists are considered the public key and s represents the secret key. At this point, we are able to distribute A and B to everybody who wishes to proceed with an encryption of a message (with the condition to keep s secret). In order to proceed with the encryption, we need to use the samples from A and B. Moving forward, based on those sample we take a bit from the message (M) and compute the following two values:

$$u = \sum\left(A_{samples}\right)\left(mod\ q\right)$$

$$v = \sum\left(B_{samples}\right) + \frac{q}{2} \times M\left(mod\ q\right)$$

- At this point, we say that the encrypted message is (u, v). To proceed with the decryption, we need to compute

$$decryption = v - s \times u\left(mod\ q\right)$$

If $decryption < \frac{q}{2}$ the message is equal with 0, otherwise 1.

The procedure described above is summarized from Oded Regev's paper [5] in order to make it easy to follow and to have a clear understanding of how to transpose the complexity of LWE in reality. Next, let's have a look at Listing 14-2 to see how this implementation will look. The output is shown in Figure 14-2.

```
D:\Apps C#\Chapter 15 - (Ring)Learning With Errors Cryptography\PublicKeyEncLWE_Case2\PublicKeyEncLWE_Case2\bin\Debug\PublicKeyEncLWE_Ca...   —   □   ×
PARAMETERS SECTION

      Message to be send: 1
      The public key (A):
      15      14      19      14      17      18      15      19      14      18      17      14      16      18
19    0       0       0       0       0       0       0       0       0       0       0       0       0       0
0
      The public key (B):
      0       1       0       1       1       1       0       0       1       1       1       1       0       1
1     1       1       0       1       1       1       1       1       0       1       0       1       0       0
1
      The errors (e) are:
      2       1       2       1       3       3       2       2       1       3       1       3       2       1
1     1       3       2       3       3       1       1       1       2       1       2       1       2       2
1
      The secret key is: 20
      Prime number is: 15
The sample is 19
The sample is 19
The sample is 20
The sample is 21
The sample is 20
[0, 1, ], end = 00
u = 7
v = 7
The result is: -13
Message is 0
```

Figure 14-2. *The output of public key encryption example using LWE*

Listing 14-2. Implementation of Public Key Encryption Example Using LWE

```csharp
using System;
using System.Collections.Generic;
using System.Linq;
using System.Text;
using System.Threading.Tasks;

namespace PublicKeyEncLWE_Case2
{
    class Program
    {
        public static int[] A = new int[30];
        public static int[] B = new int[30];
        public static int[] e = new int[30];
        public static int s = 20;
        public static int message = 1;
        public static int q = 15;
        public static int nvals = 20;
```

```csharp
static void Main(string[] args)
{
    Random randomSample = new Random();
    IEnumerable<int> q_values = Enumerable.
                                Range(0, q);
    IEnumerable<int> n_values = Enumerable.Range(
                                nvals - 1, nvals / 4);
    double u = 0;
    double v = 0;
    int sample = 0;

    foreach (int q_value in q_values)
    {
        for (int i = 0; i < q; i++)
        {
            A[i] = randomSample.Next(q_value, nvals);
        }
    }
    for (int x = 0; x < A.Length; x++)
    {
        e[x] = randomSample.Next(1, 4);
        B[x] = (A[x] * s + e[x]) % 2;
    }

    Console.WriteLine("PARAMETERS SECTION\n");
    Console.WriteLine("\tMessage to be send: {0}", message);
    Console.WriteLine("\tThe public key (A):");
    PrintValues(A);
    Console.WriteLine("\tThe public key (B):");
    PrintValues(B);
    Console.WriteLine("\tThe errors (e) are: ");
    PrintValues(e);
    Console.WriteLine("\tThe secret key is: {0}", s);
    Console.WriteLine("\tPrime number is: {0}", q);
```

```csharp
        foreach(int n_value in n_values)
        {
            sample = randomSample.Next(nvals - 1, n_value);
            Console.WriteLine("The sample is {0}", sample);
        }

        IEnumerable<int> samples = Enumerable.Range(0, sample);
        string errors = string.Empty;

        for (int x = 0; x < samples.Count(); x++)
        {
            errors = "[" + A[x] + ", " + B[x] + ", ], end
                                        = " + u + A[x];
        }

        Console.WriteLine(errors);

        double flooring = q / 2;

        v += Math.Floor(flooring) * message;

        u = v % q;
        v = u % q;

        Console.WriteLine("u = {0}", u);
        Console.WriteLine("v = {0}", v);

        double res = (v - s * u) % q;
        Console.WriteLine("The result is: {0}", res);
        if (res > q / 2)
            Console.WriteLine("Message is 1");
        else
            Console.WriteLine("Message is 0");

        Console.ReadKey();
    }
```

```
public static void PrintValues(Object[] myArr)
{
    foreach (Object i in myArr)
    {
        Console.Write("\t{0}", i);
    }
    Console.WriteLine();
}

public static void PrintValues(int[] myArr)
{
    foreach (int i in myArr)
    {
        Console.Write("\t{0}", i);
    }
    Console.WriteLine();
}
}
}
```

Conclusion

In this chapter, you tried the first practical approach for Ring-Learning with Errors cryptography using the C# programming language. It can serve as a space for multiple challenges for professionals and a starting point for significant contributions to this cryptographic primitive.

At the end of this chapter, you now have the following:

- A solid but short mathematical background of the main concepts and definitions on which R-LWE is based and without which a practical implementation will have many gaps to fill out

- An experience with the challenges brought by RLWE's mathematical concepts and their transposition in practice

Bibliography

[1] Oded Regev, "The Learning with Errors Problem," `https://cims.nyu.edu/~regev/papers/lwesurvey.pdf`.

[2] O. Regev, "On lattices, learning with errors, random linear codes, and cryptography." In *Journal of the ACM (JACM)*, 56(6), 1-40. 2009.

[3] R. Lindner and C. Peikert, "Better key sizes (and attacks) for LWE-based encryption." In *Cryptographers' Track at the RSA Conference* (pp. 319-339). Springer, Berlin, Heidelberg. 2011.

[4] O. Regev, "The Learning with Errors Problem (Invited Survey)," In *2010 IEEE 25th Annual Conference on Computational Complexity*, (pp. 191-204). Cambridge, MA, doi: 10.1109/CCC.2010.26. 2010.

[5] D. Micciancio and O. Regev, "Lattice-based cryptography." In D. J. Bernstein and J. Buchmann (eds), *Post-quantum Cryptography*. Springer, 2008.

[6] C. Peikert. "Some recent progress in lattice-based cryptography." Slides for invited tutorial at TCC'09, 2009.

[7] D. Micciancio. "Cryptographic functions from worst-case complexity assumptions." In: P. Q. Nguyen and B. Vall'ee (eds), *The LLL Algorithm: Survey and Applications, Information Security and Cryptography*, pages 427–452. Springer, 2008. Prelim. version in LLL25, 2007.

[8] O. Regev. "Lattice-based cryptography." In *CRYPTO* (pp. 131–141). 2006.

[9] NewHope – Post-quantum Key Encapsulation. Available online: `https://newhopecrypto.org/`.

[10] Jintai Ding, Xiang Xie and Xiaodong Lin, "A Simple Provably Secure Key Exchange Scheme Based on the Learning with Errors Problem." Available online: `https://eprint.iacr.org/2012/688`. 2012.

[11]   C. Peikert, "Lattice Cryptography for the Internet." In M. Mosca
       (ed) *Post-Quantum Cryptography. PQCrypto 2014. Lecture Notes
       in Computer Science, vol 8772.* Springer, Cham. 2014.

[12]   Y. Desmedt, "Fiat–Shamir Identification Protocol and the
       Feige–Fiat–Shamir Signature Scheme." In H.C.A. van Tilborg
       and S. Jajodia (eds) *Encyclopedia of Cryptography and Security.*
       Springer, Boston, MA. 2011.

[13]   V. Lyubashevsky, "Lattice Signatures without Trapdoors." In
       D. Pointcheval and T. Johansson (eds*) Advances in Cryptology –
       EUROCRYPT 2012. EUROCRYPT 2012. Lecture Notes in Computer
       Science, vol 7237.* Springer, Berlin, Heidelberg. 2012.

[14]   Tim Güneysu, Vadim Lyubashevsky, and Thomas Pöppelmann,
       "Practical Lattice-Based Cryptography: A Signature Scheme for
       Embedded Systems." In Emmanuel Prouff and Patrick Schaumont
       (eds.) *Lecture Notes in Computer Science,* (pp. 530–547). Springer
       Berlin Heidelberg. doi: 10.1007/978-3-642-33027-8_31. ISBN 978-
       3-642-33026-1. 2012.

[15]   Zvika Brakerski and Vinod Vaikuntanathan, "Fully Homomorphic
       Encryption from Ring-LWE and Security for Key Dependent
       Messages." In Phillip Rogaway(ed.) *Lecture Notes in Computer
       Science* (pp. 505–524). Springer Berlin Heidelberg. doi:10.1007/
       978-3-642-22792-9_29. ISBN 978-3-642-22791-2. 2011.

CHAPTER 15

Chaos-Based Cryptography

Chaos-based cryptography is the applicability of the chaos theory and its mathematical background to create new and unique cryptography algorithms. In 1989, it was investigated for the first time by Robert Matthews in [1] and it attracted significant interest.

Compared to normal cryptographic primitives that we use every day, to use chaos theory and systems in an efficient way, the chaotic maps have to be implemented with respect for confusion and diffusion. In this chapter, we will use the notion of a *chaotic system* for referring to the cryptography algorithm.

In order to understand the differences and similarities between chaotic systems and cryptographic algorithms, let's look over the following relations shown in Table 15-1, relations that were established by L. Kocarev in [2].

Table 15-1. *Similarities and Differences Between Chaotic Systems and Cryptographic Algorithms*

Chaotic System	Cryptographic Algorithm
Phase space: subset of real numbers	Phase space: finite set of integers
Iterations	Rounds
Parameters	Key
Sensitivity to a change in initial conditions and parameters	Diffusion
?	Security and performance

© Marius Iulian Mihailescu and Stefania Loredana Nita 2021
M. I. Mihailescu and S. L. Nita, *Pro Cryptography and Cryptanalysis*,
https://doi.org/10.1007/978-1-4842-6367-9_15

To demonstrate the similarities and differences shown in Table 16-1, we will consider as an example of a chaotic system the *shift map*:

$$x(t+1) = ax(t)(\bmod 1)$$

in which the phase space $x = [0, 1]$ represents the unit interval and $a > 1$ represents an integer.

Different functions and discrete-time systems have been proposed for use in cryptography. Once you look over them, you will see that the phase space represents a finite set of integers and the parameters are equal to the integers. One of the most common examples is represented by the discrete phase-space version of the shift map presented above as an example:

$$p(t+1) = ap(t)(\bmod N)$$

in which $a > 1$, N and p represent integers, and $p \in [0, 1, ..., N-1]$. If N is coprime to a, the second representation of the shift map is invertible. This means that all the trajectories that are within a finite phase space dynamical system are characterized as being periodically. In this situation, you can see a new concept that is being introduced, *period functions* P_N which will characterize the least period of the map F, which is F^{P_N} as being its identity and P_N represents the minimal, as being a function of system size N.

When dealing with practical chaos system, another metric that is very important is characterized by the *Lyapunov exponent* (LE) which trivially is being equal to 0. This is happening because the orbit is so periodic and it will repeat itself.

This being said, we will present two ideas of block diagrams (text encryption and image encryption) to show what an encryption scheme using the chaos approach will look like. In Figure 15-1 and Figure 15-2, you can see the process of encryption and decryption for a plaintext using logistic map. For image encryption and decryption, Figure 15-3 shows a model for example purpose.

Based on the block diagrams proposed as examples, you can take a look over the original papers and other papers listed at the end of the chapter and see that the encryption models and building them can vary depending on the chaotic map used. It is very important that you understand how a specific chaotic map works before starting to design new approaches and chaos cryptographic mechanisms. Using the following block diagrams as practical guide from theory to practical is a good starting point due to the fact that the models are created with respect for similarities and differences listed in Table 15-1.

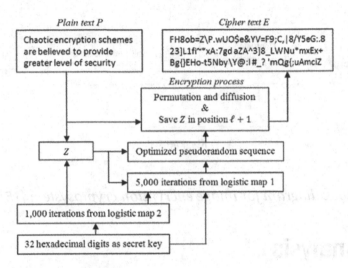

Figure 15-1. *Block diagram for text encryption using logistic map [14]*

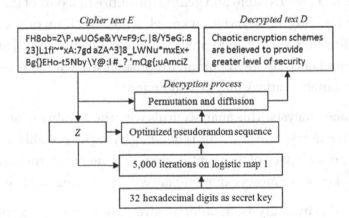

Figure 15-2. *Block diagram for text encryption using logistic map [14]*

361

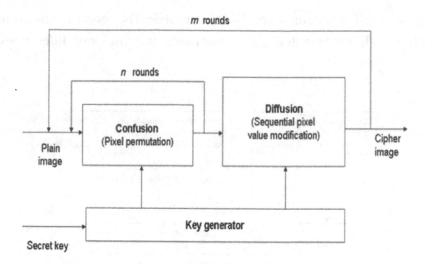

Figure 15-3. *Block diagram for image encryption cryptosystem [15]*

Security Analysis

This section will refer to security analysis as the method to find the weakness and ·
security breaches of a cryptosystem and getting the entire or a part of the ciphered
image/plaintext or finding the key without knowing the algorithm or decryption key.

Some interesting attacks over encrypted images can be found in [3] and [4]. The
following criteria and analysis are important to consider when a chaotic system is
designed or a cryptanalytic attack may be conducted:

- **Key space analysis**. This analysis deals with the number of attempts
  to find the decryption key. This is done by trying all possible keys
  within the key space of the cryptosystem. It is very important to note
  that the key space grows exponentially with the increasing key size.

- **Key sensitivity analysis**. In order to have a good image encryption
  system, the sensitivity of the secret key is important and needs to be
  taken into consideration. If only one bit is changed in the secret key,
  this will output a totally different image (encrypted or decrypted).

- **Statistical analysis**. This type of analysis is performed with the goal
  of proving the relationship that stands between the genuine and
  encrypted image.

- **Correlation co-efficient analysis**. The histogram is an important graphic tool to study the distribution of the values generated by a trajectory of a dynamic system. Besides histogram analysis, another important tool for studying the correlation of adjacent pixels of a plain image and/or encrypted image is based on the correlation of the two pixels distributed vertically, horizontally, and diagonally.

- **Information entropy analysis**. The entropy analysis is used to test the robustness of the encryption algorithm. It is very important to compare the entropy of plain images and ciphered images. By doing so, we are able to see that the entropy of the encrypted images is approximately equal to an 8-bit depth. This will help us to prove the encryption technique against the entropy attack.

- **Differential analysis**. With the help of differential analysis we will determine the sensitivity of the encryption algorithm to any slight change produced in the algorithm. There are two criteria used for testing the sensitivity. One is NPCR (number of pixels change rate) and the second one is UACI (unified average changing intensity). Once these two criteria are computed, based on the high values we can see any indication of small changes that occur in the plain image, which will produce significant changes in the ciphered images.

Chaotic Maps for Plaintexts and Images Encryption

In this section, we will present the chaotic maps based on their encryption target (text encryption or image encryption).

Most of image encryption algorithms listed in Table 15-2 were tested by the authors mentioned in the references using different security analysis, as discussed above. It's very useful to have a validation of the performance and to have an evaluation of the cryptosystem's robustness. All the references were examined and chosen as good references based on their analysis and tests.

Table 15-2. *Chaotic Map (Systems) for Image Encryption*

Chaotic Map (System)	Metrics			Key		Bibliography
	Entropy	NPCR	UACI	Space	Sensitivity	
Lorenz	7.9973	-	-	2^{128}	High	[5]
Baker						
Lorenz	-	-	-	Large	Medium	[6]
Henon Map	7.9904	0.0015%	0.0005%	2^{128}	High	[7]
Logistic Map	7.9996	99.6231%	33.4070%	10^{45}	High	[8]
Trigonometry Maps	-	0.25%	0.19%	2^{302}	-	[9]
Arnold Cat Map	7.9981	99.62%	33.19%	2^{148}	High	[10]
Chebyshev Map	7.9902	99.609%	33.464%	2^{167}	High	[11]
Circle Map	7.9902	99.63%	33%	2^{256}	High	[12]
Arnold Map	-	0.0015%	0.004%	-	-	[13]

Practical Implementation

Most of the applications of chaotic systems can be seen on *plaintext encryption* and *image encryption*. As in other areas of cryptography that we have discussed in this book, the research community offers a significant amount of theoretical contributions. The lack of practical implementations raises multiple difficulties and challenges for researchers and professionals.

There are not many practical implementations of chaos systems cryptography but some practical approaches (and here we are referring to pseudocode algorithms) can be found within [16]. The work has a very in-depth structure and gives some ideas on how different cryptosystems based on the chaos theory can be implemented by providing pseudocode. The work covers the following cryptosystems types:

- Chaos-based public-key cryptography

- Pseudo-random number generation in cryptography

- Formation of high-dimensional chaotic maps and their uses in cryptography

- Chaos-based hash functions

- Chaos-based video encryption algorithms

- Cryptanalysis of chaotic ciphers

- Hardware implementation of chaos-based ciphers

- Hardware implementation of chaos-secured optical communication systems

In [16], starting with Chapter 2, the authors propose an interesting public-key cryptosystem that uses the chaos approach and consists of three steps: the key generation algorithm (see Pseudocode 15-1), encryption algorithm (see Pseudocode 15-2), and decryption algorithm (see Pseudocode 15-3). The scenario is a typical communication between two user entities, Alice and Bob. Let's have a look at the structure of each algorithm and at the end we'll to provide a simple orientative implementation as a future reference guide for professionals.

Pseudocode 15-1. Key Generation Algorithm [16]

Start. Alice will need, before the communication, to generate the keys. For this, she will accomplish the following:

- A large integer a has to be generated.

- Calculate $G_a(p)$ based on a random number selected as $p \in [-1, 1]$.

- Alice will set her public key as $(p, G(p))$ and the private key to a.

Pseudocode 15-2. Encryption Algorithm [16]

Start. Bob wants to encrypt a messsage. To achieve this, the following must be done:

- Get Alice's authentic public key $(p, G_a(p))$.

- Calculate and represents the message as a number $M \in [-1, 1]$.

- Generate a large integer r.

- Calculate $G_r(p)$, $G_{r \cdot a(x)} = G_r(G_a(p))$ and $X = M \cdot G_{r \cdot s}(p)$.

- Take the ciphertext and send it as $C = (G_r(p), X)$ to Alice.

Pseudocode 15-3. Decryption Algorithm [16]

Start. Alice wants to read the text and to do this she will have to recover M from the ciphertext C. To achieve this, the following steps are done:

- Alice has to use her private key a and calculate $G_{a \cdot t} = G_a(G_r(p))$.

- The message M is obtained by calculating $M = \dfrac{X}{G_{a \cdot r}(p)}$.

Based on the algorithms listed above, we will move to a practical implementation as an example. Listing 15-1 shows encryption and decryption based on an automorphism of two-dimensional torus. The application has three classes: the TorusAutomorphism class (see Listing 15-1), the GenerateChaosValues class (see Listing 15-2, and the main Program class (see Listing 15-3). The application has been adapted accordingly following the pseudo-code listings from above. You can see the output in Figure 15-4.

Each class has a purpose, as follows:

- TorusAutomorphism class: The class contains functions and methods that deal with the char encryption (object CharacterEncryption), char decryption (object CharacterDecryption) and main encryption (object[] Encryption) and decryption (object[] Decryption) functions for the entire strings of characters.

- GenerateChaosValues class: The class deals with the structure functions of the automorphism, such as rotation operations and setting the index of the elements.

- Program class: The class represents the main entry point of the application.

Listing 15-1. Chaos Encryption/Decryption Using Torus Automorphism

```
using System;
using System.Collections.Generic;
using System.Linq;
using System.Text;
using System.Threading.Tasks;

namespace ChaosSystemCryptography
```

```
{
    class TorusAutomorphism
    {
        private object CharacterEncryption(char
                input_characters, GenerateChaosValues[]
                iterations, int generators, bool logging)
        {
            int spotted_difference;
            spotted_difference = iterations[(generators % 2 ==
                    0) ? 0 : 1].ItemIndex(input_characters);
            foreach (GenerateChaosValues iteration_generator
                                        in iterations)
            {
                iteration_generator.GeneratorRotation(
                        spotted_difference, 'L');
                if (logging == true) {
                        iteration_generator.PrintInConsole(
                            spotted_difference + generators); }
            }
            return iterations[2].ItemIndex(0);
        }

        public object[] Encryption(string input_locations,
                        GenerateChaosValues[]
                        generators_locations, bool logging)
        {
            object[] finalOutputObject = new
                            object[input_locations.Length];
            for (int i = 0; i < input_locations.Length; i++)
            {
                finalOutputObject[i] =
                        CharacterEncryption(input_locations[i],
                        generators_locations, i, logging);
            }
            return finalOutputObject;
        }
    }
```

```
    private object CharacterDecryption(char
                input_characterst, GenerateChaosValues[]
                iterations, int generators, bool
                logging)
    {
        int spotted_difference;
        spotted_difference =
              iterations[2].ItemIndex(input_characterst);
        foreach (GenerateChaosValues
              iteration_generator in iterations)
        {
              iteration_generator.GeneratorRotation(
                  spotted_difference, 'L');
            if (logging == true) {
                iteration_generator.PrintInConsole(
                  spotted_difference + generators); }
        }
        return iterations[(generators % 2 == 0) ?
                    0 : 1].ItemIndex(0);
    }

    public object[] Decryption(string
                encryption_locations,
                GenerateChaosValues[]
                generators_locations, bool logging)
    {
        object[] finalOutputObject = new
                object[encryption_locations.Length];
        for (int i = encryption_locations.Length - 1;
                                   i >= 0; i--)
        {
            finalOutputObject[i] =
                CharacterDecryption(encryption_locations[i],
                    generators_locations, i, logging);
```

```
        }
        return finalOutputObject;
    }
  }
}
```

Listing 15-2. Generating Chaotic Values for Torus

```csharp
using System;
using System.Collections.Generic;
using System.Linq;
using System.Text;
using System.Threading.Tasks;

namespace ChaosSystemCryptography
{
    class GenerateChaosValues
    {
        private object[] items = new object[94];
        private char last_direction;
        private readonly string generator_ID;

        //** the property will return the index of the item
        //** for a specific value as character
        public int ItemIndex(char inputValue)
        {
            int locationElement;
            locationElement = Array.IndexOf(items,
                                            inputValue);
            return locationElement;
        }

        //** the property will return the index of the item
        //** for a specific value as integer
        public object ItemIndex(int inputValue)
        {
            object locationElement;
            locationElement = items.GetValue(inputValue);
```

369

```
            return locationElement;
    }

    //** constructor
    public GenerateChaosValues(
                    string generator_name = null)
    {
        generator_ID = generator_name;
        for (int i = 32; i <= 125; i++)
        {
            items[i - 32] = (char)i;
        }

    }

    public void GeneratorRotation(int rotation,
                                    char chosen_direction)
    {
        object[] rotation_done = new object[items.Length];
        int length = items.Length;
        int rotation_location = (rotation % length);

        //** the torus will have a right rotation
        if (chosen_direction == 'R')
        {
            for (int in_direction = 0; in_direction <
                                length; in_direction++)
            {
                if (rotation_location + in_direction
                                >= length)
                {
                    int suplimentary_rotation =
                        rotation_location - (length -
                                        in_direction);
                    rotation_done[suplimentary_rotation] =
                                        items[in_direction];
                }
```

```
        else
        {
            rotation_done[in_direction +
                    rotation_location] =
                    items[in_direction];
        }
    }
    last_direction = 'R';
}
else
{
    for (int in_direction = 0; in_direction <
                        length; in_direction++)
    {
        if (rotation_location + in_direction
                            >= length)
        {
            int suplimentary_rotation =
                    rotation_location - (length -
                        in_direction);
            rotation_done[in_direction] =
                    items[suplimentary_rotation];
        }
        else
        {
            rotation_done[in_direction] =
                    items[in_direction +
                    rotation_location];
        }
    }
    last_direction = 'L';
}
Array.Copy(rotation_done, items,
            rotation_done.Length);

}
```

```csharp
public void GeneratorRotation(int rotation)
{
    object[] rotation_done = new object[items.Length];
    int length = items.Length;
    int rotation_location = (rotation % length);

    for (int in_direction = 0; in_direction < length;
                                    in_direction++)
    {
        if (rotation_location + in_direction
                                    >= length)
        {
            int suplimentary_rotation =
                rotation_location -
                    (length - in_direction);
            rotation_done[suplimentary_rotation] =
                                items[in_direction];
        }
        else
        {
            rotation_done[in_direction +
                    rotation_location] =
                    items[in_direction];
        }
    }
    last_direction = 'R';
    Array.Copy(rotation_done, items,
                rotation_done.Length);
}
public void PrintInConsole(int rotated = 0)
{
    Console.Write($"{generator_ID} rotated {rotated}
    {((last_direction == 'L') ? "left" : "right")}: ");
    for (int i = 0; i < items.Length; i++)
```

```csharp
        {
            Console.Write($"{items[i]}, ");
        }
        Console.WriteLine("");
    }
}
}
```

Listing 15-3. Main Program

```csharp
using System;
using System.Collections;
using System.Collections.Generic;
using System.Diagnostics;
using System.IO;
using System.Linq;
using System.Text;
using System.Threading.Tasks;

namespace ChaosSystemCryptography
{
    class Program
    {
        public static void Main(string[] args)
        {
            bool logging = true;
            string key = "$6G";
            string input_value = string.Empty;
            Console.Write("What to you want to do? Encryption
                                    (e) or Decryption (d): ");
            string option = (Console.ReadLine() == "encrypt")
                                        ? "e" : "d";

            int zero_location = Convert.ToInt32(key[0]);
            int one_location = Convert.ToInt32(key[1]);
            int two_location = Convert.ToInt32(key[2]);
```

```csharp
TorusAutomorphism torus_automorphism = new
                            TorusAutomorphism();

GenerateChaosValues generator0 = new
            GenerateChaosValues((logging == true) ?
            "generator0" : null);
GenerateChaosValues generator1 = new
            GenerateChaosValues((logging == true) ?
            "generator1" : null);
GenerateChaosValues generator2 = new
            GenerateChaosValues((logging == true) ?
            "generator2" : null);
GenerateChaosValues[] generators = new
            GenerateChaosValues[] { generator0,
            generator1, generator2 };

generator0.GeneratorRotation(zero_location);
generator1.GeneratorRotation(one_location);
generator2.GeneratorRotation(two_location);

if (option == "e")
{
    Console.Write("Enter the text for
                                encryption: ");
    input_value = Console.ReadLine();

    if (logging == true)
    {
        generator0.PrintInConsole(zero_location);
        generator1.PrintInConsole(one_location);
        generator2.PrintInConsole(two_location);
    }

    Console.WriteLine("");
    Console.WriteLine($"The input message:
                        {input_value}");
```

```csharp
            object[] finalValue =
                    torus_automorphism.Encryption(
                        input_value, generators, logging);

        Console.WriteLine("");
        Console.Write("\nThe output message: ");
        for (int j = 0; j < finalValue.Length; j++) {
                Console.Write($"{finalValue[j]}"); }
    }
    else if (option == "d")
    {
        Console.Write("What is the ciphertext for
                                        decryption: ");
        string ciphertext_input = Console.ReadLine();
        if (logging == true)
        {
            generator0.PrintInConsole(zero_location);
            generator1.PrintInConsole(one_location);
            generator2.PrintInConsole(two_location);
        }
        Console.WriteLine($"\nEncryption for input
                            string: {ciphertext_input}");
            object[] finalDecrypted =
                torus_automorphism.Decryption(ciphertext
                    _input, generators, logging);
        Console.Write("\nThe decrypted text is: ");
        for (int j = 0; j < finalDecrypted.Length;
                                                j++)
            { Console.Write(finalDecrypted[j]); }
    }
    Console.WriteLine("\n Press any key to exit...");
    Console.ReadKey();
        }
    }
}
```

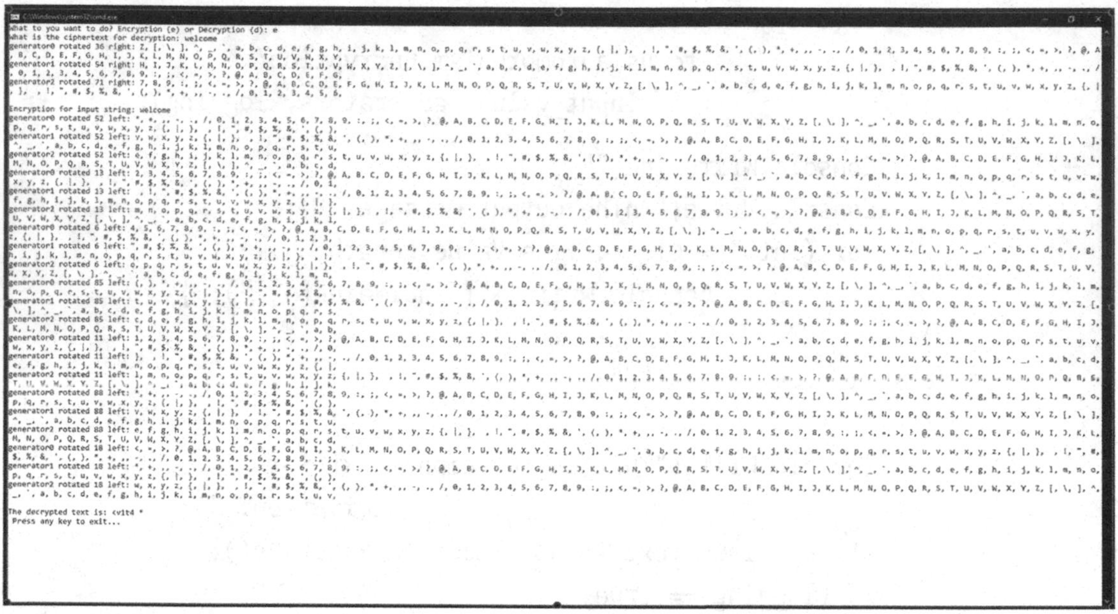

Figure 15-4. *The output of the chaos torus automorphism*

Conclusion

In this chapter, we discussed an interesting approach to cryptography, chaos-based cryptography. New cryptographic algorithms are using chaos maps to generate new cryptographic primitives in a different way from those used in the past.

At the end of this chapter, you now know the following:

- How chaos-based cryptography primitives are built and what makes them different from normal cryptographic primitives

- How the chaos system is designed for text encryption and image encryption

- How to implement a cryptographic system using chaos system and automorphism torus

Bibliography

[1]   Robert Matthews, "On the derivation of a 'chaotic' encryption algorithm," In *Cryptologia 13*, no. 1 (1989): 29-42.

[2]   L. Kocarev, "Chaos-based cryptography: a brief overview," In *IEEE Circuits and Systems Magazine*, vol. 1, no. 3, pp. 6-21, 2001, doi: 10.1109/7384.963463.

[3]   Ali Soleymani, Zulkarnain Md Ali, and Md Jan Nordin, "A Survey on Principal Aspects of Secure Image Transmission," In *World Academy of Science, Engineering and Technology 66 2012*, pp 247 – 254.

[4]   D. Chattopadhyay, M. K. Mandal, and D. Nandi, "Symmetric key chaotic image encryption using circle map," In *Indian Journal of Science and Technology*, Vol. 4 No. 5 (May 2011) ISSN: 0974- 6846, pp 593 – 599.

[5]   Anto Steffi and Dipesh Sharma, "Modified Algorithm of Encryption and Decryption of Images using Chaotic Mapping," In *International Journal of Science and Research (IJSR)*, India Online ISSN: 2319-7064, Volume 2 Issue 2, February 2013.

[6]   K. Sakthidasan Sankaran and B.V. Santhosh Krishna, "A New Chaotic Algorithm for Image Encryption and Decryption of Digital Color Images," In *International Journal of Information and Education Technology*, Vol. 1, No. 2, June 2011.

[7]   Somaya Al-Maadeed, Afnan Al-Ali, and Turki Abdalla, "A New Chaos-Based Image-Encryption and Compression Algorithm," In *Journal of Electrical and Computer Engineering*, Volume 2012, Article ID 179693, Hindawi Publishing Corporation.

[8]   Hazem Mohammad Al-Najjar and Asem Mohammad AL-Najjar, "Image Encryption Algorithm Based on Logistic Map and Pixel Mapping Table."

[9]   Sodeif Ahadpour and Yaser Sadra, "A Chaos-based Image Encryption Scheme using Chaotic Coupled Map Lattices."

[10] Kamlesh Gupta and Sanjay Silakari, "New Approach for Fast Color Image Encryption Using Chaotic Map," In *Journal of Information Security*, 2011, 2, 139-150.

[11] Chong Fu, Jun-jie Chen, Hao Zou, Wei-hong Meng, Yong-feng Zhan, and Ya-wen, "A chaos-based digital image encryption scheme with an improved diffusion strategy," In *Optical Society of America*, 30 January 2012, Vol. 20, No. 3, pp 2363 – 2378.

[12] D. Chattopadhyay, M. K. Mandal, and D. Nandi, "Symmetric key chaotic image encryption using circle map," In *Indian Journal of Science and Technology*, Vol. 4 No. 5, May 2011, ISSN: 0974- 6846, pp 593 – 599.

[13] Shima Ramesh Maniyath and Supriya M, "An Uncompressed Image Encryption Algorithm Based on DNA Sequences," In *Computer Science & Information Technology (CS & IT)*, CCSEA 2011, CS & IT 02, pp. 258–270.

[14] Miguel Murillo-Escobar, "A novel symmetric text encryption algorithm based on logistic map," 2014.

[15] K. Sakthidasan and B. V. Santhosh Krishna, "A New Cahotic Algorithm for Image Encryption and Decryption of Digital Color Images." In *International Journal of Information and Education Technologies*, vol. 1, no. 2, June 2011. Available online: http://www.ijiet.org/papers/23-E20098.pdf.

[16] Ljupco Kocarev and Shinguo Lian. *Chaos-based Cryptography – Theory, Algorithms and Applications*. Springer, 2011.

CHAPTER 16

Big Data Cryptography

Big data is defined as the process of extracting, manipulating, and analyzing data sets of big sizes (e.g. terabytes or petabytes of data) that cannot be processed normally.

Big data cryptography deals with assuring the confidentiality, integrity, and authenticity of the data. It is a sensitive topic that needs to be treated carefully as the computational models are different for each business and architectural environment. Cryptography for big data is different from the rest of the cryptographic primitives as the concepts and schemes are designed in a different way with respect for access control policies, cloud infrastructure, and storage mechanisms.

This chapter will start from a general computational model based on a cloud environment, which will allow and facilitate applications based on big-data analytics. We will start by providing a classification of the cloud compute nodes according to their roles played in big data analytics. Our journey is based on [3] and we will extend the notations a little bit by defining the following nodes:

- I_N is an *input node* used for raw data for the application that is being used. This kind of node is used for data that is entered by the front-end users or data that comes from reading or capturing sensors (such as fingerprint readers, holographic signature, face recognition, etc.).

- C_N is the *computational node,* which plays an important role due to the computational process of the application. This kind of node is based on and includes the ingestion nodes, which we will call *consuming nodes* in our example. Their goal is to scan the input data and to refine it in order to have it prepared for the analysis process and to be ready to be passed to the *enrichment nodes,* with the goal of actual analysis processing.

379

© Marius Iulian Mihailescu and Stefania Loredana Nita 2021
M. I. Mihailescu and S. L. Nita, *Pro Cryptography and Cryptanalysis*,
https://doi.org/10.1007/978-1-4842-6367-9_16

- S_N is the *storage node,* which is very important for applying cryptography mechanisms over the data. Its role is to store the data found between the computation process happening between different categories of users or third-parties. It is very important to understand that the *input data* and *output data* are stored within this node.

- R_N is the *result node,* which deals with receiving the output of some of the computation processes being executed. It is capable of automatic decisions that are using as a basis the output from above or sending the output to a specific client.

Figure 16-1 shows an example of a cloud architecture for big data analytics based on the concepts listed above. This model can be seen as a pattern to describe a wide set of applications based on big data. This being said, we will note the following set of one or more nodes of type H, as follows H^+, where $H \in \{I_N, C_N, S_N, R_N\}$.

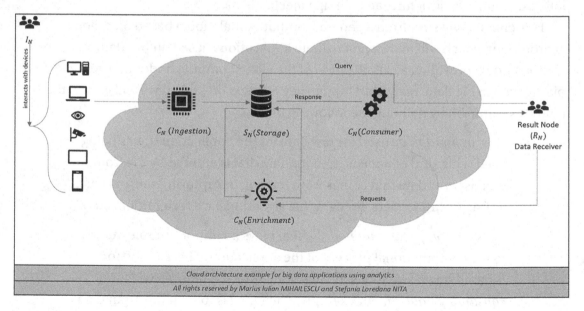

Figure 16-1. *Example of cloud architecture with big-data analytics applications*

In Figure 16-1, you can see a general cloud model that is an example of an application that is querying for data sets. The I_N in the example represents the tool that initiates the process of collecting reference datasets. The sequence data is sent by the input nodes to the C_N(*Ingestion*) node. Here, the computation process is done with respect for the sequences that need to be parsed and at end of the process to be organized into files or databases. The next step is to send the files and databases to S_N (*Storage*). From time to time, extra computations are performed by the C_N(*Enrichment*) on the stored data. This process is done offline most of the time by updating the associated metadata that is based on the needs of the user. In our example, the R_N (*Data Receiver*) represents a user who will corellate the data set with the reference one.

Cloud computing has certain risks for any sensitive data that travels between its entities. To pursue the path of protection offered by cryptography in the cloud, we will consider security with respect to the three most important security goals, known as CIA (confidentiality, integrity, availability):

- **Confidentiality**: The sensitive data, referring strictly to computation input and output, has to remain secret in order to be protected against untrusted parties or other potentially adversaries.

- **Integrity**: Any modification that is not authorized for updating sensitive data has to be detected as quickly as possible.

- **Availability**: Data owners have access to the data and computed resources.

Let's focus on *availability,* as it is addressed in most cloud environments today without any cryptographic means. We will need to bend on confidentiality and integrity of the cloud computation and on how the storage of the data is done. How the cloud is deployed will dictate how confidentiality and integrity is achieved. It is very important to establish from beginning who controls each of the components of the cloud and the trustiness between the components. Based on this we will consider the following scenarios:

- **Trusted cloud**: This type of cloud is deployed by governments and it is completely isolated from any outside networks and adversaries. The users and clients can store their files without any worries that they will be corrupted or stolen. This does not mean that the total isolation will offer full protection. Some of the nodes are exposed and they can be easily corrupted with malware or by insiders.

- **Semi-trusted cloud**: This is an interesting scenario because it is found as a real-word deployment for cloud resources. Within this type of cloud, the client doesn't need to trust the cloud totally and at the same time it is not specified/mentioned that the cloud is totally untrusted. Instead, some of the parts and components of the cloud are under control, providing solutions for monitoring adversary activity at a specified time.

- **Untrusted cloud**: The owners of the data don't trust the cloud or any of the cloud nodes. In this situation, we will not be able to keep and provide a certain level of confidentiality or integrity of the data or the computations that are outsourced to the cloud. In this case, the client needs to have solutions and protections in order to ensure the confidentiality and integrity. This model is assigned to the public cloud.

After we go through some basic elements in order to form the basis of cloud computing and big data, the *cryptographic techniques* that can be applied in such environment to ensure the security of the data in a big data infrastructure are very complex and their applicability is very difficult to achieve without dedicated third-parties software libraries or experienced professionals.

In this chapter, we will focus on three cryptographic techniques that can be used particularly for achieving security of big data applications that are deployed in the cloud:

- Homomoprhic encryption (HE) was covered in Chapter 13.

- Verifiable computation (VC) represents the first objective of this chapter.

- Secure multi-party computation (MPC) represents the second objective of this chapter.

There are other cryptographic techniques that can be applied with success for achieving security in cloud computing, such as

- Functional encryption (FE)

- Identity-based encryption (IE)

- Attribute-based encryption (AE)

Further, we will focus on the techniques we believe are promising and have applicability in real environments. This is not to say that encryption types such as FE, IE, or AE don't have applicability in real environments, but at this moment, multiple works are based on theoretical assumptions and most of them are written without taking into consideration the requirements and needs of business and industry applications. From theory to practice is a long path that theoreticians and practitioners need to travel hand in hand. They need to sit at the round table to find solutions for what is actually important nowadays to solve the problems and gaps that exist.

Verifiable Computation

Verifiable computation, or verifiable computing, is the possibility for a computer or more computers to offload the computation quantity of some function(s) to others such as clients with untrusted status, while the results are continuously verified. See Figure 16-2.

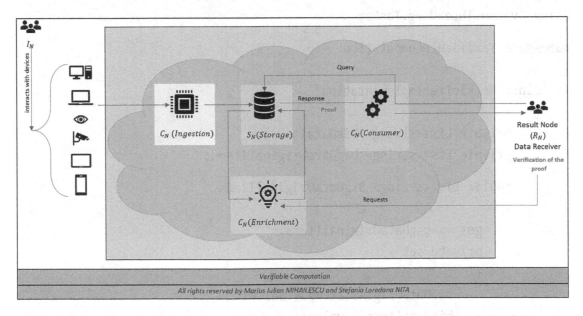

Figure 16-2. *Verifiable computation scenario. The nodes of the cloud don't have any trustiness level for integrity protection.*

A very interesting application of VC in a real environment is a Merkle tree, with the goal of verifying the integrity of the data. For a big data environment, a Merkle tree is defined as a data structure that can be used to validate the integrity of different properties of items, data, rows, collections of data, etc. The nice thing about a Merkle tree is that is works on huge amounts of data. Progresses in this direction has been made, combining verifiable computation algorithms with Merkle trees.

In Listing 16-1, we will present a scenario in which a Merkle tree is used to verify data from a database deployed in a big data environment. The example is just a simulation (see Listing 16-2 and Figure 16-3). Deploying the application in a real big data environment would require the proper adjustments.

Listing 16-1. Implementation of a Merkle Tree as a Solution for a Simple Case of Verifiable Computation

```
using System;
using System.Collections.Generic;
using System.Linq;
using System.Security.Cryptography;
using System.Text;
using System.Threading.Tasks;

namespace VerifiableComputation
{
    class MerkleTreeImplementation
    {
        private List<string> bigDataItems;
        private List<string> bigDataOriginalItems;

        public List<string> BigDataOriginalItems
        {
            get => bigDataOriginalItems;
            private set
            {
                bigDataOriginalItems = value;
                bigDataItems = value;
            }
        }
```

```
public MerkleTreeImplementation(List<string> BigData_OriginalItems)
{
    BigDataOriginalItems = BigData_OriginalItems;
    CreateTree();
}

public string GetRoot()
{
    return bigDataItems[0];
}

private void CreateTree()
{
    var data_items = bigDataItems;
    var temporary_data_items = new List<string>();
    //** using 2 element go and parse
    //** the list for items
    for (int i = 0; i < data_items.Count; i += 2)
    {
        //** Take the left element
        string left_element = data_items[i];

        //** the element from right is empty
        string right_element = String.Empty;

        //** once we have the proper item we will need
        //** to replace the empty string from above
        //** with the proper one
        if (i + 1 != data_items.Count)
            right_element = data_items[i + 1];

        //** compute the hash for the left value
        string leftHash = HashTheBigData(left_element);

        //** if we we have the item from
        //** right as being empty we will hash it
        string rightHash = String.Empty;
        if (right_element != String.Empty)
            rightHash = HashTheBigData(right_element);
```

```
                    //** if we have the hash for right empty, we
                    //** will add the sum of the left with right
                    //** into temporary_items
                    if (right_element != String.Empty)
                        temporary_data_items.Add
                                        (leftHash + rightHash);
                    //** contrary, we will add the left hash only
                    else
                        temporary_data_items.Add(leftHash);
                }

                //** if the size of the list is different from 1
                if (data_items.Count != 1)
                {
                    //** once we are here we will replace replace
                    //** bigDataItems with temporary_data_items
                    bigDataItems = temporary_data_items;

                    //** call again the function
                    CreateTree();
                }
                else
                    //** once we get 1 item then we can say that
                    //** we have the root for the tree.
                    //** we will save it at bigDataItems
                    bigDataItems = temporary_data_items;
            }
            private string HashTheBigData(string bigData)
            {
                using (var sha256 = SHA256.Create())
                {
                    //** use some big data volume
                    byte[] hasshed_bytes_of_bigdata =
                        sha256.ComputeHash(Encoding.UTF8.
                                        GetBytes(bigData));
```

```
            //** take the hash value
            //** and work with it accordingly
            string current_hash_bigdata_value =
                    BitConverter.ToString(hasshed_bytes_of_b
                    igdata).Replace("-", "").ToLower();
            return current_hash_bigdata_value;
        }
      }
   }
}
```

Listing 16-2. Simple Example of a Merkle Tree as Support for the Practibility of Verifiable Computation

```
using System;
using System.Collections.Generic;
using System.Linq;
using System.Text;
using System.Threading.Tasks;

namespace VerifiableComputation
{
    class Program
    {
        static void Main(string[] args)
        {
            //** the following items can be seen as big data
            //** items from a database
            //** as being the result of a query
            List<string> bigdata_items = new List<string>
            {
                "WelcomeToApress!",
                "Studying C# is amazing",
                "Adding extra spice, such as cryptography
                    makes it so challenging!",
```

```
            "You can master it with passion and
                dedication!",
            "Good luck!"
        };

        MerkleTreeImplementation tree = new
                MerkleTreeImplementation(bigdata_items);

        foreach (string s in tree.BigDataOriginalItems)
        {
            Console.WriteLine(s);
        }
        Console.WriteLine("Hash integrity checking is:
                                {0}", tree.GetRoot());

        Console.ReadKey();
        }
    }
}
```

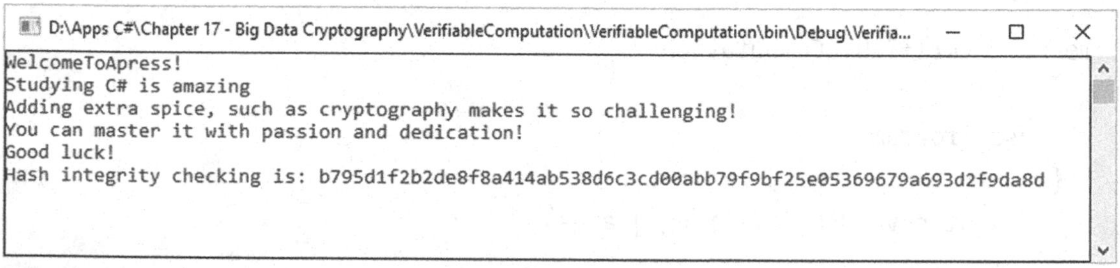

```
D:\Apps C#\Chapter 17 - Big Data Cryptography\VerifiableComputation\VerifiableComputation\bin\Debug\Verifia...   —   □   ×
WelcomeToApress!
Studying C# is amazing
Adding extra spice, such as cryptography makes it so challenging!
You can master it with passion and dedication!
Good luck!
Hash integrity checking is: b795d1f2b2de8f8a414ab538d6c3cd00abb79f9bf25e05369679a693d2f9da8d
```

Figure 16-3. *The hash checking integrity*

Secure Multi-Party Computation

Multi-party computation (MPC) represents a subfield of cryptography, the main goal of which is to provide methods for numerous parties to join the computation process of a function over their inputs and storing those inputs privately. In [10], the authors combined MPC with searchable encryption in order to provide a practical start for applying MPC (see Figure 16-4) in a real complex environment, such as big data and cloud computing.

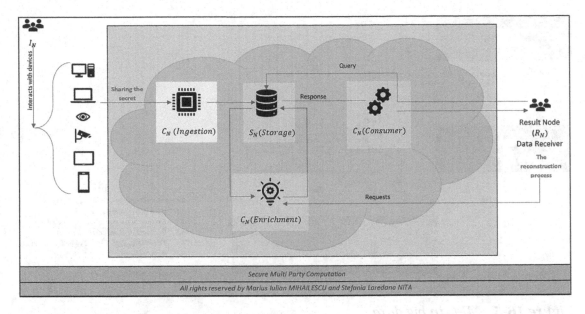

Figure 16-4. *Secure multi-party computation*

In [13], Claudio Orlandi discusses an interesting question and concerns raised about MPC applicability. MPC has multiple technical gaps that need to be filled before using it as a stand-alone mechanism in a real environment. Indeed, the research community has provided an important number of articles related to MPC but more than 80% are pure theory without any direction or sense for applying it properly. Other contributions have been done in this direction by the authors in [6-9] and [11].

Based on the MPC scenario depicted in Figure 16-4, we will consider the following MPC scenario with its components from Figure 16-5. The MPC scenario has been proposed in [10] and it represents a combination of MPC with a searchable encryption scheme and steganographic objects used as identifiers for recognizing uniquely the files and data stored in a cloud and big data environment. In order to achieve the security of the data into an MPC protocol, we will focus on *encryption* (**Step 3** from Figure 16-4) and *decryption* (**Step 4.3** from Figure 16-5). The algorithm proposed below has been designed with respect for big data applications and it has been tested in a real environment for weather forecasting and analysis as described in [10]. The encryption and decryption (see Listings 16-3 and 16-4) are achieved through the RSA algorithm (see Figure 16-7) adapted and designed properly for big volumes of data.

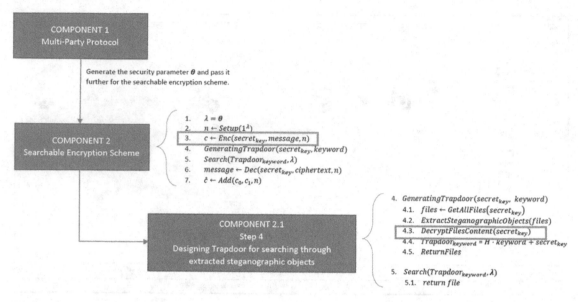

Figure 16-5. *MPC in big data*

What makes it different from a normal RSA implementation is that the private key is represented as an XML file (see Figure 16-6). You can see all the necessary parameters used for initialization of RSA.

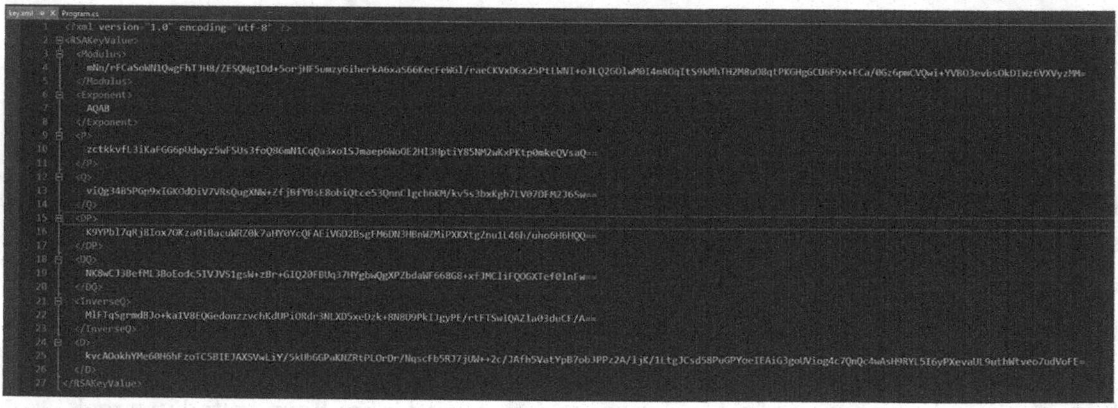

Figure 16-6. *RSA XML private key*

Listing 16-3. RSA for Big Volumes of Data (Encryption and Decryption
Operations)

```
using System;

namespace RSACryptography
{
    class Program
    {
        public static void Main(string[] args)
        {
            // encryption and decryption a password example
            var password = "P@sswrd123";

            Console.WriteLine("\n Original Password Text: " +
                                        password);

            var textToBeEncrypted =
                        CryptographyHelper.Encrypt(password);
            Console.WriteLine("\n Encrypted Password Text: " +
                                    textToBeEncrypted);

            var textToBeDecrypted =
                CryptographyHelper.Decrypt(textToBeEncrypted);
            Console.WriteLine("\n Decrypted Password Text: " +
                                    textToBeDecrypted);

            //** encryption and decryption for database
            //** connection string
            var connectionString = "Data Source=USER-
                    Test\\SQLEXPRESS;Initial
                    Catalog=OrderProcessing;Integrated
                    Security=True";

            Console.WriteLine("\n Original Connection String
                                    Text: " + connectionString);

            textToBeEncrypted =
                CryptographyHelper.Encrypt(connectionString);
```

```
            Console.WriteLine("\n Encrypted Connection String
                              Text: " + textToBeEncrypted);
            textToBeDecrypted =
                CryptographyHelper.Decrypt(textToBeEncrypted);
            Console.WriteLine("\n Decrypted Connection String
                              Text: " + textToBeDecrypted);

            //** encryption and decryption of a very long
            //** query result from DB

            var longTextForEncryption = "Literally, Blockchain is a chain
            of blocks which could be simply assumed as an immutable data
            structure. Immutability is one of the most prominent features
            of a blockchain, which leads us to build trust in completely
            unreliable environments.";

            Console.WriteLine("The encryption of the query is:
                {0}",
                CryptographyHelper.Encrypt
                    (longTextForEncryption));

            Console.ReadKey();
        }
    }
}
```

Listing 16-4. CryptographyHelper Class

```
using System;
using System.Security.Cryptography;
using System.Text;

namespace RSACryptography
{
    public static class CryptographyHelper
    {
        private static bool asymmetricEncryptionPadding = false;

        //** keys of 2048 bytes length
```

```
private readonly static string public_key = "MjAOOCE8UlNBS2V5VmFsdWU
+PE1vZHVsdXM+djFTTVVyYk5SZW50VDEyaOFhWXNRMEh3Y2hjWG9nbnFUWGpYd1NXaGGR
5Qi9aaTQ5VnF4LOlFdWxSaGFhVjdHOUtENWRmYOI4eEZaZGgyNGJOMHpZbGGFNTlFyRVB
NNnQzUEdvZXZmMXVCby9wVnhlcWFocEFkWkIwelNJcjhwTk5UOW52czV5WEN1QOOxRFo
OUUR3Q3A3b2U2aXc2ZHZ4VEZNWFZJdW9rSkcrdmlFMWhORDhnbGgOdFVsMWVBdThKT3Y
yROtyWmhvTmUxK2tnRzNNUmRueEFGTDQyRDl4eWF5NERvcmpGL2ZjYWNNc3dFYYkM3MUo
2bFNobnR2YnQ1RnYOelY1bkgOaDhqYzhnV1dQVDUvWG16TElLMmlJRDJ6L3NyeGgvbzd
MRkRhWVhXMnVwbUt5VUJQR2kOOGJLUVZKT3JjZU9rd3owwWE1nTDFJUk4yWnhRPTO8LO1
vZHVsdXM+PEV4cG9uZW50PkFRQUI8LOV4cG9uZW50PjwvUlNBS2V5VmFsdWU+";
private readonly static string private_key = "MjAOOCE8UlNBS2V5VmFsdW
U+PE1vZHVsdXM+djFTTVVyYk5SZW50VDEyaOFhWXNRMEh3Y2hjWG9nbnFUWGpYd1NXaG
R5Qi9aaTQ5VnF4LOldWxSaGFhVjdHOUtENWRmYOI4eEZaZGgyNGJOMHpZbGGFNTlFyRVB
NNnQzUEdvZXZmMXVCby9wVnhlcWFocEFkWkIwelNJcjhwTk5UOW52czV5WEN1QOOxRFo
OUUR3Q3A3b2U2aXc2ZHZ4VEZNWFZJdW9rSkcrdmlFMWhORDhnbGgOdFVsMWVBdThKT3Y
yROtyWmhvTmUxK2tnRzNNUmRueEFGTDQyRDl4eWF5NERvcmpGL2ZjYWNNc3dFYYkM3MUo
2bFNobnR2YnQ1RnYOelY1bkgOaDhqYzhnV1dQVDUvWG16TElLMmlJRDJ6L3NyeGgvbzd
MRkRhWVhXMnVwbUt5VUJQR2kOOGJLUVZKT3JjZU9rd3owwWE1nTDFJUk4yWnhRPTO8LO1
vZHVsdXM+PEV4cG9uZW50PkFRQUI8LOV4cG9uZW50PjxQPi8yY1VJS2R1MFB1b2RVaDDJ
QQ3krbFUOaWFvVWtOZOdOOVhHNmhvcll3c1ovbzdwdTJYZjZmS2E5MO90Z1RONUpqaW5
QL3grZG9ibmFiU1hNNFNwRGJlb3JVRGZBKzhYZURIxTHBCTOFtYUtUVWlkejNjMHlQRX
BQZ3l0MlpVb3poUWhjejZlUk01cUdQSlgxU29WMjczM3ZUREFtTEVWSON4eFRZOHVNSW
I30DO8L1A+PFE+djhqYlBmcHh5aXZUUelhsV2Q5L3hNK3pRUlJRSk4rTDFIYURiNHYxKz
U3dExEb3VlcGO3ajIOMkJFZ2U4dTNENmJEanZneWhBBWFIxV3IwRO9KSjBBb1ZPV2FLLz
dvZ3NHZjBnM1dzNzVicWtWSmdNTHZETnFxSVVVdOZqZml3TllONkJnNOdIdGl2SOVGdm
JldTEzcGFxVERyTnFuVOZQaWFFQK1lkQ09xVjNzPTwvUT48RFA+eWVSVDFOUTNjWC9kMU
locFhudOlVOEltRm9vVTY5UWl3YWtiUjR1dWVabXNBROOlaVJMOG9WaTFzVXpVTHNRcz
VRSk1kMklvbTFWdFF1YWtwRUZpZUJxcURRvbGtOaUpoWTNDUTNOZkp4TOszVOJ1aVNEUj
J6THEwOEZPcOJjTnpoOV2plRXIvendyUm9BYnlsZXdkXN281Z2dadDJNWHk4WVRnTSsxQk
YvODhVPTwvRFA+PERRPlRGROUxYd1JFbW9HWHFJVkF4UjVlbD1JJYTROZVcwRFhHHN1pTbz
NKMmRFMFhJSHpQRTYzelBxeGlRSlJFRnZSUEI5cVU1NU41N3UxazZzektGHUzltV2JhaX
ZCbVBHN3dJNOJTZEtQQlNleXMzMUNSMC9hQ1NGdmpTNVRkeFdzYkVU0JyTFhuZWxOS2
RkcVJPSkljNOZiTjNPdXlDY2NoVjkzZGlqNnSbEtzODO8LORRPjxJbnZlcnNlUT5rSm
YwVHZoNDZjTEQ4OElIVVVZOV3hYaDVsYlNUTWw2ZnB5cFhhUU9laUtpTy9YcnZpY21waX
dBVEhDQQpERDhYdDFFwbTc5KOhrc21sUjlrYktXR2U4WmNqZHJHdUZlZ3NDUGRpT3VGMV
NOa283NWtnblJVYOZTb1hxSzF1YVgvTWsxTEtDbVpZ3djjQOt2VC9OQUZrWVpVdVNqT3
```

pPckVrRk9VNDdML3VDVEO9PC9JbnZlcnNlUT48RD5HbTMyZUZLUOpvODYzZFRFbkFtMV
laRVJRdUZYdldWN1BUcHRLMXdrWXMxVmErcOZSQnpON3Nza1NIdEUxTXBUbytTQmk2Wj
BWYmJNY3JITOdGTUFOQO55Nkh5RzZnOU1pRWJzZWpndzQ2MHJnWUZlWkF1K1RiOG5zMU
orR2FNcGNkZGNHa2FPUXMxaOJzaURjZlFZTmMwckNoUVQrMjI5bUVmL3VqUDN6Q1IzcU
NzdkZjVTRuMkMwZzBYSWhLQ1dHYXRsbW5MOW9FMWNOMzY4aWZZKOJCUVljUExqSEO5TT
ZaSU9pMWtmR3M2bXhaTOV3cm1BWFBOTOZweW1tNlZjMUM4WGtVUENCVERtWUZTSFpiaH
NaTO9IZHpaVVlUa2lmN1VzRk4OMjdTSDVrMTNpQTVGRGJTbO53bW9kQOZrWitENGJNQ2
JUZWgwVTNvell6M3FnM1E9PTwvRD48L1JTQUtleVZhbHVlPg==";

```csharp
public static string Encrypt(string clearText)
{
    int size_of_the_key = 0;
    string xmlWithPublicKey = "";

    GetKeyFromEncryptionString(public_key, out size_of_the_key, out
    xmlWithPublicKey);

    var encrypted = Encrypt(Encoding.UTF8.GetBytes(clearText), size_
    of_the_key, xmlWithPublicKey);

    return Convert.ToBase64String(encrypted);
}

private static byte[] Encrypt(byte[] data, int keySize, string
publicKeyXml)
{
    if (data == null || data.Length == 0)
        throw new ArgumentException("There is empty data", "data");

    int maximum_length = GetMaxDataLength(keySize);

    if (data.Length > maximum_length)
        throw new ArgumentException(String.Format("The maximum
            length of data is {0}", maximum_length), "data");

    if (!IsKeySizeValid(keySize))
        throw new ArgumentException("The size of the key is not
            valid", "keySize");
```

```csharp
        if (String.IsNullOrEmpty(publicKeyXml))
            throw new ArgumentException("The key is null or empty",
            "publicKeyXml");

    using (var provider = new RSACryptoServiceProvider(keySize))
    {
        provider.FromXmlString(publicKeyXml);
        return provider.Encrypt(data, asymmetricEncryptionPadding);
    }
}

public static string Decrypt(string encryptedText)
{
    int keySize = 0;
    string publicAndPrivateKeyXml = "";

    GetKeyFromEncryptionString(private_key, out keySize, out
    publicAndPrivateKeyXml);

    var decrypted = Decrypt(Convert.FromBase64String(encryptedText),
    keySize, publicAndPrivateKeyXml);

    return Encoding.UTF8.GetString(decrypted);
}

private static byte[] Decrypt(byte[] data, int keySize, string
publicAndPrivateKeyXml)
{
    if (data == null || data.Length == 0)
        throw new ArgumentException("The data is empty", "data");

     if (!IsKeySizeValid(keySize))
        throw new ArgumentException("The size of the key is not
        valid", "keySize");

     if (String.IsNullOrEmpty(publicAndPrivateKeyXml))
        throw new ArgumentException("The key is null or empty",
        "publicAndPrivateKeyXml");
```

```
        using (var provider = new RSACryptoServiceProvider(keySize))
        {
            provider.FromXmlString(publicAndPrivateKeyXml);
            return provider.Decrypt(data, asymmetricEncryptionPadding);
        }
    }

    private static int GetMaxDataLength(int keySize)
    {
        if (asymmetricEncryptionPadding)
        {
            return ((keySize - 384) / 8) + 7;
        }
        return ((keySize - 384) / 8) + 37;
    }

    private static bool IsKeySizeValid(int keySize)
    {
        return keySize >= 384 && keySize <= 16384 && keySize % 8 == 0;
    }

    private static void GetKeyFromEncryptionString(string rawkey, out
    int keySize, out string xmlKey)
    {
        keySize = 0;
        xmlKey = "";

        if (rawkey != null && rawkey.Length > 0)
        {
            byte[] keyBytes = Convert.FromBase64String(rawkey);
            var stringKey = Encoding.UTF8.GetString(keyBytes);

            if (stringKey.Contains("!"))
            {
                var splittedValues = stringKey.Split(new char[] { '!' }, 2);

                try
```

```
        {
            keySize = int.Parse(splittedValues[0]);
            xmlKey = splittedValues[1];
        }
        catch (Exception e) { }
        }
    }
  }
}
}
```

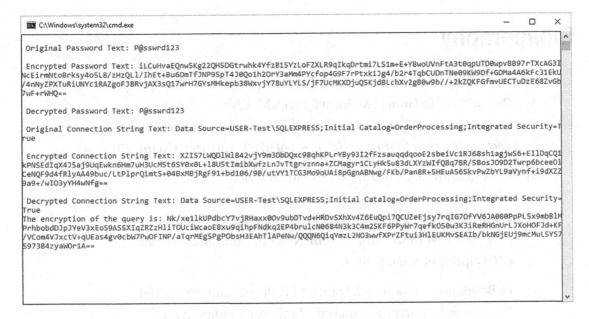

Figure 16-7. *Encryption/decryption ouput for big data volumes and other types of strings.*

For the classes `CryptographyHelper` and `RSACryptographyKeyGenerator`, see the full project at the GitHub repository.

Conclusion

In this chapter, we discussed the importance of having a big data environment and how security can be achieved through different cryptographic mechanisms, such as verifiable computation and multi-party computation.

At the end of this chapter, you now know the following:

- The main concepts of security from a cloud and big data environment

- How to put into practice complex cryptographic primitives and protocols, such as verifiable computation and multi-party computation

Bibliography

[1]   P. Laud and A. Pankova, "Verifiable Computation in Multiparty Protocols with Honest Majority," In S.S.M. Chow, J.K. Liu, L.C.K. Hui, and S.M. Yiu (eds) *Provable Security. ProvSec 2014. Lecture Notes in Computer Science, vol 8782*. Springer, Cham. 2014.

[2]   D. Bogdanov, S. Laur, and R. Talviste, "A Practical Analysis of Oblivious Sorting Algorithms for Secure Multi-party Computation." In K. Bernsmed and S. Fischer-Hübner (eds) *Secure IT Systems. NordSec 2014. Lecture Notes in Computer Science, vol 8788.* Springer, Cham. 2014.

[3]   D. Bogdanov, L. Kamm, S. Laur, and P. Pruulmann-Vengerfeldt, "Securemulti-party data analysis: End user validation and practical experiments," 2014.

[4]   B. ÖzÇakmak, A. Özbİlen, U. YavanoĞlu, and K. Cİn, "Neural and Quantum Cryptography in Big Data: A Review," 2019 IEEE International Conference on Big Data (Big Data), Los Angeles, CA, USA, 2019, pp. 2413-2417, doi: 10.1109/ BigData47090.2019.9006238.

[5] S. Yakoubov, V. Gadepally, N. Schear, E. Shen, and
     A. Yerukhimovich, "A survey of cryptographic approaches to
     securing big-data analytics in the cloud," In *2014 IEEE High
     Performance Extreme Computing Conference (HPEC)*, Waltham,
     MA, 2014, pp. 1-6, doi: 10.1109/HPEC.2014.7040943.

[6] S.L. Nita and M.I. Mihailescu, "A Searchable Encryption Scheme
     Based on Elliptic Curves." In Barolli L., Amato F., Moscato F.,
     Enokido T., Takizawa M. (eds) *Web, Artificial Intelligence and
     Network Applications. WAINA 2020. Advances in Intelligent
     Systems and Computing, vol 1150*. Springer, Cham. 2020.

[7] S.L. Nita and M.I. Mihailescu M.I. "A Hybrid Searchable
     Encryption Scheme for Cloud Computing." In J.L. Lanet and
     C. Toma (eds) *Innovative Security Solutions for Information
     Technology and Communications. SECITC 2018. Lecture Notes in
     Computer Science, vol 11359*. Springer, Cham. 2019.

[8] V. C. Pau and M. I. Mihailescu, "Internet of Things and its role
     in biometrics technologies and eLearning applications," In
     *2015 13th International Conference on Engineering of Modern
     Electric Systems (EMES)*, (pp. 1-4) Oradea. doi: 10.1109/
     EMES.2015.7158430. 2015.

[9] S. L. Nita and M. I. Mihailescu, "On Artificial Neural Network
     used in Cloud Computing Security - A Survey," In *2018 10th
     International Conference on Electronics, Computers and Artificial
     Intelligence (ECAI)*, (pp. 1-6). Iasi, Romania, doi: 10.1109/
     ECAI.2018.8679086. 2018.

[10] Marius Iulian Mihailescu, Stefania Loredana Nita, and Ciprian
     Racuciu, "Authentication protocol based on searchable encryption
     and multi-party computation with applicability for earth sciences",
     In *Scientific Bulletin of Naval Academy, Vol. XXIII* (pp. 221-230).
     doi: 10.21279/1454-864X-20-I1-030. 2020.

[11]   Marius Iulian Mihailescu, Stefania Loredana Nita, and Ciprian Racuciu, "Multi-level access using searchable symmetric encryption with applicability for earth sciences," In *Scientific Bulletin of Naval Academy, Vol. XXIII* (pp. 221-230), doi: 10.21279/1454-864X-20-I1-030. 2020.

[12]   Stefania Loredana Nita, Marius Iulian Mihailescu and Ciprian Racuciu, "Secure Document Search in Cloud Computing using MapReduce", In *Scientific Bulletin of Naval Academy, Vol. XXIII* (pp. 221-230), doi: 10.21279/1454-864X-20-I1-030. 2020.

[13]   RSA Extension for Big Data Analytics. Available online: `www.rsa.com/en-us/company/news/rsa-extends-big-data-analytics-to-help-organizations-identify`.

[14]   Claudio Orlandi, Is Multiparty Computation Any Good In Practice? Available online: `www.cs.au.dk/~orlandi/icassp-draft.pdf`.

CHAPTER 17

Cloud Computing Cryptography

Cryptography for cloud computing represents an extremely hot point in designing and implementing secure application for clients and complex network environments. Cryptography in the cloud engages complex encryption techniques with the purpose of securing data that will be stored and later used within the cloud environment.

Organizations have been rapidly adapting cloud technology as IaaS (Infrastructure-as-a-Service), PaaS (Platform-as-a-Service), and SaaS (Software-as-a-Service). The reasons consist of the benefits brought, such as efficiency and flexibility which in the end will reduce the costs.

The following cryptography primitives and mechanisms are receiving attention from research communities and industry as well:

- Homomorphic encryption (see Chapter 13)
- Searchable encryption (see Chapter 12)
- Structured encryption (SE)
- Functional encryption (FE)
- Private information retrieval (PIR)

In this chapter, we will focus on structured encryption (STE), functional encryption, transparent data encryption (TDE), and multi-party computation (MPC). The first two primitives, homomorphic encryption and searchable encryption, were presented in the chapters with the same names, due to their importance and evolution.

© Marius Iulian Mihailescu and Stefania Loredana Nita 2021
M. I. Mihailescu and S. L. Nita, *Pro Cryptography and Cryptanalysis*,
https://doi.org/10.1007/978-1-4842-6367-9_17

Structured Encryption

The role of an STE scheme is to provide encryption for data structures. An STE scheme is based on a certain token, which is used to query the structure, one being able to give an evaluation of the query and learning about the most well-defined leakage from the structure or query. Searchable symmetric encryption (SSE) (see Chapter 12) represents a special case of STE. As a quick reminder, SSE encrypts the searching structures as inverted indexes or similar with searching trees. In practice, SSE provides a natural solution for designing and implementing search engines (see Listing 12-2) with respect for

- Generating a searching structure for the data set and providing encryption for it

- Searching for a specific keyword w and based on w generating a token and proceeding with quering the encrypted structure

Similar schemes of STE can be found within graph encryption, which provides an interesting solution for the designing phase of an encrypted database using a graph structure. Encrypting graph databases in order to preserve their privacy in a social search environment is a very good example, especially since we are dealing with complex big data infrastructures in cloud computing environments, such as big data analytics and statistics.

As an example of a framework for this section, we will consider an encryption algorithm using graph-based cryptography for a database (see Pseudocode 17-1 and Listing 17-1). In Listing 17-2, you can see the working version of the framework proposed in Listing 17-1. The output is depicted in Figure 17-1. The algorithm receives as *first input n* characters that will be encrypted, $(ch_1, ch_2, ..., ch_n)$. The characters are received as records from the database. The *second input* is represented by a starting point (s^p) and an ending point for the path (e^p). The *third input* is represented by the length of the path that is being analyzed (l_p).

This being said, let's take a look at the pseudocode from Listing 17-1.

Pseudocode 17-1. The Pseudocode of the Algorithm

```
INPUT:
        ch₁, ch₂, ..., chn — characters as single records
        sp — the starting point of the vertex path
```

> *ep* — the ending point of the vertex path
>
> *lp* — length path

for i = 1 to n do

begin

> *temporary ← chi*
> *generate a next path for linking sp and ep*
> *for j = lp downto 1 do begin*
> > *temporary ← temporary XOR kj*
> > *temporary ← temporary ≪ 1*
> > *temporary ← Π(temporary)*
> *end*
> *encryptedch(i) ← temp*
> *return the encrypted character, encryptedch(i)*

end

OUTPUT:

> *encryptedch(1), encryptedch(2), …, encryptedch(n)*

Listing 17-1. The Implementation

```
using System;

namespace GraphEncryptionDatabase
{
    class DBGraphEncrypt
    {
        //** starting point
        int sp;

        //** ending point;
        int ep;

        //** path length
        int lp;

        //** constructor
        public DBGraphEncrypt() {}
```

```csharp
public void GraphEncryption()
{
        //** let's declare an instance of the context
        //** we will use Linq-to-Sql for this example

        Apress_DBGraphEncExampleDataContext dbContext
        = new Apress_DBGraphEncExampleDataContext();

        //** create an instance of the class
        //** generated for the table
        EmployeeDetail emp_details = new
                            EmployeeDetail();

        //** select the record that
        //** you want to encrypt
        var query = (from emp in
         dbContext.EmployeeDetails
            select emp.Password).Single();

        //** parse the record
        string record = query.ToString();
        for(int i=0; i<record.Length; i++)
        {
            char ch = record[i];
            Encrypt(ch.ToString());
        }
}

public string Encrypt(string ch)
{
        Encryption.useEncAlgorithm(new
        Encryption(Encryption.ALGORITHM.GraphEnc));

        string encryption_key;

        Console.WriteLine("Enter the password :");
            String password = encryption_key.readLine();
```

```
byte[] secret_key = GenerateKeys.keyGen(256,
        password, "salt/salt", 100000);

Console.WriteLine("Return the records
        (strings) that will be encrypted.");
String pathName = encryption_key.readLine();

ArrayList<string> listOfCharacters = new
                        ArrayList<string>();
listOfCharacters.Add(ch);

//** parse the listOfCharacters
//** parameters of the graph vertex for the
//** size of the data set
//** change in such way that you will get a
//** better performance
int big_block = 700;
int small_block = 120;
int size_of_data = 12000;

while (true)
{
    Console.WriteLine("Enter the keyword tosearch for:");
    String keyword = Console.Read();
    byte[][] token_encryption_key =
    GraphEnc.token(secret_key , keyword);
    Console.WriteLine(GraphEnc.
    resolve(CryptoPrimitives.
generateGraphEnc(secret_key, 3 + new String()),
generateGraphEnc.query(GraphEnc.GeneratePath(sp, ep, lp),
    GraphEnc.generateListOfCharacters(),
    GraphEnc.Encrypt()))));
    }
}
}
}
```

Listing 17-2. Encryption of SE Using Graph

```csharp
using System;
using System.Collections.Generic;
using System.Linq;
using System.Security.Cryptography;
using System.Text;
using System.Threading.Tasks;

namespace StructuredEncryptionUsingGraphEncryption
{
    class DBGraphEncrypt
    {
        //** this queries represents some constants which
       //** represents records from the database.
        public const int query1 = 255;
        //public const string query2 = "Address";
        //public const string query3 = "Phone number";

        public DBGraphEncrypt()
        {

        }

        static public byte[] Decryption(byte[] Data,
                    RSAParameters RSAKey, bool DoOAEPPadding)
        {
            try
            {
                byte[] decryptedData;
                using (RSACryptoServiceProvider RSA = new
                            RSACryptoServiceProvider())
                {
                    RSA.ImportParameters(RSAKey);
                    decryptedData = RSA.Decrypt(Data, DoOAEPPadding);
                }
                return decryptedData;
            }
```

```
    catch (CryptographicException e)
    {
        Console.WriteLine(e.ToString());
        return null;
    }
}

static public byte[] Encryption(byte[] Data,
            RSAParameters RSAKey, bool DoOAEPPadding)
{
    try
    {
        byte[] encryptedData;
        using (RSACryptoServiceProvider RSA = new
                        RSACryptoServiceProvider())
        {
            RSA.ImportParameters(RSAKey);
            encryptedData = RSA.Encrypt(Data, DoOAEPPadding);
        }
        return encryptedData;
    }
    catch (CryptographicException e)
    {
        Console.WriteLine(e.Message);
        return null;
    }
}

private static void Print(int[,] distance, int verticesCount)
{
    Console.WriteLine("Shortest distances between
                            every pair of vertices:");

    for (int i = 0; i < verticesCount; ++i)
    {
```

```
            for (int j = 0; j < verticesCount; ++j)
            {
                if (distance[i, j] == query1)
                    Console.Write("query1".PadLeft(7));
                else
                    Console.Write(distance[i,
                            j].ToString().PadLeft(7));
            }

            Console.WriteLine();
        }
    }

    public static void GraphSimulation(int[,] graph, int verticesCount)
    {
        int[,] distance = new int[verticesCount, verticesCount];

        for (int i = 0; i < verticesCount; ++i)
            for (int j = 0; j < verticesCount; ++j)
                distance[i, j] = graph[i, j];

        for (int k = 0; k < verticesCount; ++k)
        {
            for (int i = 0; i < verticesCount; ++i)
            {
                for (int j = 0; j < verticesCount; ++j)
                {
                    if (distance[i, k] + distance[k, j] <
                                    distance[i, j])
                        distance[i, j] = distance[i, k] +
                                    distance[k, j];
                }
            }
        }

        Print(distance, verticesCount);
    }
```

```csharp
static void Main(string[] args)
{
    UnicodeEncoding ByteConverter = new UnicodeEncoding();
    RSACryptoServiceProvider RSA = new RSACryptoServiceProvider();

    int[,] databaseGraphRecords = {
                { 0,    6,   query1, 11 },
                { query1, 0,    4, query1 },
                { query1, query1, 0,    2 },
                { query1, query1, query1, 0 }
                  };

    byte[,] dataGraphForEncryption = new
            byte[databaseGraphRecords.Length,
            databaseGraphRecords.Length];
    byte[] dataForEncryption = new
            byte[databaseGraphRecords.Length];
    string[] test = new
            string[databaseGraphRecords.Length];

    int k = 0;
    for (int i = 0; i <
            Math.Sqrt(databaseGraphRecords.Length); i++)
    {
        for (int j = 0; j <
            Math.Sqrt(databaseGraphRecords.Length); j++)
        {
            dataForEncryption[k] =
                Convert.ToByte(databaseGraphRecords
                                    [i, j]);
            k++;
        }
    }
```

```
byte[] encryptions = Encryption(dataForEncryption,
             RSA.ExportParameters(false), false);
Console.WriteLine("The encryption of the records
             graph from the database is:");
for(int i = 0; i < encryptions.Length; i++)
{
    Console.Write("0x" + encryptions[i].ToString()
                                      + " ");
}

Console.WriteLine("\n");
GraphSimulation(databaseGraphRecords, 4);

Console.WriteLine("\n");
byte[] decryptions = Decryption(encryptions,
             RSA.ExportParameters(true), false);
Console.WriteLine("The decryption of the records
             graph from the database is:");
for (int i = 0; i < decryptions.Length; i++)
{
    Console.Write(decryptions[i].ToString() + " ");
}
        }
    }
}
```

```
C:\Windows\system32\cmd.exe                                                   —  □  ×
The encryption of the records graph from the database is:
0x139 0x118 0x71 0x206 0x44 0x158 0x195 0x132 0x146 0x66 0x52 0x129 0x61 0x135 0x62 0x159 0x128 0x15 0x3 0x65 0x187 0x47
 0x19 0x104 0x167 0x67 0x166 0x184 0x6 0x104 0x130 0x67 0x254 0x165 0x33 0x39 0x29 0x10 0x236 0x169 0x252 0x12 0x241 0x5
1 0x15 0x26 0x245 0x73 0x53 0x166 0x157 0x232 0x156 0x101 0x126 0x171 0x154 0x26 0x216 0x243 0x33 0x34 0x89 0x125 0x3 0x
220 0x246 0x216 0x181 0x117 0x174 0x153 0x248 0x98 0x75 0x210 0x180 0x55 0x59 0x7 0x150 0x84 0x182 0x78 0x158 0x232 0x14
4 0x234 0x103 0x136 0x180 0x51 0x217 0x125 0x127 0x41 0x120 0x209 0x34 0x143 0x195 0x18 0x72 0x98 0x85 0x31 0x185 0x32 0
x22 0x234 0x188 0x144 0x196 0x102 0x200 0x103 0x169 0x242 0x136 0x151 0x238 0x244 0x16 0x106 0x80 0x147 0x170 0x149

Shortest distances between every pair of vertices:
     0      6     10     11
query1        0      4      6
query1 query1        0      2
query1 query1 query1        0

The decryption of the records graph from the database is:
0 6 255 11 255 0 4 255 255 255 0 2 255 255 255 0 Press any key to continue . . .  _
```

Figure 17-1. *Encryption of SE using graphs*

Functional Encryption

Functional encryption represents a generalization of the public-key encryption. In this type of encryption, the possession of the secret key allows one to learn a function of what ciphertext is being encrypted. FE is complex and it has several sub-classes, such as predicate encryption, identity-based encryption, attribute-based encryption (ABE), ciphertext-policy ABE, hidden vector encryption, and inner product predicate.

A functional encryption scheme represents a tuple composed of four algorithms, such as setup, keygen, encryption, and decryption. There is a condition that need to be satisfied for correctness, in such way that $k \in K$ and $x \in X$:

- $setup(1^\lambda) \rightarrow (public_{key}, master_{key})$
- $key_{generation}(master_{key}, key) \rightarrow secret_{key}$
- $encryption(public_{key}, message) \rightarrow ciphertext$
- $decryption(secret_{key}, ciphertext) \rightarrow y$

The above steps can be transposed below in Listing 17-3, in which we introduce a general framework of how a general function encryption method should be implemented. The example from Listing 17-3 doesn't represent an example that can be compile and executed. Giving an implementation for a FE can be a very challenging task due to its complexity and applications.

Listing 17-3. Simple Implementation and Startup for FE

```
//** generating master keys and FE key

//** length of input vectors
int input_vector_length = 2;

//** the upper limit for input vector coordinates
Random rand = new Random();
int bound = rand.Next();

//** length in bit of the prime modulus
int length_of_modulus = 2048;

trusted_entity = GenerateNewVector(input_vector_length,
                                 length_of_modulus, bound);
```

```
master_key = trusted_entity.GenerateMasterKey();
master_public_key = trusted_entity.GenerateMasterPublicKey();

int y = data. GenerateNewVector ([]*big.Int{big.NewInt(1),
                                        big.NewInt(2)});
functional_encryption_key =
        trusted_entity.KeyDerivation(master_secret_key, y);

//** create a simulation of encryptor
//** our encryption will hide the message (x) using
//** master public key by the trusted entity
Encryption = GenerateParameters(trusted_entity.Parameters);
message = GenerateNewVector([]*rand.Next{rand.Next(3) rand.Next(4)});,
cipher = encryption.Encrypt(message, master_public_key);

//** create simulation of the decryptor that decrypts the cipher
Decryption = GenerateParameters(trusted_entity.Parameters);

//** do the decryption in order to get the result
//** inner prod of x and y
//** we are expecting xy to be 11 (e.g. <[1,2],[3,4]>)
xy = Decrypt(cipher, functional_encryption_key, y) ;
```

In Listing 17-4 and Figure 17-4, we provide an example of an implementation of a public key encryption module for functional encryption. The example is designed to work for cloud architectures with files that contain sensitive data (such as big volumes of data, query results, etc.). Before running the project from the GitHub repository for Listing 17-4, make sure that you have properly created the certificate using the makecert command from the Developer Command Prompt (see Figure 17-2). To achieve this, you will need to run the following command:

```
makecert -r -pe -n "CN=CERT_APRESS_FUNCTIONALENCRYPTION_CERT" -b 01/01/2020
-e 01/12/2020 -sky exchange -ss my
```

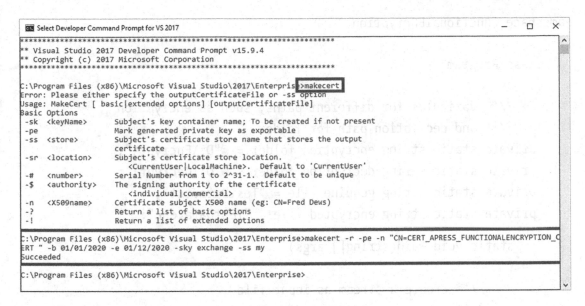

Figure 17-2. *Creating the certificate using makecert*

The next step is to verify if the certificate was imported properly by checking the Console window (see Figure 17-3).

Figure 17-3. *Importing certificates*

Listing 17-4. Implementation of X509 Public Key Encryption as Part of Functional Encryption

```
using System;
using System.Collections.Generic;
using System.IO;
using System.Linq;
using System.Security.Cryptography;
using System.Security.Cryptography.X509Certificates;
using System.Text;
using System.Threading.Tasks;
```

```
namespace FunctionalEncryption
{
    class Program
    {
        //** variables for different paths, such as encryption
        //** and decryption path for folder
    private static string encryption_folder = @"D:\Encrypt\";
    private static string decryption_folder = @"D:\Decrypt\";
    private static string genuine_file = "TestData.txt";
    private static string encrypted_file = "TestData.enc";

        static void Main(string[] args)
        {
            //** create a stream as input file
            //** for encrypting test data
            StreamWriter stream_writer =
                    File.CreateText(genuine_file);
            stream_writer.WriteLine("Data as test to be encrypted");
            stream_writer.Close();

            //** use the certificate for encrypting the key
            X509Certificate2 certificateUsedForEncryption =
                ObtainTheCertificateFromTheStore("CN=CERT_APRE
                SS_FUNCTIONALENCRYPTION_CERT");
            if (certificateUsedForEncryption == null)
            {
                Console.WriteLine("Certificate
                    'CN=CERT_APRESS_FUNCTIONALENCRYPTION_CERT'
                    was not found.");
                Console.ReadLine();
            }

            //**  Do the encryption of the file using the
            //** public key from the certificate
            FileEncryption(genuine_file,
              (RSA)certificateUsedForEncryption.PublicKey.Key);
```

```
    //** Do the decryption of the file based on the
    //** private key obtained from the certificate
    FileDecryption(encrypted_file,
     certificateUsedForEncryption.GetRSAPrivateKey());

    //** Show in the console the
    //** genuine data and the decrypted data
    Console.WriteLine("Genuine message:    {0}",
                    File.ReadAllText(genuine_file));
    Console.WriteLine("Round Trip: {0}",
                File.ReadAllText(decryption_folder +
            genuine_file));
    Console.WriteLine("Press any key to continue.");
    Console.ReadLine();
}

private static X509Certificate2
        ObtainTheCertificateFromTheStore(string
          certificate_name)

{

    //** go to the certification store and make sure
    //** that you are under the current user
    X509Store certification_store = new
            X509Store(StoreLocation.CurrentUser);
    try
    {
        certification_store.Open(OpenFlags.ReadOnly);

        //** entire collection of certificates should
        //** be added to X509Certificate2Collection object.
        X509Certificate2Collection
                collection_of_certifications =
                certification_store.Certificates;

        //** validate the certificate
        X509Certificate2Collection
            current_certificates =
```

```
                    collection_of_certifications.Find(
                    X509FindType.FindByTimeValid,
                    DateTime.Now, false);
                    X509Certificate2Collection
                    signing_certificate =
                    current_certificates.Find(X509FindType.
                    FindBySubjectDistinguishedName, certificate_name,
                    false);
            if (signing_certificate.Count == 0)
                return null;

            //** get the first certificate
            //** from the collection
            return signing_certificate[0];
        }
        finally
        {
            certification_store.Close();
        }
    }

    //** based on the public key encrypt the file
    private static void FileEncryption(string input_file,
                                    RSA rsaPublicKey)
    {
        using (Aes aes_algorithm = Aes.Create())
        {
            // Create instance of Aes for
            // symetric encryption of the data.
            aes_algorithm.KeySize = 256;
            aes_algorithm.Mode = CipherMode.CBC;
            using (ICryptoTransform
                        transforming_operations =
                        aes_algorithm.CreateEncryptor())
```

```
{
    RSAPKCS1KeyExchangeFormatter
            formatOfTheKey = new
            RSAPKCS1KeyExchangeFormatter
                    (rsaPublicKey);
    byte[] encryption_of_the_key =
        formatOfTheKey.CreateKeyExchange(
            aes_algorithm.Key,
                aes_algorithm.GetType());

    // Create byte arrays to contain
    // the length values of the key and IV.
    byte[] key_length = new byte[4];
    byte[] initializing_vector_length = new byte[4];

    int length_of_the_key =
            encryption_of_the_key.Length;
    key_length =
     BitConverter.GetBytes(length_of_the_key);
    int length_of_initializing_vector =
                        aes_algorithm.IV.Length;
    initializing_vector_length =
            BitConverter.GetBytes(
                length_of_initializing_vector);

    //** the following will written in the
    //** encrypted file
    //** - length of the key
    //** - length of the initializing vector
    //** - encrypted key
    //** - the initializing vector
    //** - the encryption of the cipher
    //** content
    int start_file_name =
        input_file.LastIndexOf("\\") + 1;
```

```
            //** change the file's extension to ".enc"
            string output_file = encryption_folder +
                input_file.Substring(start_file_name,
                input_file.LastIndexOf(".") -
                start_file_name) + ".enc";
    Directory.CreateDirectory(encryption_folder);

            using (FileStream output_file_stream = new
                    FileStream(output_file,
                    FileMode.Create))
            {

                output_file_stream.Write(
                        key_length, 0, 4);

                output_file_stream.Write(
                    initializing_vector_length, 0, 4);

                output_file_stream.Write(
                    encryption_of_the_key, 0,
                    length_of_the_key);

                output_file_stream.Write(aes_algorithm.
                    IV, 0, length_of_initializing_vector);

                //** proceed with writting the cipher
                //** text based on the cryptostream
                //** used for encryption
                using (CryptoStream
                        ouput_stream_encrypted = new
                        CryptoStream(output_file_stream,
                        transforming_operations,
                        CryptoStreamMode.Write))
                {
                //** save memory by proceeding with encryption of
                //** different chunks at a time
                    int count = 0;
```

```
//** size_bytes_of_block can
//** represent a randomly size
    int size_bytes_of_block =
            aes_algorithm.BlockSize / 8;
    byte[] data_block = new
            byte[size_bytes_of_block];
    int bytesRead = 0;

    using (FileStream
            input_file_stream = new
                FileStream(input_file,
                FileMode.Open))
    {
        do
        {
            count =
                input_file_stream.Read(
                data_block, 0,
                    size_bytes_of_block);

                    ouput_stream_encrypted.
                        Write(data_block,
                        0, count);
            bytesRead += count;
        }
        while (count > 0);
        input_file_stream.Close();
    }

        ouput_stream_encrypted.
            FlushFinalBlock();
    ouput_stream_encrypted.Close();
    }
    output_file_stream.Close();
        }
    }
}
}
```

```
private static void FileDecryption(string inFile, RSA rsaPrivateKey)
{
    //** create an object as AES for providing
    //** symmetric decryption for our data
    using (Aes aes_algorithm = Aes.Create())
    {
        aes_algorithm.KeySize = 256;
        aes_algorithm.Mode = CipherMode.CBC;

        //** declare byte arrays and obtain their
        //** length for the key encryption and
        //** initializing vector
        byte[] length_of_key = new byte[4];
        byte[] length_initializing_vector = new byte[4];

        //** generate the file name for decryption file
        string output_file = decryption_folder +
                    inFile.Substring(0,
                    inFile.LastIndexOf(".")) + ".txt";

        //** declare file stream objects for reading
        //** the encrypted file (input_file_stream)
        //** and save the decrypted file in
        //** output_file_stream
        using (FileStream input_file_stream = new
                    FileStream(encryption_folder + inFile,
                    FileMode.Open))
        {

            input_file_stream.Seek(0, SeekOrigin.Begin);
            input_file_stream.Seek(0, SeekOrigin.Begin);
            input_file_stream.Read(length_of_key, 0, 3);
            input_file_stream.Seek(4, SeekOrigin.Begin);

            input_file_stream.Read(
                    length_initializing_vector, 0, 3);
```

```csharp
//** do the conversion of
//** the lengths to integers
int key_length =
        BitConverter.ToInt32(length_of_key, 0);
int initialzing_vector_length =
        BitConverter.ToInt32(
                length_initializing_vector, 0);

//** check and get the start position for
//** the cipher text (start_pos_cipher) and
//** the length of it (length_cipher)
int start_pos_cipher = key_length +
                initialzing_vector_length + 8;
int length_cipher =
                (int)input_file_stream.Length -
                        start_pos_cipher;

//** declare byte arrays and use them for
//** encrypted AES key, initializing
//** vector, and the encrypted text
byte[] encryption_of_the_key = new byte[key_length];
byte[] initializing_vector = new
        byte[initialzing_vector_length];

//** do the extraction of the keys and
//** initializing vector by starting from
//** index position 8
input_file_stream.Seek(8,
        SeekOrigin.Begin);

input_file_stream.Read(
        encryption_of_the_key, 0, key_length);
input_file_stream.Seek(8 + key_length,
        SeekOrigin.Begin);

input_file_stream.Read(initializing_vector,
        0, initialzing_vector_length);

Directory.CreateDirectory(decryption_folder);
```

```
                //** we will use RSA to decrypt AES key
                byte[] decryption_key =
                    rsaPrivateKey.Decrypt(
                        encryption_of_the_key,
                        RSAEncryptionPadding.Pkcs1);

                //** do the decryption of the keys
                using (ICryptoTransform transform =
                    aes_algorithm.CreateDecryptor(
                    decryption_key, initializing_vector))
                {
                    //** do the decryption of the cipher
                    //** text from the file stream used
                    //** for encryption (input_file_stream)
                    //** to the file stream used for
                    //** decryption (output_file_stream)
                  using (FileStream output_file_stream  new
                        FileStream(output_file,
                        FileMode.Create))
                  {
                        int count = 0;

                            int blockSizeBytes =
                                aes_algorithm.BlockSize / 8;
                        byte[] data = new
                                byte[blockSizeBytes];

                        //** save memory
                        input_file_stream.Seek(
                                start_pos_cipher,
                                SeekOrigin.Begin);
                        using (CryptoStream
                                outStreamDecrypted = new
                            CryptoStream(output_file_stream,
                                transform, CryptoStreamMode.Write))
```

```
                    {
                        do
                        {
                            count =
                                input_file_stream.Read(
                                data, 0,
                                blockSizeBytes);
                                outStreamDecrypted.Write
                                (data, 0, count);
                        }
                        while (count > 0);

                            outStreamDecrypted.FlushFinal
                            Block();
                        outStreamDecrypted.Close();
                    }
                    output_file_stream.Close();
                }
                input_file_stream.Close();
            }
        }
    }
}
```

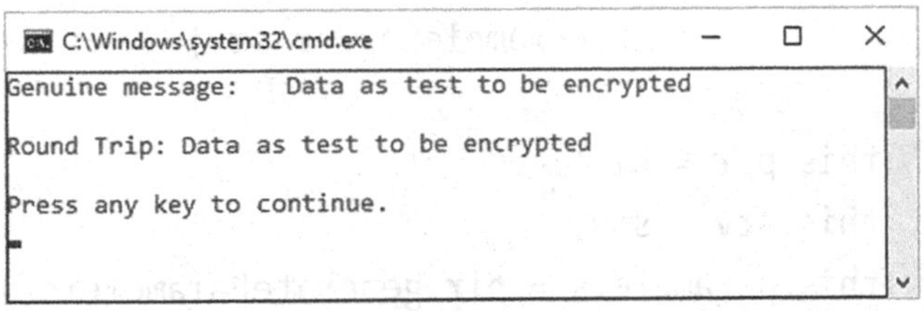

```
C:\Windows\system32\cmd.exe                    —    □    ×
Genuine message:    Data as test to be encrypted

Round Trip: Data as test to be encrypted

Press any key to continue.
```

Figure 17-4. *Functional encryption using X509 certificates for encryption and decryption*

Private Information Retrieval

Private information retrieval is a protocol that allows a client to retrieve an element of a database without the owner of the database being able to determine which elements are selected.

Below, you will see an example of implementation of PIR. The following examples cannot be compiled as they represent a general structure of a framework that can be applied in a real-life environment. It can be seen as an application that helps the end users (clients) interact with the database from the cloud environment (server). The implementation from Listing 17-5 represents a general approach for encrypting the participants with their cryptographic keys (see Figure 17-5), which need to be exchanged during the database query process. The cryptographic keys are generated using a simple homomorphic approach (see Chapter 13). The example provided is designed to work on database records, as you can see from Pseudocodes 17-2 and 17-3.

Pseudocode 17-2. Implementation of PIR – Client

```
using System;

namespace PrivateInformationRetrieval
{
    public class PIRExample
    {
        protected PIRExample pir;
        protected PIRExampleServer srv;
        protected Object parameters;

        public PIRExample(PIRExample pir,
                          PIRExampleServer srv)
        {
            this.pir = pir;
            this.srv = srv;
            this.parameters = pir.generateParameters();
        }
```

```
//** i represents the index
public Object get(int i)
{
     try
     {
          int size = srv.size();
          if (i < 0 || i >= size)
               return null;

          int maximum_width = srv.width();
          PIRExample.Query query =
          pir.generateQuery(parameters,
                              i, size, maximum_width);

          Object the_response =
                         srv.generateResponse(query);

          Object result_output =
                     pir.processResponse(parameters,
                                         the_response,
                                         i, size,
                                         maximum_width);

           return result_output;
     }

     catch (Exception e)
     {
          return null;
     }
}

public int size() {
     try
      {
          Console.WriteLine(srv.size().ToString());
          return srv.size();
      }
```

```
                    catch (Exception e)
                    {
                        return 0;
                    }
            }

        public int width() {
                try
                 {
                    Console.WriteLine(srv.size().ToString());
                    return srv.size();
                }
                catch (Exception e)
                {
                    return 0;
                }
            }

        public PIRExample pir() {return pir;}

        public PIRExampleServer srv() {return srv;}
        }
}
```

Pseudocode 17-3. Implementation of PIR

```
using System;

namespace PrivateInformationRetrieval
{
    public interface PrivateInformationRetrieval
    {
        public class TheQuery
        {
                public int maximum_width;
                public Object query;
```

```
            public TheQuery(int maximum_width, Object query)
            {
                    this.maximum_width = maximum_width;
                    this.query = query;
            }
        }

        public Object    generateParams();
        public TheQuery  generateQuery(Object parameters,
                                        int the_index,
                                        int the_size,
                                        int maximum_width);
        public Object generateResponse(List database,
                                        int width,
                                        TheQuery query);
    public BigInteger processResponse(Object parameters,
                                        Object the_response,
                                        int the_index,
                                        int the_size,
                                        int maximum_width);

        }
}
```

In Listing 17-5, we have introduced a practical approach that shows how cryptographic keys can be generated using a homomorphic method for private information retrieval.

Listing 17-5. Practical Approach for Generating Cryptographic Keys Using a Homomorphic Method for Private Information Retrieval

```
using System;
using System.Collections.Generic;
using System.ComponentModel;
using System.Data;
using System.Drawing;
using System.Linq;
using System.Numerics;
```

```
using System.Text;
using System.Threading.Tasks;

namespace PrivateInformationRetrieval
{
    class Program
    {
        static BigInteger PrivateKey;
        static BigInteger[] PublicKey;
        static readonly int val1 = 5;
        static readonly int val2 = 3;
        static string At = string.Empty;
        static string Bt = string.Empty;

        static void Main(string[] args)
        {
            Random rnd = new Random();
            byte[] rand = new byte[16];

            do
            {
                rnd.NextBytes(rand);
                PrivateKey = new BigInteger(rand);
                PrivateKey = BigInteger.Abs(PrivateKey);
            }
            while (BigInteger.GreatestCommonDivisor
                            (PrivateKey, 1000000) != 1);

            PublicKey = new BigInteger[100];

            for (int i = 0; i < 100; i++)
            {
                rnd.NextBytes(rand);
                PublicKey[i] = new BigInteger(rand);
                PublicKey[i] = (BigInteger.Abs(PublicKey[i]) *
```

```
                    PrivateKey) + (1000000 *
                    rnd.Next(10, 100));
        }
    Encryption();

    Console.WriteLine("\n The multiplication is:");
    multiplication();
    Console.WriteLine("\n The addition is:");
    addition();

    Console.ReadKey();
}

static void Encryption()
{
    BigInteger A;
    BigInteger.TryParse(Convert.ToString(val1), out A);
    BigInteger B;
    BigInteger.TryParse(Convert.ToString(val2), out B);

    if (!(A < 1000000 && A >= 0) || !(B < 1000000 && B
                                                        >= 0))

    {
        Console.WriteLine("This values are not
                    avaialble. The numbers and the results
                    obtained has to be situated between 0
                    and 1000000. These values cannot be
                    accepted");

    }
    else if (!(A * B < 1000000) && !(A + B < 1000000))
    {
        Console.WriteLine("These values are not valid
                    because neither multiplication nor sum
                    can be realized due to noise
                    accumulation. The numbers and results of
                    operations must range from zero to
                    999999  \nSuch values are unacceptable.
```

```
                        It is impossible to decrypt
                        multiplication and sum due to the NOISE
                        in ciphertext. Numbers and results of
                        operations have to be from zero to
                        999999");
        }
        BigInteger t = new BigInteger(0);

        //** Encryption for A
        Random rand = new Random();
        for (int i = 0; i < 100; i++)
        {
            if (rand.Next(2) == 1)
                t = t + PublicKey[i];
        }
        At = (A + t).ToString();

        Console.WriteLine(At);

        t = 0;
        rand = new Random();

        //Encryuption for B
        for (int i = 0; i < 100; i++)
        {
            if (rand.Next(2) == 1)
                t = t + PublicKey[i];
        }
        Bt = (B + t).ToString();
        Console.WriteLine(Bt);
    }

    public static void multiplication()
    {
        BigInteger A;
        BigInteger.TryParse(At, out A);
```

```
    BigInteger B;
    BigInteger.TryParse(Bt, out B);

    Console.WriteLine("Multiplication of A={0} and
            B={1} is {2}", A, B, (A * B).ToString());
    }

public static void addition()
{
    BigInteger A;
    BigInteger.TryParse(At, out A);
    BigInteger B;
    BigInteger.TryParse(Bt, out B);

    Console.WriteLine("Addition of A={0} and B={1} is
                      {2}", A, B, (A + B).ToString());

    }
  }
}
```

```
C:\Windows\system32\cmd.exe                                                    —  □  ×
A = 369586302133725683370472307342763566869516847254491773732058591462937216388903
B = 369586302133725683370472307342763566869516847254491773732058591462937216388901

The multiplication is:
Multiplication of A=369586302133725683370472307342763566869516847254491773732058591462937216388903 and B=369586302133725
683370472307342763566869516847254491773732058591462937216388901 is 13659403472488156561651407052133868008051257288912862
7509215933381223574339683524836669379335828581954493263494414478971680268923046278632069074504908765603

The addition is:
Addition of A=369586302133725683370472307342763566869516847254491773732058591462937216388903 and B=369586302133725683370
472307342763566869516847254491773732058591462937216388901 is 73917260426745136674094461468552713373903369450898354746411
7182925874432777804
```

Figure 17-5. *Homomorphic addition for PIR*

Conclusion

This chapter covered the most important cryptographic primitives for cloud environments. You should now understand the advanced concepts and cryptographic primitives, as well as their general implementations.

The concepts presented in this chapter will give you a strong practical foundation, which will help you go deeper into other cryptographic primitives such as multi-party computation, transparent data encryption, or property preserving encryption.

Cloud computing cryptography represents strong challenges and the huge amount of literature offers multiple theoretical frameworks but no practical direction. This gives professionals and researchers strong research directions and the goal of developing new ideas for improving the security in a cloud environment, excepting the standard security policies that are made available by the cloud solution providers.

Bibliography

[1]   Rishav Chatterjee, Sharmistha Roy, and Ug Scholar, "Cryptography in Cloud Computing: A Basic Approach to Ensure Security in Cloud." 2017.

[2]   N. Jaber and Mohamad Fadli Bin Zolkipli, "Use of cryptography in cloud computing," In *2013 IEEE International Conference on Control System, Computing and Engineering* (pp. 179-184), Mindeb, 2013, doi: 10.1109/ICCSCE.2013.6719955.

[3]   J.P. Kaur and R. Kaur, « Security Issues and Use of Cryptography in Cloud Computing." 2014.

[4]   Melissa Chase and Seny Kamara, "Structured Encryption and Controlled Disclosure," In *Advances in Cryptology-ASIACRYPT* (pp. 577-594). 10.1007/978-3-642-17373-8_33. 2010.

[5]   M. Brenner, J. Wiebelitz, G. V. Voigt, and M. Smith, "Secret Program Execution in the Cloud Applying Homomorphic Encryption," In *Proceedings of the 5th IEEE International Conference on Digital Ecosystems and Technologies* (IEEE DEST 2011).

PART III

Pro Cryptanalysis

CHAPTER 18

Getting Started with Cryptanalysis

The third part of this book will focus on cryptanalysis and its methods. As stated in the first part, *cryptanalysis* is defined as being the discipline that studies the methods and ways of finding breaches within cryptographic algorithms and security systems. The most important goal is to obtain access to the real nature of the encrypted message or cryptographic key.

Cryptanalysis is a process conducted by professionals (ethical hackers, information security officers, etc.). Cryptanalysis activity outside of the legal framework is known as *hacking*, which covers personal and non-personal interests. However, recently, the term hacking has been popularized as just writing code, hence there are people who participate in hackathons events. Hackathons generally have nothing to do with security-related programming, etc.

The mission of third part of this book is to cover the most important methods and techniques used in conducting cryptanalysis in general and in-depth. We will point out the necessary cryptanalysis tools, such as software, methods, cryptanalysis types, cryptanalysis algorithms, and penetration-testing platforms.

Performing cryptanalysis can be a tricky and difficult task. Multiple aspects must be considered before realizing the cryptanalytic process. If the cryptanalysis process is performed by a *legal entity*, things become easier. If the cryptanalysis process is realized by a *non-legal entity*, it's a more complex process and hacking methods are involved. The hacking methods will be pointed out later in our discussion. In both ways, hands get dirty. When a cryptanalysis process is performed, take into consideration the fact that it is time consuming and many obstacles can occur because of system complexity, large size of the cryptographic key, hardware platforms, access permissions, and so on.

© Marius Iulian Mihailescu and Stefania Loredana Nita 2021
M. I. Mihailescu and S. L. Nita, *Pro Cryptography and Cryptanalysis*,
https://doi.org/10.1007/978-1-4842-6367-9_18

Cryptanalysis is more fascinating and challenging compared to cryptography. The knowledge that a cryptanalyst should have is very complex. The fields on which a cryptanalyst should focus can be divided in three main categories, *informatics (computer science), computer engineering,* and *mathematics.* Let's specify the important disciplines for each of the category as follows:

- **Informatics (computer science)**: Computer networks, programming languages, databases, operating systems, theoretical cryptography

- **Computer engineering and hardware**: FPGA (Field Programmable Gateway Array), programming languages (e.g. VHDL), development platforms (Xilinx, etc.)

- **Mathematics**: Number theory, algebra, combinatorics, information theory, probability theory, statistical analysis, elliptic curves mathematics, discrete mathematics, calculus, lattices, real analysis, complex analysis, Fourier analysis

Third Part Structure

The structure of the third part of this book is as follows:

- *Chapter 19.* The chapter will cover the classification of cryptanalysis techniques. We will do a quick overview regarding the theory of algorithmic complexity, statistical-informational analysis, encoding in the absence of perturbation, cryptanalysis of classic ciphers, cryptanalysis of block ciphers, etc.

- *Chapter 20.* The chapter will cover linear and differential cryptanalysis, which are vital when cryptanalysis is performed.

- *Chapter 21.* The chapter will cover the integral cryptanalysis attack, which is used for the block ciphers that are built on substitution-permutation networks.

- *Chapter 22.* The chapter will discuss attacks and how they are applied in practice. A methodology with guidelines will be introduced and we will show how to design and implement real attacks using C#.

- *Chapter 23.* The chapter will discuss the most important techniques for text characterization. Most of the methods based on text characterization count the number of characters or string occurrences. We'll cover algorithms such as chi-squared statistic; monogram, bigram and trigram frequency counts; and quadgram statistics as a fitness measure.

- *Chapter 24.* The chapter will present case studies for implementing cryptanalysis methods.

Cryptanalysis Terms

This section discusses the most common terms used in cryptanalysis and ethical hacking. Table 18-1 lists cryptanalysis keywords and terms that are frequently used in the field. These terms are quite vital when we deal with cryptanalysis attacks and ethical hacking. The following terms will give you a clear image of the process and who interacts with what.

Table 18-1. *Cryptanalysis terms*

Keyword/Term	Definition
Black hat hacker	A *black hat hacker* is a person who has a bad intention and breaks into a computer system or network. Their intention is to exploit any security vulnerabilities for financial gain, steal and destroy confidential and private data, shut down systems and websites, corrupt network communication, and so on.
Gray hat hacker	A *gray hat hacker* is a person, known as *cracker,* who exploits the security weak points of a computer system or software product with the goal of bringing those weaknesses to the owner's attention. Compared with a *black hat hacker,* a gray hat hacker takes action without any malicious intention. The *general goal* of a gray hat is to provide solutions and to improve the computer systems and security of the network.

(*continued*)

Table 18-1. (*continued*)

Keyword/Term	Definition
White hat hacker / Ethical hacker	A *white hat hacker* is an authorized person or certified hacker who works for or is employed by a government or organization with the goal of performing penetration tests and identifying loopholes within their systems.
Green hat hacker	A *gray hat hacker* is an amateur person, but different from a *script kiddie*. Their purpose is to become a full-blown hacker.
Script kiddies	*Script kiddies* are the most dangerous form of hackers. A *script kiddie* is a person without too many skills who uses scripts or downloads tools provided by other hackers. Their goal is to attack networks infrastructures and computer systems. They are looking to impress their community or friends.
Blue hat hacker	A *blue hat hacker* is similar to a script kiddie. They are beginners in field of hacking. If someone dares to mock a script kiddie, a blue hat hacker will get revenge. Blue hat hackers will get revenge on those who address any challenges to them.
Red hat hacker	Also known as an eagle-eye hacker, their goal is to stop black hat hackers. The operation mode is different. They are ruthless when dealing with malware actions that come from black hat hackers. The attacks performed by red hat hackers are very aggressive.
Hacktivist	Also known as online activist, a hacktivist is a hacker who is part of group of anonymous hackers who can gain unauthorized access to files stored within government computers and networks They act to further to social or political parties and groups.
Malicious insider/ whistleblower	Such persons can be an employee of a company or government institution who is aware of illegal actions that are taking place within the institution. This could lead to a personal gain by blackmailing the institution.
State- or nation-sponsored hacker	A person who is scheduled and assigned by a government the goal of providing information security services and gaining access to confidential information from different countries.

A Little Bit of Cryptanalysis History

Writing a comprehensive history of cryptanalysis is challenging, fascinating, and difficult. In this section, we will cover some of the main moments in time that impacted cryptanalysis as a separate field and how it evolved through different periods of history.

The *history of cryptanalysis* starts with Al-Kindi (801-873), the father of Arab philosophy. He developed a unique method using variations of the occurrence frequency of letters. This method helped him analyze and exploit different methods for breaking ciphers (e.g. frequency analysis). The work of Al-Kindi was based on Al-Khalil's (717-786) work. Al-Khalil's work, entitled *Book of Cryptographic Messages,* describes permutations and combinations for most of the possible Arabic words, with and without vowels.

The best way to learn the history of cryptanalysis and cryptography is to divide time into short periods and consider the events within those periods. The examination of cryptanalysis history has to be done with respect for cryptography. The following events provide a quick overview of the cryptanalysis history and focus on the most important achievements of each of the periods.

- **600 B.C.:** *The Spartans* create the basis of scytale. The purpose of *scytale* is to send secret messages during their fights. The "device" is designed from two components, a leather strap and a piece of wooden stem. To decrypt the message, the wooden stem must be of a specific size. The size must be the same as the one used for the encryption phase of the message. If the receiver or malicious person doesn't have the same wooden stem size, the message can't be decrypted.

- **60 B.F.:** *Julius Caesar* designs the first substitution cipher, which encrypts a message using shifting techniques for the characters with three spots, in such way that A is D, B is E, and so on. An implementation of this cipher can be seen in *Chapter 1.*

- **1474:** *Cicco Simonetta* creates a manual for deciphering encryptions for Latin and Italian text.

- **1523:** *Blaise de Vigenère* creates the base for an encryption cipher, known as the *Vigenère cipher.*

- **1553**: *Giovan Battista Bellaso* designs the first cipher based on an encryption key. The encryption key is based on a word that is commonly agreed upon by the sender and receiver.

- **1854**: *Charles Wheatstone* creates the *Playfair Cipher*. The cipher encrypts a specific set of letters instead of encrypting letter by letter. This brings a higher complexity to the cipher, thus it's harder to crack.

- **1917**: *Edward Hebern* creates the first electro-mechanical machine based on a rotor. The rotor is used for the encryption operation. The encryption key is stored within the rotating disc. It is designed and based on a table that is used for substitution. The table is modified with every character that is typed.

- **1918**: *Arthur Scherbius* invents the Enigma machine. The first model and prototype is designed for commercial purposes. The Enigma machine uses several rotors instead of one, as in Edward Hebern's electro-mechanical machine. His invention is adopted immediately by the German military intelligence for encoding their transmissions.

- **1932**: *Marian Rejewski* finds out how the Enigma machine works. In 1939, the French and British intelligence services use the information given by Poland, which helps cryptographers such as Alan Turing break the key, which was changed on a daily basis. This was crucial for the victory of the Allies in World War II.

- **1945**: *Claude E. Shannon* revolutionizes cryptography and cryptanalysis with his work entitled *A Mathematical Theory of Cryptography*. This represents the milestone where classic cryptography ends and modern cryptography starts to gain terrain.

- **End of 1970**: Scientists at IBM design the first block cipher. The goal is to protect the data of the customers.

- **1973**: The block cipher is adopted by the United States and is set as a national standard, called DES (Data Encryption Standard).

- **1975**: Public key cryptography is introduced.

- **1976**: The key exchange protocol Diffie-Hellamn is introduced.

- **1982**: A theoretical model for quantum computers is introduced by *Richard Feynman*. At this moment, we're on the verge of having widely available cloud-based quantum computers. These aspects and advances will have far reaching implications on many aspects of computing today and in future.

- **1997**: DES is cracked with success.

- **1994**: *Peter Shor* introduces an algorithm that can be used within quantum computers for integer factorization.

- **1998**: Quantum computing is introduced.

- **2000**: Officially DES is replaced with AES (Advanced Encryption Standard). AES is declared the winner in a competition that was open to the public.

This list can be improved and contains the main events in history that contribute to cryptanalysis as a concept, model, and framework.

Penetration Tools and Frameworks

The section covers several penetration tools and frameworks that are used with success during the process of penetration testing.

We've divided the tools into two categories, *Linux hacking distributions* and *penetration tools/ frameworks*.

- **Linux hacking distributions**

  - *Kali Linux* represents one of the most advanced platforms for penetration testing. It can be installed on different devices and it can be used to attack multiple types of devices.

  - *BackBox* is a very powerful penetration testing distribution that includes powerful security assessment.

  - *Parrot Security OS* is a new distribution. It's very professionally designed and implemented. Its target is cloud environments that provide online services and other types of services.

- *BlackArch* is a very interesting penetration testing platform and security research. It is built on top of Arch Linux. As with Arch Linux, the user needs to pay attention to the installation process due to its complexity and different setup instructions.

- *Bugtraq* is a powerful and easy-to-use platform that contains a serious set of forensic and penetration tools.

- *DEFT Linux* (**D**igital **E**vidence & **F**orensics **T**oolkit) is a platform for computer forensics. There is the possibility of running it as a live system.

- *Samurai Web Testing Framework* is a powerful collection of tools. It can be used for penetration testing on the Web. It comes as a virtual machine file that can be installed in VirtualBox and VMWare.

- *Pentoo Linux* is built on Gentoo. The distribution goal is to provide fast security and penetration testing analysis. It's available as a live distribution.

- *CAINE* (**C**omputer **A**ided **In**vestigative **E**nvironment) is a complex set of tools that contains professional frameworks and modules for system forensics modules and analysis.

- *Network Security Toolkit* is a popular tool and distribution. It's easy to install and can be done as a live ISO build on Fedora. It has a powerful set of open source network security tools. It has a professional web user interface which offers important details about network and system administration, network monitoring tools, and analysis.

- *Fedora Security Spin* is a professional distro that can be used for security audits and penetration tests. It is used by various professionals, from industry to academia.

- *ArchStrike* is a pentesting distro build on Arch Linux that can be used by professionals in the field of security.

- *Cyborg Hawk* has 750+ tools for security professionals and for performing penetration tests.

- *Matriux* is quite promising. It can be used for penetration tests, ethical hacking, forensic investigations, vulnerability analysis, and much more.

- *Weakerth4n* is not well known in the field of hacking or cryptanalysis. It offers a unique approach to penetration tests and it is built using Debian (Squeeze).

- **Penetration tools/frameworks (Windows and Linux platform)**

  - *Wireshark* is a very well-known packet sniffer. It provides a powerful set of tools for network package traffic analysis and communication protocols analysis.

  - *Metasploit* is one of the most important frameworks used in pentesting.

  - *Nmap* (**N**etwork **M**apper) is a professional network discovery and security auditing tool for security professionals. The goal of the tool is to exploit the targets configured. For each scanned port, we can see what operating system is installed, what services are up and running, firewall details, etc.

Conclusions

The chapter discussed cryptanalysis in general and covered the basic foundations of practical cryptanalysis, tools, and working methods. You should now have the following knowledge:

- The mission and goal of cryptanalysis

- A quick overview of the events in history and how many ciphers and algorithms influenced the cryptanalysis discipline

- Definitions of the main terms and a clear understanding of the main differences between types of hackers

- A background of hacking and pentesting platform distributions

- An understanding of the most important frameworks and penetration tools that are used independently, according to the user flavor operating system platform

Bibliography

[1]   F. Cohen, "A short history of cryptography, 1990. *New World Encyclopedia*, 2007. Retrieved May 4, 2009, from `www.all.net/books/ip/Chap2-1.html`.

[2]   Cryptography. Retrieved May 4, 2009, from `www.newworldencyclopedia.org/entry/Cryptography`.

[3]   M. Pawlan, "Cryptography: the ancient art of secret messages." 1998. Retrieved May 4, 2009, from `www.pawlan.com/Monica/crypto/`.

[4]   J. Rubin, Vigenere Cipher, 2008. Retrieved May 4, 2009, from `www.juliantrubin.com/encyclopedia/mathematics/vigenere_cipher.html`.

[5]   K. Taylor, K. Number theory 1, 2002. Retrieved May 4, 2009, from `http://math.usask.ca/encryption/lessons/lesson00/page1.html`.

[6]   M. Whitman and H. Mattord, *Principles of information security*. University of Phoenix Custom Edition e-text. Canada, Thomson Learning, Inc. 2005. Retrieved May 4, 2009, from University of Phoenix, rEsource, CMGT/432.

[7]   *The Code Book. The Secret History of Codes and Code-Breaking*. Simon Singh, 1999

[8]   A. Ibraham, "Al-Kindi: The origins of cryptology: The Arab contributions", Crypto logia, vol.16, no 2 (pp. 97-126). April 1992. `www.history.mcs.st-andrews.ac.uk/history/Mathematicians/Al-Kindi.html`.

[9]   Abu Yusuf Yaqub ibn Ishaq al-Sabbah Al-Kindi, `www.trincoll.edu/depts/phil/philo/phils/muslim/kindi.html`.

[10]   Philosophers: Yaqub Ibn Ishaq al-Kindi Kennedy-Day, K. al-Kindi, Abu Yusuf Ya'qub ibn Ishaq (d. c.866–73). `www.muslimphilosophy.com/ip/kin.html`.

[11]   Ahmad Fouad Al-Ehwany, "Al-Kindi" in *A History of Muslim Philosophy Volume 1* (pp. 421-434). New Delhi: Low Price Publications. 1961.

[12]   Ismail R. Al-Faruqi and Lois Lamya al-Faruqi, *Cultural Atlas of Islam*, pp. 305-306. New York: Macmillan Publishing Company. 1986.

[13]   Encyclopaedia Britannica (pp. 352). Chicago: William Benton. 1969.

[14]   J.J. O'Connor and E.F. Robertson, Abu Yusuf Yaqub ibn Ishaq al-Sabbah Al-Kindi. 1999.

CHAPTER 19

Cryptanalysis Attacks and Techniques

This chapter is dedicated to the most important and useful cryptanalytic and cryptanalysis standards, validation methods, classification, and operations of cryptanalysis attacks. The cryptanalysis discipline is very complex, and writing about it takes thousands of research hours. The following sections contain a survey of the most important elements that are vital for you to use in your daily activities.

Standards

The importance of standards is vital and it should be known by any professional when a cryptanalysis attack is conducted. Most cryptanalysis attacks are conducted for business purposes only. Any cryptanalysis activity outside of government use and business purpose is not legal and should not be performed for personal gain.

Organizations are very exposed to security attacks and it is very important to make sure that the organization meets the necessary requirements regarding the security of its data. Any organization can hire security experts to perform cryptanalysis attacks in order to test its security and to find the vulnerabilities which later might be exploited by a malicious user/attacker.

The standards are provided by institutes and organizations. They contain cryptography and cryptanalysis methods, frameworks, and algorithms. The institutes and organizations are

- **IEFT Public-Key Infrastructure (X.509):** The organization focuses on the standardization of the protocols used on the Internet that are based on public key systems.

© Marius Iulian Mihailescu and Stefania Loredana Nita 2021
M. I. Mihailescu and S. L. Nita, *Pro Cryptography and Cryptanalysis*,
https://doi.org/10.1007/978-1-4842-6367-9_19

- **National Institute of Standards and Technologies (NIST)**: The institute focuses on the elaboration of standards FIPS for the U.S. government.

- **American National Standards Institute (ANSI)**: Its goal is to maintain standards from the private sector.

- **Internet Engineering Task Force (IEFT)**: It represents an international community formed out of networks, operators, and traders of services and researchers. Their main purpose is represented by the evolution of the Internet architecture.

- **Institute of Electrical and Electronical Engineering (IEEE)**: Its goal is to design theories and advanced techniques from different fields, such as electronics, computers sciences, and informatics.

- **International Organization for Standardization (ISO)**: It is a non-governmental organism that includes more than 100 countries. Its main goal is to encourage the development of standardization to help professionals to facilitate the international exchange of services.

FIPS 140-2, FIPS 140-3, and ISO 15408

ISO 15408[1] is one of the most important standards in the evaluation of IT security and it is used in the international community as a reference system standard. The standard includes a set of rules and requirements from IT field. The goal is to validate the security of the product and cryptographic systems.

FIPS 140-2 and 140-3 offer guidelines that need to be respected in order to accomplish a specific set of technical requirements which are divided and exposed on four levels.

You need to take into consideration both standards, FIPS 140-2/FIPS 140-3 and ISO 15408, when a specification or criterion is developed for a specific application or cryptographic module.

The products that are developed based on the standards need to be tested. The goal of the tests is to get validation and to confirm that the criteria were followed and respected properly.

---

[1]ISO 15408. Link: www.iso.org/standard/50341.html

Validation of Cryptographic Systems

If the business requires cryptanalysis and cryptography operations to be implemented within the software and communication systems, then cryptographic and cryptanalysis services are required. These services are authorized by certification organisms and they include functionalities such as digital signature generation and verification, encryption and decryption, key generation, key distribution, key exchange, etc.

The model in Figure 19-1 is a general model for testing security based on cryptographic and cryptanalysis modules.

Figure 19-1. *Verification and testing framework*

For a sufficient testing and verification process, at minimum you need the *cryptographic module* and the *cryptographic/cryptanalysis algorithm.* For any cryptographic product (or desktop/web software application) developed it is necessary to perform tests and submit the product to CMVP[2] (Cryptographic Module Validation Programme) in order to be tested with respect to FIPS 140-2[3] and FIPS 140-3.[4]

A *cryptographic module* is represented as a combination of specialized software and hardware processes. The most important advantages of utilizing validated cryptographic and cryptanalysis modules are

- Minimum requirements should be satisfied by the modules.

- Authorized and technical personnel should be informed and instructed within a standard. The standard is commonly agreed upon and that it was tested.

---

[2]CMVP, https://csrc.nist.gov/projects/cryptographic-module-validation-program

[3]FIPS 140-2, https://csrc.nist.gov/publications/detail/fips/140/2/final

[4]FIPS 140-3, https://csrc.nist.gov/publications/detail/fips/140/3/final

- Verify that the end user is aware that the cryptographic module has been verified and tested according to security requirements defined before developing the cryptographic module.

- A high level of reliability for security needs to be fulfilled with the goal of developing similar and specific applications.

The security requirements that characterize FIPS 140-2 have 11 metrics and criteria that can be used during the design and implementation process of the cryptographic modules. The cryptographic module has to fulfill and validate each of the metrics. During the validation process, a mark from 1 to 4 is assigned to the cryptographic module, proportional with the security level guaranteed.

Once the cryptographic modules are validated, a set of information should be included such as the name of the manufacturer, address, the name of the module, the version of the module, type of module (software or hardware), validation date, validation level, and module description.

Cryptanalysis Operations

The following principles should be followed when designing a cryptographic system. The principles are simple and should form the basis of any cryptanalysis procedure:

- The adversary should not be underestimated.

- A cryptographic system can be evaluated by a cryptanalyst.

- Before evaluating the cryptographic system, the adversary's knowledge of the assessed cryptosystem is taken into account.

- The secrecy of the cryptographic system relies on the key.

- All elements within the system such as key distribution, cryptographic content, and so on must be taken into account in the cryptographic system evaluation process.

According to Claude Shannon, when carrying out the cryptosystem evaluation the following criteria must be taken into account:

- One of the winnings of the cryptanalyst is gained once the message is decrypted with success.

- Key length and complexity

- The level of complexity of the encryption-deciphering process

- The size of the encoded text according to the document size

- The way to propagate errors

The basic operations for every cryptogram to have a solution for are as follows:

- Finding and deciding the vocabulary used

- Deciding the cryptographic system

- Reconstruction of a single key for a cryptographic system or partial or complete reconstruction for a cryptographic stream system

- Reconstruction of such scheme or determining the complete plaintext

Classification of Cryptanalytics Attacks

This section discusses the types of attacks against cipher algorithms, cryptographic keys, authentication protocols, systems themselves, and hardware attacks.

Attacks on Cipher Algorithms

Table 19-2 lists the most common attacks that occur on ciphering algorithms.

Table 19-1. *Attacks on Ciphering Algorithms*

Types of Attacks on Ciphering Algorithms	
Attack Title	**Attack Description**
Known Plaintext Attack	The cryptanalyst has an encrypted text and the plaintext as its correspondent. The purpose of this attack is for the cryptanalyst to separate the encryption key from the data.
Chosen Text Attack	The cryptanalyst has the option of indicating the plaintext that is to be encrypted. By using this type of attack the cryptanalyst may attempt to isolate the text information from the encryption key with the possibility of accessing the encryption algorithm or the key by different methods.

(continued)

Table 19-1. (*continued*)

Types of Attacks on Ciphering Algorithms	
Attack Title	**Attack Description**
Cipher-Cipher Text Attack	The cryptanalyst keeps the same text, which is encrypted with two or more different keys in plaintext and its correspondent.
Divide-et-Impera Attack	The cryptanalyst has the ability to realize a set of associations between different algorithm inputs and outputs with the intention of separating different algorithm inputs, which lets him split the problem into two or more easily solved problems.
Linear Syndrome Attack	The cryptanalysis method consists of designing and creating a pseudorandom generator-specific linear equation system and verifying the equation system with the encrypted text, thus obtaining a high probability plaintext.
Consistency Linear Attack	The cryptanalytic method consists of the creation of a pseudorandom generator-specific linear equation scheme starting from an analogous cryptographic key and checking the scheme by the pseudorandom generator with the probability that goes to 1, thus obtaining a high probability plaintext.
Stochastic Attack	Known as a forecasting attack, the attack is possible if the output of the generator is autocorrelated and the cryptanalyst manages to obtain as input data the output of the pseudorandom generator and the encrypted text. In this way the clear text is obtained.
Informational Linear Attack	Known also as a linear complexity attack, it is possible to attack if there is any chance of equalizing the generator with a Fibonacci algorithm and if the linear complexity is equivalent to the low generator. With this type of attack a similar algorithm and similar cryptographic key can be constructed.
Virus Attack	This attack is possible if it applies the encryption algorithm and operates on a vulnerable and unprotected PC.

Attacks on Cryptographic Keys

Table 19-2 lists the most common attacks that occur on cryptographic keys.

Table 19-2. *Attacks on Cryptographic Keys*

Types of Attacks on the Keys	
Attack Title	**Attack Description**
Brute force Attack	The attack requires rigorous checking of the keys and passwords and is possible if the size of the encryption key is small and the space of the encryption key is small.
Intelligent Brute Force Attack	The randomness degree of the encryption key is small (entropy is small), which allows the password to be identified because it is close to the language used terms.
Backtracking Attack	The attack is based on implementing a type of backtracking method, which consists of the existence of conditions for continuing the search in the direction desired.
Greedy Attack	The attack provides the optimal local key (the optimal global key cannot be the same).
Dictionary Attack	The attack involves searching for passwords or keys and is carried out using a dictionary.
Hybrid Dictionary Attack	This attack is achieved by changing the dictionary terms and initializing the attack by brute force with the aid of the dictionary words.
Viruses Attack	If the keys are stored on an unprotected PC, this attack is possible.
Password Hash Attack/ Cryptographic Key	This attack occurs if the password hash is elaborated poorly or incorrectly.
Substitution Attack	The original key is replaced by a third party and repeated in the network. It can be achieved using viruses.
Storing Encryption Key	If this is done in the plaintext without any physical protection measures or cryptographic, software, or hardware in the wrong way (together with the encryption data), this can lead to an attack on the encrypted message.
Storing of Old Encryption Keys	This attack will lead to a compromised version of the old encrypted documents.

(continued)

Table 19-2. (*continued*)

Types of Attacks on the Keys	
Attack Title	**Attack Description**
Key Compromise	If the symmetric key is compromised, then only the documents assigned to that key will be compromised. If the public key is compromised, which can be found stored on various servers, then the attacker can replace the data's legal owner, resulting in a bad and negative impact within the network.
Master Keys	The cryptographic system represents various phases.
Key Lifetime	It is an integral component that excludes a yet undetected possibility of a successful attack.

Attacks on Authentication Protocols

The authentication protocols are subject to various forms of attacks. We list the most relevant ones in Table 19-3, which are often used. It is very important to consider the fact that a network authentication protocol is very necessary and vitally important. Once corrupted, it is possible to expose vital information, and attackers can gain a lot of information.

Table 19-3. *Attacks on Authentication Protocols*

Types of Attacks on Authentication Protocols	
Attack Title	**Attack Description**
Attack on the Public Key	The attack within the protocol takes place for the signature. It is only available for public-key schemes.
Attack on the Symmetric Algorithm	Inside the authentication protocol the attack must take place on the signature. This is only possible through the use of a symmetric key.
Passive attack	The intruder can intercept and track the contact on the channel without interfering in any way.
Attack using a third person	The two partners' correspondence inside a channel of communication is deliberately intercepted by a third-party user.
The Fail-Stop Signature	It is a cryptographic protocol in which the sender can provide evidence of whether or not his signature was forged.

Conclusions

The chapter covered the most important and useful guidelines and methods applicable to cryptanalysis. To check and verify the implementation of cryptographic and cryptanalytic algorithms and methods, you must be able to handle the standards. You learned about

- The classification of cryptanalysis attacks

- Operations involved in the cryptanalysis process

- The FIPS 140-2 and FIPS 140-3 Standards

- The ISO 15408 Standard

- The cryptographic systems validation process

Bibliography

[1]   Adrian Atanasiu, *Matematici in criptografie*. US Publishing House, Editor: Universul Stiintific, ISBN: 978-973-1944-48-7. 2015.

[2]   Adrian Atanasiu, *Securitatea Informatiei vol 1 (Criptografie)*, InfoData Publishing House, ISBN: 978-973-1803-18-0. 2007.

[3]   Adrian Atanasiu, *Securitatea Informatiei vol 2 (Protocoale de securitate)*, InfoData Publishing House, ISBN: 978-973-1803-18-0. 2009.

[4]   S.J. Knapskog, "Formal specification and verification of secure communication protocols" (pp 58–73). https://link.springer. com/chapter/10.1007/BFb0030352.

[5]   K. Koyama, "Direct demonstration of the power to break public-key cryptosystems," (pp. 14–21). www.iacr.org/cryptodb/data/ paper.php?pubkey=279.

[6]   P.J. Lee, "Secure user access control for public networks," (pp 46–57). www.sciencedirect.com/science/article/pii/ S0140366416300652.

[7]   R. Lidl and W.B. Muller, "A note on strong Fibonacci
       pseudoprimes" (pp. 311–317). https://link.springer.com/
       article/10.1007/BF01810848.

[8]   Alfred J. Menezes and Scott Vanstone, "The implementation of
       elliptic curve cryptosystems" (pp. 2–13). https://link.springer.
       com/article/10.1007/BF00203817.

[9]   M.J. Mihaljević and J.D. Golić, "A fast iterative algorithm for a
       shift register initial state reconstruction given the noisy output
       sequence" (pp. 165–175). Advances in Cryptology—AUSCRYPT
       '90, Lecture Notes in Computer Science, vol. 453, Springer-Verlag,
       Berlin, 1990.

CHAPTER 20

Linear and Differential Cryptanalysis

In this chapter, we will go through two important types of cryptanalysis, *linear* and *differential cryptanalysis,* introducing basic and advanced concepts and techniques regarding how these two types of cryptanalysis can be conducted and implemented.

The research literature about linear and differential cryptanalysis is wide and rich in theoretical approaches and mechanisms, but only a few of the approaches can be applied in practice in a real-life environment. The difference between theoretical and applied cryptanalysis is huge, and many of the ideas published (algorithms, methods, game theory aspects, etc.) have led researches and professionals down wrong paths over the last 12 years. Doing research into cryptanalysis and increasing its potential value for being applied in practice and for different scenarios requires time, experience, and a continuous cross-collaboration between theoreticians and practitioners, without any isolation between these two types of categories.

Their importance is crucial in the field of cryptanalysis, providing the necessary tools and mechanisms to construct cryptanalysis attack schemes for block and stream ciphers.

Differential Cryptanalysis

Differential cryptanalysis was introduced by E. Biham and A. Shamir in the early 1990s. The goal of differential cryptanalysis is to test if certain positions from the key are traced with a probability bigger than others from the cryptogram. The test can be done at any risk of order 1. Actually, the test is an approximation of order 2 of a testing process much more complex.

With differential cryptanalysis we can expose the weak points of the cryptography algorithm. The following example of differential cryptanalysis is illustrated for *stream cryptography algorithms.*

© Marius Iulian Mihailescu and Stefania Loredana Nita 2021
M. I. Mihailescu and S. L. Nita, *Pro Cryptography and Cryptanalysis*,
https://doi.org/10.1007/978-1-4842-6367-9_20

The pseudocode of the algorithm is as follows:

INPUT: A base key is chosen as $K = (k_1, ..., k_n)$ with $k_i \in \{0,1\}$

OUTPUT: The sensitive and weak points of the cryptography algorithm and the resistance decision for differential cryptanalysis

1. $\alpha \leftarrow$ read the rejection rate

2. Build n sets of perturbed keys starting from the key K.

$$for\ i = 1\ to\ n\ do\ K^{(i)} = \left(\delta_{1i} \oplus k_1, ..., \delta_{ni} \oplus k_n\right):$$

$$\delta_{1i} = \begin{cases} 1, & if\ j \neq i, \\ 0, & if\ j = i. \end{cases}$$

for i,j=1,...,n. In this way, the ith key is obtained from the base key by changing the bit from the ith position.

3. *Building cryptograms.* We will build $n + 1$ cryptograms starting from the basic key, perturbed keys, and a clear text M. We will note this cryptogram with $C^{(i)}$, $i = 1, ..., n + 1$. As plaintext M we can choose for text 0 – everywhere.

4. *Building the correlation matrix.* In this step we will build the matrix $(n + 1) \times (n + 1)$ for the corellation values C:

$$c_{ij} = corelation\left(cryptogram\ i, cryptogram\ j\right),$$

where correlation c_{ij} represents the value of the statistical test applied to the sequence ($cryptogram\ i \oplus cryptogram\ j$). The matrix C is represented as a symmetrical matrix having 1 on the main diagonal.

5. *The computation of significant value.* It will count the values of significant correlation which are situated above the main diagonal. A value is called *significant* if

$$c_{i,j} \notin \left[u_{\frac{\alpha}{2}}; u_{1-\frac{\alpha}{2}} \right].$$

Consider *T* the number of significant values that represent the number of rejects of the corellation test.

6. *Decision and result interpretation.* If

$$\frac{T - \alpha \cdot \dfrac{n(n+1)}{2}}{\sqrt{\alpha(1-\alpha) \cdot \dfrac{n(n+1)}{2}}} \notin \left[u_{\frac{\alpha}{2}}; u_{1-\frac{\alpha}{2}} \right],$$

Once computed, we can decide the non-resistance to differential cryptanalysis ($u_{\frac{\alpha}{2}}$

and $u_{1-\frac{\alpha}{2}}$ representing the quantiles of the normal distribution of order $\dfrac{\alpha}{2}$ and $1-\dfrac{\alpha}{2}$

and fixes the (i,j) elements with $n \geq i > j \geq 1$, for which c_{ij} is significant). These elements represent weak points for the algorithms. Otherwise, we will not be able to mention anything about the resistance to this type of attack.

The C# source code in Listing 20-1 is an implementation of the above pseudocode (see Figure 20-1 for the output).

Listing 20-1. Implementation of Differential Cryptanalysis Example

```
using System;

namespace DifferentialCryptanalysis
{
    class ExampleOfDifferentialCryptanalysis
    {
        //** variables
        public static int[] Known_P0 = new int[10000];
        public static int[] Known_P1 = new int[10000];
```

```
public static int[] Known_C0 = new int[10000];
public static int[] Known_C1 = new int[10000];
public static int Good_P0, Good_P1, Good_C0, Good_C1;
public static int numbers_pairs;
public static int[] characters_data0 = new int[16];
public static int characters_data_max = 0;
public static int[,] characters = new int[32, 32];

public static int[] theSBOX = new int[16] { 3, 14, 1,
        10, 4, 9, 5, 6, 8, 11, 15, 2, 13, 12, 0, 7 };
public static int[] sbox_reviwed = { 14, 2, 11, 0, 4,
        6, 7, 15, 8, 5, 3, 9, 13, 12, 1, 10 };

public static int round_function(int theInputData, int theKey)
{
    return theSBOX[theKey ^ theInputData];
}

public static int encryption(int theInputData, int k_0, int k_1)
{
    int x_0 = round_function(theInputData, k_0);
    return x_0 ^ k_1;
}

public static void find_differences()
{
    Console.WriteLine("\nGenerating a differential
                    table structure for XOR:\n");

    Random rnd = new Random();

    int x, y;

    for (x = 0; x < 16; x++)
    {
        for (y = 0; y < 16; y++)
        {
```

```
                characters[x ^ y, theSBOX[x] ^ theSBOX[y]]
                                                 = rnd.Next(-1, 1);
        }
    }

    for (x = 0; x < 16; x++)
    {
        for (y = 0; y < 16; y++)
        {
            characters[x^y, theSBOX[x] ^
                                    theSBOX[y]]++;
        }
    }

    for (x = 0; x < 16; x++)
    {
        for (y = 0; y < 16; y++)
            Console.Write("{0}",
                                    characters[x, y] + " ");
        Console.WriteLine("\n");
    }

    Console.WriteLine("\nShow the possible differentials:\n");

    for (x = 0; x < 16; x++)
        for (y = 0; y < 16; y++)
            if (characters[x, y] == 6)
                Console.WriteLine("\t\t6/16: {0} to
                                        {1}\n", x, y);
}

public static void genCharData(int input_differences,
                            int output_differences)
{
    Console.WriteLine("\nValues represented as
                possible intermediate based on
                differntial has been generated: ({0} to
                {1}):\n", input_differences,
                output_differences);
```

```
        characters_data_max = 0;
        int p;

        for (p = 0; p < 16; p++)
        {
            int theComputation = p ^ input_differences;

            if ((theSBOX[p] ^ theSBOX[theComputation]) ==
                                            output_differences)
            {
                Console.WriteLine("\t\tThe certain values
                choosen are:   {0} + {1} to  {2} +
                {3}\n", p, theComputation, theSBOX[p],
                theSBOX[theComputation]);

                characters_data0[characters_data_max] = p;
                characters_data_max++;
            }
        }
    }

    public static void genPairs(int input_differences)
    {
        Random randomNumber = new Random();

        Console.WriteLine("\nGenerating {0} known pairs
                    with input differential of {1}.\n",
                    numbers_pairs, input_differences);

        //** generate randomly subkey
        int Real_K0 = randomNumber.Next() % 16;

        //** generate randomly subkey
        int Real_K1 = randomNumber.Next() % 16;

        Console.WriteLine("\t\tThe K0 Real Value is =
                                            {0}\n", Real_K0);
        Console.WriteLine("\t\tThe K1 Real Value is =
                                            {0}\n", Real_K1);
```

```
    int b;

    //** Generate plaintexts pairs using different
    //** XORs based on the differences
    //** that are provided as input
    for (b = 0; b < numbers_pairs; b++)
    {
        Known_P0[b] = randomNumber.Next() % 16;
        Known_P1[b] = Known_P0[b] ^ input_differences;
        Known_C0[b] = encryption(Known_P0[b], Real_K0,
                                            Real_K1);
        Known_C1[b] = encryption(Known_P1[b], Real_K0,
                                            Real_K1);
    }
}

public static void findGoodPair(int
                                output_differences)
{
    Console.WriteLine("\nSearching for good pair:\n");

    int c;
    for (c = 0; c < numbers_pairs; c++)
        if ((Known_C0[c] ^ Known_C1[c]) ==
                                        output_differences)
        {
            Good_C0 = Known_C0[c];
            Good_C1 = Known_C1[c];
            Good_P0 = Known_P0[c];
            Good_P1 = Known_P1[c];
            Console.WriteLine("\t\tA good pair has
                    been found: (P0 = {0}, P1 = {1}) to
                    (C0 = {2}, C1 = {3})\n", Good_P0,
                    Good_P1, Good_C0, Good_C1);
            return;
        }
    Console.WriteLine("There is no pair proper
                                        found!\n");
}
```

```
public static int testKey(int Test_Key_0,
                                            int Test_Key_1)
{
    int c;
    int someCrappyValue = 0;
    for (c = 0; c < numbers_pairs; c++)
    {
        if ((encryption(Known_P0[c], Test_Key_0,
                Test_Key_1) != Known_C0[c]) ||
                (encryption(Known_P1[c], Test_Key_0,
                Test_Key_1) != Known_C1[c]))
        {
            someCrappyValue = 1;
            break;
        }
    }

    if (someCrappyValue == 0)
        return 1;
    else
        return 0;
}

public static void crack()
{
    Console.WriteLine("\nUsing brute force to reduce
                                        the keyspace:\n");

    for (int g = 0; g < characters_data_max; g++)
    {
        int Test_K0 = characters_data0[g] ^ Good_P0;

        int Test_K1 =
                theSBOX[characters_data0[g]] ^ Good_C0;

        if (testKey(Test_K0, Test_K1) == 1)
            Console.WriteLine("\t\tThe Key is! ({0},
                                {1})\n", Test_K0, Test_K1);
```

```
            else
                Console.WriteLine("\t\t({0}, {1})\n",
                                            Test_K0, Test_K1);

        }
    }

    static void Main(String[] args)
    {
        Console.WriteLine("DIFFERENTIAL CRYPTANALYSIS\n");
        Random randomPerRunning = new Random();
        //** generating random values per each running
        randomPerRunning.Next();

        //** identify proper differentials
        //** within the SBoxes
        find_differences();

        //** defining a numerical
        //** value for known pairs
        numbers_pairs = 8;

        //** identify data inputs that will help
        //** to lead us to specific characteristic
        genCharData(4, 7);

        //** randomly, generate pairs of
        //** chosen-plaintext
        genPairs(4);

        //** based and using the characteristic,
        //** we will choose a known pair
        findGoodPair(7);

        //** use characteristic_data0 and within
        //** the proper pair we will find it
        crack();
```

```
        while (true) { }
        Console.ReadKey();
    }
  }
}
```

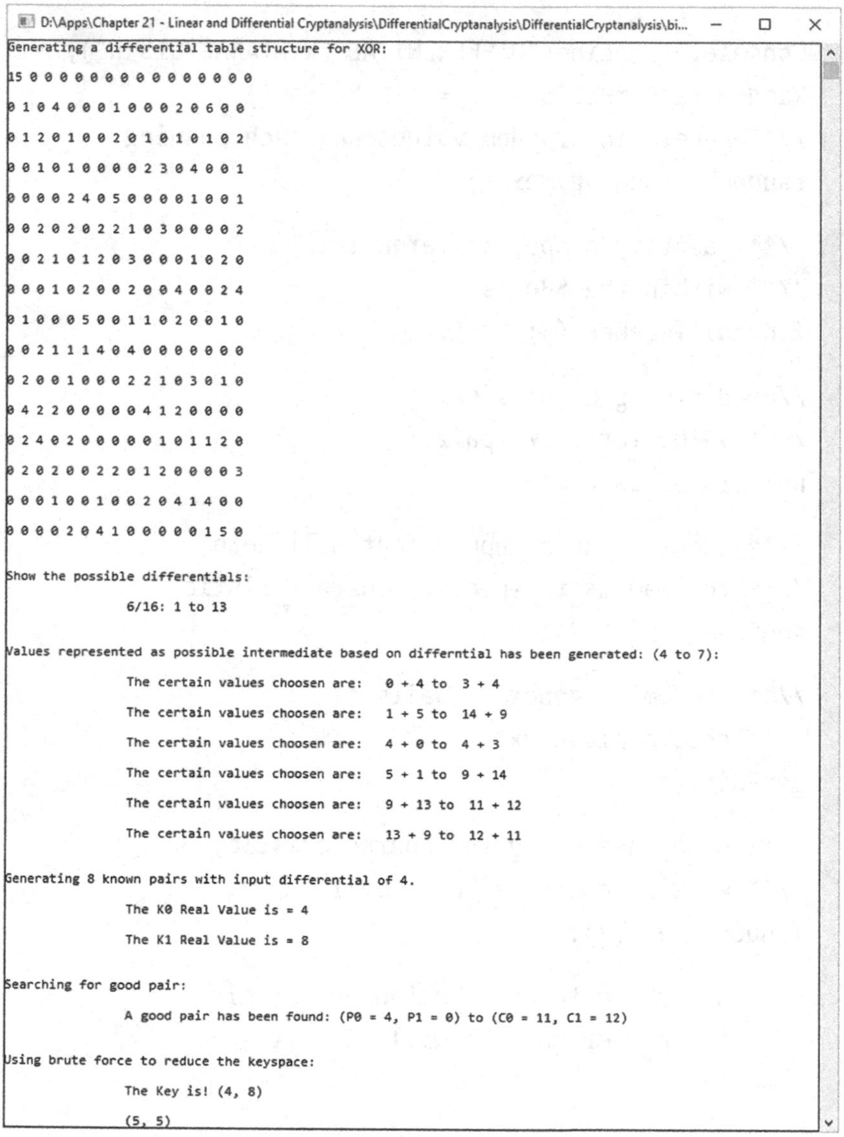

Figure 20-1. *Differential cyptanalysis example*

Linear Cryptanalysis

Linear cryptanalysis was designed and introduced in 1993 as a theoretical framework for DES (Data Encryption System). Currently, linear cryptanalysis is used within block ciphers and represents a very good starting point for designing and conducting an implementation of the complex attacks.

We can look at linear cryptanalysis as being defined as a linear relationship that is established between the key, the plaintext structure, and the ciphertext structure. The structure of the plaintext is represented as characters or bits. It is necessary to represent it as a chain of operations characterized by exclusive-or, shown as

$$A_{i_1} \oplus A_{i_2} \ldots \quad A_{i_u} \quad B_{j_1} \quad B_{j_2} \quad \ldots \quad B_{j_v} = Key_{k_1} \quad Key_{k_2} \quad \ldots Key_{k_w}$$

where $\oplus$ represents the XOR operation (which is a binary operation), A_i represents the bit from i^{th} position of input the structure $A = [A_1, A_2, \ldots]$, B_j represents the bit from j^{th} position of the output structure $B = [B_1, B_2, \ldots]$, and Key_k represents the kth bit of the key $Key = [Key_1, Key_2, \ldots]$.

Conducting Linear Cryptanalysis

In most cases, we start from the idea that we know the encryption algorithm except for the private key. Launching a linear cryptanalysis over a block cipher is represented as a model/framework, described as

- Identifying a linear approximation for non-linear components that characterize the encryption algorithm (as an example, S-Boxes).

- Performing a combination between linear approximations of substitution boxes, which includes operations that are executed within the encryption algorithm. It is very important for professionals to focus on the linear approximation because it represents a special function that contains and deals with the clear text and cipher text bits together with the ones from the private key.

- Designing the linear approximation as a guideline for the keys that are used for the first time. This will be very helpful because it saves important computational resources for all the possible values of the keys. Using multiple linear approximations is very useful for eliminating the key numbers which are necessary for trying.

In the following section, we will provide a few details in order to help figure out which components should be taken into consideration when conducting a linear cryptanalysis attack. Without understanding at the theory level the following concepts, it will be very difficult to perform any implementation of the attack.

S-Boxes

Through S-Boxes the non-linearity is introduced together with its operation, exclusive-or and bit-shift, which are found in a linear representation as well.

The *goal of an S-Box* is to create a map between the incoming binary sequences with a certain output. This being said, we will have the non-linearity provided that will build and render the affine approximation that was obtained when the linear cryptanalysis was applied. Table 20-1 shows an example of an S-Box and how the mapping works. It uses the 1st and 4th bit to find the column and the middle bits, 3rd and 4th. Based on this, the row is determined in such way that the input 1110 will be 0101.

Table 20-1. *S-Box Example*

	11	10	01	00
00	"0000"	"0001"	"0010"	"0011"
01	"1000"	"1001"	"1111"	"1011"
10	"1100"	"1101"	"1110"	"1010"
11	"0100"	"0101"	"0010"	"0111"

Table 20-2 shows the mapping operation between the examples of bits as input and bits as output.

Table 20-2. *The Mapping Between Input and Output*

The Input (J)	The Output (Q)
"0000"	"0011"
"0001"	"0010"
"0010"	"1011"
"0011"	"1111"
"0100"	"1010"
"0101"	"1110"
"0110"	"0111"
"0111"	"0010"
"1000"	"0001"
"1001"	"0000"
"1010"	"1001"
"1011"	"1000"
"1100"	"1101"
"1101"	"1100"
"1110"	"0101"
"1111"	"0100"

S-Box Linear Approximation

We will start from the idea that we want to approximate the structure of the substitution box presented above. Based on that information, we have the precision, which is quite high, of the various linear approximations. We include 256 such linear approximations having the following form:

$$d_1J_1 \oplus d_2I_2 \oplus d_3J_3 \oplus a_4I_4 = g_1Q_1 \oplus g_2Q_2 \oplus g_3Q_3 \oplus g_4Q_4$$

where J_1 and Q_i represent the ith bit characterized to input (J) and ouput (Q) with respect for d_i and g_1 which are 0 or 1. As an example, let's use the following linear approximation $J_2 = Q_1 \oplus Q_4$ and being given by $d = 0100_2$ and $g = 1001_2$.

Concatenation of Linear Approximations

It's time to move to the next step and form, design, and project the linear approximation for the whole system. To achieve this, we need two things:

- First, we need to have already computed the linear approximation for each component that is forming the system.

- Second, to do the combination, we simply *sum* by using exclusive-or the entire set of equations in different combinations. In this way we get a single equation which will eliminate the intermediate variables.

Assembling the Two Variables

Let's consider B_1 and B_2, two random binary variables. The linear relationship between them is $B_1 \oplus B_2 = 0$. Next, let's denote the probability $B_1 = 0$ by being noted with l and the probability $B_2 = 0$ by being noted with m. Based on the two random independent variables, we have

$$P\left(B_1 = a, B_2 = b\right) = \begin{cases} l \cdot m & \text{for } a = 0, b = 0 \\ l \cdot (1 - m) & \text{for } a = 0, b = 1 \\ (1 - l) \cdot q & \text{for } a = 1, b = 0 \\ (1 - l) \cdot (1 - m) & \text{for } a = 1, b = 1 \end{cases}$$

Moving forward, we can show the following:

$$P\left(B_1 \oplus B_2 = 0\right) =$$

$$= P\left(B_1 = B_2\right)$$

$$= P\left(B_1 = 0, B_2 = 0\right) + P\left(B_1 = 1, B_2 = 1\right)$$

$$= l \cdot m + (1 - l)(1 - m)$$

The next step is represented by computing the bias for $B_1 \oplus B_2 = 0$. It is given as $\zeta_1 \cdot \zeta_2$.

Now it is time to do the implementation in C# (see Listing 20-2) for the linear cryptanalysis (see Figure 20-2) and to show how the above concepts can be used in practice.

Listing 20-2. Linear Cryptanalysis Simulation

```
using System;

namespace LinearCryptanalysis
{
    class ExampleOfLinearCryptanalysis
    {
        #region Variables
        public static int[,] approximation_table =
        new int[16,16];
        public static int[] known_plaintext = new int[500];
        public static int[] known_ciphertext = new int[500];
        public static int number_known = 0;

        public static int[] theSBox =
                new int [16] {9, 11, 12, 4, 10, 1, 2, 6, 13,
                                  7, 3, 8, 15, 14, 0, 5};
        public static int[] revtheSBox = {14, 5, 6, 10, 3, 15,
                                  7, 9, 11, 0, 4, 1, 2, 8, 13, 12};
        #endregion

        //** the function will round
        //** the sbox values accordingly
        //** based on the value inputed and the sub key
        public static int RoundingFunction(int theInputValue,
                                                int theSubKey)

        {
            int index_position = theInputValue ^ theSubKey;
            return theSBox[index_position];
        }

        //** generatiing the keys
        //** and generating the known pairs
        public static void FillingTheKnowledgedOnces()
        {
            Random randomNumber = new Random();
            int theSubKey_1 = randomNumber.Next() % 16;
```

```csharp
        int theSubKey_2 = randomNumber.Next() % 16;

        Console.WriteLine("Generating the data: Key1 =
            {0}, Key2 = {1}\n", theSubKey_1, theSubKey_2);

        for (int h = 0; h < number_known; h++)
        {
            known_plaintext[h] = randomNumber.Next() % 16;
            known_ciphertext[h] =
                    RoundingFunction(RoundingFunction(
                    known_plaintext[h], theSubKey_1),
                        theSubKey_2);
        }

        Console.WriteLine("Generating the data: Generating
                        {0} Known Pairs\n\n", number_known);
    }

    //** show the the linear approximation
    //** note that the parameters
    //** a and b starts from 1
    public static void DisplayTheApproximation()
    {
        Console.WriteLine("Generate the linear
                                    approximation: \n");

        for (int a = 1; a < 16; a++)
        {
            for (int b = 1; b < 16; b++)
            {
                if (approximation_table[a, b] == 14)
                    Console.WriteLine("{0} : {1} to
                            {2}\n", approximation_table[a, b],
                            a, b);
            }
        }
        Console.WriteLine("\n");
    }
```

```csharp
public static int ApplyingTheMask(int v, int m)
{
    //** v - is the value
    //** m - is the mask
    int internal_value = v & m;
    int total_amount = 0;

    while (internal_value > 0)
    {
        int temporary = internal_value % 2;
        internal_value /= 2;

        if (temporary == 1)
            total_amount = total_amount ^ 1;
    }
    return total_amount;
}

//** the function will validate and
//** test the keys accordingly
public static void ValidationAndTestingKeys(int key_1,
int key_2)
{
    for (int h = 0; h < number_known; h++)
    {
        if (RoundingFunction(RoundingFunction
                (known_plaintext[h], key_1), key_2) !=
                known_ciphertext[h])
        break;
    }
    Console.WriteLine("* ");
}

public static void FindingTheApproximation()
{
    Random randomNumber = new Random();
```

```
//** The output the mask
for (int a = 1; a < 16; a++)
{
    //** The input mask
    for (int b = 1; b < 16; b++)
    {
        //** the input
        for (int c = 0; c < 16; c++)
        {
            if (ApplyingTheMask(c, b) ==
                ApplyingTheMask(theSBox[c], a))
            {
                approximation_table[b, a]++;
            }
        }
    }
}
}

public static void Main(String[] args)
{
    int[] key_score = new int[16];
    int[] theProperKeys = new int[16];
    int stateProgress = 0;
    int maximum_score = 0;
    int guessing_key_1, guessing_key_2;
    int x, y;

    Random randomNumber = new Random();

    Console.WriteLine("Linear Cryptanalysis
                            Simulation Program\n");

    randomNumber.Next();

    FindingTheApproximation();
    DisplayTheApproximation();
```

```
int approximationAsInput = 11;
int approximationAsOutput = 11;

number_known = 16;
FillingTheKnowledgedOnces();

Console.WriteLine("Cryptanalysis Linear Attack -
            PHASE1. \n\t\t Based on linear
            approximation = {0} -> {1}\n",
            approximationAsInput,
            approximationAsOutput);

for (x = 0; x < 16; x++)
{
    key_score[x] = 0;

    for (y = 0; y < number_known; y++)
    {
        stateProgress++;

        //** Find Bi by guessing at K1
        int middle_round =
                RoundingFunction(known_plaintext[y], x);

        if ((ApplyingTheMask(middle_round,
                approximationAsInput) ==
                ApplyingTheMask(known_ciphertext[y],
                approximationAsOutput)))
            key_score[x]++;
        else
            key_score[x]--;
    }
}

for (x = 0; x < 16; x++)
{
    int theScore = key_score[x] * key_score[x];
    if (theScore > maximum_score)
        maximum_score = theScore;
}
```

```
for (y = 0; y < 16; y++)
    theProperKeys[y] = -1;

y = 0;

for (x = 0; x < 16; x++)
    if ((key_score[x] * key_score[x]) ==
                                        maximum_score)
    {
        theProperKeys[y] = x;
        Console.WriteLine("Cryptanalysis Linear
                    Attack - PHASE 2. \n\t\t The
                    possible for Key 1 = {0}\n",
                    theProperKeys[x]);
        y++;
    }

for (y = 0; y < 16; y++)
{
    if (theProperKeys[y] != -1)
    {
        int testing_key_1 =
                    RoundingFunction(known_plaintext[0],
                    theProperKeys[y]) ^
                    revtheSBox[known_ciphertext[0]];

        int g;
        int wrong = 0;
        for (g = 0; g < number_known; g++)
        {
            stateProgress += 2;
            int testOut =
                    RoundingFunction(RoundingFunction(
                    known_plaintext[g], theProperKeys[y]),
                    testing_key_1);

            if (testOut != known_ciphertext[g])
                wrong = 1;
        }
```

```
        if (wrong == 0)
        {
            Console.WriteLine("Cryptanalayis
                        Linear Attack - PHASE 3.\n");
            Console.WriteLine("\t\tI have found
                        the keys! Key1 = {0}, Key2 =
                        {1}\n", theProperKeys[y],
                        testing_key_1);
            guessing_key_1 = theProperKeys[y];
            guessing_key_2 = testing_key_1;
            Console.WriteLine("Cryptanalysis
                        Linear Attack - PHASE 4.\n");
            Console.WriteLine("\t\tThe number of
                        computation until the key has
                        been found = 0\n",
                        stateProgress);
        }
    }
}

Console.WriteLine("Cryptanalyis Linear Attack -
                                    PHASE 5.\n");
Console.WriteLine("The number of computation =
                        {0}\n\n", stateProgress);

stateProgress = 0;

for (y = 0; y < 16; y++)
{
    for (x = 0; x < 16; x++)
    {
        int t;
        int wrong = 0;
        for (t = 0; t < number_known; t++)
        {
            stateProgress += 2;
            int testOut =
```

```
                              RoundingFunction(RoundingFunction(
                                    known_plaintext[t], y), x);

                    if (testOut != known_ciphertext[t])
                        wrong = 1;
                }
                if (wrong == 0)
                {
                    Console.WriteLine("Brute Force -
                                                    PHASE 1.\n");
                    Console.WriteLine("\t\tI managed to
                                find the keys! \n\t\t
                                      Key1 = {0} \n\t\t Key2 =
                                      {1}\n", y, x);

                    Console.WriteLine("Brute Force -
                                                    PHASE 2\n");
                    Console.WriteLine("\t\tThe number of
                                computations until the key
                                was dound = {0}\n",
                                stateProgress);
                }
            }
        }

        Console.WriteLine("Brute Force - PHASE 3.\n");
        Console.WriteLine("Computations total_amount =
                                            {0}\n", stateProgress);

        while (true) { }
    }
  }
}
```

```
D:\Apps\Chapter 21 - Linear and Differential Cryptanalysis\LinearCryptanalysis\LinearCrypta...  —  □  ×

Linear Cryptanalysis Simulation Program

==========================================


Generate the linear approximation:

14 : 10 -> 4

14 : 11 -> 11

14 : 13 -> 6



Generating the data: Key1 = 4, Key2 = 12

Generating the data: Generating 16 Known Pairs


Cryptanalysis Linear Attack - PHASE1.
                Based on linear approximation = 11 -> 11

Cryptanalysis Linear Attack - PHASE 2.
                The possible for Key 1 = 0

Cryptanalysis Linear Attack - PHASE 2.
                The possible for Key 1 = -1

Cryptanalysis Linear Attack - PHASE 2.
                The possible for Key 1 = -1

Cryptanalysis Linear Attack - PHASE 2.
                The possible for Key 1 = -1

Cryptanalayis Linear Attack - PHASE 3.

                I have found the keys! Key1 = 4, Key2 = 12

Cryptanalysis Linear Attack - PHASE 4.

                The number of computation until the key has been found = 0

Cryptanalyis Linear Attack - PHASE 5.

The number of computation = 384


Brute Force - PHASE 1.

                I managed to find the keys!
                Key1 = 4
                Key2 = 12

Brute Force - PHASE 2

                The number of computations until the key was dound = 2464

Brute Force - PHASE 3.

Computations total_amount = 8192
```

Figure 20-2. *Linear cryptanalysis output simulation program*

Conclusion

In this chapter, we discussed differential and linear cryptanalysis attacks and how such attacks can be designed and implemented. We presented the theoretical background and main foundation necessary to know before designing such cryptanalysis attacks.

At the end of this chapter, you can now

- Identify theoretically the main components on which a cryptanalyst should focus

- Understand how vulnerable those components are and how they can be exploited

- Implement a linear and differential cryptanalysis attacks

Bibliography

[1] Joan Daemen, Lars Knudsen, and Vincent Rijmen, "The Block Cipher Square. Fast Software Encryption (FSE)," In Volume 1267 of *Lecture Notes in Computer Science* (pp. 149–165), Haifa, Israel: Springer-Verlag. CiteSeerX 10.1.1.55.6109. 1997.

[2] H. Heys, "A Tutorial on Linear and Differential Cryptanalysis," In *Cryptologia*, vol. XXVI, no. 3 (pp. 189-221), 2002.

[3] M. Matsui, "Linear Cryptanalysis Method for DES Cipher," In *Advances in Cryptology - EUROCRYPT '93* (pp. 386-397), Springer-Verlag, 1994.

[4] E. Biham, "On Matsui's linear cryptanalysis." In A. De Santis (ed), *Lecture Notes in Computer Science*, vol. 950, (pp. 341–355). Springer-Verlag, Berlin, 1995.

[5] A. Biryukov, C. De Cannière, M. Quisquater, "On Multiple Linear Approximations," In M. Franklin (ed), *Advances in Cryptology, proceedings of CRYPTO 2004, Lecture Notes in Computer Science 3152* (pp. 1-22). Springer-Verlag, 2004.

[6]   L. Keliher, H. Meijer, and S.E. Tavares, "New method for upper bounding the maximum average linear hull probability for SPNs." In B. Pfitzmann (ed), *LNCS*, vol. 2045 (pp. 420-436). Springer-Verlag, Berlin, 2001.

[7]   L. R. Knudsen and J.E. Mathiassen," A chosen-plaintext linear attack on DES," In B. Schneier (ed.), *Lecture Notes in Computer Science*, vol. 1978 (pp. 262–272). Springer-Verlag, Berlin, 2001.

[8]   M. Matsui and A. Yamagishi, "A new method for known plaintext attack of FEAL cipher." In R.A. Rueppel (ed), *Lecture Notes in Computer Science*, vol. 658 (pp. 81-91). Springer-Verlag, Berlin, 1993.

[9]   M. Matsui, "The first experimental cryptanalysis of the data encryption standard." In Y.G. Desmedt (ed), *Lecture Notes in Computer Science*, vol. 839 (pp. 1-11). Springer-Verlag, Berlin, 1994.

CHAPTER 21

Integral Cryptanalysis

Integral cryptanalysis represents a particular cryptanalytic attack that is applicable to the block ciphers that are built based substitution-permutation networks. The attack was designed by Lars Knudsen as a dedicated attack against Square [1], leading it to be known as the Square attack.

The substitution-permutation networks represent one of the most important vulnerable points of block ciphers. Once the networks can be found (let's say intuitively) then the attack on the block cipher can devastatingly corrupt the entire cryptosystem. The next vulnerable points are the key and the table used to permutate the key. Once the key is close to the real one or identical, then we are close to cracking the cryptosystem. An example of such a key is

```
private byte[]PermutationTableForKey = {
    06, 30, 13, 07, 05, 35, 15, 14,
    12, 18, 03, 38, 09, 10, 22, 25,
    16, 04, 21, 08, 39, 37, 36, 02,
    24, 11, 28, 27, 29, 23, 33, 01,
    32, 17, 31, 00, 26, 34, 20, 19
};
```

In the following pages, we will go through the necessary elements required to implement a block cipher and identify the elements that are necessary to focus on in order to launch an integral cryptanalysis attack, such as building Feistel networks (see Listing 22-2) and generating a permutation table for a cryptographic key (Listing 22-4). Once there is a clear understanding of these two phases, it will become very clear how an integral cryptanalysis has to be conducted.

© Marius Iulian Mihailescu and Stefania Loredana Nita 2021
M. I. Mihailescu and S. L. Nita, *Pro Cryptography and Cryptanalysis*,
https://doi.org/10.1007/978-1-4842-6367-9_21

Basic Notions

In order to implement and design an integral cryptanalytic attack, it is very important to understand the fundamental notions first. So let's consider the following notions as the main starting point. Based on that foundation we will design and implement such an attack for education purposes only.

Let's consider $(G, +)$ to be a finite abelian group or order k. The following product group, $G^n = G \times \ldots \times G$, is the group with elements of the form $v = (v_1, \ldots, v_n)$, where $v_i \in G$. The addition within G^n is defined as component-wise. So now we have $u + v = w$ holds for $u, v, w \in G^n$ when $u_i + v_i = w_i$ for all i.

We note with B the multiset of vectors. The integral that is defined over B represents the sum of all vectors, S. In other words, the integral is defined as $\int S = \sum_{v \in B} v$, the summation operation being defined in terms of the group operation for G^n.

When designing an integral cryptanalytic attack, it is very important to know and to figure out the number of words in the plaintext and ciphertext. For our example, this number will be denoted with n. Another number that is very important to be aware of is the number of plaintexts and ciphertexts, denoted with m. Usually, $m = k$ (i.e. $k = |G|$), the vectors $v \in B$ representing the plaintext and ciphertexts, and $G = GF(2^B)$ or $G = Z/kZ$.

Moving forward to the attack, one of the parties will try to predict the values situated in the integrals after a specific number of encryption rounds. Based on this purpose, it is beneficial to make the difference between three cases: (1) where all the words are equal (e.g. i), (2) all words are different, and (3) sum to a certain value that is predicted in advance.

Let's consider $B \subseteq G^n$ be declared as before and an fixed index i. The following three cases take place:

(1) $v_i = c$, for all $v \in B$

(2) $\{v_i : v \in B\} = G$

(3) $\sum_{v \in B} v_i = c'$

where $c, c' \in G$ are some values known and fixed in advance.

The following example represents a typical case in which $m = k$, the number of vectors that are found within B equals the number of elements in the considered group. By using Lagrange's theorem, we can see if all words, i^{th}, are equal, and then it is quite clear that i^{th} word from the integral will take the value of the neutral element from G.

The following two theorems are necessary and represent a must for any practical developer who wants to translate into practice an integral cryptanalysis.

Theorem 21-1 [1, Theorem 1, p. 114]. Let's consider $(G, +)$ a *finite abelian additive group*. The subgroup of elements of order 1 or 2 is denoted as $L = \{g \in G : g + g = 0\}$. We consider writing $s(G)$ as being the sum $\sum_{g \in G} g$ of all the elements found within G. Next, we consider $s(G) = \sum_{h \in H} H$. More, it is very important to understand the following analogy: $s(G) \in H$, i.e. $s(G) + s(G) = 0$.

This being said, for $G = GF(2^B)$ we have $s(G) = 0$ and for Z/mZ we obtain $s(Z/mZ) = m/2$ when m is found in the case of being even or 0. We have also the multiplicative case for written groups (see Theorem 21-2).

Thereom 21-2 [1, Theorem 2, p. 114]. Let's consider $(G, *)$ a *finite abelian multiplicative group*. The subgroup of elements of order 1 or 2 is denoted as $H = \{g \in G : g * g = 1\}$. We consider writing $p(G)$ as being the product $\prod_{g \in G} g$ of all the elements of G. Next, we consider $p(G) = \prod_{h \in H} h$. More, it is very important to understand the following analogy: $p(G) \in H$, i.e. $p(G) * p(G) = 1$.

As an example, if we have $G = (Z/pZ)*$ where p is prime, $p(G)$ is -1, $p(G) = -1$. This is proved using Wilson's theorem.

Practical Approach

The section will show how an integral cryptanalysis attack can be put into practice using the .NET Framework and the C# programming language. The following approach represents a basic implementation of a Feistel network in C# with the possibility to override the current block size. We will use repeating sequences with the purpose of creating a weakness to show how it can be exploited and create the attack.

Listing 21-1 shows how the integral cryptanalytic attack can be built and designed. Listing 21-2 shows how the Feistel network is built. Once we have structure, to have success with the attack, it is important to "figure out" how the Feistel network is built and to create a replica of it or at least something that is similar to the original one. Listing 21-3 shows how to implement the block data and Listing 21-4 shows how to generate the keys.

Listing 21-1. The Main Program

```csharp
using System;
using System.IO;

namespace BuildingIntegralCryptanalysis
{
    class Program
    {
        static void Main(string[] args)
        {
            string theKeyword = "", data_input = "",
                    data_output = "", data_file = "";

            FeistelNetwork feist_network;
            StreamReader file_stream_reader;
            StreamWriter file_stream_writer;

            //** create a help text for the user
            const string helperData =
            @"Building Integral Cryptanalysis Attack
              Usage:
                private [-option] keyword
                           input_file output_file
                             Options:
                                 -enc Encrypt the file passed as
                                            input using the keyword
                                 -dec Decrypt the file passed as
                                            input using the keyword";

            //** show in the console the helper
            //** if we have less than four arguments
            if(args.Length < 4)
            {
                Console.WriteLine(helperData);
                return;
            }
```

```
else if(args[1].Length < 10 ||
                        args[1].Length > 40)
{
    //** Output usage if the password
    //** is too short/long
    Console.Write("The length of the password is
    invalid. The password should have between 10-40
    characters.\n" + helperData);

    return;
}

theKeyword = args[1];
data_input   = args[2];
data_output  = args[3];

//** environment input/output configuration
feist_network = new FeistelNetwork(theKeyword);
file_stream_reader = new StreamReader(data_input);
file_stream_writer = new
                        StreamWriter(data_output);

//** Read the data from the input file
data_file = file_stream_reader.ReadToEnd();
file_stream_reader.Close();

if (args[0] == "-enc")
{
    //** do the encryption based
    //** on the argument provided
    string ciphertext =
                    feist_network.EncryptionOp(data_file);
    file_stream_writer.Write(ciphertext);
    Console.WriteLine("The file has been encrypted
            with success. The file has been saved
                            to: " + data_output);
}
```

```csharp
            else if(args[0] == "-dec")
            {
                //** do the decryption based on the argument
                string thePlaintext =
                                feist_network.DecryptionOp(data_file);
                file_stream_writer.Write(thePlaintext);
                Console.WriteLine("The file has been decrypted
                            with success. The file has been saved
                            to: " + data_output);
            }
            else
            {
                //** invalid option selected
                Console.Write("The selected option is invalid.
                            Please, choose another option.\n"
                            + helperData);
            }

            file_stream_writer.Close();

            Console.ReadKey();
        }
    }
}
```

Listing 21-2. Building the Feistel Network

```csharp
using System;
using System.Collections;
using System.Collections.Generic;
using System.Linq;
using System.Text;
using System.Threading.Tasks;

namespace IntegralCryptanalysis
{
    public class FeistelNetwork
```

```csharp
{
    //** represents the size in bytes
    //** for each of the block
    public int BlockSize
    {
        get;
        private set;
    }

    //** the password code for
    //** encryption and decryption
    public string PasswordCode
    {
        get;
        set;
    }

    /// <summary>
    /// The basic constructor of Feistel Class.
    /// </summary>
    /// <param name="password_code">represents the
    /// password code</param>
    public FeistelNetwork(string password_code)
    {
        this.PasswordCode = password_code;
        this.BlockSize = 16;
    }

    /// <summary>
    /// Constructs a new instance of the Feist class, with a custom
    ///    blocksize
    /// </summary>
    /// <param name="password_code">Passcode used in this instance
    ///    </param>
    /// <param name="the_block_size">Size of the blocks to use in this
    ///    instance</param>
```

```csharp
public FeistelNetwork(string password_code, int the_block_size) :
this(password_code)
{
    this.BlockSize = the_block_size;
}

/// <summary>
/// Encryption operation of the clear text using the password code
/// </summary>
/// <param name="clearText">The string to encrypt</param>
/// <returns>The encrypted text.</returns>
public string EncryptionOp(string clearText)
{
    return DoCiphering(clearText, true);
}

/// <summary>
/// Decryption operation of the encrypted text using the password
    code
/// </summary>
/// <param name="clearText">The string to decrypt</param>
/// <returns>The decrypted text.</returns>
public string DecryptionOp(string clearText)
{
    return DoCiphering(clearText, false);
}

/// <summary>
/// Do a Feistel encryption on the text
/// </summary>
/// <param name="sourceText">The clear text or encrypted text to
    encrypt/decrypt</param>
/// <param name="isClearText">Decide if the given text represents
    (true) or not (false) a plaintext string</param>
/// <returns>A string of plain or ciphered
/// text</returns>
private string DoCiphering(string sourceText, bool isClearText)
```

```
{
    int pointer_block = 0;
    string cipher_text_posting = "";
    List<ulong> the_round_keys = new Key(PasswordCode).
    ReturnRoundKeys();

    //** Do a padding operation to
    //** the string using '\0'.
    //** The output will
    //** be a multiple of <blocksize>
    while (sourceText.Length % BlockSize != 0)
        sourceText += new char();

    //** in case of decryption, reverse
    //** the encryption keys
    if (!isClearText)
        the_round_keys.Reverse();

    byte[] the_text_bytes = Encoding.UTF8.GetBytes(sourceText);

    //** do iteration through the text
    //** moving with <blocksize> bytes per iteration
    while (pointer_block < the_text_bytes.Length)
    {
        byte[] the_block_as_bytes = new byte[BlockSize];
        Array.Copy(the_text_bytes, pointer_block, the_block_as_
        bytes, 0, BlockSize);

        Block text_as_block = new Block(the_block_as_bytes);

        //** if we have a ciphertext,
        //** swap it in halves
        if (!isClearText)
            text_as_block.SwapHalfes();

        //** each round keys will be
        //** applied to the text
        foreach (ulong the_round_key in the_round_keys)
            text_as_block = RoundOnTheBlock(text_as_block, the_
            round_key);
```

```csharp
            //** build the output by appending it
            if (!isClearText) text_as_block.SwapHalfes();
            cipher_text_posting += text_as_block.ToString();

            pointer_block += BlockSize;
        }
        return cipher_text_posting.Trim('\0');
    }

    /// <summary>
    /// Do a single round encryption on the block
    /// </summary>
    /// <param name="theBlock">The block that will be encrypted or
    ///     decrypted</param>
    /// <param name="theRoundKey">The round key which will be applied
    ///     as the round function</param>
    /// <returns>The next block in the round sequence</returns>
    private Block RoundOnTheBlock(Block block, ulong theRoundKey)
    {
        ulong theRoundFunction = 0;

        Block roundBlock = new Block(block.BlockSize);

        BitArray keyBits = new BitArray(BitConverter.
        GetBytes(theRoundKey)), funcBits = block.RightBitsOfBlock.
        Xor(keyBits);

        roundBlock.LeftHalf = block.RightHalf;

        //** do the proper casting AND round
        //** the function bits to an int
        //** set R(i+1) as L(i) XOR f
        theRoundFunction = ToInteger64(funcBits);
        roundBlock.RightHalf = BitConverter.GetBytes(ToInteger64
        (block.TheLeftBitsOfBlock) ^ theRoundFunction);

        return roundBlock;
    }
```

```
/// <summary>
/// Helper method used for conversion of BitArray to have an
    integer representation
/// </summary>
/// <param name="theArray">BitArray that will be converted</param>
/// <returns>A value of 64-bit integer of the array</returns>
private ulong ToInteger64(BitArray theArray)
{
    byte[] array_as_byte = new byte[8];
    theArray.CopyTo(array_as_byte, 0);
    return BitConverter.ToUInt64(array_as_byte, 0);
}
    }
}
```

Listing 21-3. Implementing the Block Data

```
using System;
using System.Collections;
using System.Collections.Generic;
using System.Linq;
using System.Text;
using System.Threading.Tasks;

namespace IntegralCryptanalysis
{
    public class Block
    {
        /// <summary>
        /// Represents the data that are held by the block
        /// </summary>
        public byte[] DataStructure { get; set; }

        /// <summary>
        /// Represents the left half of the data block
        /// </summary>
```

```
public byte[] LeftHalf
{
    get
    {
        return DataStructure.Take(DataStructure.Length / 2).
        ToArray();
    }
    set
    {
        Array.Copy(value, DataStructure, DataStructure.Length / 2);
    }
}

/// <summary>
/// Represents the right half of the data block
/// </summary>
public byte[] RightHalf
{
    get
    {
        return DataStructure.Skip(DataStructure.Length / 2).
        ToArray();
    }
    set
    {
        Array.Copy(value, 0, DataStructure, DataStructure.Length / 2,
        DataStructure.Length / 2);
    }
}

/// <summary>
/// Get and return as BitArray the left half of the block data
/// </summary>
public BitArray TheLeftBitsOfBlock
{
    get
```

```csharp
    {
        return new BitArray(LeftHalf);
    }
}

/// <summary>
/// Get and return as BitArray the right half of the block data
/// </summary>
public BitArray RightBitsOfBlock
{
    get
    {
        return new BitArray(RightHalf);
    }
}

/// <summary>
/// Representation of the size in bytes of the Block
/// </summary>
public int BlockSize
{
    get
    {
        return DataStructure.Length;
    }
}

/// <summary>
/// The representation of a data block. Constructor
/// </summary>
/// <param name="size_of_the_block">The size value (in bytes) of
    the block</param>
public Block(int size_of_the_block)
{
    DataStructure = new byte[size_of_the_block];
}
```

```
/// <summary>
/// The representation of a data block. Constructor
/// </summary>
/// <param name="the_data_block">the data content stored by the
    block</param>
public Block(byte[] the_data_block)
{
    DataStructure = the_data_block;
}

/// <summary>
/// Swaps the halves (left and right) of the block
/// </summary>
public void SwapHalfes()
{
    byte[] temporary = LeftHalf;
    LeftHalf = RightHalf;
    RightHalf = temporary;
}

/// <summary>
/// Converts the Block to a UTF-8 string
/// </summary>
/// <returns>String representation of this block</returns>
public override string ToString()
{
    return System.Text.Encoding.UTF8.GetString(DataStructure);
}
    }

}
```

Listing 21-4. The Key Class

```
using System;
using System.Collections.Generic;
using System.Linq;
```

```csharp
using System.Text;
using System.Threading.Tasks;
using System.Diagnostics;

namespace IntegralCryptanalysis
{
    public class Key
    {
        //** permutation table (initial)
        //** used to permutate the key
        private byte[] initial_permutation_table_1 = {
            06, 30, 13, 07, 05, 35, 15, 14,
            12, 18, 03, 38, 09, 10, 22, 25,
            16, 04, 21, 08, 39, 37, 36, 02,
            24, 11, 28, 27, 29, 23, 33, 01,
            32, 17, 31, 00, 26, 34, 20, 19
        };

        /// <summary>
        /// The representation of the key as a byte array
        /// </summary>
        public byte[] KeyBytes
        {
            get; set;
        }

        /// <summary>
        /// Encryption and decryption key for a text
        /// </summary>
        /// <param name="keyAsAString">The key to use for this instance
        ///     </param>
        public Key(string keyAsAString)
        {
            int k = 0, key_length = keyAsAString.Length;

            //** expansion of the key to a maximum of 40 bytes
            while (keyAsAString.Length < 40)
                keyAsAString += keyAsAString[k++];
```

```csharp
        KeyBytes = System.Text.Encoding.UTF8.GetBytes(keyAsAString);

        //** permutation of the key bytes using
        //** initial_permutation_table_1
        for (k = 0; k < KeyBytes.Length; k++)
            KeyBytes[k] = KeyBytes[initial_permutation_table_1[k]];

        Debug.WriteLine("The post permutation key is: "+ System.Text.
        Encoding.UTF8.GetString(KeyBytes));
    }

    /// <summary>
    /// Generate the keys that are used within the round function
    /// </summary>
    /// <returns>A list with the keys that are of 64-bit. The format is
        ulong.</returns>
    public List<ulong> ReturnRoundKeys()
    {
        //** Rounds is defined as 64-bit
        //** keys found in the Key string
        int count_of_round = KeyBytes.Length / 8;
        List<ulong> round_keys = new List<ulong>();

        for (int k = 0; k < count_of_round; k++)
        {
            byte[] round_key_bytes = new byte[8];
            ulong round_key = 0;

            Array.Copy(KeyBytes, k * 8, round_key_bytes, 0, 8);
            Array.Reverse(round_key_bytes);

            round_key = BitConverter.ToUInt64(round_key_bytes, 0);

            round_keys.Add(round_key);
        }
        return round_keys;
    }
}
}
```

Conclusion

In this chapter, we discussed integral cryptanalysis and how such attack can be designed and implemented. We presented a way of building a block cipher cryptosystem together with the vulnerable points in order to show how to apply an integral cryptanalysis attack.

At the end of this chapter, you can now

- Design and implement a simple block cipher

- Understand the two vulnerable points of such ciphers, such as Feistel networks and generating the permutation tables to permutate the key

- Understand how a Feistel network is implemented

- Use permutation tables and work with them over the keys

Bibliography

[1]   Joan Daemen, Lars Knudsen, and Vincent Rijmen, "The Block Cipher Square. Fast Software Encryption (FSE) 1997," Volume 1267 of *Lecture Notes in Computer Science* (pp. 149–165). Haifa, Israel: Springer-Verlag. CiteSeerX 10.1.1.55.6109. 1997.

CHAPTER 22

Attacks

In this chapter, we will analyze the most important attacks that can occur in a distributed environment (cloud computing [3] or big data) and how they can be exploited using the C# programming language [2] with features from version 8.0. For reference, we will use as an example an ASP.NET MVC 5 (also will work for previous versions of MVC, such as 1.0, 2.0, 3.0, and 4.0) application using C# as the back-end programming language.

The three most common attacks that occur on a daily basis on a web application are redirection attacks, SQL injections, and cross-site scripting (XSS).

The methods described here are part of the ethical hacking field and using them the wrong way can produce a major disaster for a business. The methods are very useful for the red teamers and some of them will be dedicated to post-exploitation.

Port Forwarding and How to Prevent Open Redirection Attacks

Through port forwarding a hacker cannot get access to you, but the router can be exploited in order to allow configuration on a web port.

A web application that redirects to a URL that is specified using a request based on a querystring can be easily tampered with via a redirection of the users to an external and malicious URL. This kind of attack is known as an *open redirection attack*.

To perform an attack and to encounter this vulnerability, it is very important to understand how login redirection works in an ASP.NET MVC web application project. In the example presented below, we can see that if we are going and access a controller action which has in its structure the [Authorize] attribute, this will redirect the unauthorized users to the /Account/LogOn view. The mentioned redirection to /Account/LogOn has in its structure a parameter known as returning_url querystring in such way that the user will be returned to the genuine URL that was requested after being logged in with success.

© Marius Iulian Mihailescu and Stefania Loredana Nita 2021
M. I. Mihailescu and S. L. Nita, *Pro Cryptography and Cryptanalysis*,
https://doi.org/10.1007/978-1-4842-6367-9_22

Attacks based on open redirection are very dangerous. The attacker knows exactly when we are proceeding to log into a certain website. This can make us vulnerable to a phishing attack. As an example, consider an attacker who sends malicious emails to users who are subscribed to a certain website in order to capture their passwords.

Let's consider the following example in which an attacker sends a link to users which contains a login page on a specific webpage (e.g. `http://apressprocryptoexample.com`) which has in its component a redirection to the forged page,

`http://apressprocryptoexample.com/Account/LogOn?returnUrl=http://` `apresprocryptoexample.com/Account/LogOn`. Pay attention to the returning URL, which points to apresprocryptoexample.com. Note that an "s" is missing from the word "apress." This means that the domain `apresprocryptoexample.com` is being controlled by hackers.

If the login is performed correctly, the `AccountController LogOn` action from ASP.NET MVC will redirect us to the URL mentioned in the querystring parameter, `returning_url`. In this situation, the URL is the one used by the attacker, which is `http://apresprocryptoexample.com`. If we are not paying attention, we will not notice the difference in the browser. The attacker is a very well versed person and is careful to make sure that the fake page looks exactly like the original one. The fake login page includes an error message that says that we need to log in with our credentials again. Once we retype our credentials, the fake login page will save the data and send us back to the original page, `ApressProCryptoExample.com`. At this point, `ApressProCryptoExample.com` will have already logged us in with success, and the fake authentication page is able to redirect us to that specific page. The final result is based on the fact that the attacker is aware of our credentials (user name and password) and we, the real users, are not aware that we have provided our credentials so easily [4].

Let's continue by looking at the code (Listing 22-1) for the `LoginAuthentication` action from our application. Our defined controller will return a redirection to `returning_url`. The validation is missing completely for the `returning_url` parameter.

Listing 22-1. Login Controller

```
[HttpPost]
public ActionResult LoginAuthentication(
                                LogOnModel model,
                                string returning_url)
{
    if (ModelState.IsValid)
```

```
    {
        if (MembershipService.ValidateUser(model.UserName,
        model.Password))
        {
            FormsService.SignIn(model.UserName,
                                 model.RememberMe);
            if (!String.IsNullOrEmpty(returning_url)) {
                return Redirect(returning_url);
            }
            else {
                return RedirectToAction("Index", "Home");
            }
        }
        else {
            ModelState.AddModelError("", "The credentials are
                                     wrong. Please, try again.");
        }
    }

    //** if we reach here it means that
    //** something went wrong
    //** we will show again the form
    return View(model);
}
```

Listing 22-2 shows how to perform the validation with `returning_url`. This is
done using a new method, `IsLocalUrl()`, which is part of the helper class `System.
Web.Mvc.Url`.

Listing 22-2. Validation for returning_url

```
[HttpPost]
public ActionResult LoginAuthentication(LogOnModel model, string
returning_url)
{
    if (ModelState.IsValid)
    {
```

```
    if (MembershipService.ValidateUser(model.UserName,
                                    model.Password))
    {
        FormsService.SignIn(model.UserName,
                                    model.RememberMe);
        if (Url.IsLocalUrl(returning_url)){
            return Redirect(returning_url);
        }
        else {
            return RedirectToAction("Index", "Home");
        }
    }
    else {
        ModelState.AddModelError("",
                "The credentials are wrong.
                Please, try again.");
    }
}

//** if we reach here it means that
//** something went wrong
//** we will show again the form
return View(model);
}
```

SQL Injection

For many companies, their business occurs online and in environments [5] such as cloud computing and big data, so their web sites are becoming more and more exposed to the possibility of data theft. Hackers can get important information from their data and pass it to other players on the market.

SQL injection is one of the most common methods through which malicious users can inject different SQL commands into a SQL statement using web page input. By doing so, the malicious users can break the security of the web application.

In this section, we will consider the following web application, which is built from scratch for this purpose. The reason of creating such an application from scratch is to illustrate the common mistakes developers make during the development process.

The first step is to build a database with a table that holds the login data for users. The database is created in Microsoft SQL Server v.17.9. Figure 22-1 shows the structure of the table and Listing 22-3 shows the SQL script code for generating the table. One of the common mistakes is that many web applications store passwords in plaintext. It is recommended to avoid this practice. The best practice is to use hashes of the password (such as MD5, SHA128, SHA256 etc.). For our example, we will use plaintext passwords.

Column Name	Data Type	Allow Nulls
ID	int	☐
FirstName	varchar(50)	☑
LastName	varchar(50)	☑
Email	varchar(50)	☑
Password	varchar(50)	☑
LastDateLogged	datetime	☑
		☐

Figure 22-1. *Table structure*

Listing 22-3. Login User Data Table SQL Script

```
USE [Apress_ProCrypto_SQLInjectionDB]
GO

/****** Object:  Table [dbo].[LoginUserData]
Script Date: 6/23/2020 2:51:06 AM ******/
SET ANSI_NULLS ON
GO

SET QUOTED_IDENTIFIER ON
GO

CREATE TABLE [dbo].[LoginUserData](
    [ID] [int] IDENTITY(1,1) NOT NULL,
    [FirstName] [varchar](50) NULL,
    [LastName] [varchar](50) NULL,
```

```
    [Email] [varchar](50) NULL,
    [Password] [varchar](50) NULL,
    [LastDateLogged] [datetime] NULL,
 CONSTRAINT [PK_LoginUserData] PRIMARY KEY CLUSTERED
(
    [ID] ASC
)WITH (PAD_INDEX = OFF, STATISTICS_NORECOMPUTE = OFF, IGNORE_DUP_KEY = OFF,
ALLOW_ROW_LOCKS = ON, ALLOW_PAGE_LOCKS = ON) ON [PRIMARY]
) ON [PRIMARY]
GO
```

The second step is to populate the table with some data, as in Figure 22-2. And then
we execute the script against the table from Listing 22-4.

	ID	FirstName	LastName	Email	Password	LastDateLogged
	1	Jefferson	Nicholas	nicholas.jefferson@domain.com	password1	NULL
	2	Thomas	Claudio	claudio.thomas@domain.com	password2	NULL
	3	Steven	Paolo	steven.paolo@domain.com	password3	NULL
	4	Billy	Walsh	billy.walsh@domain.com	password4	NULL
▶*	NULL	NULL	NULL	NULL	NULL	NULL

Figure 22-2. *Data for users*

Listing 22-4. Data Content

```
SET NOCOUNT ON
INSERT INTO dbo.LoginUserData
            ([FirstName],[LastName],
            [Email],[Password],[LastDateLogged])
VALUES
    ('Jefferson','Nicholas','nicholas.jefferson@domain.com','password1',
    CONVERT(datetime,NULL,121))
    ,('Thomas','Claudio','claudio.thomas@domain.com','password2',CONVERT
    (datetime,NULL,121))
    ,('Steven','Paolo','steven.paolo@domain.com','password3',CONVERT
    (datetime,NULL,121))
    ,('Billy','Walsh','billy.walsh@domain.com','password4',CONVERT
    (datetime,NULL,121))
```

The third step consists of building the web application. For this, we will not use an extra fancy web application architecture. It's just a simple web application with two web pages. The connection to the database is done using ADO.NET. With other object relational mapping (ORMs) such as NHibernate, LINQ-to-SQL, or Entity Framework, the results are the same. The single difference is the long time for processing the SQL injection.

The first page that we build is `Login.aspx`. As you can see in Figure 22-3, the page contains a simple form. The code is shown in Listing 22-5.

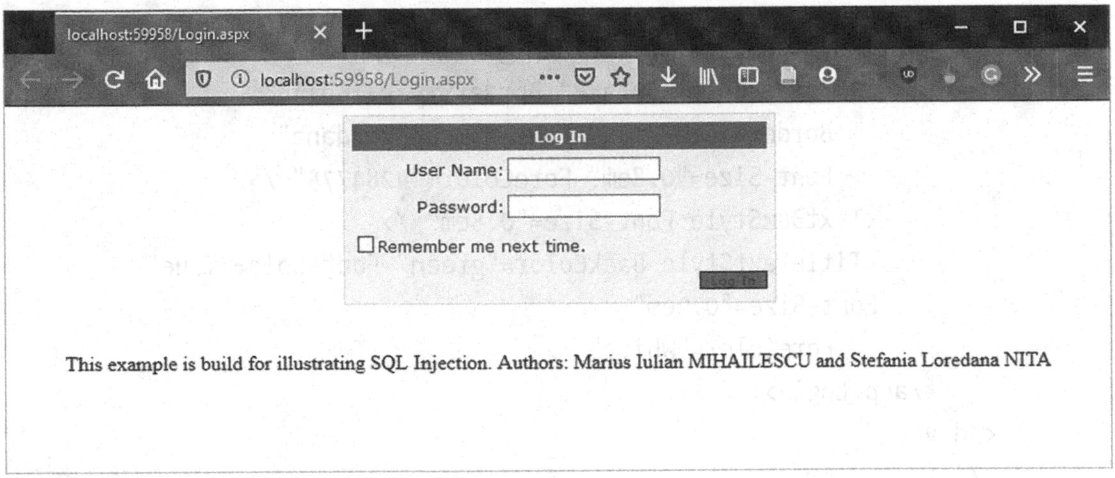

Figure 22-3. *Login.aspx page*

Listing 22-5. The HTML Source Code of Login.aspx

```
<%@ Page Language="C#" AutoEventWireup="true" CodeFile="Login.aspx.cs"
Inherits="Login" %>

<!DOCTYPE html>

<html xmlns="http://www.w3.org/1999/xhtml">
<head runat="server">
    <title></title>
</head>
<body>
    <center>
        <form id="form1" runat="server">
```

```
        <div>
            <asp:Login ID="MyLogin" runat="server"
                    OnAuthenticate="MyLogin_Authenticate"
                    Width="331px" BackColor="#F7F6F3" BorderColor="#E6E2D8"
                    BorderPadding="4" BorderStyle="Solid" BorderWidth="1px"
                    Font-Names="Verdana" Font-Size="0.8em"
                    ForeColor="#333333" Height="139px">
            <InstructionTextStyle Font-Italic="True"
                                                ForeColor="Blue" />

            <LoginButtonStyle BackColor="green"
                    BorderColor="black" BorderStyle="Solid"
                    BorderWidth="1px" Font-Names="Verdana"
                    Font-Size="0.8em" ForeColor="#284775" />
                <TextBoxStyle Font-Size="0.8em" />
                <TitleTextStyle BackColor="green" Font-Bold="True"
                Font-Size="0.9em"
                    ForeColor="White" />
            </asp:Login>
        </div>
        </form>
    </center>
    <br />
    <br />
    <center>
            This example is build for illustrating SQL
            Injection. Authors: Marius Iulian MIHAILESCU and Stefania
            Loredana NITA
    </center>
</body>
</html>
```

Listing 22-6 shows the server side code for Login.aspx. What you can note from here is that there's no kind of validation for the integrity of the password or avoiding SQL injection attacks.

Listing 22-6. Server Side Source Code for Login.aspx

```
using System;
using System.Collections.Generic;
using System.Linq;
using System.Web;
using System.Web.UI;
using System.Web.UI.WebControls;
using System.Data;
using System.Data.SqlClient;

public partial class Login : System.Web.UI.Page
{
    DataTable data_table;
    SqlDataAdapter adapter;
    protected void Page_Load(object sender, EventArgs e)
    {

    }
    protected void MyLogin_Authenticate(object sender,
                                        AuthenticateEventArgs e)
    {
        SqlConnection connection = new SqlConnection(@"Data
                    Source=SERVER_NAME;Initial Catalog=Apress_
                    ProCrypto_SQLInjectionDB;Integrated
                    Security=True");
        string query="select * from LoginUserData where
                    Email='"+ MyLogin.UserName+"'and Password='"+
                    MyLogin.Password+"' ";
        adapter = new SqlDataAdapter(query, connection);
        data_table = new DataTable();
        adapter.Fill(data_table);
        if (data_table.Rows.Count >= 1)
        {
            Response.Redirect("index.aspx");
        }
    }
}
```

The second page is called Index.aspx, which is a confirmation page for a successful login (see Listings 22-7 and 22-8). There is nothing special about the page.

Listing 22-7. Source Code for Index.aspx

```
<%@ Page Language="C#" AutoEventWireup="true" CodeFile="Index.aspx.cs"
Inherits="Index" %>

<!DOCTYPE html>

<html xmlns="http://www.w3.org/1999/xhtml">
<head runat="server">
    <title>APRESS-Example of SQL Injection</title>
</head>
<body>
    <form id="form1" runat="server">
    <div><center>
    <h1>Hello, Apress! <br/>
        Example for SQL Injection
    </h1></center>
    </div>
    </form>
</body>
</html>
```

Listing 22-8. Server Side Source Code for Index.aspx

```
using System;
using System.Collections.Generic;
using System.Linq;
using System.Web;
using System.Web.UI;
using System.Web.UI.WebControls;
```

```
public partial class Index : System.Web.UI.Page
{
    protected void Page_Load(object sender, EventArgs e)
    {

    }
}
```

Now that we have the entire project set, let's proceed with the SQL injection analysis and attack. The query is as follows:

```
select * from LoginUserData where
    Email='"+ MyLogin.UserName+"'and Password='"+
    MyLogin.Password+"';
```

Let's consider the case when in the TextBox of the login control we have entered ' or 1=1. Once the Log In button is pressed, the query will look like the following:

```
select  * from LoginUserData where Email=" or 1=1--'and Password="
```

If the attacker knows the username or rule 1=1, it will not be applied anymore. He will simply write the username + ' in the TextBox and comment everything that follows, like so:

```
select  * from LoginUserData where
    Email='nicholas.jefferson@domain.com'--and Password="
```

Another dangerous example is deleting records or dropping tables from the database. The following example shows this situation:

```
select * from LoginUserData where Email=" Delete from LoginUserData
    -'and Password="
```

Other types of SQL injections can be seen in Table 23-1. Some of them are quite dangerous and are not recommended to be used against live production databases.

Table 22-1. *Other Examples of SQL Injections*

Example of SQL injection	Description
' or ''	String characters as indicators
-- or #	Single-line comments
/*..*/	Multiple-line comments
+	Addition, concatenation (also for URLs)
||	Double concatenation
%	Wildcard attribute indicator
?Param1=foo&Param2=bar	URL parameters
PRINT	Non-transactional command
@variable	Local variable
@@variable	Global variable
waitfor delay '0:0:10'	Time delay

In case of an ASP.NET MVC web application, the procedure is similar with the one described above.

Cross-Site Scripting (XSS)

Cross-site scripting (XSS) is a security vulnerability where an attacker inserts client-side scripts, mostly JavaScript, into web pages. When a user accesses a web application, the browser will load the affected pages, and the scripts found within those pages will run, providing attackers a way to get possession of cookies and session tokens. Most of the time, XSS vulnerabilities occur when the web application takes the user input and outputs it to another page without validating, encoding, or escaping it.

From experience, we recommend that you follow these rules to protect your web application against XSS:

- Never enter sensitive data in HTML pages, such as HTML form inputs, queries, HTTP headers, etc.

- Everything that is found within a HTML element should be encoded.

- Everything that is found within a HTML attribute should be encoded.

- Any untrusted data that are, let's say, necessary (I don't like this term but let's keep it in this way) to be added in JavaScript should be first entered in an HTML element whose contents should be retrieved during the runtime process.

- Before adding any data to a URL query string, make sure that the URL is encoded.

As an example, we will consider how HTML encoding behaves with the Razor engine used in MVC, which encodes the entire output from variables. For this not to happen we need to have a workaround to prevent this situation. An HTML attribute related to encoding represents a superset of the HTML encoding type, which means we don't need to worry if we should use HTML encoding or HTML attribute encoding. We just need to be sure to use '@' in the HTML context and not when we are trying to add untrusted data as input directly with JavaScript.

Let's consider the following Razor [1] view from Listing 22-9. The output of the view will be an `untrustedInput` variable. This type of variable has in its component some characters that can be exploited and used with success in XSS attacks. These characters are <, ", and >. In the rendered output, the encode looks like:<"testing123">

Listing 22-9. Example of a Razor View

```
@{
        var untrustedInput = "<\"testing123\">";
}

@untrustedInput
```

There are some cases when we want to add values to JavaScript to be processed within our view. To achieve this, we can proceed down two paths. The safest way to achieve this is by placing the value within the data attribute of a specific tag and to take it in our JavaScript, as shown in Listing 22-10.

Listing 22-10. Using Razor and JavaScript Encoding

```
@{
        var untrustedInput = "<\"testing123\">";
    }

    <div
        id="theDataToBeInjected"
        data-untrustedinput="@untrustedInput" />

    <script>
      var theDataToBeInjected =
            document.getElementById("theDataToBeInjected");

      //** for all the clients
      var clientWithUntrustedInput =
          theDataToBeInjected.getAttribute("data-untrustedinput");

      //** for clients that support HTML 5
      var clientWithUntrustedInputHtml5 =
          theDataToBeInjected.dataset.untrustedinput;

      document.write(clientWithUntrustedInput);
      document.write("<br />")
      document.write(clientWithUntrustedInputHtml5);
    </script>
```

The code from Listing 22-10 will produce the output shown in Listing 22-11.

Listing 22-11. The Output

```
<div
    id="theDataToBeInjected"
    data-untrustedinput="<&quot;testing123&quot;>" />

  <script>
    var theDataToBeInjected =
                  document.getElementById("theDataToBeInjected");
```

```
    var clientWithUntrustedInput =
        theDataToBeInjected.getAttribute("data-untrustedinput");;

    var clientWithUntrustedInputHtml5 =
        theDataToBeInjected.dataset.untrustedinput;

  document.write(clientSideUntrustedInputOldStyle);
  document.write("<br />")
  document.write(clientWithUntrustedInputHtml5);
</script>
```

Once the script is run, the rendering result will be

```
<"testing123">
  <"testing123">
```

Also, we can call the JavaScript encoder as shown in Listing 22-12.

Listing 22-12. JavaScript Encoder

```
@using System.Text.Encodings.Web;
  @inject JavaScriptEncoder encoder;

  @{
      var someUntrustedInput = "<\"testing123\">";
  }

  <script>
      document.write("@encoder.Encode(someUntrustedInput)");
  </script>
```

Once this is rendered by the browser, we will have the following:

```
<script>
    document.write("\u003C\u0022testing123\u0022\u003E");
</script>
```

This being said, in practice it is difficult to pay attention to the encoding process. The encoding takes place on the output and the encoded values should not be stored in the database or on servers, especially in cloud computing in a big data environment.

Conclusion

This chapter presented three common attacks that occur in a web application: port forwarding with redirection attacks, SQL injections, and cross-site scripting attacks.

By the end of this chapter, you can now

- Identify three common attacks within web applications.

- Deal with the vulnerabilities in a professional way by providing latest support from the features of the programming language.

- Understand how a SQL injection behaves and how it can be encountered.

- Understand the danger of exposing applications through port forwarding with redirection attacks by understanding the disaster that could occur.

- Understand what cross-site scripts are and how they behave.

Bibliography

[1] Introduction to ASP.NET Web Programming using the Razor Syntax (C#). Available online: `https://docs.microsoft.com/en-us/aspnet/web-pages/overview/getting-started/introducing-razor-syntax-c`.

[2] Brandon Perry. *Gray Hat C# - A Hacker's Guide to Creating and Automating Security Tools*. No Starch Press, 2017.

[3] Adam Freeman. *Pro ASP.NET Core 3 – Develop Cloud-Ready Web Applications using MVC Blazor, and Razor Pages*. Apress, 2020.

[4] Stephen Haunts. *Applied Cryptography in .NET and Azure Key Vault*. Apress, 2019.

[5] Robert Ciesla. *Encryption for Organizations and Individuals – Basics of Contemporary and Quantum Cryptography*. Apress, 2020.

CHAPTER 23

Text Characterization

In this chapter, we will analyze two important metrics for cipher and plaintext analysis: the chi-squared statistic and searching for patterns (monograms, bigrams, and trigrams). When working with classic and modern cryptography, text characterization as technique is a very important part of the cryptanalysis bag of tricks.

Chi-Squared Statistic

The chi-squared statistic is an important metric that computes the similarity percent between two probability distributions. There are two situations when the results of the chi-squared statistic is equal with 0: it means that the two distributions are similar, and if the distributions are very different, a higher number will be outputted.

The chi-squared statistic is defined by the following formula:

$$\chi^2 \left(C, E \right) = \sum_{i=A}^{i=Z} \frac{\left(C_i - E_i \right)^2}{E_i}$$

In Listing 23-1, we compute an example of a chi-squared distribution.

Listing 23-1. ChiSquaredDistribution Source Code

```
using System

namespace ComputeChiSquaredStatistics
{
    class ComputeChiSquaredStatistics
    {
        static void Main(string[] args)
```

517

© Marius Iulian Mihailescu and Stefania Loredana Nita 2021
M. I. Mihailescu and S. L. Nita, *Pro Cryptography and Cryptanalysis*,
https://doi.org/10.1007/978-1-4842-6367-9_23

```
    {
        int number_of_experiments=10000;
        int number_of_stars_distribution=100;

        Random theGenerator = new Random();
            double theDistribution(6.0);

        int[] probability = new int[10];

        for (int counter=0; counter
            <number_of_experiments; ++counter)
        {
            double no =
                theDistribution(theGenerator);
            if ((no>=0.0)&&(no<10.0))
                ++ probability [int(no)];
        }

        Console.Writeline("The Chi-Squared
          Distribution (6.0):");

        for (int index = 0; index < 10; ++index)
        {
            Console.WriteLine("index {0} ", index, " -- {1}: ",
            (index + 1), ":");
            Console.WriteLine("{0}", probability[index] * number_of_
            stars_distribution / number_of_experiments);
        }

        Console.ReadKey();
    }
  }
}
```

The output of the above implementation is shown in Figure 23-1.

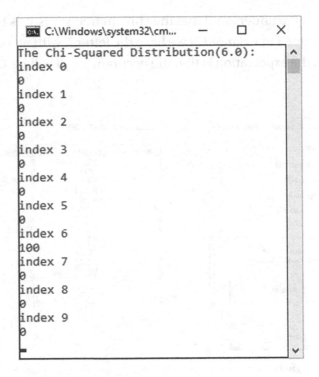

Figure 23-1. *Chi-distribution output*

How does the chi-squared distribution example help us in cryptanalysis and cryptography?

The first step that has to be made is to compute the frequency of the characters within the ciphertext. The second step is to compare the frequency distribution of the assumed language used for encryption (e.g. English) with shifting the two frequency distributions related to one another. In this way, we can find the *shift* that was used during the encryption process. This procedure is a standard and simple procedure that can be used on ciphers, such as a Caesar cipher. This take place when the frequency of the English characters is lined up with the frequency of the ciphertext. We are aware of the probabilities of the occurrences for English characters

As an example, let's consider the following example encrypted with a Caesar cipher, which has 46 characters (see Figure 23-2 for the letter frequency). The example from Figure 23-2 is computed and shown using CrypTool[1] to compute and verify the implementation and its correctness for letter frequency on encrypted text:

ZHOFRPHWRDSUHVVWKLVLVHQFUBSWHGZLWKFDHVDUFLSKHU

---

[1]CrypTool Portal, www.cryptool.org/en/

It is very important to understand that the chi-squared statistic is based on counts and not on probabilities. For example, if we have the letter E with an occurrence probability of 0.127, the expectation is that the occurance will will be 12.7 times within 100 characters.

N-Gram List of Caesar encryption of <startingexample-en.txt>, key <D, KEY OFFSET: 0>

No.	Character seq...	Frequency in %	Frequency
1	H	15.2174	7
2	V	10.8696	5
3	F	8.6957	4
4	L	8.6957	4
5	U	8.6957	4
6	W	8.6957	4
7	D	6.5217	3
8	K	6.5217	3
9	S	6.5217	3
10	R	4.3478	2
11	Z	4.3478	2
12	B	2.1739	1
13	G	2.1739	1
14	O	2.1739	1
15	P	2.1739	1
16	Q	2.1739	1

Selection: Histogram (16), Digram (42), Trigram (44), 4-gram (43). Display of the 16 most common N-grams (allowed values: 1-5000). Text options. Compute list. Save list. Close.

Figure 23-2. *Letter frequency for encrypted text*

To compute the count expected, the length of the ciphertext has to be multiplied by the probability. The cipher from above has a total of 46 characters. Following the statistic with E from above, our expectation is for the E letter to occur $46 \cdot 0.127 = 5.842$ times.

In order to solve the Caesar cipher, we need to use each of the possible 25 keys, using the letter or the position of the letter within the alphabet. For this, it's very important how the count starts, from 0 or from 1. The chi-squared has to be computed for each of the keys. The process consists of comparing the count number of a letter with what we can expect the count to be if the text is in English.

For computing the chi-squared statistic for our ciphertext, we count each letter and we see that the letter H occurs 7 times. If the language used is English, it should appear $46 \cdot 0.082 = 3.772$ times. Based on the output we can compute the following:

$$\frac{(7-3.772)^2}{3.772} = \frac{3.228^2}{3.772} = \frac{10.420}{3.772} = 2.762$$

This procedure is done for the rest of the letters and making addition between all the probabilities (see Figure 23-3).

Once the ciphertext is decrypted, the plaintext should be

WELCOMETOAPRESSTHISISENCRYPTEDWITHCAESARCIPHER

```
C:\Windows\system32\cmd.exe                      —    □    ×

The number of letters: 23
Y T A H T A A I S H N D N R E N T H W H P E I

A       13.043     8.167     4.876
B        0.000     1.492    -1.492
C        0.000     2.782    -2.782
D        4.348     4.253     0.095
E        8.696    12.703    -4.007
F        0.000     2.228    -2.228
G        0.000     2.015    -2.015
H       17.391     6.094    11.297
I        8.696     6.966     1.730
J        0.000     0.153    -0.153
K        0.000     0.772    -0.772
L        0.000     4.025    -4.025
M        0.000     2.406    -2.406
N       13.043     6.749     6.294
O        0.000     7.507    -7.507
P        4.348     1.929     2.419
Q        0.000     0.095    -0.095
R        4.348     5.987    -1.639
S        4.348     6.327    -1.979
T       13.043     9.056     3.987
U        0.000     2.758    -2.758
V        0.000     0.978    -0.978
W        4.348     2.360     1.988
X        0.000     0.150    -0.150
Y        4.348     1.974     2.374
Z        0.000     0.074    -0.074
Press any key to continue . . .
```

Figure 23-3. *Encryption letter frequency (%)*[2]

---

[2]The letter encryption frequency is generated using CrypTool, www.cryptool.org/en/

Cryptanalysis Using Monogram, Bigram, and Trigram Frequency Counts

Frequency analysis is one of the best practices for finding the number of ciphertext characters occurrence with the goal of breaking the cipher. Pattern analysis can be used to measure and count the characters as bigrams (or digraphs), a method for measuring pairs of characters that occurs within the text. There is also trigram frequency analysis, which measures the occurrence of combinations formed out of three letters.

In this section, we will focus on text characterization with bigrams and trigrams as opposed to resolving ciphers, such as Playfair.

Counting Monograms

Counting monograms represents one of the most effective methods used in substitution ciphers, such as Caesar ciphers, Polybius squares, etc. The method works very well because the English language has a specific frequency distribution. This means also that it's not hidden by the substitution ciphers. The distribution will look as depicted in Figure 23-4 and Listing 23-2.

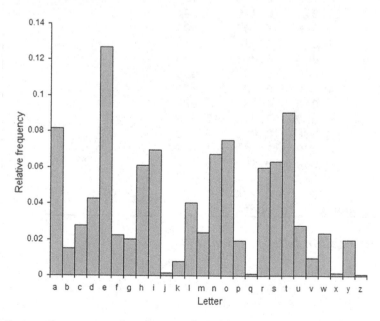

Figure 23-4. *Letter frequency for the English language*

Listing 23-2. Counting Monograms

```
using System;
using System.IO;

class Program
{
    static void Main()
    {
        //** we use the array to store the frequencies
        int[] frequency = new int[(int)char.MaxValue];

        //** look at the content of the text file
        string s = File.ReadAllText("TheText.txt");

        //** go through each of the characters
        foreach (char t in s)
        {
            //** store the frequencies as a table
            frequency [(int)t]++;
        }

        //** write all letters that have been found
        for (int letterPos = 0; letterPos <
                            (int)char.MaxValue; letterPos++)
        {
            if (c[letterPos] > 0 &&
                char.IsLetterOrDigit((char)letterPos))
            {
                Console.WriteLine("The Letter: {0}
                                    has the frequency: {1}",
                    (char)letterPos,
                    freq [letterPos]);
            }
        }
    }
}
```

The output is shown in Figure 23-5.

```
D:\Apps C#\Chapter 24 - Text Charact...    —    □    ×
The Letter: D has the Frequency: 1
The Letter: E has the Frequency: 1
The Letter: L has the Frequency: 1
The Letter: U has the Frequency: 1
The Letter: a has the Frequency: 29
The Letter: b has the Frequency: 3
The Letter: c has the Frequency: 16
The Letter: d has the Frequency: 18
The Letter: e has the Frequency: 37
The Letter: f has the Frequency: 3
The Letter: g has the Frequency: 3
The Letter: h has the Frequency: 1
The Letter: i has the Frequency: 42
The Letter: l has the Frequency: 21
The Letter: m has the Frequency: 17
The Letter: n has the Frequency: 24
The Letter: o has the Frequency: 29
The Letter: p has the Frequency: 11
The Letter: q has the Frequency: 5
The Letter: r has the Frequency: 22
The Letter: s has the Frequency: 18
The Letter: t has the Frequency: 32
The Letter: u has the Frequency: 28
The Letter: v has the Frequency: 3
The Letter: x has the Frequency: 3
```

Figure 23-5. *Output of counting monograms*

An advanced example of doing the above counting is shown in Listing 23-3. It is an advanced example using LINQ and lambda expression. Figure 23-6 shows the output.

Listing 23-3. Lambda LINQ Expression for Counting Letter Frequencies

```
using System;
using System.Collections;
using System.Collections.Generic;
using System.IO;
using System.Linq;
using System.Text;
using System.Threading.Tasks;

namespace MonogramsCounting_LINQ{
    class Program{
        static void Main(){
            var frequencies = from c in
```

```
File.ReadAllText("TheText.txt")
            group c by c into groupCharactersFrequencies
            select groupCharactersFrequencies;

        foreach (var c in frequencies)
            Console.WriteLine($"The character: {c.Key} has
the frequency: {c.Count()} times");

        Console.ReadKey();}}}
```

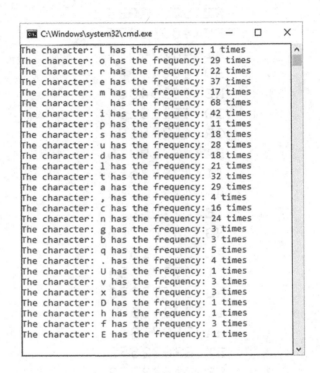

Figure 23-6. *Character frequencies using LINQ and lambda expressions*

Counting Bigrams

The method for counting bigrams is based on the same idea as counting monograms. Instead of counting the occurrence of single characters, counting bigrams means counting the occurrence frequency for pairs of characters.

Figure 23-7 lists some of the common bigrams found during the cryptanalysis process. In Listing 23-4, we have implemented a solution that deals with counting the occurrences of bigrams. Figure 23-8 shows the output.

```
TH  11699784·
HE  10068926:
IN  87674002
ER  77134382
AN  69775179
RE  60923600
ES  57070453
ON  56915252
ST  54018399
NT  50701084
EN  48991276
AT  48274564
ED  46647960
ND  46194306
TO  46115188
OR  45725191
EA  43329810
TI  42888666
AR  42353262
TE  42295813
NG  38567365
AL  38211584
IT  37938534
AS  37773878
IS  37349981
HA  35971841
ET  32872552
SE  31532272
OU  31112284
OF  30540904
```

Figure 23-7. *Examples of bigrams*

Listing 23-4. Computing Bigrams

```csharp
class Program
    {
        static void Main(string[] args)
        {
            String text = "Welcome to Apress! This book is
            about cryptography and C#.";
            String bigramPattern = "to";
            Console.WriteLine("The number of occurrences of
                    \"" + bigramPattern + "\" in \"" + text +
                    "\" is: " +
                countFrequenciesBigrams(bigramPattern,
                                        text).ToString());

        }

        static int countFrequenciesBigrams(String
                            bigramPattern, String text)
        {
            int bigramPatternLength = bigramPattern.Length;
            int textLength = text.Length;
            int occurrences = 0;

            for (int idx = 0; idx <= textLength -
                            bigramPatternLength; idx++)
            {
                int jIdx;
                for (jIdx = 0; jIdx < bigramPatternLength;
                                                jIdx++)
                {
                    if (text[idx + jIdx] !=
                                    bigramPattern[jIdx])
                    {
                        break;
                    }
                }
```

```
        if (jIdx == bigramPatternLength)
        {
            occurrences++;
            jIdx = 0;
        }
    }
    return occurrences;
}
}
```

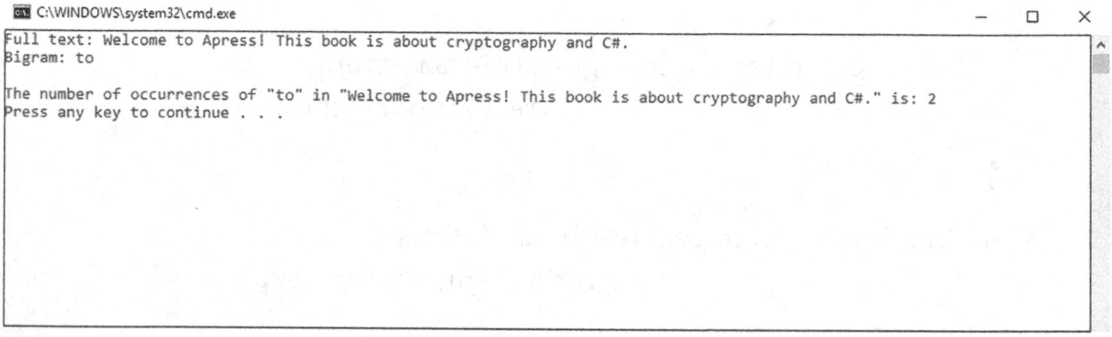

```
C:\WINDOWS\system32\cmd.exe                                                    —   □   ×
Full text: Welcome to Apress! This book is about cryptography and C#.
Bigram: to

The number of occurrences of "to" in "Welcome to Apress! This book is about cryptography and C#." is: 2
Press any key to continue . . .
```

Figure 23-8. *The output from Listing 23-4*

Counting Trigrams

Trigram counting uses the same principle as bigram counting. The difference consists in counting triple characters.

Figure 23-9 lists some common bigrams that are experienced during the cryptanalysis process. In Listing 23-5, we have implemented a solution for finding and counting the occurrences of trigrams within a text. The solution is different from the one from Listing 23-4. The output is shown in Figure 23-10.

```
THE 77534223
AND 30997177
ING 30679488
ENT 17902107
ION 17769261
HER 15277018
FOR 14686159
THA 14222073
NTH 14115952
INT 13656197
ERE 13287155
TIO 13285065
TER 12769843
EST 11956466
ERS 11823017
ATI 11227573
HAT 10900482
ATE 10712298
ALL 10501105
ETH 10304110
HES 10189449
VER 10156140
HIS 10051039
OFT 9434246
ITH 9142241
FTH 9036651
STH 9024058
OTH 8869058
RES 8835871
ONT 8757161
DTH 8745845
ARE 8741156
REA 8700830
EAR 8697937
WAS 8640940
```

Figure 23-9. *Examples of trigrams*

Listing 23-5. Counting Trigrams

```
class Program
    {
        static void Main(string[] args)
        {
            String fullText = "Welcome to Apress! This book is
            about cryptography and C#.";
            String trigramPattern = "Apr";
```

```
        Console.WriteLine("Full text: " + fullText);
        Console.WriteLine("Trigram: " +
                    trigramPattern + "\n");
        Console.WriteLine("The number of occurrences of
\"" + trigramPattern + "\" in \"" +
fullText + "\" is: " +
countFrequenciesTrigrams(trigramPattern,
fullText).ToString());

    }

    static int countFrequenciesTrigrams(String
                trigramPattern, String fullText)
    {
        int trigramPatternLength = trigramPattern.Length;
        int fullTextLength = fullText.Length;
        int noOfOccurrence = 0;

        for (int index = 0; index <= fullTextLength -
                    trigramPatternLength; index++)
        {
            int jIndex;
            for (jIndex = 0; jIndex <
                    trigramPatternLength; jIndex++)
            {
                if (fullText[index + jIndex] !=
                            trigramPattern[jIndex])
                {
                    break;
                }
            }

            if (jIndex == trigramPatternLength)
            {
                noOfOccurrence++;
                jIndex = 0;
            }
```

```
        }
        return noOfOccurrence;
    }
}
```

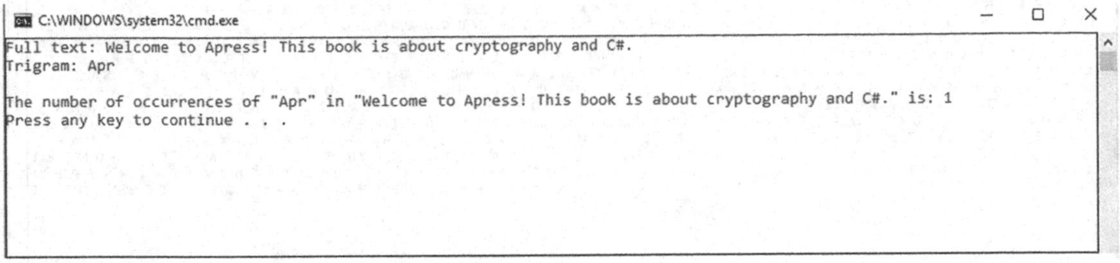

```
██ C:\WINDOWS\system32\cmd.exe                                              —    □    ×
Full text: Welcome to Apress! This book is about cryptography and C#.
Trigram: Apr

The number of occurrences of "Apr" in "Welcome to Apress! This book is about cryptography and C#." is: 1
Press any key to continue . . .
```

Figure 23-10. *The output from Listing 23-5*

Generate Letter Frequency

The array `wikiFrequencies` stores the frequencies (which are a relative percentage of the letters) as listed on Wikipedia[3] (see Listing 23-6). The provided example interprets the number as a percentage. As an example, letter "A" appears 8.167% of the time.

The program in Figure 23-11 declares a `Random` object. The defining value of the letter (e.g. "A") is as an integer. We will use this convention for later purposes. The event handler, `Load`, makes the sum of the entire values from the `wikiFrequencies.`

---

[3]Letter frequency, http://en.wikipedia.org/wiki/Letter_frequency.

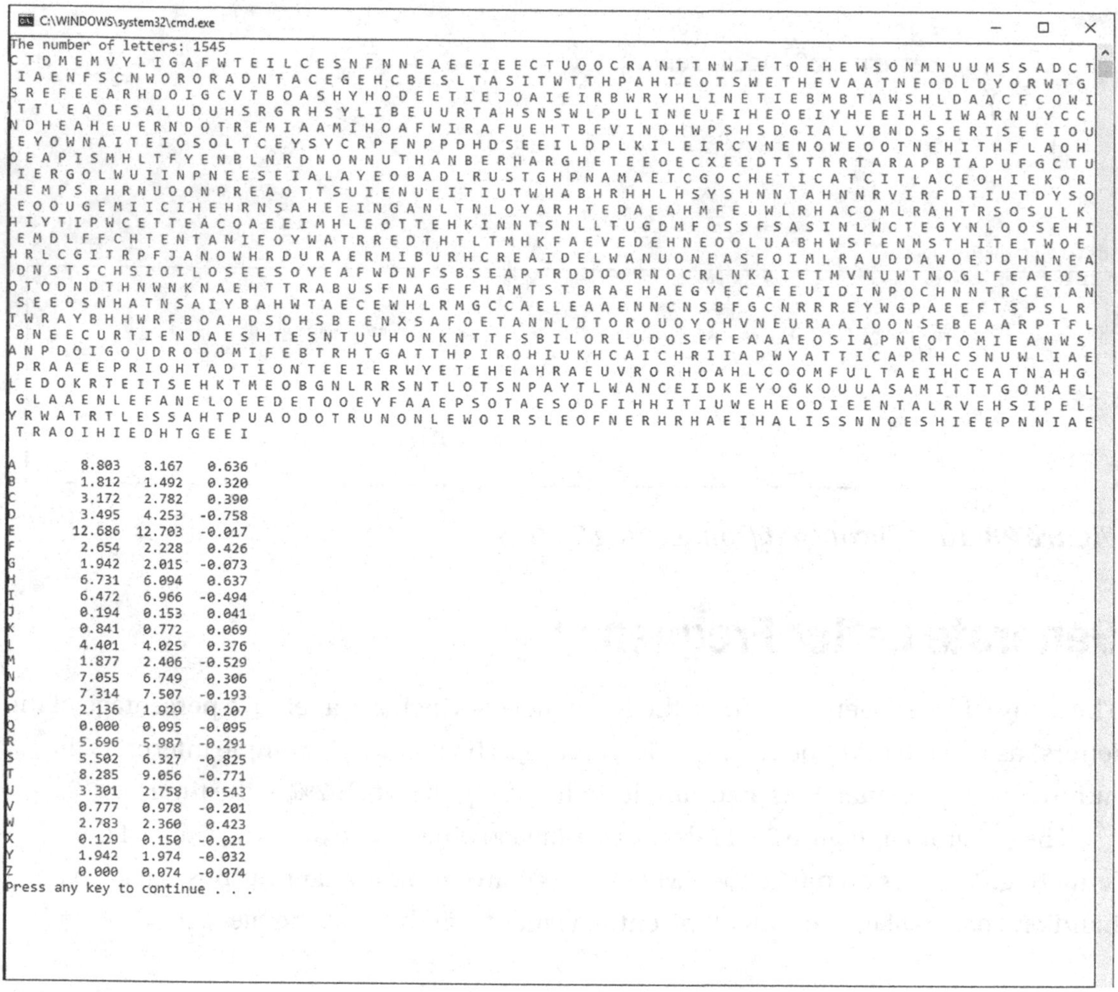

Figure 23-11. *Generation of the letter frequencies*

Listing 23-6. Randomly Generating Letter Frequencies

```
using System;
using System.Linq;

namespace LetterFrequency
{
    class Program
    {
        static void Main(string[] args)
```

```
{
    string input = "";
    VerifyFreq();

    Console.Write("The number of letters: ");
    input = Console.ReadLine();

    Compute(input);
}

//** Store the letter frequencies.
//** For more details and the values
//** stored below, see the link:
//** http://en.wikipedia.org/wiki/Letter_frequency
private static float[] wikiFrequencies =
{
    8.167f, 1.492f, 2.782f, 4.253f, 12.702f,
    2.228f, 2.015f, 6.094f, 6.966f, 0.153f,
    0.772f, 4.025f, 2.406f, 6.749f, 7.507f,
    1.929f, 0.095f, 5.987f, 6.327f, 9.056f,
    2.758f, 0.978f, 2.360f, 0.150f, 1.974f,
    0.074f
};

//** create a instance of a number
//** generator using Random class
private static Random randomNumber = new Random();

//** compute the ASCII value of letter A
private static int int_AsciiA = (int)'A';

//** verify that the frequencies are adding up to 100
private static void VerifyFreq()
{
    //** compute the difference to E
    float totalAmount = wikiFrequencies.Sum();
    float differenceComputation = 100f - totalAmount;
```

```
        wikiFrequencies[(int)'E' - int_AsciiA] +=
                    differenceComputation;
    }

    //** based on the frequencies
    //** generate randomly the letters
    private static void Compute(string txtNumLetters)
    {
        //** monitor and track each letter
        //** that has been generated
        int[] countGeneratedLetters = new int[26];

        //** randomly generate the letters
        int theNumberOfLetters = int.Parse(txtNumLetters);
        string result = "";
        for (int k = 0; k < theNumberOfLetters; k++)
        {
            //** randomly generate a number
            //** between 0 and 100
            double randomlyNumber = 100.0 *
            randomNumber.NextDouble();

            //** select the letter that
            //** this will represents
            for (int numberOfLetter = 0; ;
                            numberOfLetter++)
            {
                //** extract the frequency of the
                //** letter from the number
                randomlyNumber -=
                    wikiFrequencies[numberOfLetter];

                //** if the randomly number is
                //** less and equal than 0
                //** it means that we have the letter
                if ((randomlyNumber <= 0) ||
                        (numberOfLetter == 25))
```

```
                    {
                        char character = (char)(int_AsciiA +
                                            numberOfLetter);
                        result += character.ToString() + ' ';
                    countGeneratedLetters[numberOfLetter]++;
                        break;
                    }
                }
            }

        Console.WriteLine(result + "\n");

        //** show the frequencies
        for (int i = 0; i < countGeneratedLetters.Length;
                                            i++)

        {
            char ch = (char)(int_AsciiA + i);
            float frequency =
(float)countGeneratedLetters[i] /
theNumberOfLetters * 100;
            string str =
string.Format("{0}\t{1,6}\t{2,6}\t
{3,6} ,ch.ToString(),
frequency.ToString("0.000"),
wikiFrequencies[i].ToString("0.000"),
(frequency -
wikiFrequencies[i]).ToString("0.000"));

            Console.WriteLine(str);
        }
        }
    }
}
```

Conclusion

The chapter covered the concept of text characterization and showed its importance in the cryptanalysis process. You can now deal with chi-squared statistics and working with monograms, digrams, and trigrams for decrypting substitution ciphertexts. As a summary, you learned about

- The concept of text characterization

- Working with monograms, digrams, and trigrams

- The implementation of chi-squared statistic

- Monogram, digram, and trigram implementations

Bibliography

[1]   Simon Singh, *The Code Book: The Science of Secrecy from Ancient Egypt to Quantum Cryptography.* ISBN 0-385-49532-3. 2000.

[2]   Helen F. Gaines, *Cryptanalysis: A Study of Ciphers and Their Solutions.* 1989.

CHAPTER 24

Implementation and Practical Approach of Cryptanalysis Methods

In this chapter, we want to propose a methodology for cryptanalysis methods in general and how to apply it in a quick and efficient way. This method is for classic and actual (modern) cryptography/cryptanalysis algorithms and methods. Quantum cryptography is not included at this moment.

The proposed methodology (see Figure 24-1) is designed with the goal of letting the cryptanalyst know where they are situated and placed within their work and what tool or method they can use accordingly.

Implementing cryptanalysis methods is a very tricky task to achieve if you don't have the proper information about the cryptographic method. This being said, the cryptanalysis process consists of two general steps. *Step 1* consists of identifying what kind of cryptanalysis should be performed, and S*tep 2* what we know about cryptography algorithms. Based on these two steps, we can move on to *Step 3* for building a proper *attack model* and *Step 4* for choosing the proper tools.

Step 1. What kind of cryptanalysis should be performed? This is where the cryptanalyst decides, together with their business environment, what role they will play: a legal and authorized cryptanalyst (ethical hacker) or a malicious one (cracker). Once they decide their role, they move to Step 2.

Step 2. If they are a legitimate cryptanalyst, there are two things they should know before getting started: the *cryptography algorithm* and the *cryptographic key*. According to some cryptanalysts, this is not a necessary requirement but in some cases it will be very useful to know. Once these two things are known, they can easily perform cryptanalysis methods and test the security of the business.

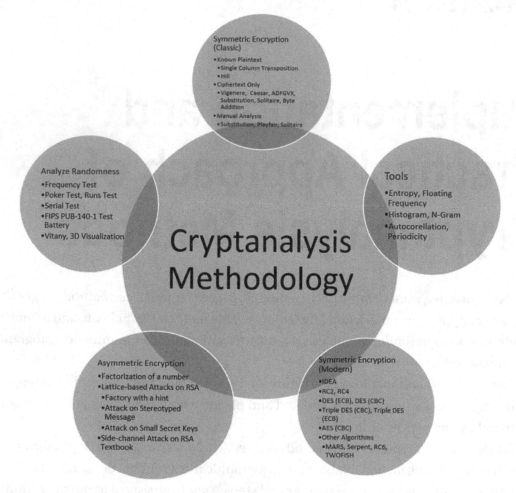

Figure 24-1. *Cryptanalysis methodology*

Step 3. Attack models or attack types will set a quantitative variable for how much information a cryptanalysis will have access to when they perform the cracking methods on the encrypted message. The most common attack models used are

- Ciphertext-only attack

- Known-plaintext attack

- Chosen-plaintext attack

- Chosen-ciphertext attack

  - Adaptive chosen-ciphertext attack

  - Indifferent chosen-ciphertext attack

Step 4. Once the attack model is chosen or another one has been created and adapted according to the situation and requirements, the next step is to choose the software tools. There are two ways, choosing from the ones that already exists or creating your own tools (this is time consuming but is good practice). The following are some examples of tools we can use in the cryptanalysis process, depending on what we are trying to "test:"

- Penetration tools: Kali Linux, Parrot Security, BackBox

- Forensics: DEFT, CAINE, BlackArch, Matriux

- Databases: sqlmap (standalone version), Metasploit framework (standalone version), VulDB

- Web and network: Wireshark, Nmap, Nessus, Burp Suite, Nikto, OpenVas

- Other tools: CryptTool (very useful and amazing tool)

The tools mentioned above represent only a selection of those that are very powerful and can produce the desired result.

Ciphertext-Only Attack (COA)

COA is one of the weakest attacks due to the fact that it can be easily used by the cryptanalyst because he just encoded the message.

The attacker (cryptanalyst) will have access to a set of ciphertexts. The attack is deemed successful if the corresponding plaintexts are deduced together with the key.

In this type of attack (see Figure 24-2), the attacker/cryptanalyst is able to observe the ciphertext. All they see is a set of scrambled and nonsense characters which is represented as the output of the encryption process.

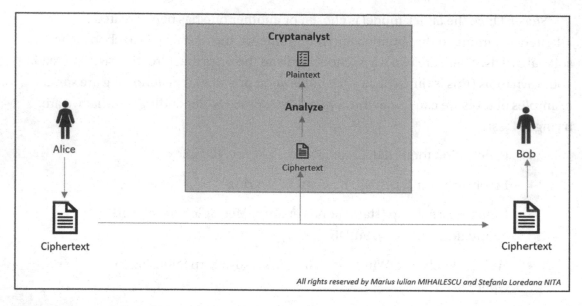

Figure 24-2. *COA representation*

Known-Plaintext Attack (KPA)

This attack (see Figure 24-3) give the cryptanalyst the ability to generate the ciphertext due to the fact that he knows the ciphertext.

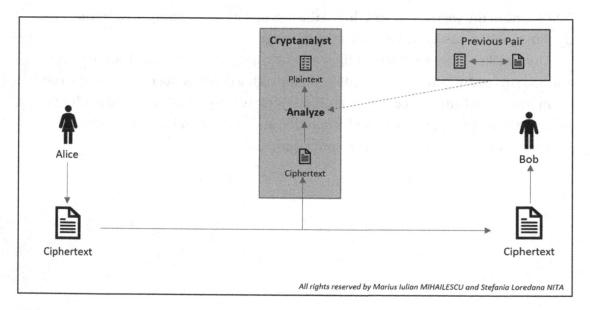

Figure 24-3. *KPA representation*

The cryptanalyst will select the plaintext, but they will notice the pair formed from plaintext and ciphertext. The chance of success is better compared to COA. Simple ciphers are quite vulnerable to this attack.

Chosen-Plaintext Attack (CPA)

The cryptanalyst selects the plaintext that has been send using an encryption algorithm and he observes how the ciphertext is generated. This can be seen as an active model in which the cryptanalyst has the chance to select the plaintext and to realize the encryption.

Having the possibility to choose any plaintext, the cryptanalyst can also observe details about the ciphertext, which gives him a strong advantage to understand how the algorithm works inside and the chance to get possession of the secret key.

A professional cryptanalyst will have a database that is populated with known plaintexts, ciphertexts, and possible keys (see Listing 24-1 and Figure 24-5 for an example of generating possible keys automatically; it is a very simple example for illustrating the main point), and to use them with the pairs for determining the cipher text input (see Figure 24-4).

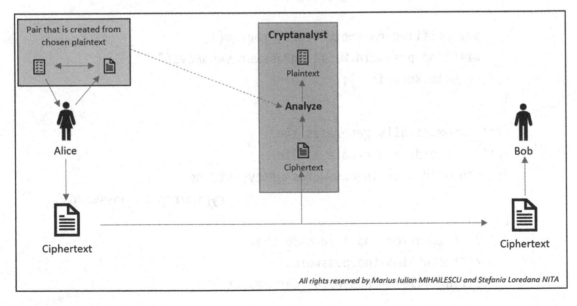

Figure 24-4. *CPA representation*

Listing 24-1. Automatic Generation of Random Keys

```csharp
using System;
using System.Collections.Generic;
using System.IO;
using System.Linq;
using System.Text;
using System.Threading.Tasks;

namespace GeneratingKeysDatabase
{
    class Program
    {
        public static string size = Console.ReadLine();
        public static int values_based_on_length =
            Convert.ToInt32(size);
        public char first_character = 'a';
        public char last_character = 'z';
        public int string_length = values_based_on_length;

        static void Main(string[] args)
        {
            var writting_password = new Program();
            writting_password.WrittingPasswordsAndKeys(" ");
            Console.ReadLine();
        }

        //** automatically generates the
        //** passwords and create a file
        private void WrittingPasswordsAndKeys(string
                                        cryptographic_passwords)
        {
            //** location and file name that
            //** contains the passwords
            string file = "passwords_database.txt";
```

```
//** add on each row a new password
File.AppendAllText(file, Environment.NewLine +
                                    cryptographic_passwords);

//** display it on the console
Console.WriteLine(cryptographic_passwords);

//** don't do anything if the length of the
//** passwords is equal with the length of
//** the string and continue with generating
//** the passwords and keys
if (cryptographic_passwords.Length ==
                                    string_length)
{
    return;
}
for (char c = first_character; c <=
                                last_character; c++)
{
        WrittingPasswordsAndKeys(
                            cryptographic_passwords + c);
}
    }
  }
}
```

Figure 24-5. *The keys and possible passwords generated. We choose three characters for short time process purpose only*

Chosen-Ciphertext Attack (CCA)

The cryptanalyst has the chance to encrypt and decrypt the information. In this attack (see Figure 24-6), they have the ability to select the plaintext, provide encryption for it, observe how the ciphertext is generated, and reverse the entire process. In this attack, the cryptanalyst will also try to find the algorithm and the secret key used for the encryption.

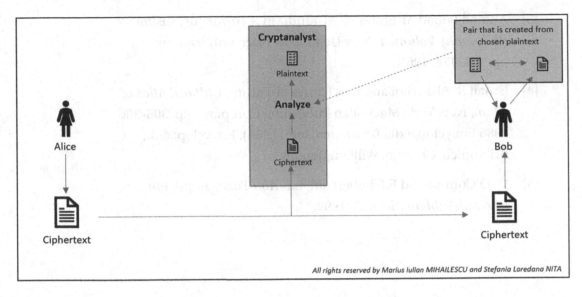

Figure 24-6. *CCA representation*

Conclusion

In this chapter, we discussed how to implement cryptanalysis methods and how to define such process for a cryptanalyst. At the end of this chapter, you will be able to

- Have a good understanding of the attack models

- Follow a simple and straightforward methodology for knowing where you are within the cryptanalysis process

- Simulate and generate a database with keys and possible passwords

Bibliography

[1]   Abu Yusuf Yaqub ibn Ishaq al-Sabbah Al-Kindi `www.trincoll.edu/depts/phil/philo/phils/muslim/kindi.html`.

[2]   Philosophers: Yaqub Ibn Ishaq al-Kindi Kennedy-Day, K. al-Kindi, Abu Yusuf Ya'qub ibn Ishaq (d. c.866–73). `www.muslimphilosophy.com/ip/kin.html`.

[3] Ahmad Fouad Al-Ehwany, "Al-Kindi" in *A History of Muslim Philosophy Volume 1*. New Delhi: Low Price Publications. pp. 421-434. 1961.

[4] Ismail R. Al-Faruqi and Lois Lamya al-Faruqi, *Cultural Atlas of Islam*, New York: Macmillan Publishing Company. pp. 305-306. 1986 Encyclopaedia Britannica, Inc. (1969). Encyclopaedia Britannica. Chicago: William Benton.

[5] J.J. O'Connor and E.F Robertson, E.F. *Abu Yusuf Yaqub ibn Ishaq al-Sabbah Al-Kindi*. 1999.

Index

© Marius Iulian Mihailescu and Stefania Loredana Nita 2021
M. I. Mihailescu and S. L. Nita, *Pro Cryptography and Cryptanalysis*,
https://doi.org/10.1007/978-1-4842-6367-9

T